EVERY OFFICER IS A LEADER
Transforming Leadership
in Police, Justice, and Public Safety

EV   R

St. Lucie Press
Boca Raton   London   New York   Washington, D.C.

Library of Congress Cataloging-in-Publication Data

Anderson, Terry D.
    Every officer is a leader : transforming leadership in police, justice, and public safety /
Terry Anderson.
        p.   cm.
    "Policing edition" of: Transforming leadership. c1998.
    ISBN 0-57444-118-3 (pbk. : alk. paper)
    1. Police administration. 2. Police--Supervision of. 3. Leadership. 4. Communication in
management. 5. Organizational effectiveness. I. Title. II. Anderson, Terry D.
    Transforming leadership.
HV7935 .A53 1999
363.2'068'4 21--dc21   99-042156
                                                                                        CIP

Visit the CRC Press Web site at www.crcpress.com

© 2000 by CRC Press LLC
St. Lucie Press is an imprint of CRC Press LLC

No claim to original U.S. Government works
International Standard Book Number 0-57444-118-3
Library of Congress Card Number 99-042156
Printed in the United States of America   4 5 6 7 8 9 0
Printed on acid-free paper

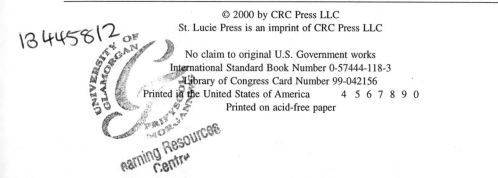

Table of Contents

Foreword

By

Barry Daniel, LLB, Chief of Police, Abbotsford Police Department, Abbotsford, B.C.
Peter Young, MBA, Chief of Police, New Westminster Police Service, New Westminster, BC.

Do you want to build a strategic leadership team? Do you wish to develop a culture that maximizes the contribution of all leaders toward achievement of organizational goals? Are you interested in managing and prioritizing change more effectively? This book will provide you with the necessary strategic, tactical and operational expertise to lead your policing organization through the challenges of the new millennium.

We have come through significant change in just the last few years. Exciting challenges that we have met include flattening of organizations, a technological revolution, getting to understand community needs, problem solving, becoming more efficient and effective in all aspects of our job while having ever increasing public scrutiny. All of our organizations have faced these issues with varying levels of success. Challenges need to be treated in a positive, exciting manner for the health of the organization and its members. Within our organizations we have used many ideas from *Transforming Leadership* to help us create enthusiasm for making change and initiating best practices in change management.

In policing there is an historical shift occurring that announces the necessity to move into the community, and to do so swiftly. While there are economic and political pressures to move in this direction, there are far better reasons. Long term efficiencies result from problem solving instead of just straight enforcement. Fear of crime is reduced and community satisfaction increases significantly when the police focus on the community's concerns. As well, problem ownership is now not a purview of just the police but that of all city departments as well as the community at large. At a recent meeting of the Police Executive Research Forum, this change was discussed under the heading of "Moving from Community Policing to Community Governance." This recognizes the continuous refinement of policing initiatives and cooperation in the interest of community safety.

As Assistant Chief Welter has stated in a recent speech to police leaders: Managing the change process to the developing Community Oriented Policing and Problem Solving (COPPS) method of policing presents unique challenges for police chief executives and commanders. One police chief described it as "similar to overhauling a car while keeping it moving down the highway" (Butts, 1995). The tactics of arrest and control in the traditional policing model worked fine and generally met the limited expectations of the community. As we move further into COPPS practices, community expectations are increasing. Neighborhood residents expect police officers to include them in crime prevention efforts and they are not satisfied with police focusing primarily on criminal apprehension. Community members are now more savvy and are beginning to expect someone in government (often the police) to help lead the effort to find solutions to many social problems that contribute to crime or a poor quality of life.

Police administrators and political leaders are raising their expectations as well. Some expect front line police officers to lead residents, business owners, and other government employees in a wide range of problem solving efforts. They also expect those efforts to have a measurable impact on the problem and not just result in reactive enforcement numbers requiring more officers and higher costs for courts and jails.

That's what this book is all about - preparing the people in our organizations to manage and make the most of some of the biggest changes that we have ever seen. The leadership development of every officer is a critical priority in preparing to cope with the future. Having leaders at all levels of the organization is crucial to becoming more efficient in a time of fewer resources and more difficult working conditions.

Over the past few years we have implemented the *Transforming Leadership* process in our organizations. This new policing edition of the book is a guide to the skills necessary to move through the process. It is a map of the transition process itself. We have not seen such a comprehensive model that contains a broad band of generic skills that can be applied directly to practical policing issues.

Although this book's focus is primarily on policing, the model, issues and skills are relevant to any organization in the justice and public safety systems and beyond. This book should be read by any member of the organization who wants to be a leader at their level and in their job. If you want to make a difference, if you want to make an impact, this book will assist you in your goals. We would go so far as to say that it should be compulsory reading for all managers throughout the justice system.

Butts, James. Chief of Police, Santa Ana Police Department. Comment made at the International Problem Oriented Policing Conference, San Diego, California, November 1995.

Preface

Why Should Police, Justice, and Public Safety Leaders Give Attention to This Book?

This book is a distillation of research and best practices in leadership and organization development. The authors have gone to great lengths to save you, the reader, time and energy in your efforts to glean from the literature and from many leaders' experiences that which is based in validated theory and verified in practice.

To our knowledge, this is the only leadership development book that provides an overarching model for leadership development and a guide for developing curricula that target—specifically and simultaneously—the means for creating the strongest impact on personal, team, and organizational effectiveness that results in positive impact on communities.

The need for such a book as this has become increasingly clear on two fronts: followers need leaders/managers who are simultaneously concerned about effective strategic management and about the human side of criminal justice organizations. They hunger for managers with credibility who inspire cooperation and creativity in reaching shared goals and dealing with planned and unexpected change.

This book is not written from fear. Nor is there any intent to create anxiety by forecasting future difficulty or doom. Rather, the intent is to assist people to develop into more fully qualified leaders who can help themselves and others become adaptable to change more gracefully and effectively—and remain healthy during the process of facing prospective adversity. The book will also assist individuals in their preparation for further clarification and achievement of their sense of purpose in the overall scheme of life and in their work. This book anticipates our best response to the likely difficult challenges we face as we are on the very edge of this millennium and moving swiftly into the next.

Transitioning Your Leaders and Your Organization into the New Millennium

During the past 7 years of implementing the knowledge and skills from the first edition of *Transforming Leadership: New Skills for an Extraordinary Future, (HRD Press, Amherst, 1992)*, upon which this book is based I have learned some major lessons. Organization development must take place alongside leadership development, and leadership development is preparation for successful strategic plan implementation. In agencies where leadership programs were initiated without the concurrent implementation of organizational and executive leadership development, the leadership program did not have much of an impact on the organization or the community. For obvious reasons, I do not want to point out the organizations where this was so apparent, but you can likely use your own observation and experience to verify these findings. Transfer of learning into the workplace did not happen just because there was a training program. Also, strategic plans very often ended up as SPOTS (strategic plan on the top shelf) in these same organizations because those who might have implemented the plans did not have the organizational and team leadership skills to implement planned change effectively. Thus, you can see that leadership development is the foundation of team and organization development and is a prerequisite for effective strategic plan implementation.

Therefore, I present, in this preface, the following summary of learning as a capstone to this book. This summary of learning will form an implementation model for *Every Officer Is a Leader* and will result in the development of an implementation workbook. Currently, research and organization-wide custom-design leadership program development is being conducted by myself and my colleague Darryl Plecas (Ed.D) at San Diego Police and Vancouver Police in Vancouver, B.C. The following best-practice recommendations can serve as a checklist to assess the extent to which you find your organization implementing what we know to be effective practices. Briefly assess below the extent to which you think your organization is implementing these performance optimization actions.

Best Practices Performance Optimization Process

Building a leadership organization to develop a learning organization in order to prepare for the future: a systems-based approach

Instructions: In the spaces provided below, insert a number from 0 to 5 to indicate how well your organization has implemented each step in the optimization process.

0=Not at All, 1=Not Very Well, 2=Slightly, 3=Moderately, 4=Quite Well, 5=Excellently

1. _____ Assess internal organizational needs, wants, problems, obstacles, strengths, opportunities, and threats. Use qualitative interview methods to give meaning to quantitative survey data.

2. _____ Assess external community needs, wants, problems, obstacles, strengths, opportunities, and threats. Use qualitative interview methods to give meaning to quantitative survey data.

3. _____ Scan future trends and prioritize best-bet opportunities, threats, and vulnerabilities.

4. _____ Conduct executive team development to maximize the potential of each contributor, clarify roles, eliminate role blur and overlap, work through conflict and past baggage, and optimize team performance. Provide executive coaching for any executives in need of specific leadership or management skill development.

5. _____ Conduct strategic planning session with key executives and stakeholders from the internal organization and external community (this is what is called the *Leadership Development Team*).

6. _____ Seek revisions or additions to and consensus on draft plan from all those who will be implementing it; at this time, deal with resistance to change and obstacles to acceptance of the plan. Achieve at least 70% acceptance and consensus support of the strategic plan.

7. _____ Assess leadership competencies of all leaders in the organization (both paid and volunteer).

8. _____ Train, coach, and/or mentor team leaders to design an operational strategic implementation plan with their teams so that the strategic priorities and plan are implemented effectively at the frontline level. Help team leaders to become comfortable with leading their teams (and developing their members as leaders) toward the implementation of strategic priorities. Accomplish this by helping leaders to learn to build their own implementation plans *with* their team members (people implement what they help create!).

9. _____ Conduct ongoing leadership development by providing coaching/mentoring learning support for leaders. Use retired personnel to accomplish some of this task, and provide training for mentors and coaches.

10. ___ All team leaders conduct monthly implementation plan review meetings with their team members and report to managers and the *Leadership Development Team* in the form of brief minutes that reflect progress on strategic priorities.

11. ___ Publish and celebrate small and large wins in ways that the "winners" experience personally meaningful recognition and reward.

12. ___ Conduct annual strategic plan review with *Leadership Development Team*. Evaluate and report the results of the year's progress to the internal organizational members and the external community.

13. ___ Redesign the strategic plan for the year(s) (we recommend at least two years and no more than 3).

14. ___ Recycle this process annually.

15. ___ Ensure that there is a competent organization development professional, or preferably a team of professionals in larger organizations, who is given formal responsibility and authority to implement the entire process above—or day-to-day operational realities will interrupt and prevent this powerful transformative process from being implemented. This last practice is, according to my experience, turning out to be the most important factor for success.

Total Score_____ (Total score possible = 70. Average organization's score = 35)

This book provides the detailed knowledge and skills that internal or external organizational consultants, executives, team leaders and change agents need in order to be able to lead such an organization development process as the one outlined above.

The Background of This Process Model

A breakthrough in the implementation of the *Transforming Leadership* model came in 1996. Terry Anderson and Doug King conducted two surveys[1,2] at the Justice Institute of British Columbia, in New Westminster, B.C., that surveyed

---

[1] Anderson, T. and D. King, Leadership Training Needs Assessment in Justice and Public Safety, Justice Institute of British Columbia, 1996.
[2] Anderson, T. and D. King, Police Supervisory Leadership Training Needs Assessment, Justice Institute of British Columbia, 1996.

the perceptions of all police supervisors and all managers in public safety and justice organizations in British Columbia. The purposes of the studies were to examine what supervisors and managers in the police community (supervisory leadership skills study for police) and in the public justice and safety sectors (managerial leadership skills) thought were the necessary skills to perform effectively in their leadership roles. Since then, similar studies have been conducted at Vancouver (B.C.) Police and San Diego Police, and another is planned for Lakewood Police Department (the department that responded to the Columbine School shootings). After consensus was reached regarding the competencies required, the participants were then asked the extent to which they saw themselves and their peers, and their supervisors (in the Vancouver and San Diego studies) as being competent in the various skills.

After the questionnaires were designed with the training officers and managers, they were sent out, returned, scored, and the data were analyzed. When we saw the results of the studies, we were not generally surprised, but realized that most of the skills of *Transforming Leadership* (the 1st edition for a general business audience was previously published in 1992, and the 2nd edition was published in 1998) were very similar (over an 80% overlap) to those described and prioritized by supervisors and managers in the field as necessary prerequisites to do their jobs effectively. Then, in 1997, spearheaded by the International Association of Chiefs of Police, and developed by the Royal Canadian Mounted Police (RCMP) and the Federal Law Enforcement Training Center (F.L.E.T.C.), another comprehensive list of competencies was released as a cutting-edge program, entitled "Every Officer a Leader." These competency lists, when combined, are the most comprehensive and exhaustive that we have seen in all the literature on leadership training in policing, public safety, and justice. This is important because there has been so much disagreement and discussion about what competencies are required to be an effective leader, and especially an effective leader in police and other justice and public safety environments. Once the competencies were identified and agreed upon, curriculum development was swift and effective, and the new leadership development program at the Justice Institute of British Columbia was evaluated in its first year, by its participants and their supervisors, as being more effective than any to date.

Appendix C presents a summary of the skills that were considered necessary for leaders to perform at the police supervisory level and management levels in a wide range of agencies, from police to courts, sheriff, ambulance, fire, and emergency rescue. **Appendix D** presents the summary of the competencies and characteristics that are similar (with some revisions) as outlined by the RCMP and F.L.E.T.C. in their "Every Officer a Leader" program. (The results of the other studies can be obtained from the respective police departments.)

This policing edition of *Transforming Leadership* has been written to respond to the need for a comprehensive leadership development model for the education and training of police, justice, and public safety supervisors, managers, and executives. There is even evidence that the more recent focus (during the past 10 years) on community policing initiatives that leadership skills training is important for frontline officers (hence the "Every Officer a Leader" program).

Overview of This Book

The review of leadership theories is retained in this edition but is included in Chapter 10 instead of at the front of the book. An examination of how leadership development can have a truly profound impact on the morale and performance of individuals, teams, and organizations is a central focus. *Transforming Leadership's* innovative conceptual contribution to the literature is a focus on how it is necessary to build "a leadership organization" before—and, to an extent, while—you move ahead in building a "learning organization" that is responsive to community and internal organizational needs. The personal, team, and organization development skills focused on in this book are the necessary prerequisites to successful implementation of any leadership development program or any neighborhood or community policing initiative.

This book addresses this issue squarely, with an emphasis on the importance of the role of executive and leadership coaching and mentoring, in addition to whatever competency-based training may be undertaken, for leadership development. When leaders have skills, they are much more capable of leading teams to achieve organizational results that meet community needs and solve community problems.

This book is front-ended with a self-assessment of skills (in Chapter 2) so the reader can get a snapshot of strengths and areas where there is a self-perceived need for training or coaching. This self-assessment can also be used as a quick 360-degree feedback tool so that a leader can get feedback on how others perceive his or her performance of fifty-six leadership skills. This book can be used as a reference tool and can be referred to over and over again during the course of a leader's development. It can be used as a skill prompter in difficult problem situations where forethought and careful consideration are clearly advantageous. The body of the book is focused entirely on gaining a more in-depth understanding of the fifty-six key leadership skills that are outlined in the book and supported by research in communication, problem solving, counseling, consulting, and leadership development. Other information that focuses on the personal development, rather than skill development, of the leader is now in Part III, Part IV, and Appendices A and B.

This book also provides a model to integrate other models into a holistic leadership development framework; it provides a map for developing critical leadership skills, and it still includes the self-assessment and developmental aspects. This policing edition, however, amplifies and augments the second edition (*Transforming Leadership: Equipping Yourself and Coaching Others to Build the Leadership Organization*, CRC Press, Boca Raton, 1998) in the following ways:

1. Examples from police, corrections, customs, immigration, private security, non-profit, and business environments are woven throughout the book. Business examples were retained at the recommendation of key leaders in the criminal justice system who advised us to include them because it was believed that often the business community is ahead of the criminal justice system in this area of leadership and organization development. Most of the members of the Consortium of Criminal Justice Leadership Program Providers supported the idea of retaining the business and community examples because many justice and public safety leaders interface with the business world and in community life on a daily basis.
2. Feedback from police leaders from all over North America has shaped the content of this book.

This policing edition aspires to add clarity, perspective, and examples to the holistic view of how individual leaders can develop themselves and one another into high-performance team leaders who lead organizations to respond to present and future issues that affect the morale, health, and safety of the communities in which they serve. It is our hope that in writing this edition, we will, to some extent, provide a practical and conceptual ladder to assist the reader to reach toward a high ideal.

A new focus in this book is an added perspective on security issues that affect police, justice, and public safety organizations. This issue of the safety of those who provide safety to others is often overlooked. Ken Gisborne adds this focus in Chapter 13.

Finally, a new focus on the future is introduced in this policing, justice, and public safety edition by including a contribution by Gene Stephens, a well-known police futurist from the University of South Carolina. This future emphasis is presented in Chapter 14.

Who Should Read this Book?

This book is intended for a diverse readership. A rich composite of competencies is needed by the wide range of professional leaders who will read this book. The reader should expect to find examples of various concepts and skills from various working environments. These include business, education, healthcare, social services, criminal justice, and government because police and other justice and public safety leaders find themselves interfacing with, and learning from, all these areas where leadership is applied on a daily basis.

Every Officer Is a Leader also provides the content, structure, and process for the development of those who want to be effective in preparing others to lead more effectively—whether they are in executive positions, managing teams, supervising squads, consulting, coaching, training, counseling, or mentoring police or other officers. An organization that initiates and sustains this kind of development is called a *leadership organization.* This kind of organization stimulates and realizes competency-driven performance improvement.

For centuries, the Japanese have utilized mentors to practice this kind of succession planning and leadership development. Europeans have done so for decades in their apprenticeship programs. In North America, formalized coaching and mentoring programs for police leaders are just now being initiated. The profession of coaching and mentoring is just becoming recognized in that coach certification training and certification programs are now being offered in various parts of North America and Europe (see http://www.coachu.com). For decades, police have instituted the Field Training Officer (FTO) program with great success in orienting and training recruits. But who is doing the LTO (Leadership Tranining Officer) program? Precious few agencies are preparing the leaders of the future before they get into the supervisory or managerial leadership roles for which they are now applying.

In policing, many policing agencies have instituted recruit orientation and coaching programs of various sorts and have trained leaders to be more effective in supervising new recruits, especially during the first six to twelve months of service. In the business sector, mentoring programs have been established in large corporations such as AT&T, Exxon, Kodak, Pacific Bell, Lytton Guidance and Control Systems, Motorola, Esso Resources, Allegheny Ludlum Steel Corporation, Varian Associates, and many others. William Gray, Ph.D., and Marilynne Miles Gray, M.Sc., principals of The Mentoring Institute of British Columbia, have conducted formalized mentor training programs for the companies mentioned above, utilizing the *Mentoring Style Indicator,* co-authored by Dr. Gray and Dr. Terry Anderson. Policing is lagging behind in the development of leaders: As one police chief recently said:

We have our recruit training and mentoring programs, but where are our leadership training and mentoring programs to get people ready to be supervisors and managers – we don't have any! We now have a severe shortage of future police leaders because many of the existing ones are dying early or retiring early, or are not adequately prepared to move up from supervisory to management or executive positions.

Also, those who are newer to their external or internal consulting and training positions are often lacking in key skills that they must have to be effective in developing leadership capabilities in others. For this reason, they may need to develop in certain areas prior to attempting specific leadership development projects or programs. This book will act as a personal and professional development planning guide for these younger professional trainers or supervisors who will mentor less experienced officers. It can also function as a challenging orientation for those who plan to enter the field of consulting or training in the criminal justice system.

Every Officer Is a Leader is also aimed at managers who have had successes in their leadership endeavors but who wish to hone their awareness and skills or develop skills they lack. Several police departments have intitiated *Transforming Leadership* initiatives and have found that they are able to have the desired impact that they wanted to have. Many may not have had training in interpersonal skills, decision making, problem management, change management, or various other skills. Most lack training in other critical leadership areas, however, such as group and team development, meeting effectiveness, organizational needs and problem assessment, culture building, and organizational effectiveness optimization. This book will serve as a catalyst to help individuals fill in some of these gaps.

This book is also for those new to the management or leadership arena, who have been timid in their leadership, or these who are fearful or rigid (in our experience this is a frequently encountered problem among untrained leaders) due to lack of training or experience. It provides an excellent introduction to leadership for those younger officers who want to get a strong preparation and a strong launch for their leadership careers.

Also, those who feel effective as leaders may want to improve their abilities by reading this book. It is often from lack of knowledge, lack of skill, lack of opportunity, or the presence of fear that many leaders fail to develop the kind of leadership impact they would really like to have.

This edition of the book can be used as an adjunct to existing texts and to update the many criminology or criminal justice university programs still functioning without any kind of comprehensive theory and skills model or competency-based leadership training program. An important move is afoot in many programs to provide both a liberal arts education and competency-based educational opportunities prior to graduation with even a baccalaureate degree. Employers in the criminal justice system are demanding a wider range of such skills.

Finally, *Every Officer Is a Leader* is for those who inevitably lead in the family unit and who wish to use this same knowledge and skills to stimulate and encourage the development of their spouses, their children, and themselves. Even though the book focuses primarily on leadership in supervisory and management-type positions, it is written in a way that individuals who are parents will find it accessible. They, too, are leaders on the grandest scale. Parents can potentially have a greater impact on our culture and our world than perhaps any other people. Also, some of the skills in this book can be used to strengthen current marriages and other significant primary relationships. In the criminal justice system, where divorce statistics soar, anything that will help in this area is a welcome gift.

A shift toward a more interdisciplinary approach is already occurring in the fields of communication, counseling, and leadership. It is essential that professionals who educate others to work in human services, healthcare, education, business, industry, the military, and government organizations shift to broader and more integrative educational models—if personal, interpersonal, organizational, and social problems are to be more potently managed and better prevented.

The broad "mission" of this book is that individual readers will find opportunity and challenge to self-examine, gain a renewed sense of purpose, clarify their foundational beliefs, and gain a broad spectrum of knowledge and skills. These new skills will ready them to build and lead the *leadership organization*. In light of this stated purpose, this book seeks to present a positive and hopeful approach: an integrative and innovative self-assessment curriculum—one that I hope can accomplish several objectives:

1. Identify and capitalize on strengths
2. Act as a tool for the assessment of training requirements to pinpoint a supervisor's or manager's (or potential ones') need to gain critical knowledge and skills to become a better leader of individuals, teams, and organizations
3. Function as an integrated knowledge and theory base that an executive, manager, or supervisor can use as a planning guide for internalizing key knowledge "chunks" in areas that are self-assessed as deficient

4. Provide a broad-based theoretical foundation for the development of leaders who will, as they become more adept, be better enabled to develop other leaders through training, coaching, and mentoring activities and programs

5. Provide concentrated focus points for needed and specific "micro" skills training until competency is attained in the areas determined to be necessary for an individual's effective leadership functioning

6. Expand upon the "awareness" and "versatility" skills needed to adapt to fast-changing, dangerous, or otherwise demanding environments (rolé, stylé, and skill-shifting skills)

7. Have this book serve to prepare designated leaders to become competent as *transforming leaders* so that they can train others

8. Point the reader toward innovative resources that can act as catalysts to facilitate further individual, group, or organization development

Acknowledgments for the Second Edition of *Transforming Leadership*

I want to thank Ron Ford for his redesign of the *Leadership Skills Inventory*, for re-sequencing the chapters of the book, and for the design, graphics, and layout of the text. His encouragement, inspiration, and friendship have made the re-write of this book an unexpected pleasure.

I appreciate Val Wilson of Val Wilson, Ink, who tirelessly rendered the reading of the second edition of *Transforming Leadership* into a less distracting, more comprehensive read.

I thank Ken Blanchard for his personal support and encouragement of my work in clarifying the issue of spirituality as it relates to personal, professional, and organization development. Ken's concern for the spirit of people, for the impact spirit can make in the workplace, and for communicating the importance of this issue has inspired me to focus on it in a separate chapter in this revision, and it is outlined as the first appendix.

I also have a deep feeling of gratitude for hundreds of students in my communication, problem-management, and leadership courses at the University College of Fraser Valley; in leadership courses at Trinity Western University; and in counseling courses at the University of British Columbia—who have given me feedback about the clarity, practicality, or difficulty they had with various parts of the first edition of Transforming Leadership over a period of several years. I believe they were honest with me. Thanks to them, I discarded one-third of what I normally would have tried to cover in one book and included some of what I may have never thought of on my own.

Finally, I most deeply appreciate and acknowledge the Spirit of my Christian heritage, the power of which I experience and know to be the driving force behind much of my work and writing.

Information and Resources Exchange

In order to learn from one another and continue to provide the latest breakthroughs in learning, we have developed a Web site where you **can register your e-mail address** and receive free updates and be notified of important additions to the site. The site's address is:

Free *Every Officer Is a Leader* Newsletter: www.policeleader.com

Terry Anderson
Abbotsford, British Columbia, Canada

Acknowledgments

I value Ken Gisborne for his friendship and for his encouragement to write this book. I also recognize him as a co-author, for contributing, as a twenty-year veteran of the RCMP and now president of Security Resource Group, Inc., a security consulting firm, his rich experience to Chapters 7 and 8 and for reviewing the entire content of the book to make improvements and suggestions. He also authored Chapter 13 on police agency, personnel, and electronic security.

I thank Assistant Chief John Welter for the professional relationship we have had while he has been in his role of leading the Neighborhood Policing Division at the San Diego Police Department. I appreciate the opportunity he afforded me to speak to the command staff at San Diego Police in 1996 about the importance of strategic planning and implementation, which led to the organization's developing a comprehensive plan in 1997 that is currently in the implementation stage. I also thank Assistant Chief Welter for discerning the value of my previous work and seeing the potential in it for policing, justice, and public safety. He has been called upon internationally to share his expertise and successful experiences in developing neighborhood policing initiatives. I was fortunate in gaining his participation in co-authoring the communication and problem management chapters (Chapters 5 and 6) in this book. The insights he has gained from his experience at San Diego Police provide powerful examples of how neighborhood and community policing can be successful.

I recognize the untiring efforts and commitment of Pat Holliday, who interwove his rich experience of over thirty years in almost every policing role at Vancouver City Police into Chapters 3, 4, 7, 8, and 12. He also reviewed the entire book and added his polish to the final draft. He deserves great honor for the depth and breadth of his experience and his ability to capture insights in language and examples that make *Transforming Leadership* come alive in a book.

I appreciate John LeDoux, a senior leader at the Leadership and Management Sciences Unit of the FBI Academy, for his early editing and comments on the first edition of *Transforming Leadership* in 1995, which encouraged me to write the second edition. His expertise, support, and feedback also encouraged me to push further to develop it into this policing, justice, and public safety edition. I also value his co-authorship contribution to Chapter 1 and his editorial contributions throughout the various chapters of the book.

I recognize and honor Chief Barry Daniel, who believed in me and the value of *Transforming Leadership* and invited me to do my best to help him, over a period of more than six years, to implement it at Abbotsford Police in Abbotsford, British Columbia, Canada. Chief Daniel led the way among chiefs of police in British Columbia to do accountable strategic planning, has systematically and financially supported the development of leadership in all members of his police cadre, and has been a promoter of leadership development in policing for British Columbia, Canada, and internationally. He forged ahead as a transforming leader who himself in many ways has become visibly transformed into a model leader for younger officers to emulate. He did this in spite of resistance and grumbling from the "old guard," who perhaps would rather have continued on in their ways of managing more and leading less. His encouragement of my work, more than anyone else, has inspired me to move ahead and believe that the knowledge in this book is real, necessary, appropriate, and effective for police personnel.

I thank Chief Constable Peter Young of the New Westminster Police Service, in New Westminster, B.C., Canada, for giving me the same opportunity as Barry Daniel to apply and prove the value of *Transforming Leadership* to the development of the New Westminster Police Service. He arrived as a new chief of police at a time when the force was ready to shift from the old to the new paradigm (from management to management plus leadership). His willingness and ability to integrate the concepts of *Transforming Leadership* into personnel and promotional practices, supervisory and management practices, strategic planning and implementation, and leadership development is second to none. Peter, with his sincerity and persistence to "make it happen," has inspired me more than anyone else to believe that it is possible to make the concepts in this book come alive and manifest into reality.

Lastly, I have a great friend in Marilyn Hamilton, who has over the years been an encouragement to my soul and a partner in our business ventures. Marilyn is also president of Consulting Resource Group International, Inc. (a publishing company I founded in 1979), the founder and senior partner of Consulting Resource Group Ltd. (the associated consulting firm), and a co-founder of the Global Consulting Group. Marilyn has taken *Transforming Leadership* to heart and built our company to a stronger and higher stature, has served dozens of clients as a senior consultant, and is now completing her Ph.D. Her contribution to this book was writing the chapter on building a leadership organization (Chapter 11), in which she illustrates how *Transforming Leadership* can help to build stronger and healthier organizations and communities.

The Author

Terry D. Anderson is a results-oriented consultant, executive coach, author, and university educator with a Ph.D. (1992) in administration and management with faculty from the University of Massachusetts School of Management and School of Counseling and Consulting, through Columbia Pacific University in San Rafael, California. His Professional Teacher Education Certification (1971) was completed at the University of Victoria, British Columbia, Canada.

As an entrepreneur, he founded and developed a successful publishing and consulting firm, Consulting Resource Group International, Inc. (1979) that is currently flourishing with over fifty publications. The first edition of his *Transforming Leadership* was published in 1992 by HRD Press, and the second edition was published in 1998 by St. Lucie Press.

For over twenty years, Dr. Anderson has been a practical, results-oriented senior consultant and executive coach. He has conducted significant organization and/or executive leadership development projects for the Abbotsford Police Department, the Correctional Service of Canada, Government of the Northwest Territories, Japan Creative Education Institute Co. Ltd. (Osaka), Management Learning Resources Ltd. (U.K.), Ministry of the Attorney General of British Columbia, New Westminster Police Service (British Columbia), and the San Diego Police Department and the Vancouver, Police Department.

As a university-level educator, his experience includes over two decades of full-time teaching, working with more than six thousand adults in the Departments of Social Work, Criminology and Criminal Justice in the areas of communication, problem management, and leadership at the University College of the Fraser Valley in Abbotsford, British Columbia, Canada. He also taught at the Justice Institute of British Columbia, and taught police, justice, and public safety managers at Simon Fraser University.

Dr. Anderson was on the Advisory Board for COMDEX, on the Justice Institute of British Columbia's Advisory Committee for the Leadership Degree

Program, and sat on the Conference Planning Committee for the Justice Institute of British Columbia and the Canadian Police College. He has served as a member of an International Network Director (1993) for the American Society of Training and Development and was certified as a Professional Consultant by the Academy of Professional Consultants and Advisors.

Contributors

Kenneth D. Gisborne, CPP, is president and founder of SRG. He developed the SRG Security Optimizer™ Model for providing security consulting services from his vast experience in corporate and government security. His twenty years of police experience, primarily spent in crime prevention, technical security, and security program management, has enabled him to broach every area that impacts the security of an organization. He holds a Certified Protection Professional designation through the American Society for Industrial Security (ASIS) and also belongs to the Canadian Society for Industrial Security and the International Association for Healthcare Security and Safety. He was recently elected chairman of the Canadian Pacific Chapter of ASIS for 1999.

Ken has provided his technical expertise and advanced security consulting training to numerous departments in the Canadian federal government on issues ranging from security program evaluation and design of security processes and systems in new construction projects to protection of the highest levels of Internationally Protected Persons. In the private sector, Ken has provided consulting assistance to numerous clients, including provincial governments, municipalities, policing agencies, universities, hospitals and public institutions, property management groups, and banks.

Ken is an informed speaker who lectures on such topics as closed-circuit video system security, information technology security, and master keying and key control system design. He was invited to speak at the Security Summit, an event that took place in Vancouver for security leaders across Canada. He has been quoted as a security expert in various publications and is currently quoted in periodicals on a major regional security issue. He has also appeared on radio and television, speaking on security-related issues. He currently contributes as a guest lecturer in criminology courses at a local university and is the editor of the ASIS Chapter newsletter.

Marilyn Hamilton, B.A., CGA, Ph.D., is an experienced facilitator and project leader in complex and changing environments. She has led projects in multiple sectors over the last twenty-five years, including professional associations. She has led and coached leaders at senior levels in multinational government and nonprofit organizations in Canada, the United States, the United Kingdom, the EEC, Australia, and the Caribbean.

Marilyn has a passion and purpose to develop wholeness in people, organizations, and communities as living systems. She has applied to leadership and organizations the theories of complexity, chaos, and ecology. Her doctoral dissertation demonstrated how learning and leadership occur in self-organizing systems.

Marilyn is co-author of *Transforming Leadership: Equipping Yourself and Coaching Others to Build the Leadership Organization* and *The Quick Style Indicator* and is the editor of two newsletters, *Leading the Way* and *The Leader*.

Marilyn received her B.A. in English (1969) and Diploma in Translation (1972) from the University of Toronto and earned her Certified General Accounting designation in Ontario (1976). She completed her Ph.D. in administration and management from Columbia Pacific University (1999).

Patrick Holliday CD, C.H.R.M., is a thirty-year veteran police officer of the Vancouver Police Department, with twenty-five years as a supervisor/manager. His broad police experience includes supervision and management in the Uniform Division, Royal Canadian Mounted Police/Municipal Joint Forces Operations and Major Crime Investigations, to name a few. He has held a senior management position in the Provincial Police Training Academy and is now the Programs Manager, Human Resources Section of the Vancouver Police Department.

His experience in policing goes beyond that of police practitioner to police educator. After serving as a law instructor in the Vancouver Police Training Academy, he accepted a position with the newly founded British Columbia Police College (now Academy), where he assisted in the development of new and innovative police training programs, curricula, and resource material.

As an educator and lecturer, he has held a faculty position in the criminology department of a local community college. He has been a guest auditor at the Canadian Police College (CPC), a guest lecturer for the CPC Executive Development Program, and a guest presenter at the 1998 Police Leadership Conference. As an advocate for quality leadership in policing, he is the Regioal Director of the Police Leadership Forum and a charter member of the Institute for Ethical Leadership.

His work has included facilitating the development and implementation of an innovative and effective strategic plan for a First Nations Police Board and Police Service based on the municipal policing model, a first in British Columbia.

John C. LeDoux, Ed.D., Supervisory Special Agent, holds a master's degree in public administration–criminal justice and a doctorate in Adult and Vocational Education from Auburn University in Montgomery, Alabama. Mr. LeDoux was appointed a Special Agent of the Federal Bureau of Investigation in 1971. He has conducted investigations in the Albany, Mobile, and Washington field offices. He is retired and operates LeDoux Leadership, a leadership consulting firm.

He was with the Management Science Unit of the FBI Academy where he was responsible for executive training. He is co-author of *A Study of Factors Influencing the Continuing Education of Law Enforcement Officers* and a contributing author to *Practical Rape Investigation: A Multidisciplinary Approach* and *Critical Issues in First Line Supervision: What Law Enforcement Executives Need to Know.* He has written a variety of articles that have appeared in such journals as *Journal of Police Science and Administration, Police Chief, FBI Law Enforcement Bulletin, Alabama Police Journal,* and *Law Enforcement Bulletin.*

John Welter was promoted to the rank of Assistant Chief of Police in September 1996. He was immediately assigned to the newly created Office of Neighborhood Policing in the San Diego Police Department. In this assignment he leads the movement to Neighborhood Policing throughout the organization. His office includes Data Systems, New Technologies, and Crime Analysis. He oversees the department-wide strategic planning process and is currently bringing a leadership development initiative to the entire police department. Chief Welter has 28 years experience with the San Diego Police Department and during his career he has served in Patrol, Traffic, Motors, Juvenile, Robbery, Child Abuse and Internal Affairs. Chief Welter has extensive leadership experience. He was both a SWAT Sergeant and Lieutenant in the high crime period of the 1980s. After separate assignments commanding the Police Department's 110 officer SWAT team and 35 officer Homicide Unit, he was promoted to the rank of captain and assigned to the newly created Neighborhood Policing Division. In that capacity he led the operational and physical restructuring of the entire 2800 member Police Department to enhance the community policing philosophy and problem oriented policing strategies. Chief Welter has worked with communities, businesses, and other government agencies to develop collaborative, productive partnerships in Neighborhood Policing. He currently sits on the City of San Diego Enterprise Community Governance Board.

Chief Welter holds associate's and bachelor's degrees in criminal justice. He is a recent graduate of the FBI's National Academy in Quantico, Virginia. John has written numerous articles on the local and national movement to community policing and speaks at various conferences and training seminars throughout the

United States. In February, 1997, the FBI sent Chief Welter to Moscow, Russia to conduct Police Management and Leadership training to Moscow Police command personnel. In June, 1997, he returned to conduct similar training in St. Petersburg, Russia. Chief Welter is a college instructor and teaches regularly at the San Diego Regional Training Center. He is presently under contract through the California Department of Justice to provide Community Policing training for police command staff, government program managers and elected officials throughout the state. Chief Welter also works for the U.S. Attorney's Office providing consulting to California police chiefs attempting to either begin, or enhance their movement to community oriented policing.

Gene Stephens has more that twenty years of experience as a consulting futurist, specializing in investigating the future of criminal justice and the world. He has presented his methods and findings to more that one hundred organizations.

Groups seeking his services for consulting/instructing/coordinating/speaking have ranged from the FBI Academy to the International Association of Chief of Police (IACP) and from the National Association of Police Planners to the U.S. Congress Office of Technology Assessment. He is also an instructor on the faculties of three of the most prestigious criminal justice management and executive training programs: the California Command College, the Florida Criminal Justice Executive Institute, and the Bill Blackwood Law Enforcement Management Institute of Texas.

Dedication

This book is dedicated to every kind of officer
who stands in that place of personal risk for the sake of others.

Introduction:
Transforming Leadership
Builds the Leadership
Organization

My premise is that leadership is not exceptional (some are born with it), but the natural expression of the fully functional personality. As Warren Bennis put it, "The process of becoming a leader is much the same as becoming an integrated human being."

—John Thompson
Corporate Leadership in the 21st Century

Transforming Leadership and the Promise of the Leadership Organization

Institutionalizing a leadership-centered culture is the highest act of leadership.

—John Kotter

"Without Vision, the People Perish"

The proverb in this heading reminds us that the vision we have in mind determines the way we respond to challenging conditions. If we have a pessimistic vision, we might tend to stalk the territory like wolves of destruction, seeking only immediate opportunities for gratifying selfish ends. If we have no vision at all, we might wander aimlessly behind others, like sheep lost in a fog of indecision. But if we have a clear vision of realistic possibilities, we can soar like birds of creative change, rising above the clouds of mediocrity to see new vistas and inspire others to achieve cooperative fulfillment.

Transforming leaders build the leadership organization. They have inwardly decided to grow into being more conscious, developed, skilled, sensitive, and creative participants. They strive to make positive differences in organizations and in the lives of others wherever they go. They climb the heavens, reaching beyond the ordinary, the predictable, the average—charting new territories and possibilities. They reach up for leadership from those who are wiser and pull others "below" them upward to greater, unseen heights on the way. This is not easy to accomplish, especially in a rapidly changing world where it seems that many cynical people belittle such lofty ideals. With vision and leadership, however, people can live increasingly meaningful and fulfilling lives. This is an important foundation to enable teams and organizations to make a serious and positive impact on the communities around them, as illustrated in the following figure.

Organization Development Stimulates
Community Development

↑

Team Development Stimulates
Organization Development

↑

Personal Leadership Development Stimulates
Team Development

There are many big themes on the horizon that executives and managers must get ready to help the other leaders in their organizations address: self-management, self-managed high-performance teams, beyond hierarchy, diversity, globalization, quality, conformance to requirements, no-doubt contracting, rapid response, international standards, focused marketing, the learning organization, continuous improvement, customerization, innovation, fashion, entertainment, multimedia, family, credibility, trust, competence, caring, ethics, spirit, transformation. All these themes are important and represent an overwhelming blizzard of change demands on the average decision maker—demands you can help your people with if you have the skills and the know-how.

Acts of Kindness Are Required

Now, more than at any other time, leaders in organizations need competent and trusted consultants (either internal or external) as associates who can work alongside them and provide the following:

1. A way to gain a visionary view of an encouraging future
2. A skilled mind at planning, managing, and leading fast in unpredictable change environments
3. An encouraging spirit
4. Coaching for their own executive and team development
5. A caring heart, so that they can, in the long term, become their own "consultants" with the skill to act with the same level of competence members of the organization have gained over time; in turn, then, they will be better able to pass this torch of knowledge and wisdom along to others.

To become this trusted associate, whether one is helping leaders manage a corporate turnaround, a (TQM) quality programs intervention, or a *law enforcement accreditation* process, one must possess the same pre-requisite sets of knowledge, qualities, and skills. Although most successful leaders may have the necessary qualities, they are not likely to have developed the full battery of technical and people skills required to lead and empower other leaders to transform their organizations into winners in the globally competitive new millennium.

Qualities that People Want from Leaders

All leadership is some form of change management. Fulfilling relationships have the following five qualities that people in organizations and families seek:

1. **Understanding** personal and organizational needs, problems, goals, and dreams helps people feel comfortable and optimistic about the relationship.
2. **Caring** that gets results inspires people to want to engage that individual as a trusted leader to help manage necessary change.
3. **Respecting** people as valuable, unique, imperfect, and developing souls gains their respect.
4. **Genuineness** is the bottom-line requirement—if one is perceived to be personally phony, or incapable of delivering one's claims, one are dead in the water.

5. **Specificity** in written and spoken communication—that leaves no doubt in anyone's mind about the intended meaning of words or contract issues—is critical to earning trust and gaining interpersonal and corporate credibility.

All decisions to change, to buy, to repurchase—or even to love—hinge ultimately on the clear content of conversations and the quality of commitments in relationships!

But if we are truly sincere, genuine in our intent to build a leadership organization and the people in it, and if we have the required qualities inside to gain credibility, that does not mean we will have developed the technical knowledge or specific skills to bring our sincerity and compassion forward to meet people's real needs.

Most Managers Lack Some of the Critical Skill Sets

There are five skill sets of *Transforming Leadership*:

1. Self-management
2. Interpersonal communication
3. Problem management
4. Consultative skills (team and organization development)
5. Style, role, and skill shifting

They are all required for successful intervention as a person or as a professional leader. These skills are more important than the staffing, investigative, patient care, policy, analytical, or technical skills you may have because they are central to your gaining credibility with others. They are also required by the midmanagers, supervisors, or people you serve in order for them to manage change, build teams, develop positive culture, and protect themselves and one another from burnout, at the same time.

Observations suggest that less than one in twenty managers has all five skill sets required to lead individuals, groups, and organizations effectively. Lacking in any one of the Big Five skill sets causes a breakdown in effectiveness when acting as a person, family leader, consultant, or manager. Also, fewer than one in fifty managers or consultants has developed the Transforming Leadership skills to the point where they can teach others these critically important skills. These skills form the foundation of building a *leadership organization*. It is a prerequisite to develop the skills outlined above in order to building a leadership organization.

What Is the Leadership Organization?

Definition: *The leadership organization creates and sustains a leadership-centered culture where leaders are equipped to develop other leaders at all levels of the organization—from the top down and from the inside out.*

To the extent that this is effective, it will result in the development of all people in the organization, who in turn will have developmental impact on their families and communities. This developmental impact occurs because learning occurs. Learning occurs because leaders are competent, caring, creative, and honest. Effective, fully functioning leaders successfully initiate community and neighborhood policing initiatives, engage in problem-oriented policing that uproots causes of crime, and build a policing organization that is successful in being responsive to community needs and problems. In policing, we have field training officers for the mentoring of frontline officers, but how many departments have leadership training officers who mentor those who are gearing up for a promotion to the supervisory or managerial level? In most departments, there is no such program. This book provides a model and process for building the skills of leadership in every officer. This is the only thing that will build the leadership organization.

The leadership organization is based on a commitment by visionary leaders to develop people (and organizations) by providing opportunities for on-the-job learning that leads to spiritual, intellectual, interpersonal, physical, career, financial, and emotional health, growth, and well-being. The obvious rationale for facilitating this development is that realizing the potential of people is a worthy endeavor and, from a professional point of view, results in higher personal, team, and also organizational performance. The leadership organization has at its helm leaders who are developmental change agents—transformation specialists who act as exemplars in the move to lead more fulfilled, service-oriented lives that make a positive difference in the lives of people who will, in turn, affect the success of their organizations the most. This is the way for organizations to regain the loyalty of so many who have grown distrustful and disloyal due to layoffs, restructuring, reengineering, and other change initiatives.

Therefore, in a leadership organization, those in senior positions are the first to make the commitment to long-term development. With consultative assistance, they assess, plan, develop, and evaluate their own personal and executive team capabilities. They learn how to become better leaders and how to develop other leaders directly through their own mentoring of protégés and/or through the development of organization-wide programs that integrate learning leadership with the management functions of the work itself. After the development of the executive team, there are identifiable steps that a leadership organization goes through to effect such a large-scale and longlasting organizational transformation.

1. Shift paradigms from mainly managing the organizational "status quo" to leading performance teams toward the realization of a preferred future.
2. Develop and communicate an inspiring vision of an ideal future that will motivate individuals and teams. Involve others in creating this vision. People get behind what they help create!
3. Assess the needs, wants, fears, and problems of the organization (including those of the internal and external "customers").
4. Using a systems approach to change management, set realistic, achievable transition goals that, when accomplished, will realize the vision.
5. Strategically plan and implement step-by-step changes, and remove obstacles to realizing the new vision and goals.
6. Prepare, train, coach, and/or mentor the key leaders—those who are willing, ready, and able—to develop self-leadership capabilities in all members of the organization.
7. Research and/or track the outcomes of change initiatives and report progress at regular strategically timed intervals throughout the process so that movement toward the vision can be celebrated and unexpected obstacles can be removed or managed.
8. Engage intentionally in continuous developmental learning that results in ongoing personal, team, organization, family, and community development.

These steps are vital to the long-term health of any organization. Without developed leaders—without a strong team at the helm—an organization will have no vision, no spirit, or will be a house divided against itself, and it will not as easily endure the storms of change we are now beginning to face.

How Is the Leadership Organization Different from Traditional Organizations?

The leadership organization prepares the leaders first, but eventually everyone in the organization learns to work *on* the organization to improve it, as well as to work *in* it. People can learn to see their individual contributions in the context of the organization as a whole if they are given feedback about their work unit. They are enlightened if they can see how the internal and external "customers" are influenced by their work. They are brought in line with reality if they understand how their decisions and actions are contributing to or detracting from the financial success or service quality of the organization. It is clear that the leadership organization is not ordinary and that, even though it is not a quick and simple transition to make, it is necessary to move forward into the preferred future that is possible through making such a transition.

The following is a comparison of traditional organizational characteristics with the key attributes of the leadership organization.

The Traditional Organization	The Leadership Organization
Controls organizational design	Is co-designed by those who work in it
Assumes it knows what is best	Assumes that what is best is always changing
Delays change as long as possible	Responds to change immediately
Clings to old paradigms	Anticipates change in advance whenever possible
A linear approach	A systems approach
Vertical command hierarchies	Collegial team relationships
Work is boring repetition	Work as meaningful self-expression
People are cogs in wheels	People as collaborators, teammates
Focus on past and present	Focus on moving toward ideal future
Sufficiency oriented	Continuous improvement orientation
Bureaucracy oriented	People and idea oriented
Management by objectives	Strategic, accountable, intuitive leadership
Traditional gender roles	Competency is recognized/rewarded
Multiple levels in organizational structure	Cross-functions: information access and role clarity
Management by position power	Leadership by credibility
Problems get attacked	Problems get processed or prevented
Conformity to rules	Creative problem solving for continuous improvement
Decision making out of consultation	Interteam brainstorming and decision making
Accountability to boss	Accountability to team
Self-interest orientation	Quality and customer service orientation
Results are top priority at all costs	Intelligent, creative people produce more results and build people at the same time
The rich get richer, the poor get poorer	Wealth and rewards are distributed by contribution

Build the Leadership Organization First, Then Build a Learning Organization

The leadership organization provides a foundation of skills for the leader of the learning organization. The leadership organization development process and *Transforming Leadership* skills provide the process and content to lay the foundation of the learning organization. For example, the five disciplines outlined by Senge (1990)—systems thinking, personal mastery, mental models, building shared vision, and team learning—assume that leaders and learners either possess or can quickly develop the requisite competencies to apply these five disciplines.

Observation during live assessment and training sessions indicates, however, that fewer than one in three trainees who claim to be good communicators can actually demonstrate effective communication skills in a live video interview where their competency levels can be assessed with a high degree of accuracy and interrater reliability. Even fewer of those assessed have demonstrated the more complicated and difficult-to-learn counseling, coaching, and consultative skills. Therefore, it is difficult for managers who are unskilled in the foundations of people-leadership skills to lead the transformation toward becoming a learning organization.

Moreover, it is possible to put into place the basics of a learning organization by installing "systems" and still not develop the leaders to the point where they can develop the people who will execute those systems willingly and competently. In a recent conversation with a health care executive, the point was made clear to me that the total quality management (TQM) process that was initiated was being undermined by over 75 percent of the mid-managers in the organization. They could not lead teams and could not gain the cooperation of workers to implement the TQM requirements—and morale sagged as never before. Numerous law enforcement students at the FBI academy have indicated that their agencies have tried to use TQM or attempted to follow the work of Senge but either have abandoned the efforts or have just pretended the efforts are working.

Senge (1990) states that the five disciplines of the learning organization "might just as well be called the *leadership* disciplines as the learning disciplines." He goes on to state:

> These disciplines span the range of conceptual, interpersonal, and creative capacities vital to leadership. But most of all, they underscore the deeply personal nature of leadership. It is impossible to reduce natural leadership to a set of skills or competencies. Ultimately, people follow people who believe in something and have the abilities to achieve results in the service of those beliefs.
>
> —Peter Senge
> *The Fifth Discipline*

There is a rising tension for leaders to get themselves ready to build "learning organizations" and high-performance teams because learning organizations promise to deliver increased quality, efficiency, productivity, morale, and profitability as they learn to learn. So do TQM organizations or ISO 9000–certified organizations. There are few if any specific training programs, however, to help people get ready to lead or participate in such advanced high-performance organizations. While there are many signs that the future success of organizations lies in their capacity for organization-wide learning, even Senge (1990) reservedly states that:

> I have yet to experience any organization that comes close to exhibiting the capacities we think of when we think of learning organizations—the ability of everyone to continually challenge prevailing thinking, the ability to think systematically (the ability to see the big picture and to balance the short- and long-term consequences of decisions), and the ability to build shared visions that truly capture people's highest aspirations.
>
> One reason that such organizational capabilities are rare is that they require individual attitudes and skills that are rare. A recent story illustrates the challenges. The "champion" of an ongoing project found herself increasingly challenged by the difficulties of operating in a truly open, non-controlling manner. She finally confessed, "It is like I have to live in two worlds—the old world of control and domination and the new world of learning. I know that the new world is what is needed, but I am so capable in the old world." Her boss, the CEO, has been a forceful advocate of the new project. But his forceful support continually sends a mixed message: We need to learn "because I say so." As the top management team has begun to actually practice dialogue (one of the core learning disciplines in our work), the CEO has described his experience as "like an 'out of body experience'"—seeing how opposite are my effects on the people around me from my intentions.

"It is like I have to live in two worlds—the old world of control and domination and the new world of learning. I know that the new world is what is needed, but I am so capable in the old world..." the above quote is so true of the realities of police managers. It is very difficult to make this shift from control to learning. However, without an unprecedented commitment to select and develop leaders, organizations will have difficulty liberating the innovation, quality, and learning required to successfully weather the storms of the coming years and decades. Future trends in policing indicate that we must get ready to become capable of managing change as never before. *Transforming Leadership* can play a critical role in preparing leaders to lead learning organizations because self-leadership is the foundation of individual success, interpersonal development is a prerequisite to team membership and leadership, team leadership is the building block of organization development, and organization development is a critical catalyst for developing healthy communities. This series of relationships is graphically displayed below.

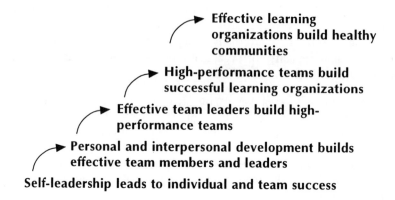

Effective learning organizations build healthy communities

High-performance teams build successful learning organizations

Effective team leaders build high-performance teams

Personal and interpersonal development builds effective team members and leaders

Self-leadership leads to individual and team success

The issue of leadership skills competencies must be taken seriously or organizations will only go through the motions of developing themselves in mechanical ways. Even the "learning organization" as described by Senge is often interpreted by less experienced managers as a quick way to install feedback systems so they can pump out productivity, often without regard to the development of the people who will execute those systems. Also at stake is the issue of leadership credibility.

People Don't Change for or with Leaders They Don't Trust

In all organizations, the catalyst for high-performing teams, productivity, and quality enhancement is people. Although change agents must understand how to assist leaders to plan for and implement change, if those leaders do not have the skills to be effective with their people, the change effort will likely be perceived as undesirable and will therefore be undermined to some extent—and momentum for positive change can be lost.

Leadership is the primary factor that distinguishes successful from unsuccessful over the long term. I accept this as true when I look at successful organizations and their leaders. Most organizations do not know how to select competent leaders because they lack a clear definition of what skills good leaders should have. Some fortunate organizations have discovered that by luck; they happened to have had good leaders. But luck is no longer good enough for even survival. Stories are told of communities where decisions are suddenly made to disband law enforcement agencies or replace emergency medical services with private companies. In most cases, these changes have resulted in reduced effectiveness.

In our complex and demanding time in history, everyone must become a leader of at least himself or herself to even live effectively. This inner strength forms the foundation of effective leadership of others. Therefore, **the successful people and organizations of the future will have taken personal, leadership, and management development seriously.** Self-leadership will become a common word, and effective leaders will become culture-change leaders. They will engage in what Kotter calls "the highest act of leadership"—"to institutionalize a leadership-centered culture." This quote expresses the most profound of insights about leadership development and its relationship to organization development.

On the one hand, I believe that it is impossible to reduce natural leadership to a set of skills or competencies. True transformative leadership includes character, spirit, vision, wisdom, and skills. On the other hand, I have observed over and over again that many well-intentioned, sincere, committed, honest, inspiring, and even wise leaders often lack self-management, interpersonal communication, coaching and counseling, and consultative skills. These absolutely critical skills deficits can seriously interfere with the leader's ability to carry out systems thinking, achieve personal mastery, use mental models, build a shared vision, and facilitate team learning.

How many managers have you personally observed who were competent in doing the task aspects of the job—often the main reason they were promoted—but who lack even the basic skills to be innovative in designing systems and building relationships, teams, and organizations with credibility? In truth, you have likely seen some of them even be destructive. The worst turn of events that I have seen too often in my consulting work is that people are promoted to supervisory or management positions because of task or technical competencies; they and the organization assume that they are competent for the systems design, interpersonal, problem management, and team development aspects of their new leadership roles. If they assume they are already competent as managers, what do they do? Stop learning! Manage more! Lead less! Think of people you know who are like this. What problems have they caused you or others? What names or words do you and other people use to describe their incompetence? *Yet, it usually isn't their fault.* They have not been trained to the level of competency in these critical skills.

In one author's personal interviews with many managers enrolled in the *Transforming Leadership* courses at the two universities where he taught them, he observed that they are often full of theories about effective leadership and that they lack many of the practical skills, know-how, and capability to implement them. Without a strong grounding in the skills of leadership, the practices of the learning organization will not get off the ground. Efforts will be undermined because people will not cooperate or change with leaders they do not like or trust. Providing people with opportunities to assess and learn the foundational skills of self-management, communication, counseling, consulting, and versatility will prepare and equip them to be exemplary leaders in their new police learning organizations.

If Managers Are Not Skilled, It's Probably Not Their Fault

Why are leadership capabilities, as Senge says, so rare among managers? Most managers have not developed the competencies they must have to lead effectively, and it is usually not their fault. They have not been able to find education or training programs that truly equip them with the competencies they need to lead teams toward higher performance and morale. Most of the universities and training programs they have attended have not coached them to competency in the critical leadership skills they must have to be effective. The reason for this is that the education they have received has rarely been competency based, comprehensive, or applied in their lives or workplaces—where it counts the most. Learning often gets lost when it is confined to classrooms or to isolated, off-site training sessions. Their program of learning is usually education about theory—with no awareness of skill—or level 2 or 3 on the five-point rating scale used to assess competency:

Level 1   Not familiar with skill
Level 2   Familiar with skill, but cannot perform it very well at all
Level 3   Can begin to perform skill on one's own with conscious effort
Level 4   Can perform skill naturally in a wide range of situations
Level 5   Can help others learn the skill

Further, in the law enforcement community, there is a prevalent presumption that training is something that is done when you are not doing real work. When you leave training, it's time to return to the real world. When you add to this assumption a general lack of support for the development and promotion of true leaders, the current lack of skills is not surprising.

Even most MBA programs in the past few years have begun to realize how important it is to provide a competency-based curriculum. Smart employers are demanding that MBAs present a wide range of demonstrable competencies before they hire them.

Many universities (City University, Trinity Western University, Simon Fraser University, Ball State University, for example) have used the first or second edition of *Transforming Leadership* to provide a map and a training program for learning the attitudes, qualities, and skills of leadership in their leadership programs. This is in addition to their traditional theory-based curriculum. In addition, more and more companies have formalized mentoring or coaching programs to ensure that those who move into management positions are realistically prepared to meet the challenge successfully. In fact, many organizations "throw their new managers into the deep end, see who can swim best, and promote the strong swimmers further," or they orient them to their new jobs by pairing them up with "politically correct" but relatively incompetent senior managers who model and pass along the "psychopathology of the average." But most of all, the job role and skills of leadership (compared to the traditional manager) have been poorly and vaguely defined; therefore, it has been most difficult to formulate a relevant curriculum for leadership development.

Another factor is that organizations may not really be comfortable with leaders in a learning organization. Law enforcement organizations often prefer the accountability afforded by the traditional hierarchy. A study of situational leadership in the law enforcement community being conducted by one of the contributors to this book contains data indicating that virtually no executives are comfortable with level 4 behavior. At this level, the leader allows the follower to take the lead. The subjects were far more comfortable using a level where the boss keeps control. Many law enforcement executives do not seem to believe they can be perceived as successful if they let go of the traditional controls.

Defining Leadership Illiteracy

Many managers are so leadership illiterate that it is difficult for them to function in the new high-performance learning organization. Many of them know this intuitively but cannot put their finger on exactly what skills they lack so they can get on track with a specific training and development program. You can use the following examples of illiteracy to compare to yourself, others, or organizations with which you are familiar.

Examples of Personal Illiteracy

Consider the following story of a business executive who looks back on a time of personal illiteracy:

> I began my conscious search for personal clarity when I was nineteen. At that time, I had a psychology professor who was into "consciousness" and the human potential movement. Through my dialogs with him, I realized that I did not know myself at all! Even though I grew up in a good, loving family and went to church, I could not

answer the basic questions of life and had most of the recognizable symptoms of the "psychopathology of the average": My religious beliefs were vague and confused; my values were not clear or prioritized; my interests were vague; I had no clear personal or career direction; I lacked a sense of an integrated core of self; I was pessimistic about my own and our planet's future; I was stressed and lacked stress management knowledge and skills; I lacked learning skills to succeed well at my university in the first year; had no sense of personal purpose; didn't manage time well; was overweight; ate poorly; and was out of shape, depressed, and didn't know it. All I wanted to do was have fun, play music, surf, and avoid responsibility.

Sound like a typical Los Angeles youth in 1964? I was typical of a person who lacked what Senge calls personal mastery skills. I didn't make a high-performance team leader (or even member), except in the band I played music in.

As I realized this, I was horrified! I wanted more! During the following several years, I took my personal search process very seriously: I took courses in philosophy and religion and psychology; attended personal awareness workshops; saw the university counselor once per week for three years; participated in encounter groups and weekend encounter-group marathons; took interest inventories and personality tests; became a health and fitness freak; learned yoga and meditation; sought (and still seek) earnestly wisdom and truth about the meaning of myself, love, and the ultimate (metaphysical reality). As I began the search process, I found that doors opened and a profound growth process had begun. I was awake to each moment for the first time! Life became richer and had more depth. Clarity did come. A sense of being on the right track came to me even though I didn't know everything I wanted to know. I learned that if I sought and did not stop seeking, I would keep on finding. I haven't stopped searching.

In many countries, law enforcement supervisors or managers never serve time as an officer or a deputy. After training, they begin immediately to function as a supervisor. In the following story, a European law enforcement executive looks back on a time of personal illiteracy:

Before I started my career in the police force, my knowledge about leadership was limited and I believed that only people with natural skills were able to drive other individuals to perform a task successfully. It seemed as if all the great historical leaders throughout the world were born that way, simply waiting until the right time and place to display their natural abilities. Leadership was a skill some people inherited that made them persons to be followed, imitated, and trusted. In fact, I was hoping these talents were in me awaiting the magical stimulus to appear from the recesses of my brain. Once they appeared

I would be transformed into the leader I presumed was hidden inside me.

The police academy training quickly destroyed my personal theory of leadership. The instructors, far from believing leadership was inherited, stressed that all persons had some natural degree of leadership, but more importantly the ability to lead could be gained through diligent study and mastery of skills through practice and feedback from mentors or coaches in real work settings. Leadership issues such as communication, knowledge of self, and motivation were stressed. These tools allowed me to continue to learn about leadership when I assumed my actual duties.

I quickly learned that I still had much to learn about leadership. Leadership is about growing, not being. I learned the importance of the ability of the supervisor in ensuring the safety of his officers. I learned how the attitude of the supervisor is transmitted to his troops. And, most helpful to me, I learned how much I could learn from my superiors. They provided the support, experience, and motivation to help me to grow. They helped me understand what I consider to be one of the most pertinent parts of leadership—accepting responsibility. I haven't finished growing yet, but I know I'll keep trying and keep helping others to grow.

Two executives were having difficulty in their marriage. The pain in their relationship was spilling over into and interfering with their work. Both of them had experienced painful relationships before, and the pain between the two of them had begun during their courting and engagement period. The premarital counselor advised them: "Whatever you do, communicate! Talk with each other regularly." They agreed that they should do so. Both of them, however, lacked some of the know-how to make their communication successful.

They did not know how to develop the inner control to give their undivided attention to one another. They did not suspend their emotions, judgments, and premature advice—and therefore often did not listen actively and accurately. They often did not convey accurate understanding of one another's feelings and ideas. As a consequence, they often were either aggressive or passive in their communication with one another. For the first two years of their marriage, they hurt and disappointed each another many times. Their confrontations were blaming and negative and did not result in resolving problems. They talked about separation and divorce. They looked around and saw that most of their relationships with other people had similar problems. They felt inadequate, ignorant, humiliated, and powerless to change. They were engaging in the same dysfunctional behaviors at work, and their own and their team members' morale was suffering as well.

Then they took a competency-based thirty-five-hour crash course in interpersonal communication skills. This short course equipped them to at least know what they could and should do. As we Shall see later, just having skills does not mean one has an open heart. They had the sincerity and the caring before, but not the competency. After the training, they had the competency, but they needed open and fully functioning hearts before they could become really good communicators. They were embarrassed! Those were the days (late 1960s) before competency-based training came to the fore. It wasn't their fault. It also wasn't their parents' fault—their parents didn't teach them because they weren't trained by their parents. Their lack of skill was typical of most people.

This pervasive interpersonal illiteracy kills intimacy, morale, and performance at work and at home. We stumble through our lives in certain areas with blind spots because **we often don't know that we don't know.** Even when people are skilled and their hearts are open, they may sometimes decide for various reasons to renege on their commitments and relationships because they do not at the time "feel love" for their partners. Even those whom you might least expect can be unfaithful or may betray commitments and loyalties in love or work relationships.

Skill development eliminates a major cause of breakdown and helps to build healthy relationships. Refusing to participate in dysfunctional relationships or partnerships can be healthy when one or more partners are not willing to engage in self-examination and problem solving. In the final analysis, however, wholeheartedness of commitment and enduring faithfulness must willingly be *given* as a gift so that both parties in a partnership can enjoy the benefits of a steadfast relationship through the tough times. Otherwise, we simply follow our emotions of disappointment or discouragement and dissolve one relationship after another when difficulties present themselves. This is how dysfunctional people can also move from role to role and job to job—people promote, transfer or fire them because they do not want to work near them!

In policing, leadership, unfortunately, is often learned by observing negative role models. For example, one law enforcement executive recounts an important leadership lesson that he learned the hard way:

> On my first day in the precinct I arrived early, as all new officers should. As I walked by the lieutenant's office I introduced myself, since this was my first day. The lieutenant looked up from his crossword puzzle, looked at me, and without a word returned to working his puzzle. He ignored me like I was some kind of lowlife trash, unworthy of his spoken word or any kind of acknowledgment.
>
> From that day on I made sure that no matter what rank I achieved, I was never going to be so important or high ranking that I couldn't speak to anyone that wanted to talk to me. Everyone deserves that much respect! I have watched this man over many years and he has never changed. No one wants to work for him, including the civilian

secretaries. His major career accomplishment has been to lead the department in grievances filed against a supervisor. If I could write down everything that man has done as a supervisor it would make an outstanding source of information for what not to do to be an effective leader.

Contrast this with the first day of another young officer who has since risen in the ranks:

On my first day in the car with him it seemed as though every pedestrian and most motorists waved to the Chief as we passed. I knew that he was quite popular, but to this extent? He said he didn't know most of those who waved, but he usually initiated the greeting. 'It may be the only time that a cop has ever extended a friendly greeting to them. I want them to know that we're on their side,' he replied. During the sixteen years I worked for the Chief, neither I nor any other officer ever recalled him raising his voice in anger to a member of the police department or the public. If an officer committed a faux pas, the trip to the Chief's office usually began with an offer to work with the officer so that the infraction would not be repeated. The officers appreciated his understanding that humans make mistakes and that shouting accomplished little.

Example of Problem Management and Counseling Illiteracy

The managers of a criminal justice organization were facing many staff problems and problems with "clients." Problems often were not faced directly because if anyone had a serious problem, or said that he or she had trouble dealing with a problem, it could affect his or her career success with regard to future promotions. Many people pretended that problems did not exist so that they would not have to be responsible for failing to deal with them effectively. CYA ("cover your ass") became the unspoken motto of this organization. Some supervisory staff ignored calls for assistance or delegated the more difficult situations to less experienced staff so that they could avoid stress, danger, political heat, or their own incapabilities. Open truth telling was not the norm in this organization.

One problem, because it was not faced and dealt with immediately and directly, escalated into mass destruction of property that amounted to millions of dollars. People were hurt physically and emotionally. Five staff members came close to being murdered. After an investigation, only a few people were assigned the blame even though most people in the organization were indirectly responsible for participating in the creation of a dysfunctional culture that led to a riot. Some of the senior managers were autocratic and attempted to solve problems by applying arbitrary policies and rules. They lacked the problem management and counseling skills to confront people head on and engage in problem solving without delay. They paid the price that many leaders in organizations pay. They demonstrated the common dysfunction of many organizations: denial and avoidance of personal responsibility. But they did so because they were afraid of failure. At some level, they knew they did not have the skills to do the job and they knew they were in over their heads. It wasn't their fault,. They had not been equipped with these more complex and difficult skills of problem management and counseling.

They realized that their lack of training and skills was a serious problem. As a result, I helped them design a training program that focused on developing the competencies for managing and solving problems and counseling others to take ownership of their own problem management processes. This course is still being taught nationally in modified form, and the skills are now listed on the job descriptions as requirements of the job. Performance reviews include feedback about how well people engage in proactive problem prevention and management. People are recognized and rewarded when they spot and attack a problem early on. To some extent, the leaders were transformed by this experience, and they have formed a leadership organization that develops other leaders. It is now expected that an officer must have this skill set. It is recognized as a matter of life or death.

Example of Consultative Skills Illiteracy

An entrepreneur started a manufacturing company in 1988. The company manufactured parts of houses to designers' specifications. This entrepreneur was exceptionally successful because of his timing in the marketplace. At the time, he was the only such manufacturer in his local area. But he was lazy. He did not want to build his organization, understand customers' changing needs, and respond in an innovative way to opportunities. By 1993, he had three competitors and was losing significant market share in spite of being in a high growth area. He had set up an assembly-line system for manufacturing that required little expertise or personal involvement on the part of the workers; he paid them low wages and counted on turnover (which had increased from 30 percent per year to 25 percent per month!). To him, people were like computer chips—if they stop working like you want them to, just unplug them and put in another one. I call this approach "computer chip management." He failed to count the costs of retraining and time off due to injuries of inexperienced workers. His turnaround time for delivery of goods improved, and word had spread that this was not the place to do business—and that it definitely was not the place to work.

My teenage son was working a summer job in a competitor's firm thirty-five miles away in another town. He liked the way his employer greeted him every day when he came to work, coached him to make continuous improvements and contributions during the assembly process, gave him raises for higher performance, and joked around with him during the lunch hour. To save two hours of commuting time and travel expenses, my son applied for a similar position in the dysfunctional firm, which was closer to home, and was hired. When he came home after his first day at the new job, he was very upset, and he said to me:

> I can't believe the difference between these two places to work! I can't stand this place! I wish I'd never changed from the other place. The owner of this company doesn't know how to build a company. He doesn't know how to treat people. He treats everyone like slaves, not people. When he's not there, people steal things from the inventory, talk about him behind his back, and work as slowly as they can get away with. When someone scraps a part, everyone laughs because they just count it as revenge on the boss for how he treats people. He doesn't even care about his customers. He is often late delivering the goods, lets flaws go through, and tells customers that if they don't like it they can go somewhere else. I was going to work here part-time while I go to the university in the fall, but I'm quitting now and looking for another job. Most of the other workers are doing the same thing.

This example illustrates how powerful a dysfunctional leader can be. He only wanted to work *in* his company, not *on* it. He wanted to see what he could get out of it, not how he could build it. He could not play a consultative role and lacked the skills to assess the needs, wants, and problems of his employees and his customers. He lacked the skills to develop programs for change and development, and he was slowly, obliviously, going out of business. Even his employees demoted him by assigning him a new title: "Joke." This is typical of leaders in some police, fire, court, prison, immigration, and customs organizations.

Example of Versatility Skills Illiteracy

Style rigidity brings to mind the image of Popeye. His favorite saying was, "I yam what I yam! I'm Popeye the sailor man." His friend Bluto was even more rigid and predictable. The chief executive officer of a major company was known by his customers as a bureaucratic, arbitrary, and rigidly manipulative man. This guy was regularly irritable, interested only in his own benefit—even at the expense of others, and engaged in put-downs and guilt trips even while trying to negotiate a contract to his advantage—more like Bluto than Popeye. He treated virtually everyone the same. His employees, his wife, his children, and one of his friends moved out of town just to get away from him. When one employee needed support and direction, he criticized her performance and demanded more, calling her a whiner. When another employee wanted two-way communication to solve a problem, he predictably gave his premature advice and demanded conformance to his "solution." When his wife sought consolation following the loss of her mother, he left for a fishing trip, telling her "everyone dies, you'll get over it." He blew up at his kids and yelled at them for over five minutes because their rooms were messy. He lacked the skills and the versatility to become anyone's problem management facilitator, communicative friend, or consultative colleague. His rationalizations made him even more intractable, as he proudly bragged: "Everyone knows where *I* stand—because *I'm* honest!"

He engaged in our self-assessment-center process using the *Leadership Skills Inventory (LSI)* from our Consulting Resource Group International, Inc., and found that he lacked most of the skills needed to be an effective communicator, coach/counselor, and consultant. Using the "other" version of the *LSI*, he received harsh and "honest" feedback from his employees in an anonymous questionnaire. He realized that if he was going to salvage his marriage, he was going to have to make some major changes. As he was on his third marriage, he began to take the feedback seriously—especially because he got the same feedback from home and work. Over a period of two years, he came to be respected as a "jerk-in-process," a person humble enough to admit to everyone that he lacked important skills but was willing to learn. He did learn most of the skills and achieved a new level of self-respect and credibility among all those who could forgive the past. His marriage survives to this day, and his teenage kids have not left home. Quite a transition!

The lack of versatility can cause serious problems. One deputy told the following story:

> The sheriff has a mental model that a good leader is autocratic and sets rules for others to follow. Often, a whole policy manual full of sometimes conflicting rules confuses or overwhelms many people. Staff meetings are held to feed the ego of the sheriff. During the meetings the sheriff provides proclamations that each attendee is expected to enthusiastically endorse. God forbid that anyone should dare to question one of the sheriff's points of view or even suggest that more research might be helpful! A vicious personal attack on the "disloyal" member is sure to follow. As you might guess sycophants abound.
>
> People are afraid to make any decision in case the sheriff disagrees. And what's okay today he may consider wrong tomorrow. Therefore, all decisions are passed up the chain. Yet if the sheriff hears someone say he would like to kick a potential decision around with others, he scolds the supervisor as someone who lacks sufficient self-confidence. The sheriff says a good leader doesn't manage by committee. Yet, the

agency has many committees. Apparently the sheriff heard somewhere that a modern leader establishes committees. But he can't break his autocratic style. The committees are meaningless. None of their suggestions are taken. Consequently people don't want to be on the committees. But you are caught in the horns of a dilemma because if you ask to leave a committee, you are marked as disloyal.

I don't know why the sheriff is like he is. But I suspect it was the type of leadership he experienced as a young deputy and he feels he just can't change. I do know he's not likely to change and it's not helping the department.

On to Part I of This Book

Part I of this book provides an opportunity for you to assess the leadership skills you have and the ones you need to develop. It will also help you to understand and learn to use the *Transforming Leadership* model to build a leadership organization.

References

Kotter, J.A., *A Force for Change: How Leadership Differs from Management*, New York: The Free Press, 1990.

Oakley, Ed and Doug Krug, *Enlightened Leadership*, New York: Simon & Schuster, 1994.

Senge, P.F., *The Fifth Discipline: The Art and Practice of the Learning Organization*, New York: Doubleday, 1990.

Senge, P.F., The future of workplace learning and performance, *Training and Dev.*, May 1994.

Thompson, John, *New Traditions in Business: Spirit and Leadership in the 21st Century*, San Francisco: Berrett-Koehler, 1992.

Part I

2

Leadership Skills Inventory: Self-Assessment

Transforming Leadership offers not only the direction and the road map for the leadership development journey, this articulate book gives us the supplies and nourishment to thrive along the way. Terry Anderson knows that leadership development is self-development.

—Jim Kouzes
Co-author of *The Leadership Challenge* and *Credibility*
and President of TPG Learning Systems,
a company in the Tom Peters Group

In this chapter, you will perform a self-assessment using the *Leadership Skills Inventory (LSI)*. The *LSI* examines fifty-six of the skills commonly used by effective leaders, skills that account for a significant amount of their success. The results of this self-assessment will provide you with a "road map" for personal and professional development as a leader through the rest of this book.

The logic of this assessment is based upon the following leadership model:

1. The core attribute of an effective leader is his or her ability "to see." Leaders can see where they are and where they are going. They have insight into the current situation and can see the problems and the oppor-

tunities. Their decisions and actions are purposeful and intentional because they are able to take advantage of what they see. Without this leadership "sight," they would have nothing to contribute to the life and mission of an organization.

2. Leaders make a difference in the lives of those who follow them. Leaders inspire followers to action and sacrifice. Leaders motivate people and organizations to make changes and tackle challenges. Leaders come in countless varieties and differ from one another in matters of style, personality, and methods. Nevertheless, there is a common, distinguishing characteristic among all leaders who are truly effective: leaders have tremendous influence upon the lives and work of others.

3. Finally, the vehicles by which a leader's "sight" is translated into influence are the skills identified and assessed in the *LSI*. These skills are central to the leader's ability to function effectively in the context of relationships and organizations.

The following figure illustrates this dynamic leadership reality.

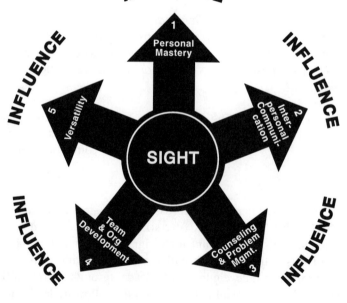

Evaluate your own ability to perform the leadership skills in the assessment below using the following scoring system

This skill is new to me. **1–2** I cannot do it.	I understand the skill **3–4** but I cannot do it.	I can perform the skill **5–6** but not reliably	I can perform the skill well **7–8** in many situations.	I can perform the skill well. **9–10** I can teach others, too

For added benefit, space is provided to gather scores about yourself from two other people who know you well enough to assess your skill levels. This will give you a very important reality check by comparing how you see yourself with the way others see you.

The Skills of Personal Mastery (For Self-Control, Improved Performance, and Development as a Leader)

These skills have been shown to be the **personal foundation** of leadership and management effectiveness. Without these foundational skills, it is difficult to become proficient in any of the other more complex skills that follow. These skills provide you with the capacity to achieve better balance in life and improved performance in all areas of professional and personal life. Your scores in this section will help you evaluate and pinpoint your need for coaching or training in specific skill areas.

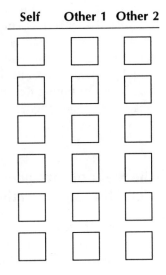

		Self	Other 1	Other 2
#1	**Grounding:** I control my attention to focus in the present (not in the past or future).			
#2	**Centering:** I maintain clear awareness of self in the context of events going on around me.			
#3	**Beliefs Clarification:** I express and live out a clear and consistent set of beliefs.			
#4	**Purpose Specification:** I identify and live out a personal statement of purpose for my life.			
#5	**Values Identification:** I identify, prioritize, and live out a set of personal values.			
#6	**Life Planning:** I formulate an integrated plan and live out an intentional life-style.			

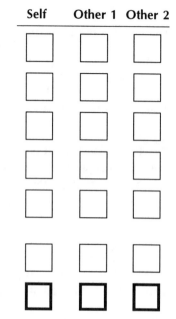

	Self	Other 1	Other 2
#7 Education Goal Setting: I specify and live a goal-driven plan for lifelong learning.	☐	☐	☐
#8 Career Goal Setting: I set and implement motivating and realistic career goals.	☐	☐	☐
#9 Time Management: I plan and implement the best prioritized use of time.	☐	☐	☐
#10 Stress Management: I apply effective stress management methods to daily life.	☐	☐	☐
#11 Health Management: I get optimum nutrition, exercise, deep relaxation, and restful sleep.	☐	☐	☐
#12 Positive Mental Attitude: I control "self-talk" and build my own sense of self-worth.	☐	☐	☐
Personal mastery skill set total:	☐	☐	☐

**Transfer the total scores for the *personal mastery* skill set
to the *LSI* scoring wheel on page 35.**

For more information on the skills assessed in this portion of the *LSI*, turn to Chapter 4 for detailed discussion and illustrations of these skills in action.

Chapter 9 provides you the opportunity to begin developing a personal plan for growing and sharpening your leadership skills, based on what you identify in this assessment and in the supportive chapters to follow.

Note: To make this comparison of the *LSI* results even easier, the *LSI* is available in two formats. The *LSI for Self* and the *LSI for Others* can be used to achieve a more anonymous assessment by providing others who are going to assess you with a separate assessment instrument to use. These tools are available from Consulting Resource Group address: 200 West Third Street, Sumas, WA 98295-8000; phone: 604-853-0566; fax: 604-850-3003; Web site: http://www.crgleader.com).

The Skills of Interpersonal Communication
(For Clear and Effective Communication with Others)

These skills have been shown to be the **interpersonal foundation** of leadership and management effectiveness. The previous skills must be in place in order for these skills to fully develop. These skills provide you with the capacity to achieve clear two-way communication, improved relationships and morale, and greater self-confidence as a communicator. Your scores In this section will help you evaluate and pinpoint your need for coaching or training in specific skill areas.

	Self	Other 1	Other 2
#13 Self-Disclosure: I reveal my personal thoughts, beliefs, and feelings appropriately to others.	☐	☐	☐
#14 Image Management: I positively manage the internal images I create in my mind of myself and of others.	☐	☐	☐
#15 Impression Management: I appropriately manage the impression others have of me through my language, dress, and decorum.	☐	☐	☐
#16 Attending: I control and focus my undivided attention respectfully toward others.	☐	☐	☐
#17 Observing: I objectively check my perceptions and avoid distortions or judgments.	☐	☐	☐
#18 Suspending: I wisely withhold emotions, judgments, and premature advice.	☐	☐	☐
#19 Questioning: I use (but not overuse) questions to elicit information effectively.	☐	☐	☐
#20 Listening: I check for the meaning others intend to convey to avoid prejudgments.	☐	☐	☐
#21 Responding: I convey accurate understanding of others' feelings and circumstances.	☐	☐	☐
#22 Assertiveness: I speak honestly and kindly and avoid using "put-downs."	☐	☐	☐
#23 Confrontation: I provide constructive criticism, direction, and positive support.	☐	☐	☐
#24 Challenging: I encourage others to capitalize on unrealized potential.	☐	☐	☐

Interpersonal communication skill set total:

☐ ☐ ☐

Transfer the total scores for the *interpersonal communication* skill set to the *LSI* scoring wheel on page 35.

For more information on the skills assessed in this portion of the *LSI*, turn to Chapter 5 for detailed discussion and illustrations of these skills in action.

Chapter 9 provides you the opportunity to begin developing a personal plan for growing and sharpening your leadership skills based on the things you identify in this assessment and in the supportive chapters that follow.

The Skills of Counseling and Problem Management (Helping Those Around You Solve and Manage Problems)

These skills have been shown to be the **problem-solving and decision-making foundation** of leadership and management effectiveness. The previous skills must be in place in order for these skills to fully develop. These skills provide you with the capacity to improve problem solving and decision making, decrease stress in relationships, engage in effective conflict resolution, and enhance your performance management efforts when working with others. Your scores in this section will help you evaluate and pinpoint your need for coaching or training in specific skill areas.

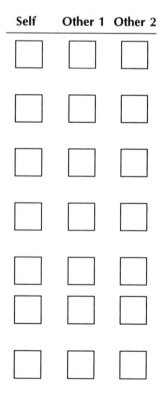

	Self	Other 1	Other 2
#25 **Advanced Empathy:** I show accurate understanding of the deeper feelings and problems of others.	☐	☐	☐
#26 **Problem Exploration:** I explore the implications of internal or external problems with others.	☐	☐	☐
#27 **Problem Specification:** I specify the nature, causes, and implications of a problem for others.	☐	☐	☐
#28 **Problem Ownership:** I specify and facilitate appropriate ownership of a problem by others.	☐	☐	☐
#29 **Goal Setting:** I help others identify realistic and motivating scenarios and time lines.	☐	☐	☐
#30 **Goal Ownership:** I specify and facilitate who is to make commitments to take action to resolve problems.	☐	☐	☐
#31 **Action Planning:** I explore specific pathways and steps for goal achievement.	☐	☐	☐

	Self	Other 1	Other 2

#32   **Implementing Action Plans:** I increase success rate through follow-up and rewards.

#33   **Confrontation:** I identify and help others and myself to address self-defeating behaviors.

#34   **Self-Sharing:** I help others see problems in a new light by sharing my own story.

#35   **Immediacy:** I point out typical problem behavior in others' present actions.

#36   **Referral:** I make an effective referral to a professional helper.

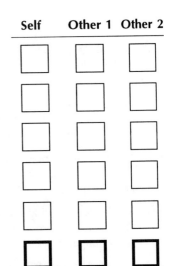

Counseling and problem management skill set total:

Transfer the total scores for the *counseling and problem management* skill set to the *LSI* scoring wheel on page 35.

For more information on the skills assessed in this portion of the *LSI*, turn to Chapter 6 for detailed discussion and illustrations of these skills in action.

Chapter 9 provides you with the opportunity to begin developing a personal plan for growing and sharpening your leadership skills, based on the things you identify in this assessment and in the supportive chapters to follow.

The Skills of Team and Organizational Development (Building Effective Teams and Organizations)

These skills have been shown to be the **team development and organization development cornerstones** of leadership and management effectiveness. The previous skills must be in place in order for these skills to fully develop. These skills provide you with the capacity to achieve consensus-based problem solving and decision making, manage the stress of working in teams, and enhance the team's and the organization's performance. Your scores in this section will help you evaluate and pinpoint your need for coaching or training in specific skill areas.

	Self	Other 1	Other 2

#37   **Informal Assessment:** I assess needs, wants, problems, and fears by one-to-one interaction with people.

	Self	Other 1	Other 2

#38 **Formal Assessment:** I assess needs, wants, and problems through surveys, research, and information systems.

#39 **Problem Management Facilitation:** I facilitate effective problem management meetings that improve performance.

#40 **Needs Clarification:** I clarify the need for change in a language others will understand and accept.

#41 **Readiness Checking:** I explore readiness for change and overcome blocks to constructive change.

#42 **Values Alignment:** I explore and facilitate team spirit and synergy through clarifying and aligning values.

#43 **Vision Consensus Building:** I facilitate consensus about the organization's mission, vision, and purpose.

#44 **Strategy Consensus Building:** I facilitate consensus regarding objectives, goals, and action plans.

#45 **Program Design:** I design and implement flexible programs to reliably achieve objectives.

#46 **Program and Team Performance Evaluation:** I evaluate and report the impact of action programs and team efforts.

#47 **TQM Leadership:** I lead teams toward continuous improvement of what our organization produces or provides.

#48 **Building Accountability:** I install accountability systems so everyone experiences "no-doubt contracting."

Team and organizational development skill set total:

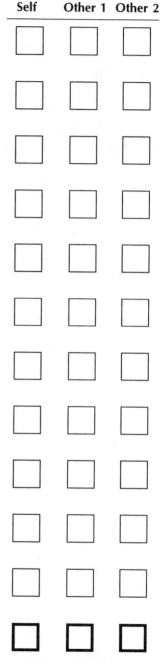

Transfer the total scores for the *team and organizational development* skill set to the *LSI* scoring wheel on page 35.

For more information on the skills assessed in this portion of the *LSI*, turn to Chapter 7 for detailed discussion and illustrations of these skills in action.

Chapter 9 provides you the opportunity to begin developing a personal plan for growing and sharpening your leadership skills, based on the things you identify in this assessment and in the supportive chapters to follow.

The Skills of Versatility in Style, Role, and Skill Shifting (Effectively Adjusting to Match the Individual, Group or Organization)

These skills have been shown to be the **versatility and flexibility cornerstones** of leadership and management effectiveness. The previous skills must be in place for these skills to fully develop. These skills provide you with the capacity to be more appropriate, flexible, and effective in a wide range of situations, including one-to-one relationships, team relationships, and relationships between teams and in organizations. Your scores in this section will help you evaluate and pinpoint your need for coaching or training in specific skill areas.

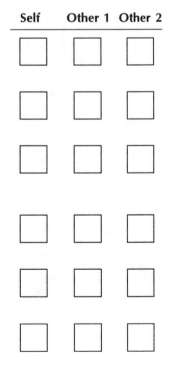

	Self	Other 1	Other 2
#49 **Assessment of Styles:** I assess the predominant style tendencies of another person, group, or organization.			
#50 **Style Shifting:** I shift into the appropriate style behaviors that match the styles of others.			
#51 **Assessment of Roles:** I assess whether the communication, counseling, or consulting role is most appropriate for a given person or situation.			
#52 **Role Shifting:** I shift into the appropriate role that matches the requirements of the situation.			
#53 **Assessment of Skills:** I assess which skills would be most appropriate to use in various situations.			
#54 **Skill Shifting:** I shift into appropriate communication, counseling, or consulting skills as required.			

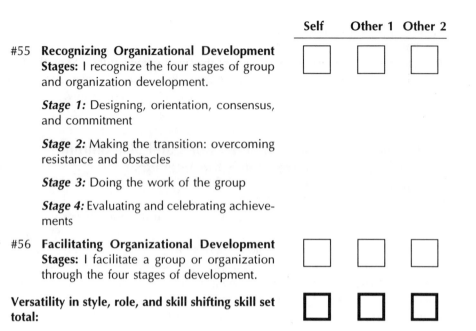

	Self	Other 1	Other 2

#55 Recognizing Organizational Development Stages: I recognize the four stages of group and organization development.

Stage 1: Designing, orientation, consensus, and commitment

Stage 2: Making the transition: overcoming resistance and obstacles

Stage 3: Doing the work of the group

Stage 4: Evaluating and celebrating achievements

#56 Facilitating Organizational Development Stages: I facilitate a group or organization through the four stages of development.

Versatility in style, role, and skill shifting skill set total:

Transfer the total scores for the versatility in *style, role, and skill shifting* skill set to the *LSI* scoring wheel on page 35.

For more information on the skills assessed in this portion of the *LSI*, turn to Chapter 8 for detailed discussion and illustrations of these skills in action.

Chapter 9 provides you the opportunity to begin developing a personal plan for growing and sharpening your leadership skills, based on the things you identify in this assessment and in the supportive chapters to follow.

Summary of Your *LSI* Results

Directions: Graph your scores in each of the five sections of the *LSI* on the *LSI* scoring wheel to visualize the results of your self-assessment. Place a "dot" on the line for each skill to correspond to its total score. Then connect all the "dots" with a continuous line. This will give you an overview of the extent to which you have developed each of the five skill sets, an important part of your leadership effectiveness. In addition, ask two other people, who know you well, to complete the *LSI for Others* for you. This will give you a valuable reality check and useful feedback. Graph their scores in different colors to distinguish them from you own self-assessment scores.

LSI Scoring Wheel

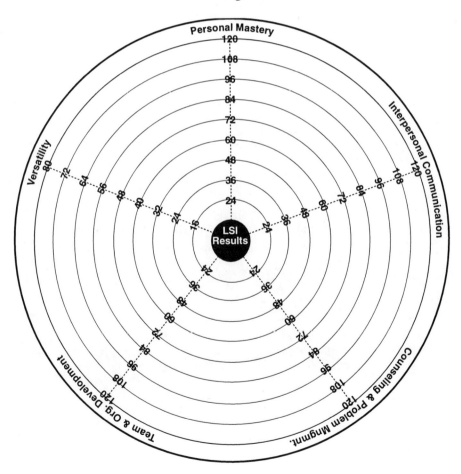

3

Introduction to Transforming Leadership and the Transforming Leadership Model

...The original purposes of police organizations were difficult enough, but superimposed on these difficulties are these modern problems which aggravate the situation and complicate it enormously. All other governmental activities are dwarfed in comparison...Executive capacity of the very highest degree should be demanded and universities should vie with each other in turning out from their institutions people adequately trained to serve their country as efficient police leaders.

—August Vollmer
The Wickersham Commission Reports, 1931

Introduction

In this chapter, we will look into the nature of transformative leadership by examining the following:

1. Examples of *Transforming Leadership*
2. The emergence of *Transforming Leadership*
3. The *Transforming Leadership* model

4. Principles of *Transforming Leadership*
5. Roles and functions of *Transforming Leadership*
6. Attitudes and characteristics of transforming leaders

As expressed by Germann in his book *Police Executive Development* (1962):

> The police administrator of today is faced with an ever increasing complexity of responsibilities. Society is making demands upon him unheard of twenty-five years ago—demands of complex technology, of increased services, of more effective operations. If the police administrator is to meet the challenge, he must be prepared by adequate training.

If the preceding quotes were true in 1931 and 1962, they are even truer at this time as we approach the new millennium. The *Transforming Leadership* model addresses this need for learning that prepares us to respond in complex ways to complex problems, to anticipate and lead the future, and to build teams that respond to community needs and problems in creative ways.

Examples of *Transforming Leadership*

Some examples of leadership that have a transforming effect will help to clarify the important differences between traditional and *Transforming Leadership*:

1. A police chief realized, after he had completed both a compliance audit and an organizational culture audit, that his organization was doing great in the compliance areas but not very well in the organizational culture area. The audit elucidated the fact that three of his senior managers and eight of his mid-managers were perceived to be a demoralizing force within the ranks. They were identified as having engaged in demoralizing behavior of various sorts. Then, after some internal investigation and confidential interviews, there was corroborating evidence of harassment; discrimination; unfair treatment; playing favorites with friends; a general failure to build teams and prevent, manage, and solve problems; and in some cases overt avoidance of responsibility and laziness. He met with each of those who were suspected to be engaging in demoralizing behavior and confronted them with the evidence. Most of them admitted their mistakes. He asked them to make a commitment to change and to agree to a peer review (along with all managers and supervisors who also underwent confidential 360-degree feedback). They agreed, and further reviews were done after three and six months. A year later, less than half of these eleven leaders remained with the department (they were fired

with just cause); the others changed their behavior and continued to serve on the force.

2. A top-level government executive realized that his management team lacked cohesion and harmony, that team meetings were fraught with tension and competition, and that some of the more important goals of the organization were not being reached because of poor relations among the management "team." He privately surveyed each of his managers, summarized their individual perceptions and concerns, and called them together to present his findings. The main trouble seemed to stem from the fact that the team was thrown together in a hurry during a time of available funding, and no one spent much time discovering strengths of others, clarifying roles, or agreeing upon goals of the organization. The group called in a consultant to run a three-day team development session, followed by a three-day strategic planning session. By the end of that year, the group had not only achieved its goals—it surpassed them. Tension levels dropped, job satisfaction increased, and cohesion and creativity developed within the group.

   Traditionally, there would have been no systematic intervention, with the resulting effect of either increased tension and backbiting with lowered performance or increased turnover, or both.

3. After a serious riot in a maximum security prison, the deputy warden decided to call in a stress and health consultant to work with staff whose lives had been threatened. Some of the officers had been trapped in their living unit offices while inmates set fire to them, and there was evidence of posttraumatic stress syndrome in a number of officers (anxiety attacks, insomnia, depression, irritability, distractibility, absenteeism). After an assessment of officer needs, the deputy warden decided to offer health and wellness training to all the officers who wanted it and personal stress counseling sessions for all who wanted to speak to a psychologist. Also, a consultant was called in to assess the organizational climate and predisturbance factors that precipitated the riot. As a result of this intervention, changes were made that, over a period of a year, resulted in a significant drop in absenteeism, a reported increase in morale, and significantly fewer stress symptoms reported among staff. Moreover, there were no further riots at this institution for five years.

4. A relatively large police department decided to implement a system of "report cars." These cars responded to low-priority, nonemergency calls. Activities consisted primarily of interviewing victims and witnesses and reporting. One of the issues that arose was staffing. Due to the perceived low-stress, nonemergency type of activities, staffing of report cars was often seen as analogous to "hiding" those who were deemed less than

fully productive. When asked to provide staffing for the new units, some supervisors used the opportunity to "dump" those members they felt were underproducing. The leader of one group of selected report car members took a very different position. She brought them together to facilitate determining their vision of their new role in the organization. She made responsibility and ownership a rallying cry. They were allowed freedom in the planning stage to determine days and hours of duty based on their own research into effective deployment. Risk taking was encouraged. They were also encouraged to work with each other on quality-of-life issues such as determining which shift best suited their own life-styles while optimizing service. They prepared and presented justifications to the leader for specialized equipment. The leader "fought" their case successfully (with some skepticism from senior managers), and they got the equipment. The report car program was implemented with the unit members doing their own evaluation. The leader brought them together at regular intervals to discuss their successes (and nonsuccesses). Part of the group's planning process included clearly defined success criteria. Group members were allowed to criticize the program only if the criticism contained something productive. Shifts and procedures were adjusted based on their experiences. Reports were evaluated for quality and suggestions for improvement were made. The leader transmitted and reinforced positive feedback from senior levels. More importantly, however, the leader brought "acknowledgment" of their contribution by their peers. Within several months, production and service quality of the unit far exceeded the original targets. As positive feedback increased, so did the level of service. The experimental program became an integral part of the organization's service delivery.

5. No situation evokes a greater image of a call to leadership than when someone must replace a "fallen" leader. Such was the case for a member of a police tactical unit. Its leader had died during a tactical operation. The new leader, who was elevated from the ranks, was faced with numerous crucial and some potentially crushing issues. One of these was the use of this horrific incident by some as an emotion-based challenge to police management to make immediate and costly changes in the equipment and resources provided to the tactical unit. The incident added fuel to an already contentious situation. The new leader was faced with this challenge when rational thought clearly indicated that a slower, more research-based approach was necessary to ensure that the unit was equipped only after an objective and thorough evaluation of its needs. The pressure on the leader to act swiftly came from within the unit and from outside. But the new team leader, emphasizing a cognitive-based personal style, was able to mitigate the emotional tide through interpersonal communi-

cation skills. The skills of listening, responding, and, where necessary, confronting helped move the unit toward a shared vision and purpose. Although it took longer than some might have wished, the unit achieved new levels of professional growth in terms of training, skills, and the acquisition of resources under the new leader's stewardship.

Obviously, such results do not occur simply because a program is inserted into the environment. The people involved must accept and utilize such a program, and the program has to be introduced in such a way that it is perceived as a welcome addition. This is where the comprehensive approach taken by *Transforming Leadership* can lead to greater success in anticipating, managing, and planning change.

These examples illustrate the essence of *Transforming Leadership* in several different environments. Next, we turn to the aspects of gaining a better understanding of the foundational theories of *Transforming Leadership*.

Leadership and Management: Interrelated but Different

There are clear differences between a management and a leadership orientation. As the chart below reveals, however, the integration of the two orientations presents a complete view of what is necessary for effective creation and trans-

Relationship of Management and Leadership Functions

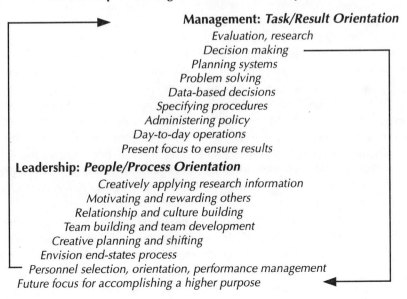

Management: *Task/Result Orientation*
Evaluation, research
Decision making
Planning systems
Problem solving
Data-based decisions
Specifying procedures
Administering policy
Day-to-day operations
Present focus to ensure results

Leadership: *People/Process Orientation*
Creatively applying research information
Motivating and rewarding others
Relationship and culture building
Team building and team development
Creative planning and shifting
Envision end-states process
Personnel selection, orientation, performance management
Future focus for accomplishing a higher purpose

formation of an organization and the people in it. Also, the recyclical nature of the *Transforming Leadership* approach illustrated in the chart provides a sense of the fluidity of the process. Rather than a cycle, perhaps it could be better represented as a spiral moving through time.

The Leading Manager: Integrating Diverse Orientations

As you look at the steps in the chart, you can see how important each of the tasks and functions is in management and leadership and how certain functions must be performed prior to others, in a step-by-step but flexible process. It is also useful to think of management and leadership as two separate but interrelated areas because there has been so much confusion about their separate identities and purposes. Unless both work together in a balanced manner, each will suffer and be less effective. Without leadership as the foundation of management, management cannot function effectively because it is undermined by a lack of humanity, clarity, focus, adaptability, and creativity. Without management, leadership might never follow through enough to get the results needed for long-term success.

The Nonprofit Society Case Study

A group of people concerned about unwed mothers facing pregnancy who, for religious reasons, did not want to abort the unborn formed a nonprofit society by registering with the appropriate government agency. This example is similar to many community-based policing and corrections initiatives where it is important for leaders to facilitate the development of teams, consult with community members, lead advisory boards, etc.

The board members of this society were dedicated professionals who were very sincere and very busy, but had no previous experience in the process of developing a new organization. A rough constitution was written up, but it was not ratified by all members. Staff members were hired, and the operation opened its doors. The staff agreed that the first priority was to conduct counseling sessions with unwed mothers to assist them in making an independent decision as to whether to keep the child or find parents who wished to adopt the child. Those who chose the adoption route had an opportunity to select the parents to whom their babies would go. In nearly all cases, the adoptive couple was unable to have natural children.

Things went well for a few months, until conflicts among staff members began to emerge. Who should decide which of the qualified applicants on file should be permitted to raise the child: the birth mother, the director of the agency, or the staff person involved in the interviews with the adoptive parents? Should prospective adoptive parents have to reveal whether or not they had ever had an abortion in the past, used illegal drugs, had a criminal record, etc.? Staff members disagreed and could not resolve their disagreements on these issues. Board members disagreed and could not resolve their differences either.

The board of directors had not specified the extent of the director's authority, even to the director. When the chairman of the board was informed of the conflicts, some arbitrary "management" decisions were passed "down," and the staff members felt that their views were not being heard or respected. There wasn't really a team approach, which had been so generously spoken of by everyone, at least in principle.

In the beginning, there was little *Transforming Leadership* to provide clarity of vision, purpose, philosophy, goals, and policies about which people could agree. The process of seeking consensus was sidestepped. Therefore, it was very difficult for the board, director, or staff to set forth procedures based on these vague organizational foundations. The moral of this story is: Where there is lack of clarity on issues that require leadership to facilitate team or organizational consensus, various individuals withdraw their energies or try to **overmanage** so that at least some decisions are made and action occurs. Had clarity on the key organizational issues been established from the beginning, many of the problems of the new agency could have been averted. It is preferable to lead more in the beginning and manage less as the organization develops.

The chairman of the board eventually exercised leadership influence and acquired the services of an external consultant who understood the goals of the agency and who was experienced in organization development and team development. He met with the board and the staff members to facilitate the specification of a vision, mission, and values statements (where the agency wants to be in five years, whom it wants to serve, in what manner, etc.) on which board and staff members could agree. This eliminated power struggles, bonded staff members together around a common purpose and values, and eliminated confusion and downtime due to disorganization or people working at cross-purposes. The consultative leadership intervention transformed the character and performance of the organization and the people in it for the sake of the parents and children being served. After this leadership intervention, the organization was ready to once again be managed.

Leading for a Change

The necessity of integrating management and leadership knowledge and skills within each key decision maker, or at least on each team, is becoming more critical as we are faced with increasing complexity, spastic change, and unpredictability. Each manager must lead and each leader must manage in a world where both leadership and management dimensions must be developed in order to respond to constant change and pressures, both internal and external to an organization. Increasing pressures of a technical, interpersonal, and organizational nature are already upon us and are not likely to diminish.

Change must be envisioned, anticipated, managed, and adapted to by key leaders, and this leadership must be exercised on a global scale. In this way, we can better cope with the acceleration of the rate of change that is happening now and will likely occur in the future.

The focus at a recent policing conference in Vancouver, British Columbia, was "Challenge the Future with Best Practices in Police Leadership." The theme at this international conference was to compare the best of what has worked (and what has not worked) in facing a number of problems that are current and many that are anticipated in the future.

Dr. William L. Tafoya, a law enforcement futurist, was the keynote speaker at the conference. He noted that we can expect massive urban unrest and civil disorder by 1999. Drug abuse and spouse and child abuse, like a cancer, will continue to spread widely. Political terrorism, already epidemic elsewhere in the world, will worsen in the United States, putting pressure on not only federal law enforcement agencies but local agencies as well. The much-feared nuclear terrorism may become a reality, calling for an increasing array of security measures, including planning for mass evacuations.

Another finding of his study of law enforcement practices and opinions nationwide is that computer-related crime will emerge as a threat to the American economy and national security. Computer criminals in the workplace already cost American businesses up to $3 billion a year. Crimes committed using high technology will become so complex that some police agencies will be unable to do more than take initial reports, although other law enforcement agencies believe they will develop enough expertise in this area to handle the threat, just as they have in other areas of criminal endeavor.

Law enforcement must begin to learn to deal with hacking, phreaking, piggybacking, data diddling, superzapping, scavenging, trapdoors, Trojan horses, logic bombs, and a whole host of other computer threats promoted not only by professionals but also by precocious but naive youngsters. To deal with such threats, law enforcement needs not only computer-literate officers, civilians, and managers but a new sophistication to deal with such complexity.

At present, too few agencies are well equipped to deal with high-tech crime, Tafoya said. Even so, many in the field have faith in the ability of law enforcement to understand and use computers and other technology and faith that law officers will keep pace with the ability of criminals to use that same technology.

On another computer-related topic, it is predicted are that we will see an upswing in successful lawsuits charging invasion of privacy due to inadequacies of and inaccuracies in police computerized files.

Law enforcement, Tafoya said, needs greater computer capabilities to do sophisticated crime analysis, including modus operandi, mug shots, field interviews, and in-car terminals.

The pressure on our jails will not diminish, Tafoya predicted, as Americans become increasingly concerned about crime. Some suggest that the cure to jail and prison overcrowding is increasing reliance on home electronic monitoring.

Community involvement and self-help by citizens (community-oriented policing) will become common practice in much of the nation, his report said. Even so, policing in the future may, in large part, be contracted out to private security firms.

Finally, most police executives will have to adopt a nontraditional (proactive/goal-oriented rather than top-down) leadership style.

The bottom line, said Tafoya, is that law enforcement's technical knowledge and skills need to be honed to deal with future crimes, and we should not wait for these types of crimes to become rampant before we start preparing our officers. Not only is computer knowledge vital, but it is expected that a bachelor's degree from a university—instead of a high-school diploma—will be the mandatory qualifier for a law enforcement career in the near future.

Higher education for police officers has been recommended by every blue-ribbon law enforcement panel convened since the 1931 Wickersham Commission. In the next four decades, Tafoya concludes, we will see advanced formal education become the standard in law enforcement. Obviously, those better qualified people—who will be more analytical and more tolerant police—will have to be paid a higher salary.

Other predictions are that law enforcement will:

- Become more rather than less specialized.
- Become better trained to deal with emerging threats (blood-borne pathogens, domestic violence), provide better survival training to deal with more sophisticated firepower, and develop new strategies and tactics to deal with the resurgence of militias and their ilk.
- Become part of a communications revolution. Our agencies will be individually wired into the World Wide Web, and each police car will probably have a mobile data terminal and a cellular phone. Identification by means of electronic telecommunications fingerprints, facial ratios, retinal patterns, etc.) will increase.
- Become part of world-wide policing. In a world in which a person wanted in Moscow can be in New York in less than eight hours, and fraud in Los Angeles can be committed by someone sitting at a terminal in São Paulo, traditional jurisdictional lines will blur.
- Become involved in the revolutionary changes besieging the workplace. We are looking at not only privatizing jails but perhaps contracting out

law enforcement as a whole to private concerns—rent-a-cops or temp-cops to cover shifts or even whole jurisdictions. It has already been done.

While leaders get ready to deal with all of the above issues, they must also develop the leadership capabilities required to capitalize on the power of consensus around a common vision of justice and order and to lead teams, organizations, and communities. *Transforming Leadership* is a comprehensive model for the development of leadership that becomes capable of developing other leaders while the job gets done.

We can influence the direction of events in the future only as we anticipate future trends, formulate alternative responses to these future scenarios, and are prepared to implement alternative action plans in concert with community leaders and community awareness and support. In this way, we can continue to correct-course as the winds of change shift direction unpredictably. For further reference on this issue, refer to *The Future of Policing* (published by Oxford University Press in 1997).

Community leaders (city councilors, mayors, and citizens) involved in making funding decisions about police, justice, and public safety must gain perspective on the **necessity to plan for more than minimally adequate funding** of services in order to address the complexity of issues that are coming toward us in the future. Otherwise, communities will find that their forces for dealing with crime, fire, emergencies, etc. may be seriously lacking. In this time of dramatic and sweeping change, it is important to help funding decision makers to articulate the difference between minimally adequate, adequate, good, and excellent policing, fire, emergency, correctional, and court services.

A Time for Vision in an Era of Change

Our planet has likely never seen such a complex and difficult time in human history. For this reason, leaders need to understand the kind of leadership that stimulates positive transformation and breakdown prevention. Egan (1985) most aptly states some basics of a theory of transformative leadership by describing clearly what a transformational leader does:

> Transformational leaders are shapers of values, creators, interpreters of institutional purpose, exemplars, makers of meanings, pathfinders, and molders of organizational culture. They are persistent and consistent. Their vision is so compelling that they know what they want from every interaction. Their visions don't blind others, but empower them. Such leaders have a deep sense of the purpose for the system and a long-range strategic sense, and these provide a sense of overall direction. They also know what kind of culture, in terms of beliefs, values, and

norms, the system must develop if it is to achieve that purpose. By stimulating, modeling, advocating, innovating, and motivating, they mold this culture, to the degree that this is possible, to meet both internal and environmental needs (p. 204).

This clear vision of some ways a transformative leader can achieve positive results will assist you to further identify the somewhat elusive nature of *Transforming Leadership*. In addition to clarity of vision, the use of positive power is a necessary aspect of *Transforming Leadership*.

Power for Change

Bennis and Nanus (1985) reintroduce the seemingly lost concept of power as a key to transformational leadership. They observe that many, if not most, leaders have visibly lacked wholehearted commitment to the challenge of leadership, have been overwhelmed by the rapid change and complexity of our era, and have lacked the necessary integrity and credibility to earn the trust and respect of followers. They claim that the kind of leadership needed is transformative leadership and that this leadership power is exemplified by what they call "the Iacocca phenomenon."

> Power is the basic energy needed to initiate and sustain action or, to put it another way, the capacity to translate intention into reality and sustain it. Leadership is the wise use of this power: Transformative Leadership. As we view it, effective leadership can move organizations from current to future states, create visions of potential opportunities for organizations, instill within employees commitment to change, and instill new cultures and strategies in organizations that mobilize and focus energy and resources (p. 17).

Leaders who are particularly successful in acquiring and sustaining power have a number of things in common. In his studies on the use of leadership power, Kotter (1979) observes that there are several keys to success for those who are effective in the use of power. They tend to be very sensitive to where power exists in their organizations. They use specific methods to develop power, as long as the methods are ethical. They take calculated risks in which they "invest" some of their power in the hope of gaining it back with interest. They recognize that all of their actions can affect their power, and they avoid actions that will accidentally decrease it. In their career development, they try to move both up the hierarchy and toward positions where they can control some strategic contingency for their organizations.

We can see that it is possible that one of the reasons some people are not very successful in developing leadership effectiveness is that they do not know how to establish their own "power" image in the minds of others. To do this, it is necessary to assess the different kinds of power one could possibly have and set about to develop these different types of power for positive purposes. Image management (managing one's own self-image and self-presentation) can have a positive impact on the images others have of us in their minds.

Kanter (1982) found that formal authority was less important to managers attempting innovation than the power and influence they exercised beyond the formal mandates of their organizational positions. Clearly, a greater understanding of power, how to develop it, how to keep it, and how to use it effectively is important in *Transforming Leadership*.

The Subtle Nature and Potency of Transforming Leadership

Burns (1978) further clarified the character of *Transforming Leadership* when he stated that it is more than mere power holding and is the opposite of brute power. He described the relationship between most leaders and followers as a transactional, favor-for-favor type of interchange. He does, however, point us to a view beyond the transactional tit-for-tat relationship of jobs for votes, subsidies for campaign contributions, or raises for more production.

> Transforming leadership, while more complex, is more potent. The transforming leader recognizes and exploits the existing need or demand of a potential follower. But, beyond that, the transforming leader looks for potential motives in followers, seeks to satisfy higher needs, and engages the full person of the follower. The result of transforming leadership is a relationship of mutual stimulation and elevation that converts followers into leaders and may convert leaders into moral agents of change.
>
> ...Moral leadership emerges from and always returns to the fundamental wants and needs, aspirations, and values of the followers. I mean the kind of leadership that can produce social change that will satisfy followers' authentic needs.

Greenleaf (1977) had foresight in predicting the terrain of leadership theory today when he wrote:

> A fresh look is being taken at the issues of power and authority, and people are beginning to learn, however haltingly, to relate to one another in less coercive and more creatively supporting ways. A new moral principle is emerging that holds that the only authority deserving one's allegiance is that which is freely and knowingly granted by the led to the leader, in response to and in proportion to, the clearly evident servant stature of the leader. Those who choose to follow this principle will not casually accept the authority of existing institutions.

Rather, they will freely respond only to individuals who are chosen as leaders because they are proven and trusted as servants. To the extent that this principle prevails in the future, the only truly viable institutions will be those that are predominantly servant-led (p. 9).

A more recent view on *Transforming Leadership* is presented by Kanter (1983). She encourages a responsible, balanced leadership in serving the needs of the followers and the needs of the organization simultaneously through participative leadership.

While encouraging participation, innovators still maintain leadership. "Leadership" consists in part of keeping everyone's mind on the shared vision, being explicit about "fixed" areas not up for discussion and the constraints on decisions, watching for uneven participation or group pressure, and keeping time bounded and managed. Then, as events move toward accomplishments, leaders can provide rewards and feedback, tangible signs that the participation mattered (pp. 275–277).

The Qualities Followers Want to See in Leaders

Kouzes and Posner (1987) conducted a most interesting study of over 1,500 managers to discover the positive practices in which their leaders engaged. They identified four key qualities and ten leadership practices that can be found in the behavior patterns of effective and admired leaders.

Most of us tend to admire leaders who have credibility, those who are:

1. Honest
2. Competent
3. Forward-looking
4. Inspiring

These credible leaders tend to be committed to consistently implementing ten leadership practices:

1. Search out challenging opportunities to change, grow, innovate, and improve
2. Experiment, take risks, and learn from the accompanying mistakes
3. Envision an uplifting and ennobling future
4. Enlist others in a common vision by appealing to their values, interests, hopes, and dreams
5. Foster collaboration by promoting cooperative goals and building trust
6. Strengthen people by sharing information and power and increasing their discretion and visibility

7. Set the example for others by behaving in ways that are consistent with one's stated values
8. Plan small wins that promote consistent progress and build commitment
9. Recognize individual contributions to the success of every project
10. Celebrate team accomplishments regularly

These ten practices represent central issues important to the understanding of *Transforming Leadership*. *The Leadership Challenge* (Kouzes and Posner, 1987) is recommended highly as a book that has a very practical focus on understanding and integrating these ten most effective leadership practices. Also recommended is a more recent work by Kouzes and Posner (1992) entitled *Credibility*, which corroborates their previous findings and outlines critical ways that leaders must develop credibility or fail to have the impact they could.

The Intertwining of Management, Leadership, and Power

Kotter (1990), in *A Force for Change: How Leadership Differs from Management*, outlines how subtly various successful executives behaved as they artistically intertwined the various aspects of their approaches into a powerful force for positive change.

Specifically, the most effective executives created agendas for themselves, made up of loosely connected sets of short-term plans, medium-term strategies, and long-term visions. They each built resource networks that could accomplish these agendas by staffing and structuring the jobs reporting to them, by communicating their plans and visions to people, and by establishing cooperative relationships with a broad range of individuals whose help they might need. They then actively sought to influence people in those networks when necessary to assure the achievement of their agendas, and did so in a wide variety of ways, sometimes trying to control people and activities, sometimes attempting to inspire others to new heights of performance. Overall, this behavior was extremely complex and, as has been reported in other in-depth studies of executives at work, did not look much like traditional management.

What these executives were doing, in the language of this book, was a combination of management, leadership, and still other things (chief among which was the development of sources of power that could help them manage, lead, and get promoted), but all of these various aspects of behavior were highly intertwined. They did not manage for fifteen minutes and then lead for half an hour. Instead, in the course of single, five-minute conversation, they might try to see if some activity was proceeding as planned (a control part of management), gather information relevant to their emerging vision (the direction setting part of leadership), promise to do someone a favor (an aspect of power development), and agree on a series of steps for accomplishing some objective (the planning part of management). As a result, to the observer, what they were doing did not look much like management or any other recognizable activity. The managers themselves even found their own behaviors difficult to describe and explain.

With the kinds of complex demands placed upon those in positions of leadership, it is not surprising that a wide range of skills should be displayed in the behaviors of those who are most successful. A model that can capture the components of this complexity and render them transferable to others is needed. Such a model will provide guidance for self-assessment, planning for training, and for evaluating the effectiveness of one's own or others' leadership behavior. *Transforming Leadership* provides a model that is an attempt at this integration of the various complex parts of the effective leadership behaviors exhibited by the executives Kotter studied—whose leadership helped turn around NCR, P&G, and Kodak and stimulated business growth at American Express, PepsiCo, and ARCO.

The *Transforming Leadership* Model

In developing this model, an interdisciplinary approach was taken to capture specific philosophical, theoretical, and scientific investigative results that together have a range of practical applications. The following theory and practice bases should be recognized as important in the formation of a more integrative and comprehensive model such as *Transforming Leadership*.

1. Interpersonal communication
2. Counseling and problem management
3. Human development
4. Human resource development
5. Organization development
6. *Transforming Leadership* theory and principles

From the above bodies of research and theoretical formulations have emerged "chunks" of applicable knowledge or sets of easily learned and teachable qualities and skills. As a result of learning these skills or developing such qualities, it is easier to bring forward into reality not only competencies but some sense of the "art" or charismatic (character) power involved in *Transforming Leadership*.

A model is an approximate map of what reality could look like, and it is clear enough to give us a reference point for evaluation of our own effectiveness when we try a particular leadership intervention. With this clarified reference point and increased evaluative ability, we are able to make the necessary shifts to fine-tune our responses to people, teams, organizations, and communities so that we can have more positive and potent impacts.

Transforming Leadership: A Research- and Philosophy-Based Model

There are so many theories and philosophical assumptions about what one should do to become more effective that it is difficult to trust just anyone spouting off about another panacea, wonderful training, or action-oriented program. The concepts in the *Transforming Leadership* model are based on applicable theory in communication, counseling, and consulting (organization development and human resource development). Philosophers and practitioners often attempt to simply convince others that their school of thought is the correct one. I am not doing that with the *Transforming Leadership* model. What I am doing is providing dozens of practical examples of how each skill in the model can be applied in concert with other skills to form a comprehensive approach to the development of people, teams, organizations, and communities. A visual overview of the *Transforming Leadership* Model is presented below.

Transforming Leadership Model

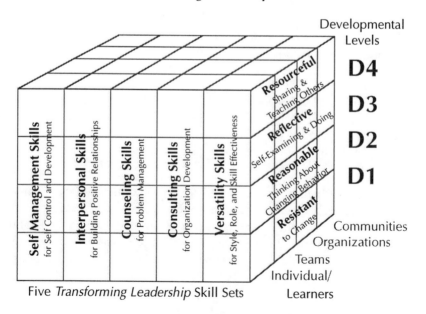

An explanation of the details of each section of this model is contained in the chapter of this book. For example, the self-management skills, are explained in Chapter 4, the interpersonal communication skills are the focus of Chapter 5, and the counseling and problem management skills are defined and illustrated in Chapter 6. The meaning and application of the model will become clearer as you read through this book.

Leaders who utilize the five *Transforming Leadership* skill sets and knowledge areas in the model have greater potential to shape organizational climate and the interpersonal environment to achieve the desired results. Except for the management functions, these skills and knowledge areas are discussed in greater detail in Chapters 4 through 8. It is not the purpose of this book to introduce the reader to the knowledge and skills of effective management because there are a wealth of good books that accomplish this goal more than adequately. First, it is important to understand that, in reality, *Transforming Leadership* is not a rigid, linear, step-by-step process, even though a series of steps can be outlined to assist in understanding how the process can work.

Steps in the Transforming Leadership Process

Leadership can be viewed as a complex process involving a fluid series of steps (which may overlap or reverse into one another, depending upon the circumstances). When this process is understood, it can assist leaders to develop people and to bring a vision of human and organizational transformation into reality. Without a compelling and clearly communicated vision, the status quo often remains, and innovation and development are arrested.

Learning to use the steps in the *Transforming Leadership* process model can increase your leadership behavior appropriateness "score."

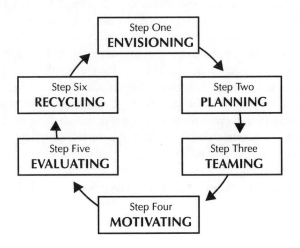

The following summary further delineates what is entailed in each of these steps:

1. **Envisioning**: This first step requires imagination, creativity, and an understanding of the history of a group or organization so that what is possible in the future can be more accurately and realistically specified and articulated. For most people, this is the most difficult of all the steps because it requires originality and stepping out of the ordinary ways of thinking and doing things. Because habits are strong and new ideas are accepted slowly, there is more risk involved than many people are willing to take. It is the critical step, however, because innovation and improvement usually happen because some person conceived of a better way to work or a better way to live. Envisioning must also be based upon specifying and meeting some kind of human need, or there will be no market for the new service or product being offered by a person or an organization.

2. **Planning**: Once a vision is captured (with or without dialogue with others), it can be built upon through carefully specifying just how, where, and when a thing can best be done and by whom it might best be done. This may involve family or committee meetings, brainstorming sessions, team development sessions, conflict resolution, and negotiation. As the plan develops, if it is to succeed, there must be enough acceptance of it and enough enthusiasm about it and the vision for it to be truly shared by all involved. Otherwise, the likelihood of it succeeding can be seriously diminished. When those involved have an opportunity for involvement that challenges them personally, they are more likely to invest themselves at a deeper level in making it work. Finally, this planning process must include highly specific and concrete goals, objectives, and program steps for the timely accomplishment of worthy and realistic aims.

3. **Teaming**: Selectively giving responsibility to others involves building harmonious and productive teams by placing people in appropriate groupings that they see as desirable (whenever possible), giving them tasks appropriate to their strengths and interests, and supporting them emotionally and physically in the process of their taking on responsibility. This ensures that they will more likely meet the challenges they hopefully chose to meet. Matching the nature of a person with the nature of the job and matching people with people is an effective way of exercising leadership discernment.

4. **Motivating to action**: Once some acceptance is established, motivation must develop inside of people (for internal or external reasons) on a continuing basis, or the plan will not be realized to the level of quality

originally envisioned or within the time allotted. A system of rewards must be established and valued so that motivation can be kept at a challenging and yet comfortable peak. People will not work hard when they feel that what they give is a great deal more than what they get— they find it demoralizing. Many things act as rewards, and identifying people's "hot buttons"—a whole range of them—and giving them reasonable rewards and opportunities that encourage them to stay motivated are key factors in transforming people and organizations. Motivation leads to the most important aspect of organizational life: action. Higher levels of motivation and achievement can be accomplished by meeting the deeper needs of people: needs of recognition, accomplishment, challenge, belonging, meaning, and purpose. This is not manipulation but rather respect for people who have a sense of need for both internal and external rewards in return for the sweat of their lives.

5. **Evaluating**: Evaluation of the results of a change effort is tricky but necessary business. It is important in terms of making improvements in the plan and being able to jointly celebrate a specific level of success. The more carefully specified the plan is in terms of identified accomplishments to be reached for, the easier the evaluation of the results. In designing the plan, evaluation criteria should be made a part of the plan. They should be realistic, desirable, concretely defined in terms of accomplishments, and measurable.

6. **Recycling the process through evaluation**: Periodically, after a time of evaluation, all the steps in this process need to be repeated so that false assumptions are not made about how events are going or how they should best go. Rethinking the vision, reformulating and renegotiating the plan, finding new motivators, regrouping for greater harmony and productivity, and reevaluation all keep people and organizations alive to what is real and to what has positive change potential.

Using the skills and understanding in the *Transforming Leadership* model and these process steps as a backdrop, we can now examine the twelve principles that lie at the heart of *Transforming Leadership*.

Twelve Principles of Transforming Leadership

As a part of this summary of *Transforming Leadership*, an outline of principles involved in the model is important. Principles of *Transforming Leadership* are general operating guidelines that can be applied in a wide variety of situations. These principles are as follows:

1. Every person in every situation is having an impact, for better or worse, on the people and the situations that are present.

2. Learning to observe this impact alerts us to the reality of positive or negative leadership opportunities and events. Increasing our level of awareness of people and events can be fruitful for everyone.

3. Every person can choose to try and make a positive difference in each moment with each other person and, at least within that immediate sphere of influence, can likely exert some positive, and therefore *Transforming, Leadership*.

4. The use of positive and respectful power and influence is necessary for leadership to have enough impact to be effective. Knowing your own strengths, gaining strategic position power, developing a power network of like-minded people, and communicating your personal and position power in a positive way to others will assist you to reach higher goals.

5. Everything begins with the initiative of each individual. Privately, inwardly, individuals determine within themselves what to do, how to act, and how to treat people. If we are each clear within about our own beliefs, purpose, goals, and objectives, we will be much more likely to achieve them from this solid and well-defined center within ourselves.

6. Leadership, in its deepest sense, is the understanding and meeting of the deeper needs of the people being led/served. Even when achieving goals of increased innovation or productivity, our meeting of the deeper human needs of worth, recognition, reward, accomplishment, and personal development of others are cornerstones of motivation and satisfaction.

7. *Transforming Leadership* has a moral component that is centrally important to all other aspects of leadership, because few people will trust a leader who has lied, embezzled, or hurt others.

8. *Transforming Leadership* understands and involves others, so that they can gain a critical sense of belonging and experience the mutual sense of respect and trust that follows. Personal ownership in any venture can potentially increase motivation, morale, creativity, energy, and productivity.

9. There is opportunity for leadership in every environment, in every interaction, in every situation, in every moment. Leadership is intentionally making a positive difference in the development of organizations and individuals for a specific purpose. Being awake to these opportunities and seizing them increases our personal meaning and impact in life and work.

10. *Transforming Leadership* looks for long-term impact and long-term development, rather than just immediate results. Satisfaction increases when we can see continuing positive development over longer periods of time, rather than just short-term successes.

11. *Transforming Leadership* begins deep within a person's belief and value structures, and a solid sense of purpose or mission in life is necessary for leadership effectiveness to be sustained. Have a well-defined, achievable sense of purpose that "sets you on fire" and distinguishes you from the herd of people who follow along with a more vague purpose of some relatively unknown leader–heroes (such as in politics, sports, science, etc.).

12. *Transforming Leadership* isalways open to the possibility that there may be another, higher, or deeper understanding of reality beyond what is presently comprehended. An attitude of humility as opposed to being "puffed up with pride" characterizes a transforming leader. The globular nature of the earth, the sun and planets, the splitting of the atom, and the development of radio, television, and radar are practical examples of how what used to be hidden is now revealed. Other areas of life may be the same: What was once "metaphysical" or speculatory can be known in new ways.

These principles, when internalized and implemented in a leader's life, will result in greater leadership impact in the wide range of roles leaders must play. These roles are examined further in the next section.

Comparing Traditional and Transformational Functions and Roles of Leadership

Classical theories as outlined by Stogdill (1974) in his monumental review of leadership theory and research suggest that the primary functions of a leader are planning, organizing, and controlling. Various theorists have added coordinating, supervising, motivating, and other functions to the list. Functions that have been identified by behavioral theorists and researchers include:

1. Defining objectives and maintaining goal direction
2. Facilitating team task performance
3. Facilitating team action and interaction
4. Maintaining team cohesiveness and member satisfaction
5. Providing and maintaining team structure
6. Providing means for goal attainment

Functions of *Transforming Leadership* are necessary for greater impact on the development of individuals and the organizations in which they live and work. These functions are

1.   Creating and communicating vision and purpose
2.   Doing strategic and versatile thinking and planning
3.   Facilitating peer, subordinate, and team development
4.   Facilitating the development of the organization
5.   Protecting individuals from destructive forces
6.   Protecting the organization from destructive forces
7.   Seeking and communicating consensus between teams
8.   Specifying philosophy and values and creating culture
9.   Creating insight
10. Motivating people to action

Traditionally, the roles of leadership have been divided into three main categories (Mintzberg, 1973): interpersonal, informational, and decisional roles. *Transforming Leadership* theory asserts that the informational and decisional roles are primarily management functions, even though they can be handled creatively from a leadership as well as from a "hard-line" management perspective. Therefore, these three traditional roles exclude some important dimensions that can make a critical difference in leadership effectiveness and potency. The important roles that encompass some of the traditional roles and introduce some new ones form the structures and avenues for the effective execution of *Transforming Leadership*. These roles are graphically introduced and expanded upon in the table on the next page.

Although these roles and functions are not exhaustive, they capture some of the essence of what is believed to produce a transforming effect on individuals, groups, and organizations. It should also be kept in mind that effective management practices form the solid platform from which these additional functions can be carried forward.

Now that we have reviewed the roles and functions central to *Transforming Leadership*, we can examine the critical attitudes and characteristics of transforming leaders.

Attitudes and Characteristics of Transforming Leaders

This part of the chapter can be used as a means for you to look at yourself in relation to what have been discovered to be effective attitudes and characteristics of transforming leaders. In doing this self-examination, you can discover areas that are in need of development, and you can devise a short-term and long-term plan for your development as a leader. Highlight or underline parts of the following that you think will help you to formulate such a plan.

Roles and Functions of *Transforming Leadership*

Role	Function
Communicator	Get to know others Manage personal image Communicate corporate image Understand others accurately Communicate concern Recognize achievements of others Suspend judgements and emotions Resolve interpersonal conflicts Build effective, enjoyable relationships Build self-worth in others Empower and encourage others Confront others effectively
Counselor	Help others define and own their problems Help others to set achievable goals Help others explore and evaluate plans Motivate others to take action Sustain and support others to achieve plans Reward and recognize achievement Confront low performers Make referrals effectively Share your experience at the right time Coach people to reach goals Mentor people to prepare for new roles Evaluate performance and give feedback
Consultant	Act as public relations person for the organization Apply the consulting process Develop corporate values and culture Delegate to achieve goals through others Legitimize your leadership Facilitate group and team development Clarify norms, values, and beliefs Communicate vision and purpose Assess organizational needs and problems Deal with distracting members Research and report important information Plan and coordinate human resource development and hiring

A Portrait of the Transforming Leader

General Characteristics: The transforming leader is critically involved in envisioning, communicating, and creating an improved future for self, other people, and the group or organization. The transforming leader has clear personal beliefs. Without clarity about one's own stance on life's major questions, an individual can be easily swayed by situations—which are becoming increasingly complex, unstable, polarized, and unpredictable.

The transforming leader also has a well-defined sense of mission, purpose, values, goals, and strategies, based upon a deep understanding of the people and the overarching aims that are being served, and a clear understanding of the cultural, political, and economic environment surrounding the change endeavor being attempted. The transforming leader is able to arouse a sense of excitement about the significance of the organization's contribution to society or a team's contribution to the organization. The transforming leader has working knowledge and skills in the areas of human development, organization development, interpersonal communication, counseling, consulting, and problem management/solving.

Transforming Leaders Need Exceptional Physical Health: Being in a leadership position often requires an ability to deal with stress and difficult situations with some degree of resilience. The fitness required to sustain higher levels of energy and performance is described and prescribed very clearly by Schafer (1987). The energy to achieve higher levels of performance must also come from the nutrition program appropriate for each individual. A wide range of books on fitness and nutrition are available to assist you in developing your understanding in these two key areas.

Transforming Leaders Are Peak Performers: Garfield (1986) has, for the past two decades, researched top achievers through all strata of business, science, and the professions. He provides an illuminating profile of those people he calls peak performers: They are individuals motivated by a personal sense of mission; they possess the twin capacities of self-management and team mastery; they have the ability to correct course and manage change. These qualities are similar to the findings of other theorists mentioned above, except Garfield has gone to great lengths to specify some of his findings.

Summarized below are some of these findings about peak performers—that are similar to others' findings about transforming leaders.

Exercise Self-Management Through Self-Mastery
1. **Self-confidence**: Being willing to hear "no," and move on to focus on the next opportunity.

2. **Bimodal thinking**: Combining macro and micro forms of attention. Analyzing a problem situation within a company requires the overall macro view.
3. **Mental rehearsal**: Preparing for action so that both the mind and the emotions are conditioned positively for the upcoming events.

Use Course Correction

4. **Mental agility**: Having the flexibility to change perspective and do the creative thinking necessary to deal with challenges.
5. **Concentration**: Consists of the stamina to work long hours, adaptability to change, and the hardiness that could also be called resilience under stress.
6. **Learning from mistakes**: Taking appropriate actions based upon updated information.

Have a Results Orientation

7. **As individuals**: Envisioning and communicating a clear mission, and following up with a plan of action that includes specific goals, complete with benchmarks necessary for assessing timing, quality, and quantity of results.
8. **As collaborators**: Using a "magnet mentality" to draw in what they need from other people.
9. **As innovators**: Understanding that there is no guaranteed path from A to Z and being prepared to make new paths in the service of results.

Cultivate Necessary Skills

10. **Develop new skills**: Assessing what new skills are needed and then developing those skills though readings, courses, workshops, and tapes. Then asking for and getting feedback.
11. **Use leverage**: Maximizing opportunities to use the skills they already have so they stay in their "peak performance" zone.

Develop Teams to Accomplish Results

12. **Delegate to empower others**: Empowering (releasing power in and from) others by giving them tasks and assignments that they do best, and never doing themselves what others can do better.
13. **Stretch the abilities of others**: Challenging others to develop to their potential and offering opportunities and projects for them to do so (with the necessary support to succeed).
14. **Encourage educated risk taking**: Encouraging others to take higher payoff risks if there is reasonable chance for success.

Manage Change for Future Success

15. **Are students forever**: Seeking lifelong learning opportunities, which means there is a willingness to admit sequential ignorance and that a degree is not the end of the game.
16. **Expect to succeed**: Having confidence and the ability to visualize at least one way in each moment that things can work.
17. **Map alternative futures**: Having alternate game plans to shift into if the present one does not materialize as expected.
18. **Update the mission**: Having an open mind to restate the mission—or critical paths to it—can be a necessary ability in times of spastic change.

Refined Self-Awareness and a Broad Base of Self-Development

The transforming leader has a refined self-awareness; is able to acknowledge and compensate for limitations; has the ability to use self as an instrument for change; has developed good interpersonal communication skills, counseling skills, and problem-solving and problem management skills; and has an optimistic attitude in general.

The transforming leader takes initiative in transforming all parts of an organization where there is opportunity for positive change. Ideally, the person who has been placed "in charge" of any family, group, department, or organization would facilitate development at the personal, interpersonal, and organizational levels. All too often, traditional leaders attempt only one level of impact, or at best two, and fail to comprehend the breadth of influence they could have (Egan, 1985).

Consciousness: An Openness to New Perspectives

The transforming leader values increasing consciousness of self and others without overloading awareness with clutter and detail. It is important to have an ability to see patterns in the past and project them into the future to sense new directions. The transforming leader understands that a personal commitment to become a more conscious, clear-minded, and intentional person results in important personal growth that attracts others and wins their trust. Some call this personal "presence," presence of mind, alertness, or expanded awareness (beyond the average).

Caring: The Critical Factor

Most of all, the transforming leader cares deeply about self and others and is committed to the higher goals of both developing the inner lives and affirming the worth of individuals. The transforming leader is committed to developing positive organizational climates that result in high morale and increased quality and productivity. For example, one police chief was exceptional in his commitment to caring for people. He went to great lengths, but quite naturally, to show concern about the stresses and tragedies of others, listened compassionately, and made judgments mercifully whenever possible. He thought the best of his members until they proved him wrong consistently and would support them even when it was not in his political interest to do so (in the case of many public complaints against officers). The transforming leader knows that increased morale in general means increased productivity and that, to an extent, increasing productivity and quality of products or services can boost morale. Facilitating the personal development of people as individuals adds depth and character to an organization over the long term, and workers are more likely to have a positive self-image, which often results in improved performance in producing quality goods or delivering quality services. The transforming leader builds a learning organization capable of continuous improvement.

Bennis and Nanus (1985) quotes Irwin Federman, president and CEO of Monolithic Memories, one of the most successful of the high-tech companies in Silicon Valley:

> If you think about it, people love others not for who they are, but for how they make others feel. We willingly follow others for much the same reason. It makes us feel good to do so. Now, we also follow platoon sergeants, self-centered geniuses, demanding spouses, bosses of various persuasions, and others as well, for a variety of reasons. But none of those reasons involves that person's leadership qualities. To willingly accept the direction of another individual, it must feel good to do so. This business of making another person feel good in the unspectacular course of his daily comings and goings is, in my view, the very essence of leadership.

Caring about the well-being and development of others is a quality that not only is necessary but when absent from an otherwise good leader, most of us feel a sense of having being deceived, or at least having been let down or sadly disappointed, as is exemplified in the extreme by such leaders as Napoleon, Hitler, and Nixon. It would seem that the tragic flaws of deceptiveness, lovelessness, and the insane tragedy of destructiveness are, to most of us, unacceptable, no matter what the promises or other accomplishments of a leader are.

The Secret of Leadership Success

Kouzes and Posner (1987) claim that love is the secret of leadership success. I agree. They define love as encouragement, loyalty, teamwork, commitment, and respect the dignity and worth of others and claim it is an affair of the heart and not of the head. If any one thing will cause people to be distrustful of a leader, it is when they sense that the leader *does not care.* In contrast, Kouzes and Posner write, "When we encourage others, we give them **heart**. And when we give heart to others, we give love." To further explain what is meant by love, an ancient wisdom on this point is worthy of quotation: "Love never gives up. Love cares more for others than for self. Love doesn't want what it doesn't have. Love doesn't strut; doesn't have a swelled head; doesn't force itself on others; isn't always "me first'; doesn't fly off the handle; doesn't keep score of the wrongs of others; doesn't revel when others grovel; takes pleasure in the flowering of truth; puts up with anything; trusts God always; always looks for the best; never looks back; but keeps going to the end" (*The Message*, pp. 424–425). This quote summarizes some of the underlying assumptions of this book, but the following section will assess the extent to which you really "buy into" the principles of *Transforming Leadership.*

Assessment: Identifying Your Own Position in Relation to Transforming Leadership Principles

Rate the extent of your agreement with the twelve principles of *Transforming Leadership.* This will give you an opportunity to discover the extent to which you "buy into" these basic "beliefs" of *Transforming Leadership.* Doing this assessment will assist you to identify how much you are committed to the idea of seeing yourself more and more as an agent of positive change. You can rate each of the twelve principles from 1 to 5 to indicate your acceptance of them in your value structure.

> 1 = rejection
> 2 = avoidance
> 3 = neutrality
> 4 = general acceptance
> 5 = complete acceptance and agreement

Score

1. Every person in every situation is having an impact, for better or worse, on the people and the situations that are present.

2. Learning to observe this impact alerts us to the reality of positive or negative leadership opportunities and events. Increasing our level of awareness of people and events can be fruitful for everyone.

3. Every person can choose to try and make a positive difference in each moment with each other person and, at least within that immediate sphere of influence, can likely exert some positive, and therefore *Transforming, Leadership.*

Score

4. The use of positive and respectful power and influence is necessary for leadership to have enough impact to be effective. Knowing your own strengths, gaining strategic position power, developing a power network of like-minded people, and communicating your personal and position power in a positive way to others will assist you to reach higher goals.

5. Everything begins with the initiative of each individual. Privately, inwardly, individuals determine in themselves what to do, how to act, and how to treat people. If we are each clear within about our own beliefs, purpose, goals, and objectives, we will be much more likely to achieve them from this solid and well-defined center within ourselves.

6. Leadership, in its deepest sense, is understanding and meeting the deeper needs of the people being led/served. Even when achieving goals of increased innovation or productivity, meeting the deeper human needs of worth, recognition, reward, accomplishment, and personal development of others is the cornerstone of motivation and satisfaction.

7. *Transforming Leadership* has a moral component that is centrally important to all other aspects of leadership, because few people will trust a leader who has lied, embezzled, or hurt others.

8. *Transforming Leadership* understands and involves others so that they can gain a critical sense of belonging and experience the mutual sense of respect and trust that follows. Personal ownership in any venture can potentially increase motivation, morale, creativity, energy, and productivity.

9. There is opportunity for leadership in every environment, in every interaction, in every situation, in every moment. Leadership is intentionally making a positive difference in the development of organizations and individuals for a specific purpose. Being awake to these opportunities and seizing them increases our personal meaning and impact in life and work.

10. *Transforming Leadership* looks for long-term impact and long-term development, rather than just immediate results. Satisfaction increases when we can see continuing positive development over longer periods of time, rather than just short-term successes.

11. *Transforming Leadership* begins deep within a person's belief and value structures, and a solid sense of purpose or mission in life is necessary for leadership effectiveness to be sustained. Have a well-defined, achievable sense of purpose that "sets you on fire" and

Score

distinguishes you from the herd of people who follow along with a more vague purpose of some relatively unknown leader–heroes (such as in politics, sports, science, etc.).

12.   *Transforming Leadership* is always open to the possibility that there may be be another, higher, or deeper understanding of reality beyond what is presently comprehended. An attitude of humility as opposed to being "puffed up with pride" characterizes a transforming leader.

Total score:

Interpretation of Scores: If you scored between 52 to 60, you have a high degree of agreement with the underlying principles of *Transforming Leadership* and are likely willing to move ahead with further development of the skills. If you scored between 44 to 51, you have a moderate degree of agreement with the principles of *Transforming Leadership* and you may have some reservations about proceeding with further development of the skills. If you scored below 43, you likely have serious reservations about the underlying assumptions of *Transforming Leadership* and likely will not proceed with further training.

References

Bennis, W. and B. Nanus, *Leaders: The Strategies for Taking Charge,* New York: Harper and Row, 1985, 17, 66–67.

Brown, A. and E. Wiener, *Supermanaging: How to Harness Change for Personal and Organizational Success,* New York: Mentor Books, 1985.

Burns, J., *Leadership,* New York: Harper and Row, 1978, 4.

Egan, G., *Change Agent Skills,* Monterey, CA: Brooks/Cole, 1985, 204.

Garfield, C., *Peak Performers: The New Heroes of American Business,* New York: William Morrow and Company, 1986.

Germann, A.C., *Police Executive Development,* Springfield, IL.: Charles C Thomas, 1962, 5.

Greenleaf, R., *Servant Leadership, A Journey into the Nature of Legitimate Power and Greatness,* New York: Paulist Press, 1977.

Hickman, C., *Mind of a Manager, Soul of a Leader,* New York: John Wiley and Sons, 1990.

Hickman, C. and M. Silva, *Creating Excellence: Managing Corporate Culture, Strategy, and Change in the New Age,* New York: New American Library, 1984.

Kanter, P., *Power and Entrepreneurship in Action: Corporate Middle Managers, Varieties of Work,* Beverly Hills, CA: Sage, 1982.

Kanter, R.M., *The Change Masters,* New York: Simon and Schuster, 1983.

Kotter, J. *Power in Management,* New York: AMACOM, 1979.

Kotter, J., *A Force for Change: How Leadership Differs from Management,* New York: The Free Press, 1990, 103–104.

Kouzes, J. and B. Posner, *The Leadership Challenge, How to Get Extraordinary Things Done in Organizations,* San Francisco: Jossey-Bass, 1987.

Kouzes, J. and J. Posner, *Credibility,* San Francisco: Jossey-Bass, 1992.

Kouzes, J. and B. Posner, *The Message,* New York: Zondervan Publishing, 1995.

Mintzberg, H., *The Nature of Managerial Work,* New York: Harper and Row, 1973.

Morgan, Rod and Tim Newburn, *The Future of Policing,* New York: Oxford University Press, 1997.

Naisbitt, J., *Megatrends,* New York: Warner, 1982.

Naisbitt, J. and P. Aburdene, *Re-Inventing the Corporation,* New York: Warner Books, 1986.

Naisbitt, J. and P. Aburdene, *Megatrends 2000. Ten New Direction for the 1990's,* New York: William Morrow and Company, 1990, 13

Schafer, W., *Stress Management for Wellness,* New York: Holt, Rinehart and Winston, 1987.

Schlenker, B., *Impression Management,* Monterey, CA: Brooks/Cole, 1980.

Stogdill, Ralph M., *Handbook of Leadership,* New York: The Free Press, 1974.

4

The Skills of Personal Mastery

If I have all the other leadership skills, but fail to build the foundation of my life on these, I will live a stressed, shaky and regretful life. But if I develop these as the foundation of my life and police work I can have health, balance and can lead with hope.
——Trainee, Justice Institute of British Columbia

Introduction

In this chapter, you will gain a more in-depth understanding of the skills you will need to have greater positive impact as a leader while you are in the process of developing yourself and others. The following *Transforming Leadership* (TL) skills are discussed in this chapter:

You may want to pay special attention to those skills in which you felt stronger and weaker when you took the *Transforming Leadership* skills assessment in Chapter 2.

In the future, when you come across a workshop or course outline you think may be relevant for your development, you will be able to evaluate immediately whether or not that particular professional development opportunity fits your individual learning needs in this foundational area of personal and professional development.

The Need for Identity, Clarity of Beliefs, Vision, and Purpose in the Face of Chaotic Change

As we approach the end of this millennium, we face changes of a magnitude never faced before. In the next ten years, nearly one and a half billion babies will be born. The world's population will be tilted toward the Pacific Rim, with 60 percent living within two thousand miles of Singapore. Vast cities, with all their problems, will prevail on the planet. More than twenty-two mega-cities will be populated with more than ten million people each. The health of our environment is seriously threatened. There is more than a slim chance that a terrorist group will attack an area on the planet with nuclear weapons. Disease, wars, and crime are on the increase globally. Information is exploding at a rate faster than the average person's ability to process and use it, and computer crime is the new threat upon the horizon that is already visiting us. The cost of crime in dollars for some industrialized nations easily exceeds the entire economic wealth of emerging nations. National economies are rising and falling, with international consequences. The whole environment is rapidly transforming, but no one is certain where it will end up.

Technological Changes Overshadow Our Ability to Manage Their Effects on People

We have created a technologically advanced environment that outstrips our ability to integrate and manage it! In addition, the knowledge and skills on the people side of managing change are falling behind the demands to cope with the new technologies. "Inner" technologies are lagging behind the demands of "outer" technologies. Many fear that we cannot keep up with what we are creating. "Future management" will have to become a new skill! Stress management has to become the new life style.

The Competencies Needed to Adapt to Profound Change and Help Others Adapt

The competencies needed to be an effective emergency services leader in the face of this rate of change are many and complex, but it is possible to learn them. Are the police, fire, corrections and emergency medical services executives and managers ready to lead the way? Do they have the inner clarity and grounding to avoid losing their balance as the "top" spins faster and faster? And the most important question for the longer term: Can they prepare younger leaders to become ready to assume the helm in the decades to come?

Of all the areas of awareness and skill focused on in this book, the most difficult are beliefs and values. Many of the people I have taught in university and college classes have given up, to some degree, on the hope of achieving inner clarity and resolution regarding their personal beliefs or life stance. They have become somewhat numbed to the challenge of tackling life's most difficult of questions. Many have even consciously resorted to a kind of waning scientific materialism they also describe as lacking in vitality and inspiration. Srivastva and Cooperider (1990) have so aptly described the precipice near which so many stand:

> While the voices sometimes clash and the arguments reel in complexity, there is one powerful consensus that reverberates throughout: The scientific materialism that so confidently dominated the postindustrial era and so thoroughly insinuated itself into virtually every aspect of institutional life is now a dying orthodoxy. While there is little agreement as to exactly what we are moving toward, there is no question that the shift now taking place in society's dominant metaphysic—Who are we? What kind of universe are we in? What is ultimately important?—will have a transforming effect on all our institutions.

With this ominous prospect of huge paradigm shifts in the minds and belief positions of large numbers of people, we turn to the process of self-assessment that will trigger the beginning of a new, careful, and conscious clarification within.

This book provides you with an opportunity to begin your search for clarity and resolution. If you have not consciously begun your search, you can do so with the assistance of some structure and process provided in the pages to follow. If you have already intentionally begun your search process, you can more easily monitor your clarity and progress. If we are to function as ethical people of justice in an unjust world, we must become clear and resolved about what we believe to be true, good, right, wrong. The foundation of justice is clear beliefs and the ethical bringing forward of those beliefs.

Values are perhaps the next most perplexing area of life to clarify and resolve so that a sense of inner peace and integrity is in place within each person. How can we move ahead in teams in emergency response situations, in our communities, in our families? Because there are so many criteria for judging which values are more correct or appropriate, which criteria shall we trust? Should we trust our inner sense of what our priorities should be? Should we trust evidence from history regarding the consequences of certain values being implemented? Are there any absolute values? Should we adjust our values to fit each situation? Or are some values situational in nature and others absolute? These questions and others are very difficult for most people to answer to their own satisfaction. Even so, clarification and regeneration of values are nevertheless greatly needed. As pointed out by Gardiner (1990):

> The truth is that disintegration of the value framework is always going on—but so are regenerative processes. Some people see little hope that such processes can be effective, believing that we have lost the capacity to generate a new vision. A still gloomier view is that we may have lost the capacity to tolerate a new vision. The debunking reflex is powerful today. We are sick of past hypocrisies. We have seen the fine words of morality used as a screen for greed, for bigotry, for power-seeking. Granted. But to let that estrange us from all attempts to regenerate the moral framework would be petulant and self-defeating.
>
> Creating value systems is something that the human species does. "It's our thing," as the recently popular saying goes, and without that irrepressible impulse, civilization would not have survived. Destroy every vestige of lay and morality, demolish every community, level the temples of justice, erase even the memory of custom, and one would see—in the midst of chaos, savagery, and pillage—an awesome sight: the sight of men and women, bereft of all guiding memory, beginning to forge anew the rudiments of order and justice and law, acting out of the mysterious community-building impulse of the species.

If it is true that we by instinct seek order, peace, and benevolent control—and I agree with John Gardiner that it is, then let's get on with the task of clarification and teach others to do the same.

Inner Skills of Self-Mastery for the Transforming Leader

TL Skill #1. Grounding:
Focusing Awareness in the Present

The awareness skill of *grounding* involves taking responsibility for placing your attention in each present moment, and not in memory about past events or in fantasy about future events. When you focus your attention in the "here and now," you are grounded in the present, fully available for interaction with self, the environment, and people in each passing moment. Individuals who are grounded have more personal presence, and people who are in fantasy or memory seem to be "spaced-out," somewhere else, or in some ways "out of it."

Example of Grounding: You can probably think of someone who is very spaced-out most of the time and someone else who is grounded most of the time. I know a person who has abused a great deal of drugs in his lifetime, and this has caused him to become inwardly distracted, lacking in memory power. He is, as a result, socially dulled. He is wrapped up in himself, and his nervous system is so stressed that it is very difficult for him to be grounded in the present with others. I have seen a number of inmates in prisons who are in a similar state because of lifelong stress accumulation. I have observed the same in workaholic executives who just cannot inwardly focus their attention to "be here, now." I have also observed those who have decided to be grounded and live a life that is grounded. Their "command presence" is visually and psychologically evident. I know one police chief who, when he walks into a room, is so conscious that others come to attention more because of the intensity of his consciousness than because of his position as chief.

Developing the Skill of Grounding: This skill involves a commitment to and the practice of inner wakefulness, and the commitment to strengthen it. It is the foundation of all other skills, for if we are psychologically unavailable to present events, our interactions with ourself and others will be interrupted or blocked. In policing, such lack of grounding can be dangerous.

The development of this skill requires a willingness to work toward continually being more vigilant, wakeful, sober, on the watch, alert in the present, etc., and as one practices this "self-remembering" training, it becomes more enjoyable, more natural. It becomes the foundation of all other strength. This kind of awareness comes with rigorous training in sports or martial arts, intellectual development, determination, and raw commitment.

TL Skill #2. Centering: Including Self in the Context of Events

Centering is an important prerequisite for being a conscious, alert, and intentional person, especially when exercising leadership. It is an awareness skill that enables you to intentionally be conscious of your own presence as a person with your specific beliefs, biases, creative ideas, intuitions, revelations, emotions, physical experiences, and judgments in each moment. This awareness level is distinct from your awareness of external events. This deeper self-awareness can develop more quickly through self-conscious effort and through the practice of being very still (deep relaxation, meditation, or prayer states). Centering is the opposite of selfishness because this part of yourself that can be more aware of you is the same part of yourself that can be more receptive, sensitive, and giving to others.

Examples: You have probably observed a person who is easily "knocked off center." I recall the example of most of my classmates in my first public speaking class in college. Most of us forgot what we wanted to say and became overly "self" conscious to the extent that we lost the capacity to inwardly keep track of the task at hand, which was to focus the self and speak clearly and articulately. How embarrassing it was to be unable to think and speak clearly in front of others! Some people feel this way all the time. They are so shaky in the self-worth department that their sense of being connected to themselves is destroyed—they become "beside" themselves and lose control. In contrast, some people are smooth-performing speakers, musicians, or athletes. They are on dead center with their inner strengths and talents and have the practiced confidence that enables them to bring forward their message, music, or athletic performance with ease and grace.

This inner strength was clearly demonstrated by individuals when drunken revelry turned into a full-scale riot in a large Canadian city. Individuals in the fire, medical, and police services "rose to the occasion" to deliver services under unimaginable conditions. For some, this was the first time in their careers that they had come under physical attack. Yet despite the justifiable fear (that many readily acknowledged in later interviews), individuals recognized that they had a task to perform. Many were ill-equipped, and the communications system and command structure had collapsed. Many were separated from their comrades. Rank or position within the service became irrelevant. Those who did not hold supervisory rank became supervisors; more importantly, they became leaders. They knew what had to be done and they took control. Their inner strength and confidence "blossomed" as they rallied those around them to deliver the emergency services they were trained to provide.

Developing the Skill of Centering: The capacity to be centered and maintain one's center under stress comes from being still in mind and body. It comes from practicing being quiet for longer periods of time, from twenty minutes to one hour. Some people call this process meditation. It also comes from having an unbroken and clear awareness of one's own feelings, thoughts, intuitions, values, beliefs and priorities. When we are clear and focused, we are in the "eye of the storm," and it is difficult to knock a strongly centered person off center. Centered officers are able to exude a "command presence" based on a deep inner sense of calm and stability.

TL Skill #3. Beliefs Clarification and Resolution: Taking a Stance on Life's Basic Issues

This awareness skill area requires the longest discussion because of its importance; it is also the most difficult to explain because of its complexity. This area of skill or "wisdom" in discerning the nature of things is the primary cornerstone for the development of the other skills to come. If, when a person looks inside, there is fog or "mush," that is too vague or soft a foundation on which to build. We all could benefit from further clarification or a deepening of understanding of our operating assumptions about life. This skill focus will help you move ahead toward enhanced clarity of your beliefs.

Science defines and explains the "what and how" of observable life and in the last hundred years has delved more into the powers of previously unseen forces—radio, electronic, and atomic. Beliefs—philosophy and religion—deal with the questions of "who and why." These questions are much more difficult to answer, but they are, at the same time, more essential to our integrity because the answers we give to key questions determine our whole approach to our lives, to others, and to life itself.

What Is Beliefs Clarity?

This awareness "skill" is developed by examining carefully the main questions of existence and, over time, searching for and discovering workable answers to them and validating or invalidating their authenticity or "truth." If we are, however, to have any confidence in our answers, they must be validated in at least some of the following ways of knowing (epistemology): through empirical investigation (science), historical evidence, personal experience (phenomenology), archeology, intuition (psychological), revelation (spiritual), etc. Otherwise, we have little confidence that our assumptions about the nature of life are grounded in any kind of reality that is substantial and therefore believable. That we should be able to validate our positions at all of the levels listed above may also be of critical importance. If there is historical evidence to support the validity of our belief position but no other evidence (or conflicting evidence), we should be suspect! Perhaps our beliefs should be true at every level, or they are only partly true.

For example, most people in the free world believe absolutely in the sanctity of life, that murder is wrong, and that the only justification for the use of force that may kill another person is to stop unjust, immoral, or illegal killing (but only with the appropriate and necessary amount of police or military use of force). Evidence that murder for self-gain has negative consequences can be supported by historical documentation, empirical investigation, archeological findings, intuition, and possibly revelation (depending upon the belief system of the investigator). Therefore, the assertion for the sake of discussion is that premeditated murder of an innocent child, for example, is truly and absolutely wrong because under no circumstances does it have positive consequences that can be validated in the long term—it only has negative consequences. Some questions are not so easily answered, however, as we shall see.

Some people maintain that addressing the most difficult of life's "belief" questions is irrelevant to a meaningful existence in the here and now and that mere values and goals are adequate for living. Values and goals are very important, but the presumption that it is irrational for us to expect to clarify metaphysical issues and arrive at resolute beliefs does nothing for those of us who want to grasp some further essence of life, to go beyond what is visible, to comprehend life in new and deeper ways.

The Personal Nature of Beliefs Clarity

Beliefs are by their nature intensely personal. They are our operating assumptions about life, love, safety, happiness, leadership, management, etc. If we want to know a person intimately, we might first ask what he or she believes to be most real, true, good, unreal, false, or bad. Then we will begin to get a picture of his or her position on some of the basic issues of life, which are really the twenty major questions in life. In an annual survey (over four years) of college and university students, twenty of "life's most unanswered problem questions" were identified in their order of estimated difficulty to answer:

1. What is really happening here on this planet? What is the purpose of matter and existence, if any?
2. Is it really possible to know at all, or should I just skip it as an issue I can't resolve?
3. What criteria do I use to discern what is true from what is not true, good from bad, real from unreal?
4. How can I know whether these criteria are reliable and true, and what are the sources of these criteria?
5. Who am I: In relation to others, the world, the universe, God, etc.?
6. What should I do with my life: a purpose for living, goals to accomplish, a career or "life calling" (vocation)?
7. What is truth? What is my definition of truth, where did I get it, and how do I know it is true?
8. What is the nature of human beings? Good? Evil? Neutral? Where did I get my belief? How did this human nature I believe in get to be the way it is: creation, the environment, the "fall into original sin," conditioning, parents, all of the above, etc.?

9. Is there a supreme being or ultimate cause, or did everything just evolve from nothing, and how do I know?
10. Where did matter come from? Creation by some conscious designer, statistical happenstance, or evolution?
11. Is everything absurd, or is there underlying and inherent purpose in life and in the universe?
12. Are there any absolutes (truths that are immovable) or is "reality" relative to each person's perspective?
13. What is the source(s) or cause(s) of negativity ("evil") and positivity ("good") in life? Are there many sources, one, none?
14. Is there life after death? If so, what kind, where, and with whom? If not, what happens, and how do I know this?
15. Is it possible to communicate with a higher being(s)? If so, how? If not, what difference does that make in my life?
16. What should I value? What is most important in life and what are my priorities?
17. Whom should I join up with in life: to marry, live with, work with, etc.? What criteria should I use to choose these people with whom I ally myself?
18. Where (geographically) on this planet do I want to live and why?
19. How do I prepare myself to fulfill my purpose and goals?
20. How do I know if I am doing okay in life?

These questions are among many critical questions people ask, attempt to answer, or attempt to avoid answering. The fact that different people come up with clashing answers to these questions accounts for much of the discord, misunderstanding, and conflict in relationships, in organizations, and even between nations.

Why Some People Give Up on Gaining Clarity of Beliefs

For most people, getting to the bottom of the above kinds of questions is a meaningful task (or quest, depending upon one's view of the issue). When I asked over six hundred students over the past twelve years if they had generally either given up on answering these kinds of questions or found them to be irrelevant, approximately 32 percent answered yes. They gave the following reasons for giving up trying to answer the difficult questions of life:

1. Confusion, or a feeling of being overwhelmed by the complexity of both the questions and the diversity of answers
2. Lack of satisfying criteria for validating what is true or good
3. Lack of interest in the issue of clarification

4. Lack of understanding of the benefits of being more clear
5. Lack of information and knowledge about alternatives
6. Laziness or fear

About 30 percent of these six hundred students reported that they were determined to "crack the code" to some kind of "higher reality." They said that they had already had some experiences that had led them to believe there was a discernible reality beyond what they could see with the eye. One person explained that if radio and television waves are not hard to believe in, then why should other "waves" of communication be so hard to fathom?

Another 32 percent of the six hundred claimed to have satisfying answers to these and other more difficult-to-answer questions. They seemed to have some kind of clear frame of reference, stance, faith, or belief about questions of death, a supreme being, the nature of humans, why we are here, who we are, and where we are going. Some of these students admitted that they had not really examined or searched for their beliefs but simply accepted them because of their family and cultural upbringing. Approximately 6 percent decided not to respond to the questions put to them.

The Advantage of Beliefs Clarity

It would seem in one way that those who have greater clarity of beliefs enjoy an advantage over those who have not dealt with these questions. There is research (a good starting place is David Larson's 1992 article in the *American Journal of Psychiatry* that summarizes twelve years of psychiatric literature) to suggest that people with clear belief systems have less anxiety, more success, lower divorce rates, and lower stress-related illness rates. In a state of conscious awareness, they act on specific assumptions and are more likely aware of the consequences of taking action based on each specific belief position. This enables them to gain feedback from their environments about the validity and workability of their assumptions. Contrast this clarity of mind with the person who is unsure and unresolved or who wavers from situation to situation and gets mixed feedback.

Some of those who claimed to know specific answers were criticized by others for not having ever really searched and opened their minds in the first place, because they may have simply "swallowed" what was "fed" to them when they were children. This is a good point. Someone said that the unexamined life is not worth living.

It would appear from this informal study that the issue of beliefs is a highly charged and intensely personal one to most people. When challenged to rate the importance of the issue of beliefs clarity on a scale from 1 to 10, the average person gave the issue an 8.6 out of 10 (with a range of 4 to 10).

The Process of Developing Beliefs Clarity

It is for this reason that I developed a self-guided process for clarification of beliefs. The process is clearly a developmental one—usually there is no sudden flash of blinding light on the road to Damascus, as Saint Paul is reported to have had, although slightly over one-third of those who claimed to have achieved some clarity of beliefs said there was a definite time when an internal "light went on."

Before outlining the steps in the search process, I recommend that you refer to a summary of the developmental stages delineated by Fowler (1981). These are longer and are called *Stages in the Development of a Personal Faith Position* (see Appendix A). I have also developed a systematic way to explore these critical issues of life and build a personal life plan; this process is called *Deep Structure Strategic Planning* (see Appendix B).

Steps in the Process of Clarification of Your Belief Stance

The process of clarifying one's beliefs is very complex and often happens— unintentionally—because of significant events in one's life. If you want to embark on a conscious search, however, that can involve a series of steps. By following these steps, your own belief stance will become clearr as time passes. The steps for clarifying beliefs can be done by yourself, or you can help an individual or group of people gain resolution by coaching them through the following steps.

1. As best you can, specify in writing your present answers to life's major questions, which were outlined above, or attempt to answer your own problem questions.
2. Search out where you got your beliefs and write what you can remember about these sources for later comparison.
3. Examine your criteria for accepting these beliefs as true, and write down the various validations for your beliefs that you accept.
4. Write a clear and concise position paper about your stance on life's twenty major questions and issues.
5. Read this paper over once a week while you consistently attempt to take on this position in a real way, living it out on a daily basis as congruently as you are able.
6. Review your position statement every three to six months, and examine how your position helps you to deal with problems or better appreciate the joys of life.
7. Note any "holes" or inconsistencies in your belief position that you think may be invalid, incomplete, or problematic.

8. Examine other differing belief positions (ones you think are incomplete or false, if any) that validate for you how true your position is in a course on world religions or through additional reading. Or, note how there are parts of other belief positions that seem to have truth in them on the premise that "truth is truth wherever it is found."

To assist you in getting started with this last step, I suggest you consider reading Chapter 9 in *Megatrends 2000,* by Naisbitt and Aburdene. This book will give you an overview of what is occurring in the world of beliefs. Using this chapter as an introduction, you can move ahead with a more thorough study of each of the various philosophical or religious belief positions.

Students who have generally followed this series of steps in my courses on self-awareness and interpersonal communication have reported in the course evaluations at the end of term that this exercise was the most challenging and meaningful of the semester; some even reported that it was the most important step in their whole lives. The process outlined above, however, is a structure for cognitively oriented people. Some people do not learn well this way, by following steps. Some students have indicated that they have gotten better results by simply asking, as though they will get an answer through circumstances, from thoughts coming into their minds, dreams, etc., from a source they do not fully understand. They are convinced of the "magic" of simply asking to know, like a child would ask his or her parent an innocent question and not give up until satisfied that he or she got an answer. This childlike approach, oddly enough, is the approach I have found to be even more powerful than the cognitive approach, and I have tried both. If you would like to read the story of my own personal search, you may contact me by e-mail at: drcoach@home.com.

The Downside of Failing to Clarify Beliefs

People who avoid the whole issue of belief clarification, or give up on its resolution, perhaps are less deeply "rooted" in a life position. They may be more easily influenced to move in a number of directions, depending upon which way a personal, social, political, or economic "wind" is blowing at the time. They often claim that this "flexible" tendency is a strength, that they are open-minded and willing to change with the times. They also often say, however, that they have little inner peace, that decision making is difficult without a clear reference point, and that their relationships suffer because they often clash with individuals who have clear beliefs, who do not really align well with people who do not have clear assumptions.

Those who have a metaphysical understanding of and an orientation to life (answers to the "why" questions) have a distinct advantage, even if their orientation may be ultimately incorrect in the end. They are more "solid," act more consistently, can get feedback from the environment as to the validity and workability of their assumptions (because they have a position as a reference point), and many times are better able to understand the position of others—a "tolerance" skill important when leading people. Some people who are "clear" are not tolerant, however. Some people are narrow, intolerant, have to be "right" about everything, are not very compassionate of others' struggle for clarity, and want others to "swallow" their truths. But not all of these people who claim to be "sure" are "fundamentalist fanatics" who would negatively judge you for not being clear or for not wanting to agree with their positions. Some really are clear, truly peaceful, kind, patient, and caring people who just quietly "know." You likely know at least a few people like this. Ask them what they believe and listen to their stories.

Beliefs form the solid foundation of a clear purpose in life, and a clear set of values is a structure upon which to build goals, strategies, and actions. With only values to live by, the "why" of life is not addressed, explored, or resolved in the least. Beliefs address the "why" and "what" questions of life directly. The hierarchical relationship between beliefs, purpose, values, goals, strategies, and actions is illustrated as follows:

When people can share some basic beliefs, they are more likely to join together to create something productive. This is true for marriage partners or any other type of endeavor in business, health, education, community development, the military, or human services—where team effort is required.

Furthermore, if you understand others' beliefs, you are more likely to comprehend why they have given their "hearts" to them, why they feel they need them, and why they need to keep them, and you can then be even more tolerant.

Finally, beliefs are the cornerstones upon which all stable *ethics* rest. Ethics are those codes that we are sworn to when we take our oaths, and we hold one another accountable to our ethical commitments the same as professionals in

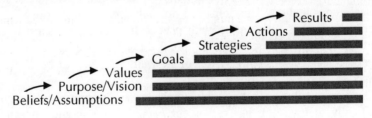

medicine, accounting, the clergy, etc. do.

TL Skill #4. Specifying Your Personal Purpose/Vision: A Critical Life Skill

A **purpose** is a reason to do anything, such as a reason to get up in the morning. A **vision** is clear picture of a preferred future where you can imagine yourself accomplishing this purpose. As you gain a greater sense of clarity about what you believe or assume to be real and true, it is easier to move ahead to specify a keener sense of purpose and vision in your life that is in harmony with your beliefs. If your beliefs are fuzzy or unresolved, you will have more difficulty in specifying a definite purpose or vision. A desire for clarification and a belief that it is possible are good requisites for making progress in this area.

Finding or developing a clear sense of personal purpose and vision is not an easy task. One of the contributors to this book tried for a number of years to state, on paper, his purpose for living. He did not have a sense that he had actually captured the essence of it. His life was less focused and organized because of this. He found himself saying yes to things others wanted him to do and things he could not see a good reason to say no to, and as a result, his life became filled with tasks, goals, and even obligations that didn't "click way down deep." He would get up in the morning and say to himself, "What am I _really_ up to today, anyway?"

As a leader, it is imperative that you understand the importance of purpose and vision so that you can understand it (or the lack of it) in others. Understanding the importance of purpose and vision in yourself will help you recognize that the absence or "fuzziness" of the preferred future in others may be the harbinger of problems by which you, as a leader, may be challenged. For example, a young man with strong spiritual beliefs became a police officer. He did so partly due to external pressures from family and friends who felt that his honest and caring way would make him a good police officer. His lack of clarity in his vision allowed him to be convinced that this career choice was best for him. As soon as his practical training began, it was evident to classmates and staff that there was a problem. His "purpose" of choice was to assist, support, love, and provide guidance to those in need. He found that this clashed with the role of a police officer, which often required impartiality, nonemotional responses, and even physical confrontation. This impacted not only his ability to do what was required but also his relationship with peers. His career was short-lived as he found himself in an irreconcilable "moral dilemma." He agreed that policing was not consistent with his vision of how his life was to be lived, and he resigned.

The French phrase that roughly translates as "purpose" is _raison d'être._ Specifically, it translates as "reason for _being._" Why should you and I even bother to _be_ at all? If we can answer that question so that we have a burning sense of mission or purpose about which we are passionate, then we will be internally motivated, better able to clarify and set priorities, and better able to specify high-drive goals that match our strengths and abilities.

My personal purpose statement reads as follows:

> My purpose in life is to be a whole man while I support and develop leaders who can build other leaders, resulting in the development of teams and organizations that make positive impacts on communities.

So, I am an author, encourager, facilitator, helper, knowledge resource, consultant, and supporter of other leaders (or leaders-to-be) who have, as their purpose, a desire to impact human and organization development for positive community ends. I include my family in this purpose; my two sons are leaders in some ways and becoming better at it. My identity is steeped in this purpose. I plan my days around this purpose, set my priorities and goals around this purpose, and encourage and assist willing others to do the same. I have also learned to have fun and enjoy each moment of life—thanks to my precious wife. In the midst of all of their endeavors, this is something many people forget to do when they become too goal oriented. I am now teaching my first-year university students this foundational lesson in life—*enjoy each moment*!

I feel fulfilled with this purpose and a charge of excitement when I see it realized. It is highly motivating to me. Try to write your own purpose statement in the space provided below

Your First-Draft Personal Purpose Statement

My purpose in life is to...

A **personal vision statement** captures the essence of your preferred future. It captures what your ideal life will look like in the future, who you will be, what career you will have, whom you will be with, where you will live and work, and where your future life will ultimately lead. Most people find it very difficult to formulate such a statement of a vision because they are used to being so realistic and practical that they cannot dream dreams and stretch their hopes into the nearly impossible reaches of the future. It is true that we cannot know if our vision of a preferred future will come true. Likewise, if we have no vision, we will not likely reach it. On the other hand, it is also true that a portion of our vision of the future will come true because we will consciously move in that direction.

My own vision statement reads as follows:

> God willing, in ten years I will be a senior consultant to world leaders in the back rooms of the palaces of the world, comforting and coaching them to make critical decisions carefully, discerningly, and thoroughly, in the most complex and trying of times. I will live with my wife, Jo-Anne, in a smaller two-bedroom flat that has an ocean view, and we will travel abroad several times a year to enjoy the world and help key leaders. I will be retired from my university teaching job and will be supporting and spiritually coaching leaders around the world from my office. I will be writing very focused books and developing a Web site that will touch and transform people's lives with hope and inspiration—that they may see their true worth and discern the Source and Ultimate Purpose of their lives. Then they will lead others toward that mysterious Peace that silently awaits us on the horizon of time until the end of this age.

Your First-Draft Personal Vision Statement

In five and ten years, my spiritual, financial, interpersonal, health, and life-style will look like...

It is challenging for anyone to complete the above statements. Therefore, additional help in defining and writing your personal purpose and vision statements is provided in Appendix B, "Stages in the Development of a Personal Faith Position." If you are having difficulty specifying your sense of purpose, a course in career and life planning, a workshop in personal life planning, or counseling can be a very worthwhile investment. Readings in this area could also be useful.

TL Skill #5. Identifying Your Values: Setting Priorities in Life

The clearer your purpose, the greater ease you will have in identifying what is important to you. Confusion rules when one's sense of purpose is vague and one's vision is unclear. Clarifying and identifying values (personally important or of high priority) is a somewhat difficult matter of prioritizing various things in one's life, such as spirituality, family, career, education, money, geographic location, etc. When you know what you find to be most important—more valuable in relation to other values—it becomes easier to set goals.

I have, as my highest value, human life and human development. I value the quality of the inner life of myself and others more highly than anything else. Developing a quality inner life and learning to express high quality to others through caring and the use of knowledge and skills are very important to me. I value high-impact activities where the payoff is primarily human development. It is because of these values that this book was written.

An example of an organization where people often have conflicting values is a prison. In one prison I visited, not only were the inmates pitted against one another with conflicting values, but the staff was as well. Some staff members valued respecting and trying to rehabilitate inmates, and others wanted nothing to do with "the slugs." Some didn't care one way or the other, but just wanted to collect a paycheck and get to retirement at the end of the road. This conflict of values is like a house divided, unable to stand the stresses and strains of longer term oppression from some of the inmates. The negativity was triggered one Christmas Eve when a manager ordered a cell search, found an alcoholic fruit-juice brew in a number of cells, confiscated it, and precipitated a million-dollar riot. Those people who had clear values, no matter what they were, believed they were right—no matter what happened. Staff members who suffered the greatest stress were the ones caught in between, with little or no clarity of their values. Because they stood for nothing, they had no reason to stay in such a high-stress environment, and many of them chose to leave their jobs. Those who had clear and positive values were the ones who chose to stay on after the riot and help rebuild a better culture where both the keeper and the kept must live together, hopefully in greater peace.

Another example relates to our values outside the workplace. As previously asked: how do you establish what has value in your life to determine what is "important"? After becoming a single parent, one police officer quickly had to establish a new relationship with his young children. Through counseling, he learned to "connect" with the children and establish the communication needed to work on the healing process. During one of the discussions about the past with his children, he was shocked when one of them said, "We never saw you." They went on to tell him about school events and baseball games that he had missed and school plays where they looked into the audience of dutiful parents only to find his face still not present. Later ,when he had time to reflect, he knew they were right. He had set lofty career goals at the expense of family goals. Promotion in the police culture required higher education and thus off-duty hours in class away from home. It required working extra hours (usually without compensation) and placing his career first, both in word and deed. His priorities, although ostensibly noble, had cost him the bond with his wife and years of memories with his children.

Another way to get at our values, especially in relation to work, is to assess our patterns of interest in relation to others. Testing in this area with interest inventories is available for free in most counseling centers at colleges and universities.

If you want to go through a more complete values preference prioritization exercise, obtain a copy of Robinson's (1990) *Values Preference Inventory* from www.crgleader.com. As you gain clarity of purpose and identify your values in order of priority, you will be able to more easily and clearly set motivating goals in specific areas of your life, development, and career. Effective goals are based upon clear beliefs and assumptions, a deep sense of purpose, and clear values. They must be desirable, concretely defined, realistically achievable within the time you have available, measurable so you know when you have reached them, owned or chosen by you instead of imposed on you by others, and celebrated when achieved. The next three skills focus on this proactive approach to these three key areas of life.

TL Skill #6. Life Planning: Setting Motivating Goals

Someone once said that we spend more time planning our vacations than we do our lives. One study of over six hundred students found this to be true. Is it for you? This area-of-living skill is so often overlooked that up until the last twenty years few courses were available on life planning. Until fairly recently, it was not something for which one would ask a professional counselor for assistance. I did a search on the Internet for "life planning" and found a number of resources that were not available in years past. Life planning is not a skill that our children are regularly being taught in school. The earliest we see this skill being taught systematically is in a student success course in the freshman year of college. A few high schools are teaching it in career-planning courses.

But leaders—or prospective leaders—need this skill perhaps more than most people do. The one great hazard for leaders is that they tend to overload their lives and their work to the point of being addicted to the adrenal high of workaholism, lifeaholism, or love of money. This is due to lack of focus on a higher sense of purpose and vision, and therefore a leader tries to accomplish too much—and thus the addiction to accomplishment or success overtakes his or her life. One accomplishment leads to the next, until there is not time left to enjoy the moment, to do things like take a walk for no purpose, to enjoy just *being* or being *with* the ones we truly love.

We can sell our souls to success, drugs, food, money, power, security, sex, pleasure, laziness, or whatever. Designing and living out an intentional life plan can help us live more balanced lives. However, planning too much and robotically living our lives can kill risk taking and spontaneity. This "balance" area of skill should be taken seriously and be developed. Balance and joy in life are perhaps more important in the long run than you might think at first. If you lose joy of life, or health, you can lose all else! This book does not cover this area in depth. If you want to look into this area further, obtain the resources that are available from Strategic Resources (http://www.strategia.com). They are co-authored by Ron Ford and Bill Bean, such as the workbook *Living on Purpose*, or other material that is available through libraries or the Internet.

TL Skill #7. Educational Planning: Setting Motivating Goals

Today, we must have a learning plan because our fast-changing environment will leave us behind unless we are plugged into relevant, meaningful, and targeted learning opportunities. Unless we know what our beliefs, values, careers, and life goals are, however, it will be difficult to develop an educational plan. Hopefully, your learning plan will be based on your life plan and not just your career goals. Otherwise, you could become like many people who have good careers and hollow or wrecked lives.

Most people do not consider what their true interests and passions are when they choose a career and then decide how long they need to attend school and what courses to take there. In the past thirty or so years, most people have enrolled in courses that struck their fancy at the time or a close relative took. Before that, most people enrolled in the standard career programs, of which there were relatively few. Now there are so many learning choices available that you really must focus on who you really are and prioritize what you really want—or you could go to school forever and never accomplish anything else! Many people have become professional students to a certain extent. But that can also be a trap. Richard Bolles, in his book *What Color Is Your Parachute?: A Practical Manual for Job-Hunters and Career-Changers* (updated annually), asserts that there are three "boxes" of life in which we can get caught: school, career, and leisure. If we spend too much time in any one day or week on any one of these things, we can feel boxed in by that activity. But if we balance our lives with learning, working, and leisure each day—so we continue to stay abreast of changing knowledge and skills, engage in meaningful work, and enjoy life—we will be much happier and more productive overall. This seems to me to be wise. In summary, a good learning plan should be based on a good life plan and should be linked to a solid and clear career plan.

A trend in recent years has been the recruitment of emergency services personnel from a pool of well-educated men and women. As the level of education for recruits rises, so does the level of education for promotion in the services. Succession planning models are being introduced. Most people with years of experience in these services are seeking both horizontal and vertical movement in the organization. Many have not made the effort to include educational planning in their career plans. After spending years in organizations that used seniority-based promotion and transfer systems, they now find themselves in a highly competitive market where higher education is a mandatory prerequisite. The only avenue available is a significant financial and time commitment to education in order to compete with those hired in more recent years. They are faced with a financial burden as education costs soar. They struggle with study habits long dormant. But often most difficult is the impact on their personal and family lives as hour upon hour is spent in the classroom or cloistered away in intense study. In order to prevent this "overload," it is wise to plan to complete educational goals as early as possible or to schedule them so that they can be completed without throwing your life, health, or relationships out of balance.

TL Skill #8. Career Planning: Setting Motivating Goals

"To thine own self be true and thou can'st not then be false to any man." This line by Shakespeare is worthy of consideration when it comes to career planning and setting wise career goals. Most people tend to choose a career goal and then revolve their lives around that one goal. It controls their daily schedule (especially those who are involved in shift work); it controls the environment in which they work, often the location where they live, their daily stress level, their economic future, and their overall destiny to some extent.

Leaders need to be especially sure that what they are doing is connected directly to their strengths, gifts, talents, interests, and life goals; otherwise, people will tend to look at the leaders' lives to see how integrated they are, and if people see that the leaders have problems, that can hurt the leaders' credibility. People will see that the leaders talk the talk but have a difficult time walking the walk. This is why life planning as a skill is listed before career planning. It is better to base our careers are based on our life plans that include how we want to live, where we want to live, how we want to spend our waking hours, and with whom we want to spend them. A career is, at best, a vehicle to get us to the destination we want to reach in life, not just a job in isolation from the rest of life.

It is especially important for leaders to have a career path plan or succession plan so they can see how their current role is preparation for the next level of promotion or development they want to achieve. It is important that they find and develop mentors and coaches (such as counselors and career coaches at colleges and universities) to help them optimize their real job and career skills. That will help them avoid running headlong into the Peter Principle: being promoted to one's level of incompetence and staying there. This is another reason why a life plan, a learning plan, and career plan truly go together to form an integrated approach to living an intentional life. If you have not already done so, it is recommended that you invest in these three areas lavishly as the foundation of building your vision for your future and preferred life here on planet Earth.

TL Skill #9. Time Management

After teaching this skill for years, I estimate that few people actually want to practice time management to increase their own productivity and balance in life. It is a skill that sometimes appears to be in opposition to the very existence of emergency services personnel. Fire fighters, paramedics, and police officers all begin, and continue for many years, in positions that are primarily reactionary in nature. These practitioners do not go to work to carefully compartmentalize the tasks of the shift. They can't. They simply respond to whatever occurs during the shift. A phrase frequently heard is, "Hours of boredom occasionally interrupted by a few minutes of utter chaos." When they reach supervisory and management positions, the concept of "managing time" is foreign. Most of us tend to just live from day to day, get done what we can, and avoid what we can in terms of stress. Many people become discouraged when they start to plan their personal and work lives. At first, they are not very realistic; their plans do not work out as expected. They often try to do too much in too short a time; they find that time management is an additional hassle and distraction. They experience some "burnout" and give up on any kind of systematic approach to planning and living. This is unfortunate because it is possible to find a more comfortable and productive way to more effectively use of time. I have discovered a very practical approach to dealing with the complexities we face in our work and personal lives. I create three "bins":

Priority 1   Must be dealt with today
Priority 2   Would like to do today if there is time for it
Priority 3   Will get to it if I can, someday

Each task is placed in one of the "bins." As time goes by, various tasks can be moved up into a higher priority "bin." If everything just keeps piling up, then, of course, I have to ask myself if I really want to live or work in that way!

Another important way to manage time is to block out periods of time by the type of task: All phone calls returned between 9 A.M. and 10 A.M, all letters written between 10 A.M and 11 A.M, etc. This approach is very effective for some people and eliminates distraction and complexity that can interfere with effective performance.

When your beliefs, purpose, values, and goals are clear, it is much easier to decide in which of the three piles things belong. My experience is that I become better at managing time as I do it over and over. It is an art as well as a logical planning activity. Sometimes I allot a block of time that is not structured or goal oriented, except that my goal during that "loose" time is to free myself from any regimen. There are fine workshops in time management, good resources to read, and excellent time management systems that can be purchased. But as a leader, it is necessary that you find your own style of managing time. You will continue to get better at it as you go along. When we manage our time, what we are really managing is our lives.

TL Skill #10. Stress Management

This skill is often learned after people become so stressed that they have to find a way to unwind. It is often with reluctance that emergency services personnel even acknowledge the existence of personal stress. Incidents that by "normal" standards would cause a great deal of stress are often treated by emergency services personnel with apparent nonchalance and even disdain. The culture is seen as demanding this strength as a sign of an individual's ability to "get the job done." In the course of time, people haphazardly find stress management techniques that work well and others that work well but have undesirable side effects (such as the use or overuse of anything that temporarily relieves stress—drugs, food, sex, work, exercise, leisure, etc.).

Culturally acceptable are the early morning parking lot "tailgate parties" which include the obligatory alcoholic "stress reliever." An upstream approach to the prevention of stress accumulation is more desirable. The very best stress prevention method is a well-designed and well-lived life that is not overloaded—one that is balanced and enjoyed. The two most powerful tools for stress management, to knock down the stress that we do accumulate, are a regular, daily program of cardiovascular exercise and deep relaxation. Twenty to thirty minutes a day of exercise combined with twenty to thirty minutes of deep relaxation can do an incredible job of reducing pent-up stresses in the body and preventing the accumulation of stress. Talking through problems to resolution can release emotional tension and promote a sense of well-being. People who are good self-managers and have developed the skills outlined in this chapter will likely have lower stress levels, look younger, be healthier, and enjoy life more. If you want to look into this area in greater depth and learn more, refer to Walt Schafer's (1991) book, *Stress Management for Wellness.* If you want to do a self-assessment, you can complete the Stress Indicator and Health Planner, co-authored by Terry Anderson and Gwen Faulkner (available from www.crgleader.com). Another way to look at stress management is to look at each leader's life as an energy system. The next section provides that useful perspective.

TL Skill #11. Energy Management
for Improved Health and Performance

Energy management is the preventive approach to managing stress. If you can "get the jump" on stress accumulation in your mind and body by nourishing, strengthening, and resting yourself physically, then you will have a much greater reserve of energy to cope resourcefully with more difficult or demanding situations. In addition to avoiding harmful substances such as tobacco, alcohol in moderate to large quantities, and various medical and nonmedical drugs, there are four areas where increased knowledge and development can result in a greater resilience and hardiness.

The Four Life Style Management Keys to Increased Energy and Performance: Optimum Nutrition, Exercise, Deep Relaxation, and Restful Sleep

The wide range of opinion about what makes up the optimum amounts and best types of nutrition, exercise, deep relaxation, and sleep is overwhelming and confusing for most people. Just what sources or experts should one rely on when attempting to establish an appropriate balance in these four energy resource foundations? After reviewing the literature in the four resource areas that has been published over the last twenty years, the following basic guidelines become evident:

1. There is little disagreement among various experts in the fields about things one might do in general to best increase baseline energy and performance levels.
2. Individual differences between people are significant enough that a generic prescription for any one person may not be appropriate. Therefore, a health care specialist should be consulted before any major changes are made.
3. Assessments of a particular individual's unique physiology, needs, and style are prerequisites to any appropriate health and fitness program designed for that person.
4. Monitoring progress on any program is necessary in order to determine if, in fact, changes made in diet, exercise, relaxation practices, or sleep patterns make any worthwhile difference.
5. Life-style changes (clarity of purpose, values, goals, plans, and activities) often accompany increased control and balance of energy resources, which result in higher performance and vitality. These life style changes need to be protected and supported if the programs are to promote sustained higher energy and performance.

6. Once new and more effective habit patterns have been well established—habits that are preferable to the old patterns—the side benefits are increased self-awareness, self-esteem, and therefore self-confidence.
7. A combination of professional medical advice and personal experimentation with various programs yields improved health and wellness and increased performance and well-being.

It is not the purpose of this book to look in depth at this area; rather, the purpose here is to introduce you to the importance of learning to manage this part of life well. The benefits of healthful practices are obvious, and the limitations that can occur when we allow stress to overtake us are also obvious.

TL Skill #12. Positive Mental Attitude: The Inner Skill of the Winner

In his studies of professional athletes, Waitley (1979) found that there were specifically identifiable patterns of thought and action that distinguished winners from losers. The major differences were found in mental attitude, and other less significant differences were found in physical ability. He studied winners from many fields and found similar success patterns.

The ability to face an apparent problem and see it as a positive challenge is one internal ability winners have. They inwardly control their reactions to an event and assign it the weight of importance appropriate to the situation, rather than assess the situation by the intensity or depth of their emotions at the moment.

Winners accept failure and use it to improve their next performance. Their rationale is, "The more times I fail, the more practice I get, and the better I get." Because they practice more often without presuming they cannot achieve a particular goal, they succeed more often.

References

Anderson, T. and G. Faulkner, *The Stress Indicator and Health Planner,* Abbotsford, B.C., Canada: Consulting Resource Group, 1990.

Fowler, James W., *Stages of Faith: The Psychology of Human Development and the Quest for Meaning,* San Francisco, Harper and Row, 1981.

Gardiner, John A., Crime and Criminal Justice: Issues in Public Policy and Analysis, 1990.

Larson, David B., et al., Associations between dimensions of religious commitment and mental health reported in the *Am. J. Psychiatr, Arch. Gen. Psychiatr.*, 1979–2989, *Am. J. Psychiatr.*, 149 (4), 557, 1992.

Naisbitt, John, et al., *Megatrends 2000*, New York: William Morrow, 1990.

Robinson, E., *Values Preference Inventory*, Abbotsford, B.C., Canada: Consulting Resource Group, 1990.

Roglieri, J.L., *Odds on Your Life*, New York: Seaview, 1980.

Schafer, W., *Stress Management for Wellness*, New York: Holt, Rinehart and Winston, 1991.

Srivastra, Suresh and David Cooperider, *Appreciative Management and Leadership*: *The Power of Positive Thought and Action in Organizations*, San Francisco: Jossey-Bass Publishing, 14, 1990.

Waitley, D., *The Psychology of Winning*, New York: The Berkeley Publishing Company, 1979.

The Skills of Interpersonal Communication

In order to wholly be with another person, I have to first be inwardly connected with myself—then I am in a position to be awake to others, to see them, hear them, and understand them. Then, and only then, will I gain their trust and the cooperation that is required for us to reach together toward deeper friendship, higher achievement, and service.

—Terry Anderson

Introduction

This chapter continues the in-depth exploration of the skills involved in being a transforming leader. If we manage ourselves and our lives well, as indicated in the previous chapter, we will be in a better position to be fully present, whole, and influential in our relationships with others. Even one serious deficit in a skill area in these foundational skills of self-management and communication can undermine our leadership credibility, diminish our influence with others, and result in our not being as effective as we could be. This is especially true when it comes to learning the more complex skills of counseling, coaching, and consulting that are expanded on in the chapters that follow.

We have all seen how few people around us are really consistently good self-managers and communicators! Most of us seem to have a blind spot or undeveloped skill (or two) that continues to frustrate others and that interferes with our gaining credibility or resolving interpersonal difficulties. This has been demonstrated in my unpublished research studies which indicate that others see us as less effective than we see ourselves (on a 10-point scale, the average person rates himself or herself about 7.5 ["good"], and "others" rate him or her at 6.0 ["minimally acceptable"]. In addition, when people come into our university-level courses in interpersonal communication and do a first videotaped assessment, they exhibit typical communication problems regardless of their educational background or level of professional experience. In other words, most of us have blind spots that can be quite easily corrected with competency-based training or coaching. Also, most of us can learn quickly to avoid doing some things that undermine our effectiveness when we become aware of what we are doing. When the skills are presented as "microskills," they are more transferable, more easily learned, and certainly easier to understand.

As police agencies across the United States move toward community policing models, the need to effectively communicate becomes most critical. Police officers are no longer entirely driven by calls for service or merely reacting to crimes in progress. They are expected to be leaders in the community. Community-oriented policing and problem-oriented policing are much more proactive and focus more on crime prevention than criminal apprehension. Problem-solving strategies frequently call for participation by other governmental agencies and the resident community.

The police officer or deputy sheriff is expected to identify neighborhood problems that contribute to crime and bring various resources together to work on those problems. The success of those problem-solving partnerships often depends upon the leadership and interpersonal communication skills of the police officer or supervisor leading the crime prevention effort.

Under the professional model of policing, practiced throughout most of the twentieth century, police supervisors, managers, and administrators were expected to simply manage the system rather than inspire, act creatively, or lead change (Geller and Swanger, 1995). The accountability of individual officers was a fundamental issue for police executives (Kelling et al., 1988). Geller and Swanger (1995) also describe the traditional style of police management being practiced for the past several decades. They refer to this style as "old age" managerial skills. These skills include setting goals, establishing procedures, organizing, and controlling. They also describe the militaristic structure in most police agencies that causes managers to "rely on authority rather than competence and respect among peers as the basis for influencing subordinates." As a result of the changing culture of policing, the first-line supervisor and middle manager roles (generally a sergeant and lieutenant in most departments) have taken on much more responsibility for coaching, leading, and communicating.

Even the frontline officer is expected to be more of a leader and facilitator than was expected under the Professional model of policing. The transformation from traditional policing to Community Oriented Policing and Problem Solving (COPPS) will challenge the leadership ability of all members of the police organization.

The following *Transforming Leadership* skills are the focus of this chapter:

TL Skill #13	Self-Disclosure	Page 101
TL Skill #14	Image Management	Page 102
TL Skill #15	Impression Management	Page 103
TL Skill #16	Attending	Page 106
TL Skill #17	Observing	Page 108
TL Skill #18	Suspending Frame of Reference	Page 109
TL Skill #19	Questioning	Page 111
TL Skill #20	Listening	Page 113
TL Skill #21	Responding with Understanding	Page 114
TL Skill #22	Assertiveness	Page 115
TL Skill #23	Confrontation	Page 118
TL Skill #24	Challenging	Page 124

You may want to pay special attention to those skills in which you felt strongest and weakest when you took the *Transforming Leadership* skills assessment in Chapter 2.

What Are Interpersonal Communication Skills?

Interpersonal communication skills are the vehicles by which all interactions between people are made clear. Much of the communication that occurs between people is one way, without either party truly hearing the other and accurately understanding the feelings, thoughts, or reasons for these feelings or thoughts. In fact, if you think about it, our modern culture, especially in cities, teaches many people not to have two-way communication because it is too personal and imposing or too time consuming

Have you ever taken a course where you were trained in interpersonal communication skills, so that it was confirmed you had competencies and not just knowledge? Where do people go to get such training? Not many places offer it: not most schools, not most families, not most churches, not even most business schools, medical schools, or law schools. Schools of social work, education, and counseling often offer such courses as a required part of their programs. But few of us get the opportunity to gain confirmed competency in the use of these all-important foundational skills.

Serious Problems Can Be Traced to Communication Skill Deficits

I recently bought my son a three-month trial membership in a gym as a birthday gift. Unfortunately, at the time, he was working so many hours a week that he couldn't use the membership. We decided to cancel it and get a refund. After the owner finished a twenty-minute phone call (she knew I was waiting to see her), I explained the circumstances to her. She briskly and efficiently pulled out the contract and told me that I would lose the money I had paid. She took this position even though the staff person who sold me the contract had previously told me that if my son didn't want the membership, my money would be refunded. The owner acted in an officious manner, using the contract for justification, and seemed to see the situation only from her perspective. She expressed no understanding of, or empathy toward, my feelings or my views.

By handling the situation in that way, she followed the letter of the contract rather than the spirit of the agreement. I had no desire to become a return customer at that point. Then, when I further explained that my son had not used the membership at all, she said, "I don't know that he hasn't been here. We don't keep records." In making that statement, she expressed distrust in me, the customer.

As you might have guessed by now, I was becoming less and less comfortable as this interchange progressed. In an effort to help her understand, I explained that it seemed only fair that I receive a partial refund because my son did not decide to buy the membership but received it as a gift and had in fact not been to the gym even once.

She said, "I don't think a refund is necessary."

I said, "Do you want to create a satisfied customer or a dissatisfied customer?"

She said, "It's up to you whether you are satisfied or not." I left my business card with her and told her that if she thought about it, she might change her mind, and if she did, she could give me a call. She looked away. I left the gym feeling unfairly treated not only about the money but mostly because I was treated in such an officious and distrusting manner.

Will I recommend that gym to others? No. Will I go out of my way to caution others from doing business there? Yes, but not vindictively. She simply did not gain my respect of her operation. She "won." I lost. Adept communication skills could have made the whole difference in this situation. (She went out of business six months later.)

Exploring the Skills of Communication

The practice of good communication skills results in two-way communication that builds intimate relationships or solves practical problems, whichever is the intent. This chapter will assist you to review and self-assess the extent to which you have the skills that have been researched as critical to the development of effective interpersonal communication in any setting (Carkhuff, 1971).

TL Skill #13. Self-Disclosure: Appropriately Sharing Yourself with Others

Self-disclosure refers to the ability to appropriately reveal deeper and deeper levels of self to others, as the other person in the relationship earns trust, which warrants such deeper and more genuine disclosure. This skill is critical in the development of both one's self-concept and one's relationships with others.

It seems that we earn trust and intimacy to the extent that we can be genuine, from the heart. Being open, but not unwisely risking too much information too soon, promotes this type of trust and can even encourage the development of intimacy. If no one knows you very well, you will probably not feel much of a connection to others. Perhaps a sense of belonging and being connected with others is one deep need we all have, and if that need is frustrated, some people experience the pain of loneliness and emotional difficulties. If you are shy— fearful that others will use any knowledge they have about you against you, you will likely have difficulty with this skill of appropriately sharing yourself with others. If you are outgoing—can easily share your feelings with others, you may find that this tendency makes more introverted people uncomfortable. There- fore, self-disclosure appropriate to the level of familiarity with the style of the other person is an important factor to consider.

Self-disclosure, to be most effective, must be well timed, not too deep or too shallow for the purpose of improving the relationship, and shared in confidence and trust. As an example of how truth telling in relationships is healthy, a special friend recently said to me:

> My wife and I have had relational problems develop over the years that we sort of ignored and adjusted to without really realizing it. But the romance and closeness grew faint as the years passed and we became distant to one another. She has wanted to work on facing these things but I have avoided it for years. It was just too humiliating that a professional like me would have to admit failure in this area of life when I teach communication to people as a profession! But in the past few months, I made a commitment to really listen to her and tell her the truth about what I am feeling in the relationship. We asked each other two questions: (1) Where is our marriage from your point of view on a ten-point scale, and why? (2) What could I do to make it a ten for you? Wow! Did that ever open up the communication on both our parts! The truth hurt, but we didn't hurt one another! As a result, we are closer than ever, the romance is back in a new and deeper way,

and this is in spite of the fact we are both busier than ever in our careers. I can't tell you how important this is to my overall happiness and optimism for the future. And our kids are getting the bonus of seeing us be joyful and playful together as they grow up!

Self-disclosure can also be valuable in community policing practices. Police officers must first build trust if they truly expect to develop the relationships necessary to partner with others in crime prevention efforts. We have led too many for too long to believe that police officers alone can solve complex neighborhood crime problems. Community support is needed. Many communities, especially in moderate to large cities, have a general mistrust of the police. It is not uncommon to see or hear news accounts of police brutality or corruption. Police misconduct may not be acceptable or commonplace, but even isolated instances of it can get top news coverage. Even the most recent dramatic drop in crime is contaminated by news accounts of large East Coast police agencies falsifying crime rates in order to bolster their dramatic reductions in crime rates (*San Diego Union,* August 3, 1998).

To overcome the general mistrust that may be unspoken, police officers must be open and honest at all times. Openness has not traditionally been a strong attribute of the law enforcement community. Police agencies typically guard crime information as though it was a national security secret. Neighborhood residents probably have a very clear understanding of crime problems as a result of living in the middle of the problems. They do not need to be protected from the reality of crime, and they should be trusted with specific crime prevention tactics. Officers must share crime statistics and noncritical crime data if they want to truly build trust and working partnerships. By being open and sharing as much as possible, the officer gives residents the knowledge to understand problems and the opportunity to contribute to solutions.

TL Skill #14. Image Management:
Taking Responsibility for How You See Yourself

This skill refers to your ability to be conscious of how you see your own self. This means that you self-monitor any negative images or internal "voices" that would undermine your effectiveness as a person or leader and manage them in a number of ways to ensure that you remain positively focused, no matter what external circumstances occur. This critical skill area is often neglected by many people. It is mainly a skill activated by awareness and by carefully choosing and affirming a positive self-image. Also, it is important to live congruently (with integrity) to that image so that it can develop as a part of the very fabric of your being. No one enjoys the tension of being divided internally and presenting himself or herself as "duplicitous" to others. Studies on successful people reveal that this inner capacity and strength of managing self-image and inner integrity is an important contributor to success in career and life (Glasser, 1984; Waitley, 1983).

Career opportunities in policing are diminishing. Greater numbers of citizens are seeking lifelong careers in law enforcement. Community policing also promotes a move to downsize, restructure, and flatten organizations. These management decisions result in fewer promotion opportunities for competent career officers. Increasing, outstanding officers are "passed over" for promotion. The lack of perceived success results in spiraling poor performance. Rather than recognize that the job can continue to be rewarding, they begin to question their self-worth. Their dissatisfaction prevents them from taking on new challenges or taking the risks necessary for problem-oriented policing to work.

There are also those who resist the movement to COPPS because they perceive it as too much like "social work." They do not see themselves as successful in COPPS practices, and so they refuse to try. They do not know how to manage self-image and integrity. They continually see their cup as half full, and they eventually become discipline problems, even resorting to dishonest practices in order to obtain recognition or promotion. Many good officers simply leave the profession because of negative images of themselves or the job.

Even experienced police officers must be coached into remaining self-confident. If I believe that I can climb the mountain, then I will get at least part way to the top! If I believe it is useless to even try, I will not attempt it. I will stay where I am. Failure to perceive and to take advantage of opportunities is just another kind of failure. Seeing just one way that things can work out well produces some success for me. I do not have to be perfect or exceptionally successful to enjoy life and be a respectable person. Even when I fail, I can treat myself as I would treat my best friend when he is suffering from a failure of some kind, with compassion and understanding. This more tolerant and supportive attitude is needed in the "macho" policing world and in various other parts of the justice and public safety systems, such as corrections, immigration, customs, private security, ambulance, fire, and emergency response. Keep in mind that confident officers communicate well with themselves and others, and they even communicate their weaknesses, problems, and difficulties; then they process these through to resolution.

TL Skill #15. Impression Management: Taking Responsibility for How Others See You

This skill involves awareness of the impact of your behavior, appearance, and mannerisms on other people. It is also choosing your behavior intentionally to alter this impact in a desired manner. It is related to the foregoing skill in that it involves bringing forward the positive images of self that have been created or discovered. The skill includes the following.

1. Learning to dress appropriately for various social situations
2. Learning to speak effectively and articulately
3. Expressing strong, effective, and pleasant nonverbal messages to others
4. Creating the image in others' minds that you want them to have of you
5. Avoiding being "pigeonholed" by others' limited perceptions of you

One very successful police lieutenant has a reputation as an outstanding "tactical" leader. His twenty-year career was primarily in patrol-related assignments. He worked as a SWAT sergeant and lieutenant and handled numerous critical incidents. When he recently interviewed for a promotion to captain, he was perceived as being too rigid and inflexible. This perception by command staff personnel was founded on specific behaviors observed during field situations when quick decisive action was necessary. All of us want a decisive field commander to be in charge of a major crime or disaster scene. We also want that same commander to be seen as approachable and willing to listen to other points of view when the situation requires versatility and creativity.

Very few people saw this lieutenant as capable of possessing the skills necessary for participatory decision making. He was rarely seen involved in complex negotiations with other city departments or facilitating community meetings where various competing interests were being discussed. Even though he possessed these skills, he had been "pigeonholed." He also did not have the skills necessary to create the image he wanted others to have of him.

After being passed over for promotion, I gave him specific feedback on how others saw him. His facial expressions (rarely smiling or using humor), continuous criticism of others, and by-the-book decision-making process (with little explanation) were sending an unintended message: "I don't have time for you or your concerns." Specific examples of his past behavior were discussed and recommendations made. He realized that he needed to intentionally model the behavior that might change the image he intentionally worked so hard to develop when he went after the SWAT commander's position. He accepted an administrative assignment that gave him more exposure to command personnel in more business management settings. He took the opportunity to discuss his past job-related experience with command personnel. He was also able to demonstrate his current skills in upper management problem solving. He is currently on the list for promotion to the rank of captain. Even if he doesn't get the promotion, he has changed many people's perceptions of him, and new job opportunities are coming his way.

The following brief story illustrates how impression management works. For twenty-five years, I have trained university students to get ready to go out into the business, justice, and public safety systems and find jobs that fits their newly acquired skills and qualifications. Most of them struggle with anxiety when preparing for the first job interview. Most of the students have not had validation and confirmation that they are perceived as competitive and are desirable as prospective employees. Many have severe self-doubts even though the track record of the program from which they are graduating is that over 90 percent of the graduates find employment in their area of their interest. What I do to get them ready is to "grill" them as though I were the interview panel. We know in general what questions they will be asked. We know what the employers are looking for in terms of personal appearance, conceptual understanding, and specific kinds of answers to questions.

When we finish with students after about an hour or two, they report feeling strong relief from anxiety and much greater confidence. Many of them have said that the experience is like a "rite of passage." They know what to do to capitalize on their strengths and what to stop doing to minimize their weaknesses. The top ten of the many main things the students learn in the "grilling" session are:

1. Dress the way the interviewers dress. Find out ahead of time what this code is and match it.

2. Eliminate "uh" and "um" and such phrases as "and stuff like that" and "you know what I mean" from your vocabulary.

3. Match the strength of the handshake, if you are offered a handshake. Do not give either an overpowering grip or a "gentle flower" handshake to the interviewer.

4. Dress looking business, not fashion; look professional, not masculine or feminine.

5. Talk about your strengths without an apologetic tone, and let the interviewers know how you really believe you have demonstrated job-related skills in your training and field work experiences. Be specific and tell short stories about how you made a difference.

6. Make consistent eye contact without staring in order to maintain an image of poise, confidence, and receptivity to the interviewers.

7. Remember that interviewers are not comfortable making you uncomfortable. Acknowledge your understandable nervousness and move on to answering the questions with energy and specific examples.

8. Don't take the situation too seriously, as though the outcome is a measurement of your worth. Treat the interview like a practice session, and remember that you will get better at it with practice. You will get a job. You are qualified. You have been trained for this career and specifically for this interview. Some interviewers will likely prefer you over the competition. The average student has to go through eight interviews to land the job he or she wants.

9. Laugh at yourself and inject humor into the situation whenever it is natural to do so. But be careful not to be seen as trying to be funny to win the interview. Your response must be natural.

10. Hold your head and body up! Don't stoop or slump. Would you want to hire someone who has poor posture? It is often a sign of low self-esteem.

This list gives you an idea of how we help students to manage the image of themselves they project when they are getting ready for an interview. Being a leader is like preparing for a whole range of interviews in varying environments. You need to be appropriately flexible, yet genuine in how you present yourself. You want to earn respect, credibility, and the right to influence people in positive ways through the trust you gain. Learning to be intentional about understanding what "images" and "languages" (both verbal and nonverbal) people are comfortable with and shifting into them will have a bearing on your success as a leader.

TL Skill #16. Attending:
Giving Undivided Attention to Others

Attending involves both appearing to be attentive to others and actually (inwardly) giving your undivided attention. Attending behaviors that give the appearance of being interested in others are facing the other person, squaring your shoulders, appropriate eye contact, an open and relaxed posture, leaning into the relationship (instead of leaning back), and observing appropriate distancing (usually three to six feet in North American culture, farther away in Asian cultures, and often closer in Mediterranean, some European, and South American cultures).

Genuinely giving attention to others is something that others can sense as well as observe. Focused attention from the heart is what most people want and expect from one another but receive all too infrequently. Attending forms the basis for observing another person accurately and is a prerequisite skill for observing without distorting your perceptions. Review your attending behaviors and your ability to inwardly direct your attention where you want it to go on a continuing basis.

This skill is critical in all police settings. Whether on the witness stand in court, talking to a crime victim in the street, or obtaining a confession from a suspect, giving undivided attention can enhance the effectiveness of any officer. The overall success of a police officer will rest, in part, on his or her attending ability.

The officer or deputy responding to any number of garden-variety disturbance calls develops this skill through trial and error. Experienced officers use the skill of attending subconsciously. Eventually they survive the stress and conflict of police work by developing this skill.

I clearly remember the primary method used by police officers in years past: "If I get called back out here again, someone is going to jail!" I was taught that method in 1971, when I first graduated from the police academy. That tactic rarely solved any problems, and it did not require trying to give undivided attention to anyone. In fact, the old style was to say, "I'm too busy to listen to your problems and I don't care how you work them out." Not exactly "protecting and serving." People are less likely to call the police for help with any type of problem (domestic violence, juvenile delinquency, etc.) if the only resource the officer offers is the criminal justice system.

Many times, people call the police just to be heard. They can solve many of their own problems if they feel they are getting the support, attention, and resource referrals they deserve. By giving undivided attention, people will be encouraged to release more information, which can lead to an officer more accurately assessing the underlying problem, thereby enabling him or her to make the proper referral to a support agency. Providing an effective referral can reduce repeat calls for service and free up officer time to work on more serious crime problems. The general success of COPPS can be largely attributed to the street cop's ability to give undivided attention to community members.

As an illustration related to daily life, you have probably gone into a bank and found that the teller or loan officer is so busy with the task part of the job that he or she forgets the relationship part. You stand there waiting to get his or her attention, but you don't get it. You find yourself becoming impatient because the teller is there to serve you and you are waiting. The same thing can occur in a restaurant, a doctor's office, or a law office. Most of us just don't have the "time of day" for people who don't have it for us. People who won't even look at us are communicating some form of preoccupation, lack of availability, or caring, and we never know which it is unless they tell us. If you are busy and preoccupied, then say so. Tell the other person when you will be able to give him or her your undivided attention. That is better than not giving attention at all.

In your personal life, you probably already know that giving attention is so powerful that it is the foundation of expressed love. Most of us have seen lovers in a restaurant, eyes as big as saucers, looking "goo-goo-eyed" at one another. This is what we enjoyed as babies when our parents tossed us up in the air and held us on their laps. In our Western culture, eye contact is what we appreciate from others, especially when we seek it or want it for various reasons. Those who cannot give steady, comfortable, pleasant eye contact are often not trusted, are suspected of perhaps being devious, or are seen as weak or withdrawn.

Making eye contact can be nourishing, can encourage communication, can be welcoming, and can put others at ease, especially if you are a genuinely kind person seeking to serve or to make things better for everyone. If you are not genuinely kind or really do not care that much about people, it may show up in how you fail to make contact with your eyes.

One employee who worked for a leader I was coaching told me, somewhat humorously, about her frustration with her boss's inattentiveness. She felt so discounted and undervalued that she said to me, "The next time I go into his office and he keeps shuffling his papers and doesn't look at me, I am going to tell him that he had better look at me or I will set his desk on fire! Maybe that will get his attention!"

TL Skill #17. Observing:
Simply Seeing Another Person Without Distorting or Judging

Observing skills involve consciously receiving information about another person from all visible sources: a person's physical tension and energy levels, facial expressions, skin flushes, body posture, manner of dress, expressive mannerisms, hand movements, gestures, and the sum total of all other body language. When you can simply look and see what another person is doing, and keep those observations separate from any judgments you might be making, then you are being more objective in your understanding of others.

Using the skills of observing prevents the development of assumptions and alerts us to judgmental tendencies we all seem to have at times. Observing is the prerequisite skill for effectively and temporarily suspending one's own frame of reference (judgment or value system). Consider the effectiveness of your ability to observe accurately and keep your personal reactions separate from what you see as you read this chapter.

This skill is the one that connects you with the world of another person. If you want to motivate an individual to learn, perform better, engage in problem solving with you, trust you, or find you credible, then it will help if you demonstrate that you are sensitive and observant. Noticing how people feel and processing that information as a part of your communication with them is a more subtle and advanced way of developing credibility and influence with others. If I want to understand the extent to which someone is motivated to work on a project, it helps to notice his or her face and eyes. Women seem to notice these nonverbal cues more keenly and immediately than men. This may be one of the major causes of the "battle of the sexes." Men often complain to women, "You're too sensitive!" and women often complain to men, "You're so insensitive!" To resolve the differences that may be accounted for by temperament and by gender, we need to be aware that different people have differing capabilities in their ability to be sensitive to others in their environment. If I tend to be less observant, then I need to even more consciously decide to focus on, observe, and note what is going on with others nonverbally. If I assume I am never perfectly accurate in my perceptions, I am in a position to reserve judgment and check for the accuracy of my perceptions, thus avoiding much grief and misunderstanding in relationships.

Successful police officers develop this skill consciously. There are specific classes in interviewing and interrogation techniques that teach recognizing and reacting to nonverbal behavior. Many confessions have been obtained as a result of knowing exactly when to physically move in close to a suspect during an interrogation. Moving in too early can threaten the suspect and cause him or her to retreat and deny any involvement in the crime. Moving in too late will prolong the interrogation and can result in missing the only opportunity to gain a confession.

Gaining cooperation from an uncooperative witness at a gang homicide scene requires being nonjudgmental and understanding the witness's perspectives of the situation. Officers need to gain support and trust by seeking to understand the gang culture.

Getting neighborhood residents to become involved and begin grass-roots crime prevention efforts is based on the beat officer's ability to be understanding of the residents' fears and perceptions. Working with those fears can frequently mobilize a neighborhood to take action.

TL Skill #18. Suspending Frame of Reference: The Key to the Golden Rule

The skill of temporarily suspending your frame of reference is perhaps the most critical and important of all skills in that your credibility and effectiveness can at times rest solely on your performance of this skill. Your frame of reference is made up of your beliefs, assumptions, values, feelings, judgments, emotions, advice, mood, thoughts, perceptions, and stress level at any given moment. Because our frame of reference is so personal and deeply imbedded in each of us, it is very difficult to practice suspending it on a regular basis. Most interpersonal, counseling, and leadership problems stem from this difficulty we all seem to have by needing to interpret reality from our own vantage point and reacting in a self-oriented manner. It is very important that we learn to react in such a way that we take into consideration others' points of view and feelings, as well as our own.

This skill, simply put, is inner strength for self-control of emotions, judgments, and premature advice. Practicing this suspending skill involves putting others first before self, checking things out before jumping to conclusions or reacting emotionally, and giving others the benefit of any doubts we might have about them. Making snap judgments, reacting emotionally to a situation before we really understand it, "writing a person off" before we give him or her a fair chance, or assuming that something is true before we check it out are all signs of not suspending.

Suspending is especially appropriate when others need to be understood so that their tension or stress can be defused. In this way, we can help them become ready to hear our own thoughts, feelings, or points of view and, from a leadership point of view, help them take action on a project that is important. Suspending, which is based on the facts of accurate observation, is the foundation of patience, gentleness, kindness, respect, and effectiveness in all leadership, counseling, and communication situations.

The skill of suspending frame of reference is probably one of the most difficult for a police officer to learn and maintain. Today's young recruits frequently come directly from home or college with no military background. Many of them have limited life experience to draw upon and their frame of reference is very narrow and shallow. Many are very naïve when they hit the streets.

Of course, there are also those who have developed this skill and immediately put it to use when dealing with a wide range of people. Many young officers, however, are conned by the streetwise crook who feeds them a faulty alibi for why he is in a business district alley at 3:30 in the morning. They fail to get the confession from the experienced child molester, and this failure means that the case goes to court without a confession. They turn off a potentially great witness with their quick judgments or emotional reaction to a stressful situation. Experiences like these pull an officer in the direction of not trusting anyone, being suspicious of everyone, and giving no one the benefit of the doubt.

Even though it is believed most law-abiding people support their police or sheriff's department, officers generally get very little exposure to that support. Being exposed to criminals on a daily basis forms a new frame of reference for a one- to five-year veteran.

COPPS has given police officers an opportunity to practice the skill of suspending frame of reference by working with residents in a nonthreatening and cooperative relationship. Police officers regain the trust and support of the community. Accurately observing what is happening in a neighborhood, both positive and negative, gives an officer the experience needed to be more understanding, patient, observant, and successful.

The importance of using the skill of suspending frame of reference can also be seen in a business environment. Bill, the new vice-president of sales and marketing for a wholesale distribution company, came into the company with an MBA from an Ivy League graduate school. He was commissioned by the president to accelerate the effectiveness of the marketing and sales functions. When he joined the firm, it had over 30 locations with over 240 salespeople, and no one was attending to marketing issues. Bill was brazen and proud in his approach, presuming that he, based on his MBA and his previous track record of building his own company, was the most qualified to decide what needed to be done. He used his own frame of reference almost entirely to assess the current state of affairs in the sales area and wrote a prescription for disaster by diagnosing the sales team's weaknesses and taking a remedial "I'll-fix-it-and-get-all-the-credit" approach to "making change happen." He thought that was what he had to do to please the president and justify his salary.

Most of the salespeople had been with the company a long time and had enjoyed a successful track record in getting the company to the $180 million in sales that it currently enjoyed. The sales team was operating at perhaps 70 percent efficiency, and Bill treated the staff and the sales managers as though they needed his expert advice and he needed none of theirs. As a result, they rejected him. Within the first year of Bill's arrival, over 15 percent of the salespeople quit the organization (over half were higher performers) because, as one sales manager explained, they refused to deal with such a "condescending bastard." Sales plummeted and the organization lost $35 million that year! Bill rationalized that the drop in sales was due to his having to get rid of the "dead wood" on the sales team and that he would more than make up for the loss with outstanding progress the following year. The president believed him. A further loss in sales occurred the following year. No one asked the people who quit why they quit until I did follow-up interviews with them. The same thing occurred in a large police force in North America when a new chief arrived with the same attitude and approach—and achieved the same kind of results!

These are classic cases of "know-it-all" managers trying to work "on" a team of people to get "desired results" instead of working "with" them to make things happen for the better, for everyone. Bill—and the president—were presumptuous, domineering, unreceptive, inattentive, and did not suspend their frames of references enough to even listen to what people were saying. They paid a dear price. The new chief of police, it is rumored, will not be allowed to continue his Machiavellian approach for more than the next year. The union will recommend a vote of no confidence and communicate the result to community officials.

TL Skill #19. Questioning: Appropriate Gathering of Information

Questioning is a much overused skill that can puts others on the defensive. An appropriate and effective leadership behavior when we want a person to expand on a particular topic without influencing the direction of his or her response is to use open questions like "What do you think about that?" As we shall see, however, active listening and checking for what people intend to convey to us is often more effective than questioning. Questioning makes it seem that we are the ones controlling the situation, much like interrogation during a police interview. Of course, carefully framed questions can be effective during an interrogation but are not as effective when we want to establish trust and open communication. Closed questions like "How many times did you beat your wife?" leave little room for discussion and force a person toward the answer we hope to hear.

Questioning is used effectively when we need to gather information about a person's address, what he or she thinks about a specific issue, or directions to get particular place. In general, questions are less personal than active listening and should be reserved for less personal interchanges, when correctness or completeness of information is the main focus. It is risky to use questions on a habitual basis because when we question others, we often "take the ball" from them and lead the conversation—usually unconsciously—in the direction we think it should go (and we thereby fail to suspend frame of reference and truly listen). Questioning often prevents people from just "telling their stories."

In hundreds of videotaped leadership interviews, when questions are overused (and therefore not much listening is going on), an accusatory, blaming, or suspicious tone of voice is often evident while the interrogation is being conducted. This tone can make people even more defensive and interrupt the flow of their own version of the story they are telling. Many times, just listening carefully, and using gentle probing questions sparingly, can elicit more information than direct questions.

If your style of interacting with others is to use questions as the main theme, consider achieving more of a balance among listening, sharing, and questioning. This will increase the amount and quality of two-way communication that leads to problem solving and conflict resolution in your personal relationships and will lead to performance improvement when you are leading others.

As an example, experienced police officers recognize the difference between interviewing a witness and interrogating a suspect. Interrogation is a more controlling and leading form of questioning. Obviously, both methods are used to gain specific information and both prevent the speaker from going off on an irrelevant tangent.

When leading COPPS program, supervisors need to ask questions to ensure their officers are receiving the support they need to solve neighborhood crime problems. Questions should also be asked to ensure officers are not subjecting themselves or the organization to civil liability by their problem-solving actions. However, too much questioning can inhibit the "risk-taking" process that is so important. Officers need to experiment with nontraditional responses to intervening in criminal activity. They need to develop unique partnerships and support nonenforcement activities of trained citizens, and this requires listening more than questioning. Problem-Oriented Policing (P.O.P) relies on bringing new partners and new ideas to old crime problems.

Officers need the room and support to try out new ideas. To the experienced supervisor, these new ideas may seem like a waste of time. Supporting nonenforcement activities may seem unnecessary. Questioning the likely outcome of a particular tactic may also discourage innovation. Most supervisors of the 1990s are not problem-solving officers and have little practical problem-solving experience to rely on when they call into question what may or may not work. They were raised in a time when there was a clear line between what was considered "police work" and "social work." COPPS has blurred that line and encouraged police officers to think outside of the box of the traditional police response.

Supervisors would do best by limiting the amount of questioning and increasing the amount of active listening. Also, by asking clarification questions, a supervisor can help an officer think through the problem-solving process. In this way, a balanced approach of listening and questioning appropriately produces the best overall results.

TL Skill #20. Listening: Checking for What Others Intend to Mean

A person who listens well actively checks for the intended meaning of a message from the sender's point of view. A good listener is grounded; centered; gives undivided attention; temporarily suspends emotions, advice, and judgments; uses questions in a limited and appropriate manner; and checks with the sender to see if there is mutually understood meaning.

The skill of active listening also involves letting others finish, even when you feel like "butting in" to make your point. Helping others to feel heard and to finish with what they are saying only increases the chances that the door of their perceptual system will be open when you do send a message and that it will get through to them from your frame of reference.

To some people, letting someone else finish talking and then checking for accurate understanding so that the other person feels understood (and says so) seems to be a phony way to interact (because they are holding themselves back), and they are uncomfortable with it as a skill. Perhaps it can be seen that way, but nevertheless, careful listening works to clarify confusing messages and defuse tensions that are often at the root of conflicts or misunderstandings in all kinds of relationships. The following are some language formats that can be used for active listening:

"You mean _____?"

"Maybe you're saying _____?"

"What I hear you saying is _____. Is that right?"

"Could it be that you mean _____?"

"Can you clarify that for me?"

"I'm not sure I get what you mean. Can you explain further?

Notice that all of the above formats suggest a tentative, not presumptuous, approach to checking with the other person to see if you are grasping a good part of the meaning that he or she intends to send to you. Also notice the questioning tone at the end of each format. By asking the other person if you understand accurately, you are stating that you have an open mind and can learn more. You are showing interest and respect. This is an opportunity for you to ask questions all you want and not make the other person so uncomfortable!

Inexperienced police officers need to feel supported. They also need to learn how to think through the problem-solving process. Active listening gives them the opportunity to take ownership of problems in their areas of responsibility. It also gives them the feeling that what they have to say is important. After all, we expect them to make important decisions and use discretion every day. If officers are continually directed as though they were responding to a radio call, they will be slow to take charge of situations and less likely to feel competent enough to take on complex neighborhood problems.

TL Skill #21. Responding with Understanding: Getting on the Inside

The skill of responding with understanding is a more powerful, personal, and intimate skill, and using it can even sometimes require the other person's permission. To carefully understand what someone is feeling, all of the foregoing skills discussed in this chapter must be applied first. Many people will resist or even resent your responding to their feelings directly. Many others will experience relief or satisfaction when you show understanding of their feelings in a specific way. Yet, one of the most frequent complaints of employees, spouses, children, and relatives is,, "You don't even understand how I *feel*." The most important point here is that this particular skill is best used when others want us to use it with them. Otherwise, we might be accused of being like "phony bleeding-heart social workers."

The use of this skill requires greater expertise and sensitivity than any of the other skills reviewed to this point because careful observation of nonverbal cues is required, which is how responding gets you inside another person's emotional world. Responding with accurate understanding also enables you to see and feel things from the other person's point of view.

That is why this skill is the foundation of the quality called empathy. Empathy is defined as communicated understanding, so that you can prove to other people you understand what they feel and think and why they feel and think the way they do. The following language formats can be used to convey empathy.

"You seem to feel (*feeling word*) because (*reason*)."

"Maybe you're feeling (*feeling word*) because (*reason*)."

These formats are just general guidelines and can be changed to fit the situation or person, but they must contain a direct and accurate response to a person's feeling state and the reason why he or she feels a particular emotion. Empathy training is available as a part of most communication skills training courses or workshops. Understanding others' feelings (until they tell us we understand) is an important cornerstone of building leadership credibility and trust in the minds and hearts of those with whom we work.

Police officers are frequently criticized for not being concerned with or responding to local neighborhood problems. Frequently, police priorities for crime control tactics are not consistent with neighborhood priorities. Several surveys support this perception. Neighborhood residents are more frequently concerned about the social conditions in the neighborhood that contribute to crime than about the more serious crime problems themselves. Police officers think community members would list murder, gang activity, and other forms of violence as top priorities. Instead, residents are more concerned about low-level drug dealers, graffiti, and abandoned cars.

Police officers must understand community concerns and respond to them if they are to gain community support in any problem-solving effort. Police officers can facilitate a discussion where community concerns are heard and tactics are developed to address them. Tactics must take into consideration the feelings and priorities of the neighborhood residents. Once success is achieved in any one problem-solving effort, residents will be more likely to join in on the next crime prevention effort.

TL Skill #22. Assertiveness:
Speaking Honestly and Kindly with Self-Control

Practicing the skill of being assertive means that you send a part of your frame of reference to others in a respectful manner, letting them know your feelings, ideas, opinions, reactions, beliefs, judgments, or points of view. If you want leadership credibility, it is important that you be genuine and up-front—without being overly pushy—to avoid being walked on by others' behaviors, false expectations, and assumptions about you. Assertiveness involves speaking the truth about yourself to others in a patient, kind, and understanding manner, thus giving others the opportunity and the right to do the same thing. If you want to make the communication and relationship even better, then model putting the other person first! Being assertive also involves not getting your frame of reference "emotionally hooked" and then overreacting emotionally in anger— which can add fuel to an already blazing fire.

Combining assertiveness with responding skills prevents your communication with others from seeming aggressive or passive and promotes two-way completed communication that can result in problems getting solved. Therefore, if you are angry with someone because of her or his behavior, you might use a format such as:

> "When you (*describe behavior*), I end up feeling (one word) and then (*describe what else tangibly happens to you*)."

If the other person is having difficulty receiving your message, you can respond in an empathic way ("You seem upset when I tell you how I feel") and help the other person to process your message. Combining the skills of assertiveness and responding allows you to manage your half of the communication and provides every opportunity for two-way communication to take place. By taking this responsibility, you can more often than not solve problems and develop relationships. Some people, however, may choose not to enter into two-way communication for a number of reasons. If this occurs, at least you know that you have done your part well.

Police officers frequently need to move from being very assertive to being somewhat passive based upon the situation they face. They must approach each situation with the ability to suspend their frame of reference and at the same time be assertive enough to maintain control for the safety of all involved. Maintaining control must also be done in a manner that does not fuel a volatile situation. Some studies have shown that the manner in which a police officer responds can incite more violence. Experienced officers develop the skill of being assertive with self-control. One particularly effective officer warns suspects *in a quiet tone of voice* that if they escalate their violent behavior, he will have to escalate his use of force. His sober, centered, calm, and steady demeanor is so disarming and powerful that he generally gains their cooperation.

These same principles apply to police supervisors. Being too assertive (in other words, being aggressive) with subordinates can inhibit cooperation and innovation. The overly assertive supervisor can encourage officers to remain reactive to crime and wait for someone else to develop problem-solving strategies. Not being assertive enough with subordinates can enable officers to become passive about crime and remain uninvolved when developing problem-solving strategies. Effective problem solving requires practice on the part of street cops. Nonassertive supervisors will be left with sole responsibility for solving area crime problems.

I recall a conversation I had with a young officer. I was on patrol with him and he was describing the crime problems in his area. He described a series of purse snatchings that occurred near a popular restaurant. The victims were elderly women in the community who walked to the restaurant. I asked him what strategies were being employed to solve the crime series. He told me about a stakeout his sergeant had organized three weeks earlier. The entire squad of six officers wore street clothes and sat in various locations throughout the neighborhood, hoping to catch the robbers. They were unsuccessful. When I asked what he was going to do next, he said he was waiting for the sergeant to come up with another strategy. It was obvious the sergeant was not assertive enough in expressing his expectations for officers to practice problem solving. COPPS relies on problem-solving strategies developed at the street level. These strategies must be designed around all sides of the crime triangle, victim–suspect–location, and officers must feel as though the sergeant supports their efforts and can even brainstorm with them to generate new approaches, test them and evaluate their effectiveness. In this example, the nonassertive sergeant was developing a passive squad of officers.

The old style of policing required little feedback from supervisors on cooperative team or innovative performance. Officers were merely expected to answer radio calls and engage in an acceptable level of reactive enforcement. It is very easy for the sergeant and officers to fall back into this passive relationship where no one is challenged to be innovative and solve the problems that contribute to criminal activity. COPPS expects all police personnel, from the chief to the street cop, to be leaders in the community. Leading other agencies and community members in problem-solving strategies requires being open enough to share feelings, ideas, opinions, beliefs, and points of view without offending others or being seen as too pushy.

Self-Control: A Worthwhile Responsibility

A major goal of personal development and the key to effective assertiveness is self-control. It only makes sense that the more self-control people have, the better they will be able to use the abilities and skills that are at their disposal.

Control is achieved through knowledge, practice, and maturity. For an individual to develop tennis skills, he or she needs to exercise control over her or his body on the tennis court. The same is true for personal relationships in that those individuals who have solid relationships usually also have self-control and interpersonal skills.

A very important part of controlling self is self-discipline. Egan (1977) states, "Discipline means, at least in part, self-control. A person is disciplined if he or she makes whatever sacrifice is necessary in order to achieve a goal. Thus, discipline often involves some kind of hardship—doing things that aren't pleasant and giving up things that are."

This kind of self-control and self-sacrifice is an essential ingredient for personal satisfaction and successful relationships. Individuals who lack control over their frames of reference become more self-centered and tend to have shallow relationships with others. As a result, they can be lonely people who neither give nor receive much love in their lives.

People who behave assertively, rather than aggressively or passively, tend to be more in control of self. This occurs because these individuals accept both their rights and their responsibilities. They do not aggressively take what belongs to others or passively let others blame them for what is not their responsibility. Assertive individuals think of others as having equal value and attempt to treat them as they would like to be treated.

On the other hand, people who are aggressive are usually not in control of their thoughts, feelings, and behaviors. They either cannot or will not take charge of their frames of references. Therefore, they have trouble controlling their actions, and others suffer as a result. They suffer, too. These types of individuals are labeled aggressive or "hotheads" because they attempt to take others' rights away from them so that they themselves can have more control to get what they want. They also attempt to make others assume their responsibilities so that they will not have to do so. These individuals often put themselves before and above others.

People who are passive tend to go to the other extreme in that they often overcontrol their frames of reference to the point of self-suppression. They place others before themselves even if they (or others) have to suffer for doing so. While this sounds noble, often it is for selfish reasons. Passive individuals, like those who are aggressive, are most worried about their own needs first and others second. Notice some of the qualities, behaviors, and skills of the three style characteristics in the chart of interpersonal style characteristics on the following page.

In the gym membership story, the owner treated me in an aggressive manner and did not use even basic communication skills. Had she been assertive, a "win–win" situation could have been achieved.

TL Skill #23. Confrontation:
Telling People the Truth about Unacceptable Behavior

Assertiveness is mainly concerned with presenting yourself honestly and realistically in tight social situations. Confrontational communication, on the other

Interpersonal Style Characteristics		
Aggressive	**Asssertive**	**Passive**

	Aggressive	Asssertive	Passive
Qualities	Insecure	Secure	Insecure
	Insensitive	Sensitive	Oversensitive
	Domineering	Respectful	Submissive
	Impatient	Patient	Patient
	Self-oriented	People oriented	Other oriented
	Win–lose attitude	Negotiable attitude	No-win attitude
	Dishonest	Honest	Dishonest
	Decision maker	Decision maker	Indecisive
	Unreliable	Reliable	Reliable
Behaviors	Verbal/physical	Respectful	Manipulative
	Abuse	Communication	Negative messages
	Lies by distorting	Truthful	Lies by omission
	Power oriented	Respect oriented	Escape oriented
Skills	Physical	Centered	Attends
	Verbal	Attends	Observes
		Observes	Gives
		Listens	LIstens
		Understands	
		Communicates	
		Challenges	
		Solves problems	

hand, is more focused on other people's problem behaviors or attitudes and your need for them to change in order for them to be more effective with you, in their jobs, in their own lives, or with others.

Sometimes it is important or even necessary (in the case of performance reviews) to give critical feedback to others about how their behavior is ineffective, stressful, or inappropriate. This is a difficult skill to perform effectively because it requires development of a certain level of trust in the relationship before others will receive your feedback in a positive manner and therefore engage in positive change. In a sense, you have to earn the right to confront by proving ahead of time to others that you care about their development as individuals. You have to show them that you are seeking to develop a relationship with them, that you are attempting to build rather than tear down, and that you are willing to accept confrontational feedback as well as dish it out.

Get Agreement to Confront in Advance.   It is possible to get agreement in advance with others that your relationship with them will be characterized by genuineness and honesty for the purpose of mutual personal development and for the purpose of your developing your work or personal relationship with them. With this advance permission, giving difficult feedback can be easier and more effective. The predominant culture in an organization can be honesty about difficult things, with a firm resolve to deal with them quickly. Also, using confrontation and responding with understanding skills can assist others to process your confrontational feedback to them. This can be helpful in defusing the stress and tension often involved in giving and receiving feedback.

This skill is the most risky of all communication skills and is actually least likely to succeed. If the maturity or personal security of the person you are confronting is marginal, he or she will likely not handle your confrontation very well. In such cases, it is advisable not to confront but to use challenging skills (Skill #24) if possible. Sometimes it is necessary to confront people with the ultimatum that they must either perform up to expected standards or they will be fired. In a personal relationship, sometimes it is better for the relationship to end if it is destructive, without hope of restoration.

In policing, accountability of individual officers has always been a fundamental issue for executives. However, holding police officers accountable for acceptable behavior and confronting unacceptable behavior was much easier in the traditional model of policing. Measuring arrests, traffic tickets, and field interviews was the primary means of measuring productivity and effectiveness. Much of an officer's activity was reacting to calls for service. An officer could be successful in meeting expectations by answering radio calls and performing a minimal amount of proactive enforcement activity.

Even managers and first-line supervisors were held to a simpler level of performance under traditional policing practices. As Trojanowicz and Bucqueroux (1994) observed, under a paramilitary, authoritarian model of management, the focus was on control. Management determined the department's mission and dictated strategies and tactics. Management set forth and enforced the policies and procedures and described how the work was to be done by those at lower levels in the organizational hierarchy. Managers were judged on the basis of how well their employees followed the rules and whether the managers succeeded in improving productivity—defined primarily as answering more calls and making more arrests. Kelling et al. (1988) also observed that the style of management practiced in the professional model of policing emphasized top-level decision making. Orders from executives were passed down to line personnel, and information exchange went primarily up the chain through dense layers of supervision

Confronting unacceptable behavior is much more difficult today. Acceptable behavior is much more complex and demanding. Being successful at COPPS involves a change in attitudes as well as developing new complex performance behaviors. Police officers are some of the most sensitive people I have met. They are much more educated and professional than in years past. Even though they have to put on a strong, rough exterior at times to survive, officers are very sensitive to personal criticism. They are frequently judged and evaluated on their ability to be independently successful, either in the arrests they make, the crimes they solve, or the quality of their individual testimony in court. Police officers are continuously in the individual spotlight. They are also expected to respond to calls for help, be sensitive to the needs of others, and solve complex problems in the shortest period of time.

The movement to community policing requires street-level officers to work more in teams, be less reactive to calls for service, and possess the interpersonal skills necessary to bring nonlaw enforcement resources together in problem-solving efforts. Measuring success is not limited to the number of arrests officers make. In San Diego, the crime rates fell dramatically in the period from 1993 to 1998. Murder was down almost 50 percent and robbery down 45 percent. Even property crimes like burglary and auto theft decreased by 45 percent. Yet the number of arrests officers made was also down. Arrests for property crimes went down from 9,507 to 7,121 and felony narcotic arrests decreased from 6,020 to 5,549.

Success in many police departments is now being measured by successful problem-solving efforts, developing new partners in crime prevention, and reducing the fear of crime in neighborhoods. Officers and deputies are encouraged to take risks and be proactive in crime prevention. All of these new expectations present new challenges to supervisors and managers when confronting unacceptable behavior.

The developing role of the COPPS police officer is moving law enforcement personnel even further into areas in which they have little experience or expertise. Officers are expected to mobilize communities, identify or develop unique problem-solving resources, and lead neighborhood groups in taking responsibility for the social conditions that contribute to crime. Officers are now expected to successfully resolve myriad organizational, social, and emotional problems that contribute to crime problems in a neighborhood. Supervisors and managers need to develop their subordinates and confront them in an agreed-upon productive manner when expectations are not met.

For example, one small company had five executive level managers who worked together quite well in most ways. One of the managers, however, was very critical of how the CEO was performing and would sometimes lash out at him without any seeming justification. Small things would trigger his near-rage reaction! As an external consultant, I was asked by the CEO to confront this person about the negative impact of his behavior. In my first conversation with this angry executive, I was told all the reasons why the manager felt justifiably angry at the CEO. I listened until he felt secure that I understood his point of view, and then I asked him if I could confront him about something I saw in him with which he was having difficulty. Note here that I respected his boundary, his right to say no. He consented, and I told him that even though he may have justification for feeling angry, venting at the CEO in an executive team meeting was not considered responsible or effective behavior on his part.

I told him simply that his approach did not work to build a better relationship with the CEO and that it did not help anyone to resolve the problems for which the CEO may, in fact, be responsible. I told him that his behavior alienated the CEO, poisoned the team atmosphere with negativity, and was not matched with two-way communication and problem-solving behavior. When I stated it this bluntly, and in a kind and patient tone of voice, he said, "Wow, you're right. How stupid of me to think that I was doing anything constructive!" We then explored alternative behaviors for him to apply to the situation, and he decided to confront the CEO directly for the first time and tell the CEO the truth in the same way that I had told him the truth about his behavior. He asked me to come along and facilitate, which I did, and because of the willingness and maturity of the CEO, this became the turning point in the relationship between the two executives. Team morale was no longer in jeopardy in future meetings and the performance of the team was enhanced by the new problem-solving capabilities released in the new relationship between the vice-president and the CEO.

Another clear example of confrontation occurred when a new police chief came into office and discovered that a "good ol' boys" network of several sergeants was demoralizing many of the younger recruits. They justified their treatment of the younger officers by saying, "That's the way we were initiated into this organization." As the new chief interviewed some of the subordinate officers, he found that the sergeants were awarding overtime hours to their longtime friends and treating the younger officers with disdain and giving them the more dangerous and difficult assignments without adequate supervision or backup.

When the chief corroborated that these practices were typical of 20 percent of the sergeants, he called them into his office one by one in the presence of his deputy chief as a witness. He confronted them with the unacceptable behaviors, asked them to own up to or deny the allegations, and made it clear to them that they would be fired if the behavior they did own up to continued. Over a period of one year, the chief fired several sergeants for continuing these dangerous and morale-destroying actions. The other sergeants confronted for their behavior changed their approach and engaged at least satisfactorily in upholding the new values of treating all employees with dignity, respect, and equity.

The Four-to-One Law

For people to receive "bad news" and internalize it, take ownership of it, and change their behavior, they do need to know that they are seen as having "worth" as individuals and that their worth is a separate issue from their value to the organization.

Experience in giving confrontational feedback reveals that the following results are true for the average person:

1. He or she can process fairly well one negative confrontational statement if it is prefaced with four positive statements about how positive past behavior is valued.
2. He or she can tolerate two negative statements when they are prefaced with three positive statements.
3. He or she can barely process three negative statements when they are prefaced with two positive statements.
4. He or she cannot process four negative statements when they are prefaced with only one positive statement.

This "four-to-one law" is supported by research, but it is really common sense when you think about how you feel when receiving negative feedback. Perhaps this is where the "golden rule" applies very strongly: would treat others the way we would like to be treated if we were being confronted by them, especially if they have position power over us!

Finally, leadership in this delicate situation can be positive if a person, regardless of past behavior, is told in various ways that he or she has worth and that we are willing to work with that person to increase his or her value to the organization. As soon as we communicate verbally or nonverbally that someone has little or no value or worth, it is unlikely that the confrontation will produce positive results in the short or long term. Shaking your head from side to side, frowning at the corners of your mouth, and rolling your eyes are all nonverbal signals to many people (especially insecure people in high-pressure situations) that you are writing them off as having little or no worth!

The following sample formats for the language of this skill can be used as guidelines to assist you to plan your next confrontation with someone:

"I appreciate (*specify behaviors*) that you do well."

"I appreciate (*specify behaviors*) that you do well."

"I appreciate (*specify behaviors*) that you do well."

"I appreciate (*specify behaviors*) that you do well."

"You have been observed doing (specify unacceptable behaviors)."

"Which, if any, of these alleged behaviors do you take ownership of?"

"If you continue to do (*unacceptable behaviors*), the consequences will be (*specify reasonable consequences*)."

These formats are guidelines to assist you in formulating statements that are factual and nonblaming in their tone. They help you focus on the issue of the confrontee taking ownership of behavior, get the message across that the behavior is not acceptable, and provide clear understanding of the consequences of continuing the unacceptable behavior. Of course, the consequences must be in line with labor laws and personnel policies and procedures in your workplace and cannot be arbitrarily assigned by you if you are in a formal business or organizational environment. If you are using this skill in the context of a personal, marital, or parental relationship, you can decide what your boundaries are, what is acceptable and not acceptable, and can often enforce those boundaries by saying no to unacceptable behavior and making the reasonable consequences happen.

Keep in mind the mutual quality of the interpersonal communication role and skills in this chapter. Even the police chief invited critical feedback of his performance from his subordinates by sending around an anonymous questionnaire. He also had an open-door policy, managed by "walking around talking with people," and rewarded people for speaking their truth to him even when he disagreed with them.

TL Skill #24. Challenging: Helping Others to See Strengths and Opportunities and Move Toward Positive Change

Challenging is a skill that is especially reserved for encouraging people to look at unused opportunities or personal strengths, spurring them on to take positive action. This skill differs from confrontation (which confronts smokescreens, blind spots, performance deficits, weakness, or discrepancies) in that it is focused more on the positive potential of other people and the hidden or unseen creative opportunities that exist within their current relationships or environments. This skill is also less risky and easier to handle by those on the receiving end.

An example of this skill in action is the same police chief who also met one on one with all sixty supervisory officers in his policing organization. His deputy chief was also present in those very positive interviews. The chief's goal was to recognize the worth of each dedicated officer, acknowledge specifically his or her value to the organization, and make it known to each officer that he personally appreciated the individual's good work, support, and continuing commitment. In each of these interviews, personnel files were reviewed beforehand and specific, positive feedback was given for all past achievements, length of service, heroic behavior, and loyalty to the force and the community. Later in the year, plaques were given to all officers in leadership positions for their exemplary service, including the officers who had been given formal warnings. Career-path planning sessions were held during the chief's second year to give encouragement and feedback to all those seeking promotions in the organization. The officers were given opportunities to plan for further training that would prepare them to compete more effectively for promotional opportunities.

This team of police leaders moved on to build one of the world's most effective community policing forces. Although the exceptional leadership that was exercised here is not typical of every organization, this challenging skill can have a positive impact on the future of any organization and the community it serves.

Conflict Management: Putting the Communication Skills Together

When managing an interpersonal conflict, all the skills examined in this chapter must be utilized to the fullest to have as positive an impact as possible. Conflict management involves managing your own frame of reference and your feelings, words, wants, and needs and assisting the other person to feel respected and yet understand your position at the same time. This is why the conflict management process is the most difficult of all applications of the interpersonal skills: Often, you have to manage your half and the other person's half at the same time. This is the case because most people do not have well-developed interpersonal skills.

Research on conflict management (Burke, 1977) has produced a general list of methods used in managing conflict. These methods, which form parts of the interpersonal conflict management process, are outlined as follows:

1. **Forcing**: Using power to cause the other person to accept a position; each party tries to figure out how to get the upper hand and cause the other person to lose.
2. **Withdrawal**: Retreating from the argument.
3. **Smoothing**: Playing down the conflict (differences) and emphasizing the positive (common interests), or avoiding issues that might cause hard feelings.
4. **Compromise**: Looking for a position in which each gives and gets a little, splitting the difference if possible; no winners and no losers.
5. **Confrontation and/or problem solving**: Directing energies toward defeating the problem and not the other person; encouraging the open exchange of information; discovering the best solution for all. The situation is defined, the parties try to reach a mutually beneficial solution, and the situation is resolved as "win–win."

A problem-solving approach to conflict management is the ideal choice to implement when attempting to resolve a conflict. It should be your first choice. If it doesn't work, back off to the fourth method, compromise, and so on.

In the problem-solving approach, it is best to begin your communication in the following way:

1. Set a time to communicate with the person with whom you are having a conflict. Set a mutually convenient time instead of releasing your tension and demanding that the problem be solved now.

2. Then, whenever possible, take into consideration your personal style and the other person's style, and get ready to shift styles, if necessary, to encourage the other person to engage in two-way communication and problem solving with you.

3. Agree together on a clear definition of the problem by redefining it several times from one another's point of view, using listening and understanding skills. Express your own point of view when the other person is able and willing to listen, or the session will turn into a power struggle (a lose–lose position).

4. Then agree on mutually satisfactory goals for your session. State and come to consensus about what you hope to achieve at the beginning of the session, so that there are no gaps in expectation that can lead to disillusionment or bitterness.

5. Take turns sharing honestly, in a nonblaming tone, each person's views, needs, wants, etc.

6. Explore alternative solutions to the problem that could potentially be satisfactory to both parties. Consider the consequences of each alternative, both short and long term.

7. Implement the agreed-upon solution(s) by deciding together who will do what, when, where, etc. Set a date to review how things are going and to see if any adjustments need to be made for the plan to work better in the future.

8. When you cannot agree or come up with a plan that is satisfying to both parties, it is acceptable to negotiate time for reevaluation and then plan another meeting.

9. After a time of further exploration, if a solution is not forthcoming, then withdrawal from the situation, putting the conflict into the hands of others for management, or proceeding in your own direction may be the only alternatives possible.

10. There are always consequences to pay when you decide to walk away, get help from a mediator or person in a position of authority, or just take your own course of action without compromise. Weigh the con-

sequences carefully before acting. You want to be as constructive as possible without giving up your own sense of integrity.

Conclusion

In this chapter, we have examined interpersonal communication skills in particular from the point of view of establishing a base of mutuality, respect, and openness in personal and work relationships. The most respected leaders are those who are honest without putting others down, are willing to solve a problem so that as many people are respected as possible, and who show caring about other people without being manipulated (the "bleeding-heart" syndrome).

In the next chapter, we will examine the skills of counseling and problem management. These skills and the counseling/coaching role differ in character in that it is often difficult to maintain the predominantly mutual quality in the relationship. In counseling and problem management, the transforming leader exercises a more direct influence and accepts even more of the responsibility for facilitating communication and the problem-solving process.

References

Burke, R., Methods of resolving superior–subordinate conflict: the constructive use of subordinate differences and disagreements, in *Readings in Interpersonal and Organizational Communication,* 3rd ed., R.C. Huseman, C.M. Logue, and D.L. Freshley, Eds., Boston: Holbrook Press, 1977.

Carkhuff, R.R., *The Development of Human Resources,* New York: Holt, Rinehart & Winston, 1971.

Egan, G., *The Skilled Helper,* 2nd ed., Monterey, CA: Brooks/Cole, 1977.

Geller, William A. and Guy Swanger, *Managing Innovation in Policing: The Untapped Potential of the Middle Manager,* Washington, D.C.: Police Executive Research Forum, 1995.

Glasser, W., *Taking Effective Control of Your Life,* New York: Harper and Row, 1984.

Kelling, George L., Robert Wasserman, and Hubert Williams, Police accountability and community policing, *Perspectives on Policing,* 7, 1–7, November 1988.

Trojanowicz, Robert and Bonnie Bucqueroux, *Community Policing: How to Get Started,* Cincinnati, OH: Anderson, 1994.

Waitley, D., *Seeds of Greatness,* Old Tappan, NJ: Fleming H. Revell, 1983.

6

The Skills of Counseling and Problem Management

Leaders are effective at problem management to the degree that the people they work with are better equipped to manage their problem situations.

—Terry Anderson

Introduction

This chapter is divided into two sections. First we will take a careful look at each of the twelve *Transforming Leadership* skills included in this problem management skill set. You may want to pay special attention to those skills in which you felt strongest and weakest when you took the *Transforming Leadership* skills assessment in Chapter 2. Remember that these skills build upon the self-mastery and communication skills explored in the previous chapters.

The second part of the chapter explores the larger steps and processes involved in problem management when using these twelve skills.

The following *Transforming Leadership* skills are discussed in this chapter:

I have coined the phrase "problem management skills" to clarify what people often mean when they use the words "counseling," "coaching," or "mentoring." In counseling, coaching, and mentoring relationships, the same generic problem management skills are used to help people become more effective at learning to work through change and solve various types of problems. In police, justice, and public safety environments, these skills can be used with yourself, other individuals, teams, organizations, and communities. They are important aspects of the practice of *Transforming Leadership* because these skills can help to move people you lead toward greater self-understanding, self-responsibility, and performance. Each leader needs to develop these skills for personal use and to encourage others to develop and perform to their full potential. The result of developing these skills will be (to some extent) personal, team, organizational, and community development.

Perhaps nowhere is there a greater need to develop these skills than in the movement toward Community Oriented Policing and Problem Solving (COPPS). Many policing agencies are either failing to successfully move toward COPPS or are progressing far too slowly because of a lack of skills in counseling and problem management. Moving too slowly fosters resistance and encourages many officers to fall back into traditional law enforcement styles of policing. At the same time, moving too quickly leaves many in the organization feeling as though they have been left out of the change process. The behaviors exhibited by both groups may look similar. But without competency in the counseling and problem management skills, many good employees will be less effective or even become cynical because they will find that their interventions do not get very positive results. Officers who have this skill set can be efficient when orienting, training, and coaching volunteers and more effective in face-to-face encounters with other officers or with difficult people on the job. These skills apply in community corrections, volunteer fire fighting, and a wide range of other environments.

Personal applications of this skill include self-examination and problem solving (counseling oneself) and assisting family members to gain self-understanding and to solve problems they may encounter in everyday life. These skills may also be used with peers in organizations so that people in these settings can become more effective and enjoy a greater sense of well-being. Corporate applications may include counseling, coaching, and mentoring others who may need assistance in overcoming blocks to performance, help in dealing with personal or work-related crises, or guidance in career planning. Problem management skills are necessary prerequisites to effectively coaching others' performance and mentoring to facilitate their development.

There has been a great deal of confusion about the differences between counseling and coaching and mentoring. As stated above, it is simple and clear to think that all three of these unique types of relationships require the same generic set of problem management skills. Another feature that the three roles have in common is that they occur in the context of a formal or informal agreement with another person with whom it is your role to engage in solving problems in a specific way. To many people, counseling, coaching, and mentoring are just different words that describe the same thing. This is untrue, confusing, and often causes problems with conflicting expectations between leaders and their team members, bosses and employees, parents and children, etc.

Therefore,the following definitions of counseling, coaching, and mentoring are presented. In examining these definitions, notice how the problem management skills apply to all three of these distinctive ways of helping others to self-examine, remove obstacles to change or growth, and move ahead to greater learning and performance.

Definition of the Counseling Relationship: Counseling is often personal in nature. The counseling relationship is often based on the role you have agreed to play in your organization. You are engaging in some kind of counseling relationship if you are a supervisor or manager and it is an expectation in your job description that you engage people you lead in conversations of a personal nature that will help them resolve personal or family problems to improve their job performance. This is especially true of small businesses or smaller police or fire departments where counseling in the workplace is done by co-workers, supervisors, or owners. This is often true when the nature of the problem is not perceived to be the employee's fault, such as a tragic loss in the family or when a marriage partner is abandoned.

Counseling relationships in larger companies and organizations can often occur in the context of employee assistance programs or when an employee visits a psychologist during a time of distress. It is also possible that these skills would be appropriate with, for example, a victim of spousal assault who has to decide if he or she will testify against the spouse, move out, or continue to put up with the abuse. It is possible for a wide range of people to provide good, skilled counseling even though they have not had formal training in counseling. It is almost always better to have been trained as a professional counselor if longer term counseling is what is required. It is possible, however, to learn and be effective in practicing the effective short-term counseling skills outlined in this chapter.

Definition of the Coaching Relationship: Coaching is most often job performance related. Supervisors do performance coaching of their subordinates, to orient and get their performance up to speed on certain tasks. Again, if it is the supervisor's job to coach, there should be an agreement between the employee and the supervisor that coaching will take place. The relationship may shift into counseling at times but primarily is focused on coaching for continually improved performance.

I do executive coaching with police chiefs, CEOs, presidents, and other leaders. We always agree in advance that this is the relationship we will have. We set up a list of things, on the phone or in person, we want to work on in each session, and I provide the coaching relationship so the leader can develop and apply specific skills to deal with identified personal, team, or organizational problems. Sometimes, we agree that counseling of a more personal nature is needed and, because my training is in counseling as well as consulting, I may shift into providing this more focused service or make a referral to another professional.

Definition of the Mentoring Relationship: Mentoring can be both formal and/ or informal. Perhaps one of the best learning experiences people can have is when, at the right times in their lives, a mentor appears and helps them learn exactly what they need to know to succeed. This happens by providence or by chance. More often and more preferably, a formalized mentoring program can be built into an organization's strategic plan, so that it becomes a part of the culture that people, especially leaders or potential leaders, are mentored. Mentoring programs identify those who would be the best mentors and pair them up with those with the greatest potential for promotion to receive formalized mentoring. Specific goals are set for the protégé's development. Often, the mentor and protégé make a commitment to work together for a year or more. The relationship is free of any formal job performance evaluation.

Counseling, coaching, and mentoring can happen in the context of the same relationship, but often it is helpful to be clear with the other person about what it is you are agreeing to do with and for the individual. If you are doing coaching and it appears that it would be beneficial to shift into a counseling relationship for a period of time, it is helpful to get agreement with the other person for you to do so.

Understanding the Twelve Problem Management Skills

These skills are presented with the idea that it is possible to be proactive in one's approach to managing and preventing further problems. It is also possible to divide the skills into specific language and observable behaviors that can be demonstrated, modeled, practiced, learned, and passed on to others. This approach to learning skills has been described as the microskills approach. Learning skills in this micro fashion, however, can make the whole process seem mechanical or robotic. Therefore, when you practice or apply a particular skill, keep in mind that each skill flows into another. Although the skills are presented below in logical, progressive order, the process of problem management is fluid. Therefore you may find yourself moving from one skill back to another, based on what the other person needs. Genuineness on your part is more important than perfectly performing each step of the process in order!

Just as when you learn any new skill, you will feel awkward at first because it may be different than the way you have done things in the past. When you learn a skill and see it work, you will enjoy the power and ease with which you can assist yourself and others in the problem management process. It can become enjoyable!

TL Skill #25. Advanced Empathy

Sharing your hunches with others about their experiences, behaviors, or feelings can help them move beyond blind spots and develop the new perspectives they must have for breakthrough thinking to emerge. In using the skill of advanced empathy, you can help others express what they are implying; help them to identify themes in their stories; assist them in connecting islands of experiences, behaviors, or feelings; and help them to draw conclusions. This skill is critical in facilitating deeper understanding in others, but must be approached with caution and respect because of the powerful and intensely personal nature of the material likely to emerge.

As an example of how this skill can work, I recently coached a CEO who continued to complain about personal and work overload. He couldn't keep up with all the demands, phone messages, e-mail messages, pager messages, meetings, and family obligations and complained that he had no time of his own. He was having difficulty sleeping, was losing weight, and was experiencing the beginning symptoms of depression. I responded with deeper understanding of what this exhausted man was saying with his whole being when I said, "You seem overwhelmed to the point of losing hope because you realize you are caught in a pattern of overextending yourself that you can't stop." His response was a deep sigh, and a big, "YES! That's it! I say yes to everything but I don't know why and I can't stop it! I am really making myself miserable living this way." When I said what I did to him, the situation came together for him like the pieces of a puzzle, and a light of truth went on. That truth set him free to make significant changes.

A somewhat mechanical language format illustrates how language can be structured to capture the feeling, the behavior, and the cause: **"You feel (*one feeling word*) because you realize that you are (*accountable in some way for the consequences you now face*)."**

This personal realization of a blind spot helped him to later change his relationship with his wife, children, partners, and community. During the next few weeks, he clarified his personal purpose statement, dropped out of his overenrollment in too many committees that did not fit his purpose, made wife and kids a high priority in his daily time planner, and even took some time for himself to regenerate and relax. After twenty-six years of living a compulsively driven life without a clear vision or purpose, all this change was precipitated by just one turning point realization during our executive coaching interview.

In another example, I watched a sergeant who worked for me struggle with his feelings of overall responsibility for the success of an investigations restructuring project in the police department. The chief of police assigned to me and two other assistant chiefs the task of restructuring the investigations section in order to provide more support for problem-oriented policing in the police department. Very few police agencies had developed COPPS roles and responsibilities for detectives. The restructuring project was intended to examine the entire structure of the investigations section and recommend any changes to the chief of police.

The sergeant was assigned the job of facilitating the various restructuring meetings and preparing a final report on any recommendations. Unfortunately in this case, the chief of police failed to assign individual responsibility for overall project coordination. In addition, the other two assistant chiefs and I failed to clearly communicate our expectations to each other or to the sergeant. His specific overall responsibilities for the project were not clear to him. The subsequent restructuring meetings were heated and controversial as individual units battled to protect their turf and individuality. Few units saw any need to change their operations. Few units developed new roles or responsibilities to enhance problem-oriented policing. The project slowed to a crawl.

After several months of meetings and much discussion, the chief of police was becoming very impatient with the time it was taking to develop any specific recommendations. The assistant chiefs were putting pressure on the sergeant for a final report. We had left it to him to design the meeting structure, identify the committee members, develop the process for expressing opposing opinions, and produce a final report that captured all of the relevant discussion and opposing opinions. He was also expected to make a final project presentation to the chief's executive committee. As assistant chiefs, each of us thought one of the others was closely following the project.

The sergeant was feeling overwhelmed as he perceived little direction or support from the chief officers. Committee chairs (captains) used different processes for gathering information in committee, and they were preparing their final recommendation reports in different formats. Some committees could not agree on what their own group had heard or was recommending. There were no suggestions for how to make sense of all of the conflicting opinions and recommendations. I could sense the sergeant's frustration. It was having an impact on his performance on this project as well as other assignments. He was feeling as though he was failing the chief of police. I could see the confidence he once had in all of his work begin to disappear. I sat down privately with him and discussed my observations. I acknowledged my perception of his situation. I pointed out his specific responsibility in the project compared to the responsibilities of the assigned assistant chiefs. I also accepted my responsibility for not providing more leadership and for not being timely in assisting him with the project.

Our ensuing discussion helped him regain his confidence. We met with the other assistant chiefs and discussed strategies to complete the project. The sergeant began to focus on his tasks and make recommendations as to what the other two assistant chiefs and I could do to support the project. He began to take the initiative and develop additional specific strategies for finishing the work. I could sense his relief when he realized he had been given permission to make the decisions he felt were his responsibility without having to wait for direction from the assistant chiefs. He was also relieved that the assistant chiefs were not expecting him to shoulder the entire burden for the delay in the project. In a short period of time, the project was successfully completed.

TL Skill #26. Problem Exploration:
Exploring External and Internal Problems

This skill requires that you follow other people through their own understanding of their problem situation first. Then, if they are ready or developed enough, assist them to see the personal *internal* problems they are having with those external problems. This step is best done prior to setting goals, exploring alternative courses of action, and giving any advice from your perspective. Understand the specific problem first—and its causes—and then offer advice when the other person's own ideas have been exhausted.

The facilitative process of helping others see and take ownership of problems is much like a quarterback leading a runner by throwing the football. If the ball is thrown too far ahead, the runner will miss it, and if the ball is thrown too far behind, no yardage is gained. You may have to lead a bit, but only in the direction the other person is already going. Difficult but necessary confrontations, of course, are exceptions to this general guideline of passing the ball to people.

You can offer your own hunches about what you think the real problem is and see if the other person can use your view of it—but only if you are not so busy doing this that you interrupt the other person's self-examination process with your "wise ideas." People receiving help—especially premature advice (before the problem is specified and owned)—often find it more difficult to use ideas offered by others when they are busy trying to define and understand their own thoughts and feelings. If you follow this advice, you will avoid the second most prevalent of the major problems beginning problem managers have: failing to define the problem and giving premature advice.

Perhaps the ideal time to share your definition of a problem with others is when they are stuck or when you want to add some alternative ways for them to consider a problem. Do this tentatively and watch (use observing skills), and then check with the other person to determine the usefulness of your ideas or responses. Do not assume that your perspectives will be internalized and used by the other person. We usually do not take advice from others carte blanche and then act on it! Give focused input at the right time.

The more thoroughly a problem is explored and the more specifically it is defined, the greater the probability a high-impact solution will be reached. The exploration of an internal or external problem with another person—or with self—begins by using all of the communication skills outlined in Chapter 5. As you understand meanings and feelings and define the situation that has occurred, you will begin to get a sense of a pattern emerging.

As you lay a base of understanding using the communication skills—especially the skills of listening and responding—you are in a better position to formulate a specific problem statement using a format such as: **"Now you realize that you cannot/have not** (*specify what the person cannot or has not done*) **because** (*specify the reason*), **and that makes you feel** (*specify the predominant feeling, using one word*)."

You can also use a somewhat different format that gets at the same issue: **"You seem** (*identify the main feeling*) **because you cannot** (*specify what cannot be performed*) **due to** (*identify internal lacks or causes of the problem, which could be overcome if identified*)."

Example of a Problem Exploration Dialogue in a Coaching Relationship

An example of a problem specification dialogue is presented in this section. An executive (Helen) was engaged in a dialogue with a manager (Merle) who was having a difficult time meeting deadlines. He turned in most assignments two weeks late. He had been a high-performing employee in his previous job, where he moved around and talked to people, but now was in a job role where much of what he did was an audit function at his desk. He had more critical managerial responsibility in his new role but less opportunity for innovation and human contact. He was also having medical problems in his family, his parents were aging and lived 1,500 miles away, and he didn't really like the stress of living in a big city with all the traffic and smog.

Helen: Merle, I've noticed that you have been turning in several projects late during the past few weeks. Could we talk about this now, or do you want to set up a time to meet tomorrow?

Merle: Yes, we can talk now. I know I have been late on three important projects, but I'm in a slump and can't seem to keep myself on track. I don't really know what is wrong.

Helen: I noticed that you looked stressed just now, Merle [a response to an immediate, observable feeling, to facilitate a supportive climate]. I'm not trying to make you feel guilty, but I'd really like to work through this with you if I may be of any help. Your previous contributions have been on time and high quality, and I want to do what I can to support you to continue the super job you normally do. [Recognizing previous strengths and achievements in the context of confronting weakness is respectful and supportive leadership behavior.]

Merle: I've even been avoiding trying to face why I am repeatedly late with the projects. It's been bothering me a lot since the first one was late two weeks ago. I just feel depressed and I don't know why.

Helen: Yes, when I have glanced at you during the past few weeks, I have noticed your energy level is down and you seem to be in a slump—sometimes your posture is actually slumped over, as it is even now. You seem to be sort of in pain, somehow. Does that fit for you? [A response to the predominant feeling nonverbally exhibited is often facilitative of deeper self-disclosure.]

Merle: Yes! I feel pain in my neck and back when I sit down to do these projects. I thought I would be motivated in this new area, but now that I am into it, I don't find it challenging—it's too repetitive, and I don't see any promotions sideways or up for quite some time. I feel trapped, like I'm just doing time here all day long, not using my talents as I was in my other role. [At this point, because she went out of her way to help Merle get this promotion, Helen could have become hooked and said, "But I thought you wanted this job, you jerk," but she did well and suspended her frame of reference.]

Helen: Okay, Merle, I think I am getting a clearer picture. Right now you seem down on yourself because you haven't taken responsibility for processing this off-key feeling for over two weeks and you have allowed your performance to drop because you can't see any way out of your dilemma.

Merle: Yeah. I know I'm stuck because I said I would take on this job for two years. And I can't go back on my word.

Helen: So you feel trapped because you believe you can't have integrity if you change your mind, due to your high standards about giving your word?

Merle: Yes. If I say I'm going to do something, I do it. No whining!

Helen: So it's like you're sapped of enthusiasm because you can't see another way to maintain your integrity other than making yourself march through this job for a few years—even though you now realize it doesn't fit your goals and talents?

Merle: Is that what I'm doing?! I'm not that rigid, am I? I guess I am. I think I want to do something about that! I don't think I will be giving myself or this organization the best I can by being so rigid. What other options do I have? [Merle now recognizes and takes ownership of his part of the problem.]

Helen: I'm not sure because I haven't thought about it. Maybe we could both jot down some ideas between now and Monday and see what we come up with. Can we meet at 10:00 in the morning?

Merle: Yes, definitely. Thanks for supporting me on this one, Helen. It's not everyone who is willing to look at more than one way things can work out for the better.

Helen: I need to be in the right spot, too, if I am going to use my talents and enthusiasm to produce good results. I'm thinking about making a move in about a year. I'll be ready for a change by then. Thanks for your trust in going through this personal area with me. Do you think you can get the report in on time tomorrow afternoon now that we have a better idea of what is happening?

Merle: Count on it.

Helen: Thanks.

It Doesn't Have to Take a Long Time

The preceding sequence of problem identification responses gives you a clear idea of some interventions that may be appropriate in a three- to five-minute conversation. It doesn't have to take a long time to facilitate a person through the process. In the long run, it will save many lost person-hours if Merle's performance improves or if he moves into a more appropriate job role—or even if Helen helps him find another company so she can replace him with a person with a nature that fits the job.

TL Skill #27. Problem Specification: The Most Complex Skill

This specification skill is the main one nearly everyone who attempts to develop these skills has difficulty implementing effectively. This is the case because problem exploration requires a complex set of qualities and abilities—patience; temporarily suspending personal hunches, judgments, emotions, and premature advice; careful empathic listening; a creative mind; and a perceptual receptivity to the other person's nonverbal cues. It also requires the ability to craft language that clearly defines the problem and a belief that the root causes of a problem should eventually be explored when the person being helped can handle greater depth. Although difficult to master, the skill of problem specification is very powerful in assisting others to move ahead in their understanding of their problems and solving them—which can improve their morale and their work performance.

The following is an example of language that can be appropriate for a problem statement a leading manager might make to a co-worker in trouble: **"You seem to be saying you're depressed because you realize that you can't stop drinking so much, because it's so difficult right now for you to face the painful reality of your wife's cancer."**

This is a complex sentence that captures the problem behavior, the difficult inner self-control problem, and the harsh external reality. The statement also contains no words that could be accusatory—just the facts as presented, for the most part. These statements are difficult to formulate, and therefore many people tend to oversimplify problems and give trite advice or pat answers they honestly hope will be helpful.

Problem specification in policing is valuable when trying to understand why officers or deputies "refuse to go along with the program." Their activity and commitment are low. They refuse to get involved in problem-solving efforts. They shy away from engaging the community in a productive manner. Many supervisors jump to the conclusion that the uncooperative officer is a malcontent. The reality may be that the officer feels lost in this new concept of policing. Moving to COPPS is difficult. As a result, the police officer's job becomes more difficult. And, of course, supervision becomes much more difficult.

Officers are expected to look at crime problems from other than the law enforcement perspective. They may have been trained in the concepts of COPPS but may not have had the benefit of proper leadership in the practical realities of implementation. By identifying the problem accurately, a supervisor can work to develop strategies to address the specific problem. This can result in retaining and further developing a once-valued employee.

The More Solvable Problems Are Best Addressed First

It is also important that problems with a high probability of being solved or managed effectively are focused on first so that motivation to take action will be greater. Searching for supports in the environment, strengths within the person, and problem-solving potentials inherent within the problem itself is important. Success will then more likely be the result. We all need the encouragement of early small wins.

TL Skill #28. Problem Ownership: Helping Ourselves and Others Own Up

This is a difficult skill because many people often assume that if people were really motivated, they would "get the lead out" and solve the problem. When people face difficult and stressful problems, they are often stunned. They can be temporarily mentally or emotionally frozen, unable to think or function well. Helping others to take ownership of their part of an overall problem they believe they can do something about is our primary task as problem-managing leaders. If people unable to willingly and honorably take ownership of their part of the problem, there will not be change.

What if people will not take ownership of their problems? This is often because they feel humiliated, ashamed, embarrassed, or fearful of not getting a hoped-for promotion—or they dread the pain of facing the problem and would rather live with the pain of the problem itself. As we create a culture of facing the truth about problems (and our personal responsibility in them), we can provide a climate where mistakes or difficulties can be overcome and dealt with honorably. It is even possible to create a culture where celebration and recognition can be given to those courageous souls who, with honor, face the facts and engage themselves in dealing with the problem.

The fact remains that some people will not take ownership, no matter what we do. In such cases, it is our job to act in good faith and continue to do our part in facilitating problem solving even though others are frozen, unable, or just plain unwilling to face things. As long as we have the leadership responsibility to work with people—and we have decided not to fire them or they cannot be fired—we must act as though the glass is half-full and we are going do what we can to fill it up until it runs over.

The following language format can be used to specify a problem so it facilitates ownership: **"You seem to feel (*one feeling word*) because you can't stop (*problem behavior*) due to (*internal cause of problem*)."**

Once we help someone crystallize the language that captures the essence of his or her internal difficulties and obstacles, we are in a position to help that individual set goals to overcome the internal difficulties causing the external manifestation we call the problem. Most often, external problems are caused by these internal difficulties that must be dealt with before progress can be made. This is where we can see that helping someone through this impasse can be very powerful in creating a climate where learning can occur.

Some people are good at personalizing problems (taking ownership) so they can get into personal action to solve them. Others are not as good at it. An inability to personalize problems is most often an issue of personal development rather than stubbornness. An inability to personalize can also be due to previous emotional abuse or learning disabilities. Therefore, it is much more economical and effective to hire good problem solvers in the first place than it is to coach and develop them to maturity and competence. If, however, we have to work with people who are not competent at present and need to grow or need to be facilitated through this process, the problem management process can work quite well.

Jack Welch, CEO of General Electric, held morning meetings during which he had managers go through this kind of processing of problems in a large group. He led the process himself, and all those present dealt with emerging problems on a daily basis; they went through the problem management process for each problem. Sometimes people had to own up to personal responsibility in front of the group. Sometimes Jack did. Those who did were honored and recognized for their courage and humility. Could this have something to do with the fact that General Electric is the largest and most profitable company in the world?

An Example of How Supervisors Can Help Officers Accept Ownership When Solving Crime Problems

The success of COPPS is founded on the ability of the street-level police officer or deputy to be a problem solver. As mentioned earlier, police officers involved in COPPS are expected to be less reactive to crime and more proactive in crime prevention problem-solving strategies. Sir Robert Peele recognized the responsibility of the police to work with the community in policing strategies as far back as 1872. This early recognition of community engagement was lost in the last half of the twentieth century and is just now gaining popularity as the century draws to a close.

A good supervisor helps employees develop into successful problem solvers. The skill of effective problem solving is difficult to teach and even more difficult to coach. Many police supervisors and managers were not problem-solving officers early in their careers. Many will claim they practiced problem solving years before it became a popular policing strategy. However, they will admit they had few independent resources to apply to the wide variety of problems. There also were very few outside public or private agencies willing to support their problem-solving efforts. Their form of problem solving did not include a role for the community member living in the middle of the crime problem. In addition, they rarely followed a problem-solving model like Scanning, Analysis, Response, and Assessment (SARA), which forces the problem solver to perform a detailed analysis of the situation in order to correctly identify the problem.

In the traditional policing model, officers would frequently race to the obvious crime scene (i.e., robbery, burglary, or drug dealing) and identify the suspect as the target of any problem-solving effort. True problem solving demands analyzing all three sides of the crime triangle, suspect–victim–location, and developing a tailor-made response which does not focus entirely on enforcement tactics. Under COPPS, officers are also encouraged to look for unique resources outside of the policing agency that can be applied to the crime problem.

Many times, the best ideas for a response or potential solution come from street officers or deputies. They need to be encouraged to take risks and work through problems on their own. All too frequently, a well-meaning supervisor provides an immediate solution to the problem before the officer has had time to take ownership of it. The solutions sergeants or lieutenants come up with are often stuck in the traditional policing bag of tricks. Many problem-solving efforts fail to go far enough to get at the core of a problem. The responses remain traditional tactical operations that are heavy on enforcement, with no community engagement and no or little focus on the victim or location.

A good example of this occurred when a young police officer faced a series of robberies on his beat. Elderly female residents were the victims of purse snatchers as they walked to and from two local restaurants. The well-meaning sergeant developed a response to the crime problem by assigning the entire squad to a stakeout on a night when one of these robberies was likely to occur. For reasons obvious to more experienced cops and robbers, the stakeout produced no arrests. Crooks frequently spot cops, even on stakeouts. From my past experience, even if the stakeout had resulted in arrests, there were more than enough robbery suspects working this area to take the place of those arrested.

When I asked the patrol officer what he was going to do next, he responded,

"My sergeant hasn't come up with anything yet." I then encouraged him to perform a more detailed analysis of the problem. He realized that the other two sides of the crime triangle had been ignored. We discussed educating the victims through flyers and personal meetings using the existing neighborhood watch and other volunteer programs. He considered contacting the restaurants and gaining their support by pointing out their potential loss of business if the robberies continued. He also thought about encouraging the restaurants to consider allowing certain customers to run a tab on their meals, thereby eliminating the need for patrons to carry purses.

In this case, I could see the patrol officer taking ownership of the problem, and he was truly excited about testing his potential solutions. His success is not guaranteed, but he will likely analyze his problem-solving effort, look at new resources, and develop new responses if necessary. This one experience will help him develop new skills he can use on other problems, both professional and personal. All of this was made possible by including the officer in the discussion when deciding what to do about the robbery problem. First-line supervisors need to develop this skill if they are going to get officers to change from being crime responders to problem solvers.

TL Skill #29. Goal Setting: Identifying Realistic and Motivating Targets

Goal setting is the "what to do" part of the problem management process. Action planning, the skill we will examine after goal setting, is the "how to get there" part of the process. For now, let's turn to a self-assessment of your goal-setting skills.

Attacking high-yield problems, where there is opportunity for both personal development and improvement in external circumstances, is preferable to setting goals that will alleviate only a personal problem or improve external circumstances. This is the case because personal difficulties often cause problem situations, and problem situations can in turn cause additional personal difficulties. The skill of goal setting is important because it provides a focus for defining future accomplishments which, when reached, can ideally alleviate the problem inside a person and improve the external problem situation at the same time. Goal setting is a practical and powerful skill for becoming a more intentional and successful person and for assisting those with whom you are involved in leadership interventions to do the same.

Goals that are set should be specific enough to solve a defined problem and give direction for action. Goals statements that are the most effective have the following attributes.

1. Measurable and verifiable

2. Realistic and achievable within a reasonable time
3. Genuinely owned by the person with the problem
4. In accord with the values and beliefs of the person
5. Clearly envisioned and attractive enough to be motivating
6. Desirable enough to give rise to genuine commitment
7. Evaluated on an ongoing basis to check for realism

Thus, specific and careful goal setting that challenges our own unused potential or that of others is often not easy to specify. Often, people offer one another premature advice or "pat answers." Goal setting, however, requires time and careful consideration for effective formulation. By providing yourself and others with a clear sense of direction for managing problems, stress can be alleviated and constructive action, increased energy, and improved performance can result.

An example of a clear goal statement is the one that Merle made to Helen during a subsequent meeting, when he realized that, for a number of reasons, he had to change jobs and geographic locations. After Helen and Merle met the following Monday morning, Merle not only realized that he was disillusioned with his new job role but also faced the fact that he did not want to live in the city where he was presently located, wanted to move closer to his aging parents, and wanted to live in a city where pollution would not be such a problem.

His problem was related to a complex set of factors pushing him away from not only the job he was in but away from the company he was working with, too. After Helen helped Merle sort through a clearer understanding of these factors, she helped him respecify his problem as a career and life-planning problem. Then Merle formulated his own goal statement based on the increased clarity he found through his dialogue with Helen: "I want to take the initiative to explore other career options and other cities so I can relocate and start a new life by next summer—where there are ample career opportunities, good family emphasis, clean air, and affordable housing."

Note how clearly the goal is defined here, with a time line and Merle's values considered in the statement. Helen did a good job of helping Merle to be quite specific and concrete in his goal setting.

Helen began searching for another employee who could better fill Merle's position, instead of keeping Merle in the same job or switching him to another job in the same company in a city where he did not want to live. Helen is likely to see an overall increase in corporate performance if she does more careful staff selection for that same position and other positions the next time she has the opportunity.

Another example of goal setting is the narcotics lieutenant who gave up his preferred assignment in order to accomplish specific goals he set for himself in order to get promoted to captain. He decided he needed to become more knowledgeable and technically proficient in specific areas. He volunteered for a less rewarding assignment (no take-home car, no special investigations pay, no overtime). In his new assignment, he developed some new skills within the two-year target time frame. When he failed to be promoted to the next available position, he set new goals and moved to another assignment. When requesting his next assignment, he considered the opportunity to demonstrate the new skills he had developed. He set new goals in his new assignment and began working on strategies to achieve them.

Regardless of reaching his goal of promotion, he challenged his status quo. He became a much more valuable employee. His confidence and enthusiasm were enhanced, and his improved performance and contributions to the organization were recognized. In this case, his goal setting paid off with a promotion to the rank of captain within months of his new assignment.

TL Skill #30. Goal Ownership: Securing Ownership to Get Commitment to Action

In the same vein, it is important to facilitate others to take ownership of goals that will resolve their part of the overall problem being faced. In my experience, until people come up with the language to move ahead successfully, they do not change their approach or perform any differently. Although some people are visual, it still seems that language locks goals into people's action systems. Observations indicate that goals that are written down are more than 50 percent more likely to be achieved than goals thought or spoken about. Goals that are prioritized are more likely to be accomplished than those that are on a long list of things to be achieved "someday." If we are always working primarily on our top three or four goals, we are more focused, less distracted, and more successful. Goals for which a time line is established are also more likely to be achieved. If I want to get commitment to action, then I help people set goals that follow the specificity guidelines set out here.

As an example, consider how one CEO took ownership of a goal. For years, he was preoccupied with business. He agreed with his wife and friends who thought he was neglectful in his marriage. Even though he had admitted his problem and set a goal to change, he had never really taken personal ownership for the goal. I challenged him by asking him to open up his daily planner and find a place during the last month where he had written his wife's name. He looked and was stunned to find that he still had not planned "a date" with her, even though he had committed to do so. This time, he agreed with me that he would meet with her that evening and plan a two-week vacation. He was also going to schedule time for them to spend special evenings together, doing things they could both enjoy. He agreed to phone me the next day to tell me he had followed through with his plan. He did and he had.

A resource well worth mentioning is a fascinating workbook called, *Living on Purpose,* written by Bill Bean, Ron Ford, and Richard Edler. It outlines over three hundred well-formulated goals from which you can select, then prioritize and create an action plan to build a more balanced and meaningful life. The same *Strategic Planning Technology* that has worked so well in business can now be applied to personal life, too. Those interested in accessing a copy of this work-book can do so at http://www.strategia.com. Although not yet in its published form, it is accessible at this time online.

The movement to COPPS requires personal and organizational goal setting and ownership. The best strategic plan and commitment from the top of an organization will not guarantee a successful change to community policing. In fact, without individual commitment, any plan for meaningful change is subject to failure. It's just too easy to fall back into the comfort zone of traditional policing. All ranks in the organization need to set individual goals that are in line with COPPS organizational goals. They must then use their leadership skills to assist subordinates in doing the same.

The San Diego Police Department's entire forty-person command staff spent months developing seven organizational goals. They used a strategic planning process to develop objectives and strategies for reaching the seven goals. When over one hundred new strategies were developed by hundreds of people inside and outside of the organization, the command staff prioritized the top twenty strategies and assigned names to their top five priorities. In this way, each had a vested interest in the success of reaching those goals. Each could be called upon individually to support specific strategies as the implementation phase began. Throughout the next year, all command staff members regularly reported to one another on the progress of their respective strategies.

In addition, each was required to develop four to eight specific individual objectives for the annual performance evaluation report. The supervisor evalu-ated their performance in part on their ability to accomplish their personal objectives. This process is still in the developmental stage and is not eagerly accepted by all of the command staff. It was so much easier to be a manager of systems and operations and not be responsible for leading the police department into COPPS.

TL Skill #31. Action Planning:
Exploring and Evaluating Specific Pathways for Achievement

Once a goal has been defined, it is time to examine alternative pathways to reach it; then it is time to develop a realistic plan to implement that goal in a step-by-step fashion.

Exploring Alternative Strategies to Reach the Goal

Quite often, people fail to achieve goals for a number of reasons. Some of the main reasons are unclear strategies, the steps involved are too large for the time line that has been set, or lack of the required material or emotional supports. It is important, therefore, to ensure that all possible alternative strategies are explored and evaluated before one is decided upon prematurely. Often, there is a better way to "get there," but people tend to do what is familiar and not explore other options thoroughly enough to evaluate better action alternatives. Being exhaustive in searching out alternative courses of action almost always reveals attractive, motivating, and encouraging steps to take that were not previously clear.

Evaluating and Selecting Alternative Strategies to Reach the Goal

Once alternative strategies have been explored, it is important to evaluate which ones best fit your own or others' values and motivational structures. The action plan has to "turn us on" for some reason or we do will want to "go for it." Therefore, to evaluate the potential of an alternative action plan, we need to specify what is important to the person with the problem and assess how well each alternative course of action fits what is felt to be important.

For example, Merle wanted to choose a new location in which to live. After exploring what was important to him, his family, and others in his social setting, he created a comparison chart similar to the one below. He rated each city on a scale of one to five in terms of how much it might fulfill the values he deemed important.

	Alternatives		
Values	**Chicago**	**Denver**	**Dallas**
Clear air	2	5	3
Family city	2	4	3
Good economy	3	4	4
Affordable housing	2	4	2
Proximity to aging parents	2	5	3
Total	**11**	**22**	**15**

It may not be necessary to actually put the chart on paper unless the problem is quite complex, but the steps you would go through in considering various alternatives—or helping someone else to consider them—would be the same:

1. Identify alternatives.
2. Identify values in order of importance.
3. Weigh alternatives against criteria.

4. Get a clearer sense of which alternative course of action seems most desirable after careful assessment.

TL Skill #32. Implementing Action Plans: Increasing the Success Rate

Helping self and others to reach goals and succeed in taking planned action steps is important to the problem management process, perhaps ultimately the most important step. If we do not succeed in counseling ourselves and others to accomplish worthwhile goals, then how effective is our helping or problem management?

Action plans may not get off the ground because people tend to cling to old, less functional patterns of behavior. It can be scary to give up familiar patterns of action in favor of more effective but foreign ones. If action plans are implemented, they tend to fall apart over time, or fade in intensity, and quite often, are replaced by old patterns of behavior.

Leaders may become discouraged by how often people "fail" to live up to their expectations for improved performance. We can also become discouraged with ourselves in certain areas of our lives when we want change and it doesn't come easily. It would be good for us to accept that deeper changes often come about after great struggle, much encouragement, and quite a bit of time. Just because people set goals and plan to take new actions does not mean that the leader's task has ended and the "follower" is now fully capable and responsible.

An implementation plan includes a clear—often written—statement of what will be accomplished, when, and by whom. When implementation breaks down, ongoing coaching or counseling may be required. With people who are more stuck or resistant, confrontation may be required.

This is so true in implementing the wide range of action plans needed for COPPS to take hold. A simple implementation plan must be developed that involves a wide variety of areas in policing. Implementing is not the responsibility of a small group in the organization. Implementation requires the commitment of most if not all members in the organization. In the San Diego Police Department, several committees developed forty-two recommendations for changes they felt were necessary if the department was to move from traditional to neighborhood policing. Recommendations included changing the basic patrol beat structure, size of squads, and responsibility for lieutenants and detectives and diverting various patrol duties to civilian personnel.

As change began to occur, there were successes and failures. Each person in the organization focused on what supported his or her patterns of behavior. Some true leaders in the organization used the success to support more change and take greater risks. Others used the failures to resist any change so they could hang on to their old, comfortable style of policing. Some even intentionally subverted any progress toward change.

Often, people resist change because they cannot see alternate paths that can still fit their policing style. An organization must have leaders capable of helping others see their way of getting to the vision of COPPS. After specific training, coaching, and counseling, some of the more resistant San Diego Policy Department supervisors were confronted with negative discipline. A senior patrol sergeant can cause considerable damage if cynical, subversive behavior continues unchecked.

It is ultimately the responsibility of every supervisor, manager, and executive officer to provide the organizational structure, training, and resources to make the change to COPPS. Each is responsible for his or her span of control and organizational turf. Implementing action plans will reward the employee, supervisor, organization, and community. These problem management skills are what enables leaders to assist those who are resistant to working through managing change on the *inside,* one officer at a time.

TL Skill #33. Confrontation: Facing Self-Defeating Behaviors

You can challenge the discrepancies, distortions, smoke screens, and games that others seem to use to keep themselves and others from seeing their problem situations and unused potentials—or you can use confrontation to challenge people to move beyond discussion to action.

This skill is the most risky of all the skills because it involves getting another person to confront self directly. A great deal of trust is required for people to feel comfortable enough to allow you to challenge what you think may be self-deception, self-defeating behavior patterns, or destructive interpersonal "games." It would seem we have to earn the right to confront by developing the relationship over time, prior to engaging in confrontation.

Strength Confrontation: You challenge others to focus on strengths you observe are present, but ones they tend to ignore or deny. Berenson and Mitchell (1974) found that more facilitative helpers used strength confrontation significantly more often than less facilitative helpers. They also found that people used this type of confrontation least often! The following is an example of a strength confrontation: "You have lots of ability to perform and enjoy sports that you aren't using right now—and yet you say you want to get fit. Maybe you could find a sport you really like and use that to help you reach your goal."

In promotion feedback interviews, I frequently challenge candidates to apply their traditional policing strengths to the COPPS culture. Good officers find the time to go after specific criminals they have targeted on their beat. Yet these same officers will say there is never enough time to perform problem-solving activities. Good detectives find some of the best resources when trying to track down a suspect wanted for a major crime. These same detectives do not recognize their responsibility to actively support the patrol officer or community member in developing the resources needed to solve some of their own problems. I remind promotional candidates that if they want to be promoted, they must apply their strengths in the direction in which the organization is moving.

Weakness Confrontation: You can challenge others to face their weak spots if they tend not to see them. This is the more risky type of confrontation because it requires that the other people have enough self-worth to face their deficits without feeling like losers. Many people cannot face weaknesses or faults directly without feeling shaky in the self-worth department. They may also feel threatened and fearful that others will judge them negatively and discriminate against them when it comes time for a promotion. In some environments, this is probably a realistic fear.

Recently, I confronted a CEO I was coaching. I told him I believed he was underutilizing his superior visionary leadership abilities (a strength confrontation) and then confronted him with the fact that his implementation of action plans was not nearly as strong in view of his track record of execution. He agreed and realized that if his organization was to function at its optimum level, he would have to hire someone with an excellent track record in operations and execution to complement his visionary abilities. He also agreed that such a person should be able to more than generate his or her salary because only someone with proven experience in that area would be hired.

Weakness confrontation with police officers is no different. Officers have a keen sense of honesty and open communication. They can read someone who is not being "totally open" with them. That is what they are paid to do—recognize dishonesty. As long as you base your comments on identifiable behaviors and not rumors or judgments, most officers will respect your direct confrontation style. Weakness confrontation should be coupled with some suggestions for improvement. Use your experience and knowledge to make meaningful recommendations, so the person being challenged sees a possibility for strengthening the weakness in order to become more successful. Officers have a strong desire to succeed.

Didactic Confrontation: In this type of confrontation, you are sure that the other person simply has wrong information, and it would be irresponsible or uncaring for you not to confront him or her about it. You could say, "I have different information that might help you solve this problem you are facing. Are you willing to hear it?" Asking people if they are willing to hear a confrontation and getting their permission to confront is an important step in ensuring that they will even hear you. Using confrontation to build the relationship and build others' successes makes you a more appreciated and credible leader.

This skill will probably be more difficult for police supervisors to develop. We are not accustomed to asking people if they are willing to hear a confrontation. Street experience taught many cops to confront first and ask questions later. Sometimes this learned behavior negatively affects personal relationships at work and at home. Leaders in the organization should refine this skill and promote it in others in order to lower stress and actively value and respect the worth of others to the organization and the community.

TL Skill #34. Self-Sharing:
Giving Others Additional Perspective with Your Own Story

You can share your own experience with others as a way of modeling nondefensive self-disclosure, or as a way of helping them move beyond blind spots, and as a way of seeing possibilities for problem-managing action.

This is perhaps the most encouraging of all the types of challenging. When you are genuine enough to share an experience—which shows the other person that you have some true sympathy with their experience—a sense of camaraderie or mutuality develops. This is trust building and eliminates a tone of judgment so often feared by many.

It is important that your sharing of your experiences does not dominate the dialogue, that it be well timed, and most importantly, that it be useful in facilitating further understanding or insight in the other person. It is an especially valuable skill to use when a person is stuck when attempting to specify his or her own part of a problem or when attempting to come up with action alternatives.

I used this skill when I shared my own experience of having difficulty in specifying my own purpose statement with a CEO with whom I was doing executive coaching. He really wanted clarity about his own purpose but was expecting his purpose statement to take shape out of thin air in one try. When I shared with him that my own purpose statement is continuing to evolve, and that it took a few weeks of revision after revision for me to feel comfortable with the first one, he relaxed and made more realistic progress.

I frequently share my negative and positive experiences while serving in various police units. It is a good idea to be careful that it does turn into sharing old "war stories." The experiences must be related to the particular situation. This can be a valuable way of demonstrating that even experienced officers need to continuously monitor their weaknesses and blind spots. I have allowed irate citizens to drag me into the gutter emotionally. I have failed, on occasion, to remember I am expected to be a role model on and off duty, *at all times*. And I have taken for granted the power of a police officer to develop partnerships in problem solving, within city government and the private community.

Take the opportunity to pass on successful strategies for handling problems. Officers are tactical and appreciate real-life examples that are applicable at the street level. Many officers who were great problem-solving cops have been promoted to the ranks of sergeant. For various reasons, too many fail to make great problem-solving supervisors. The skill of self-sharing would enable the supervisor and employee to apply proven tactics to similar problems or take risks and try new strategies. Either way, both supervisor and employee will benefit from the process.

TL Skill #35. Immediacy:
Helping People Get Unstuck in Their Immediate Context

This is a very versatile and widely applicable skill that enables you to deal with issues that must be addressed before other problems can be tackled. It can be considered a "process" skill that enables you to help get yourself or others "unstuck" when things are not moving forward. This skill can assist you to improve your working alliance with others in two ways:

1. By using relationship immediacy—which focuses on your ability to discuss with another person your relationship with him or her, with a view to managing whatever problems have existed and maintaining strengths in the relationship
2. By using here-and-now immediacy—which focuses on your ability to discuss with others whatever is standing in the way of working together right now

Immediacy is a powerful skill in establishing your genuineness as a person and as a helpful leader. It expresses your concern that the relationship go well and expresses your commitment that problems get solved. Using immediacy is an excellent way to "cut through" tension and a stuck feeling in the relationship if the other person is the type who can handle direct, face-to-face honesty. If the other person is too intimidated to deal directly with such intensity and openness, then this could be a risky skill to use, especially in the beginning of a relationship.

A police supervisor and the new middle manager to whom she reported were having difficulties relative to the amount "upward delegation" that appeared to be occurring. The middle manager spent countless hours instructing the supervisor on decision-making techniques and efficient administrative practices, but problems went unresolved and communications strained. During a counseling session, the manager pointed to the stripes on the uniform shirt and asked, "What do those mean to you?" After her answer, the manager told the supervisor that his expectation was that only information that was needed at the manager level or higher and only problems that needed to be resolved at those levels would be forwarded. His message was that "The responsibility to act like a supervisor comes with that rank you wear." Almost with a sense of relief the supervisor told of having all decisions made, regardless of importance, by the previous manager and she just wasn't sure where she stood with the new manager, until now. Removing the doubt improved performance as well as her relationship with the manager.

TL Skill #36. Making an Effective Referral to a Professional Helper

When you realize the person with whom you are working is facing a personal problem that is beyond your capability to handle, it is appropriate to make a smooth referral to a professional helper. In making an effective referral, it is best to refer the person to someone he or she already knows and respects. When this is not possible, try to identify some good helpers you personally know and can recommend to others when they are in need.

The following steps can be followed when making a referral:

1. Gather as much information about the counselor or therapist to whom you might make a referral.
2. Make sure the counselor is formally qualified (through university training and certification, as is appropriate in certain states and provinces) and, whenever possible, verify that he or she has a track record of reputable practice.
3. Meet this professional helper face to face so that you get a sense of who the person is and what approaches this individual prefers.
4. When you are satisfied that you have located a good counselor, suggest to the person needing assistance that you would like to make a personal introduction to a new helper who can help more effectively than you can in this instance, for very specific reasons.
5. Personally introduce the two and leave them alone for their first session.
6. Follow up with both parties to see how things went (you may have to make another referral if the first one does not click).
7. Make sure that confidentiality agreements are specified and agreed upon by you, the person, and the therapist or you will lose trust and integrity in the eyes of others.
8. Continue supporting the person receiving help, but do not enter into confidential conversations that could counter the work being done by the therapist; if you do, you may find a frustrated therapist or counselor on the phone asking you to stay in your own territory.

Understanding the Processes of Counseling and Problem Management

What Is the Problem Management Process?

The problem management process is a step-by-step manner of approaching and solving all kinds of problems. It emerged from theory, research, and models of problem solving and decision making. This process is becoming more popularly integrated into counseling, leadership, and management practice because of its logical and systematic approach to defining problems, setting goals, exploring and implementing action alternatives, and evaluating the results.

Effective counseling or helper training programs have effectively used a problem management approach (Egan, 1990). In his book, Egan offers a theoretical backdrop for the model he has developed. He reviews and integrates applied behavioral psychology, applied cognitive psychology, applied personality theory, and social influence and decision-making approaches and weaves them into a comprehensive counseling model. This model has a three-stage process that assists practitioners in assessing what they are doing and what they need to do next in the problem management process.

Expertise in the use of a step-by-step process model such as this is developed as you apply it to real problems. The problem management process gives structure to the application of appropriate skills at various stages. We will examine the stages, steps, and skills in this process later in this chapter.

Who Needs You to Be a Skilled People-Problem Manager, Anyway?

Almost anyone may need you to assist them in some way. The knowledge and techniques for facilitating problem solving within and between individuals is perhaps more subtle and advanced than any other problem-solving body of knowledge. It can be applied to personal and interpersonal matters that affect overall human performance and morale in families and in work settings. If there is truth in the above statement, then everyone with whom we come in contact (including ourselves) could potentially benefit from others who possess these skills.

During a consulting contract where my job was to assist twenty-eight managers to better understand and deal with high stress levels on the job, I heard one manager say: "Managers don't have time to deal with 'whiners' or people with problems. We are too busy dealing with more important operational issues and decisions and shouldn't be slowed down by ineffective people. If people can't hack it, get rid of them and get people in there who can do the job. If you have a disgruntled customer, tell him or her to leave—we don't have to put up with 'guff' from customers."

This general attitude of impatience, seeming unkindness, and intolerance is a signal that this person lacks what the research of Kouzes and Posner (1988) reports that employees like very much in their leaders: a heart for people. The insensitive "bottom-line" response to people with "problems" is what I call the "computer chip approach" to management: If it is defective, just unplug it, and put in another one that works."Sometimes, because of collective agreements or labor legislation, managers are forced to make the best of employees with problems. Parents are leaders who definitely are "stuck" with their children who almost always seem to have some kind of problem prior to leaving home. Business owners are stuck with finicky customers who will leave and bad-mouth them and their business. Police leaders cannot tolerate poor performance that may have dangerous consequences.

Someone Close to You May Need Your Help: It May Be You

It is realistic to say that some of the personal relationships that managers or leaders have may require a deeper level of helpful understanding and skills. Certainly for oneself, family, and friends, they are enviable skills to possess. Problems do not really happen between people in a relationship; they happen inside of each person interacting within the context of a relationship. That is where problems must be solved—on the inside. This is the great contribution counseling skills can make toward strengthening our personal and even our business relationships. Another encouraging point is that you can learn the skills of solving (and helping others to solve) internal personal problems that interfere with personal relationships and work performance.

Often, someone in our immediate family or the person working beside us is going through a separation that could end in divorce, a battle with alcoholism, drug abuse, grief, depression or a mid-life crisis. Leaders are in strategic positions to support, problem solve, and intervene in the lives of many people. The results of counseling others can be increased morale, increased productivity, and a more positive organizational culture. Sometimes we find ourselves in the advantageous position of having established trust with someone—and that can enable us to assist that person in more powerful and deeper ways than anyone else could. Most people do not go to a professional psychologist or counselor for help but find it through more informal channels.

The most impressive studies I have seen on the efficacy of good communication, problem management, and effective culture building are those by Kravetz (1988). A total of 150 well-established companies were evaluated as to the effectiveness of their human resource practices and attitudes. The ones that came out on top were also the ones assessed as having the highest morale and greatest revenues (compared to the other companies surveyed).

There is also some evidence that the best counseling occurs right in a person's own environment and that most people facing a personal problem will not or do not seek the help of a professional (Carkhuff, 1971).

Furthermore, it is also true that if everyone who needed help were to go to a professional helper (and no one else) for assistance in solving problems, there would likely be more than two hundred people crowded into each psychologist's waiting room at any given time. This is another reason why it is, ideally, everyone's responsibility to learn to help others for the benefit of all.

Finally, you may need to help yourself solve a problem. Perhaps you have some problems that are too personal to share with some others. Watson and Tharpe (1981) have devoted a whole book to self-management and problem solving that outlines how to apply the problem management process to yourself.

When do Managers Have Time to Counsel?

Because managers often do not have time to become involved in longer term or in-depth counseling relationships, it is important that they continually seek a balance between task and relationship factors in the environment. If supportive and helpful relationship factors are neglected for too long a time, performance can be affected. If the task aspects of the environment are not attended to properly, then they simply may not get done. This type of balance is much like surfing: If you step too far ahead trying to catch the wave, it will come crashing down on you; if you step back too far, you will miss the wave entirely.

It is true that leaders cannot deal with all people with personal problems just because they happen to cross paths, but it is very desirable and advantageous for good leaders to selectively understand and be able to show genuine and skilled caring for some of the people they encounter. This can increase trust, commitment, morale, and productivity.

It is also a fact that people who are ordinarily effective go through periods of time when they face developmental crises; times of grief when performance is lower; times of personal, family, or marital stress when concentration is distracted; or times of physical health difficulties when performance is temporarily on the decline. An attitude of support, encouragement, tolerance, and compassion is what most of us would deeply appreciate from others around us— and is perhaps what we especially need from those "above" us in leadership positions.

When time or pressure does not allow a leader to take on counseling responsibilities, then a transforming leader will develop other helpers within the organization or effectively refer the burdened person to a professional helper.

Does Counseling Really Help?

A review of research literature on counseling outcomes reveals basic themes that might be best summarized by saying that some approaches do help some people, with some problems, in some situations, some of the time. We are not able to say with confidence that all helpers are helpful, but we can say with some confidence that some helpers have been and can be destructive!

A summary of three statements from the literature on counseling effectiveness, provided below and in the next section, will give you with a clearer picture of some relevant findings that have been established through research:

#1 Counseling can be effective and can encourage personal development and can also enhance job performance (Bergin, 1971; Emrick, 1975; Landman and Dawes, 1982; Smith and Glass, 1977; Smith et al., 1980).

In view of the evidence in the studies referenced above, that counseling can be valid and helpful is not really in question. The studies referenced below indicate that the reliability of counseling may be in question:

#2 Counseling can also be questionable because there is some evidence that it can be ineffective and/or destructive (Levitt, 1963; Bergin, 1980; Mays and Franks, 1980; Orwin and Cordray, 1984).

This statement may summarize why so many managers, leaders, and others are fearful of trying to help people solve problems that interfere with morale or performance at home or on the job. It is clear that if you do not know what you are doing when you enter someone else's personal world, you might inadvertently damage self-worth, morale, and performance—and perhaps even increase turnover and absenteeism at the same time. Therefore, it is important to be able to recognize the major mistakes of counseling and to develop the key skills to be a facilitative helper.

Three Major Mistakes Untrained Leaders Make When Attempting to Do Counseling

In videotaping sessions of untrained (in counseling skills) leaders and managers at the beginning of a counseling skills training session, I see several frequently made mistakes:

1. The first mistake is simply that most leaders are so task focused that they fail to actually hear the content and check for the intended meaning of the messages being sent to them.

2. The leaders presume that they accurately understand—without checking with the other person.
3. The leaders give premature advice without jointly arriving at a specific definition of the problem. This advice is usually not followed by the other person because the solution offered does not fit the real nature of the problem.

Other problems showed up less frequently, such as failing to temporarily suspend personal judgmental reactions,and emotions—and giving inappropriate or even destructive advice.

The Good News about Transferable Skills Training

We know from many other studies on the efficacy of training people in interpersonal and counseling skills that it is possible to train them in a relatively short period of time to be effective in counseling others to solve problems not long term and pervasive in nature. We know it is possible to help most trainees quite rapidly give up ineffective patterns.

> **#3 Helper training programs that bring forward core facilitative conditions through systematic skills training have been demonstrated to be most effective** (Carkhuff, 1971; Carkhuff and Berenson, 1967; Ivey and Authier, 1978; Larson, 1984).

Based on the positive statement of skills-training outcomes like the ones above, counseling skills have powerful potential to assist transforming leaders in producing positive changes in self, in others, and therefore in organizations.

Gain Self-Confidence and Self-Esteem

After managers had developed a minimum level of competency in counseling skills in my college and university courses, they reported in their evaluations that they felt a greater sense of calm, confidence, and self-esteem because they knew they could now really be of help to others in need without feeling they were "fumbling around in an area I don't know anything about." They also reported being glad to learn how to make effective referrals to professional helpers when appropriate to do so. We will review this skill at the end of the chapter. You will also have the opportunity to assess your knowledge of it.

Dispel Fears of Judgment and Earn Trust

By developing in your group, organization, or family a culture where people agree in advance to face problems openly and see one another as resources rather than judges, there can be a resultant increase in morale and performance. There are decreases in productivity and increases in absenteeism, staff turnover, and stress-related illnesses in situations where people are supervised in negative culture environments by overly task-oriented managers who miss out on the people side of the enterprise. When they fail to attend to the relationship dimensions of their supervisory or managerial roles, these managers contribute to a higher level of corporate stress. The same is true when children are put down and undervalued: They often rebel or even run away from home.

Problem Solving, Not People Blaming

Many, if not most, problems are a result of a person not having a more effective response to a given situation. In most cases, people can learn new ways of perceiving, thinking, and acting that will enable them to solve problems. This approach of defining a situation as a problem to be better faced through learning and development avoids people feeling like they are losers, "basket cases," or "unpromotable."

When Is Counseling Appropriate?

It is inappropriate to counsel people when trust has not been established, when there is no cause to counsel, and when there is no permission to counsel. Peters (1985) suggests counseling is most needed when an individual follower shows some or several of the following indicators:

1. Has a solid track record but is not performing
2. Has been educated and coached but without results
3. Asks for help in solving a personal problem
4. Is "stuck," unsure about how to proceed
5. Is having difficulty coping with organizational change
6. Cannot bounce back after a failure or loss

More specifically, counseling can be used constructively in several ways:

- **For improving performance:** It is appropriately used for leadership impact when co-workers, colleagues, subordinates, or learners are having personal difficulties that are interfering with their performance on a task or in relationships with others. Assisting them in specifying and taking ownership of their own problems in a problem situation is germane. Supporting or guiding them in setting realistic goals and taking effective action can also be a great help in keeping people, groups, and organizations "unblocked."

- **For supporting others:** The problem management process and counseling skills are also appropriately used with those seeking or in need of brief personal assistance, whether with those in your own family, with friends, or in work situations. These skills do not replace professional counseling or long-term psychotherapy when it is needed. By understanding and practicing the skills of counseling, you can better specify, manage, and solve problems yourself.
- **When you get permission to counsel:** Most people have to be willing to enter into a helpful type of communication with you and often will do so only because they trust you. They will be more likely to trust you if you have integrity and if you are genuine, respectful, empathic, and skilled. You must have people's permission to enter into a deeper level of communication with them, which can involve your seeing their personal difficulties that are interfering with their relationships at home or their performance at work.

Getting and Giving Mutual Commitment through Formalized Mentoring Relationships

As reported by Gray (1987), it is clear that a key set of skills identified as effective in the process of formalized mentoring are the skills of supporting and helping protégés through the stages of the problem management process. The mentor/protégé relationship is a further development and extension of the leader-helping-follower relationship, as there is agreement in advance to engage in problem management, personal growth, and professional development. This agreement avoids the often uncomfortable crossing the "line" into what is traditionally considered to be the personal territory of the follower. The importance and impact of developing a mentoring or consultative type of relationship with subordinates is discussed more fully in Chapter 7.

Example of a Major Problem and an Appropriate Counseling Intervention

The Assessment

The CEO in a large government department became aware of a serious stress problem among most of the managers in his region. They were ill more often than usual and did not deal well with problems he thought should have been dealt with swiftly and effectively; he was suspicious that there was a "hidden" problem.

The senior executive talked with some of the managers in an attempt to identify the causes of the problem, but not one of the managers wanted to come right out and say what the real problem was. The senior executive sought assistance from a consultant who interviewed him and the five top managers in the region. Aside from the fact that management positions had been trimmed due to budget cuts, it became clear from the interviews that all five managers felt afraid that their job security was threatened. This was because they had received virtually no feedback from the senior executive in over a year, had observed him firing two other managers for "confidential" reasons, and found his leadership style to be very authoritarian—he did a great deal of telling. He was distant (he held only one weekly meeting where he informed them of new developments and changes) and threatening (he yelled frequently and listened very little).

The Intervention

The consultant confidentially presented his findings in summary written form to the senior executive and asked him for his assessment of the validity of the findings. Surprisingly, he responded very openly and said he had been very domineering all of his life, had felt close to hardly anyone, and had alienated his wife and three children with his intimidating stance to the point that his wife had threatened to leave him. He asked for direct counseling assistance in overcoming this problem.

Then, with the CEO's permission, the consultant shifted into a supportive counseling mode—because he had the skills and ability to do so—and had several productive two-hour sessions with him. After these sessions, the consultant shifted back into the consultant "mode" so he and the CEO could plan and arrange a team development session. He and all twelve managers clarified the purpose and concrete goals of the team for the first time, clarifying each of their roles and the goals they were attempting to reach, and negotiated an appropriate and agreeable leadership style for the senior executive to use with this group of managers.

Transforming leaders can be "outside consultants," as in this case, or they can act as a flexible counselor–consultant–coach within their own organizations if they have the knowledge and skills to do so. It would have been preferable if the CEO himself had the personal and interpersonal development and counseling skills to deal with these problems.

The Results

The absenteeism levels dropped, two-way communication was established among nearly all members, problems were managed more effectively, goals were reached more swiftly, and the CEO sought continuing marriage and family counseling outside of the work setting. This is an unusually ideal series of events where almost everything worked out well, but without the *Transforming Leadership* intervention, the outcome otherwise have been far worse.

The main point in the above example is that the consultant was able to shift into a helpful, supportive, developmental mode to assist the senior executive to develop in a problem area that was causing distress among twelve managers—and their employees, their families, etc. If the senior executive had these skills from the beginning, the stress and morale problems would likely not have developed to the degree they did. The advantage is clear when communication and counseling skills are present within individual leaders, regardless of their role.

Counseling Skills Training: It's Becoming More Recognized

On the basis of extensive research on the impact of counseling in various environments, Carkhuff (1969) has stated two propositions that suggest counseling can be a potent tool for leaders. The first one states, "All interpersonal processes may have constructive or deteriorative consequences." This implies that management, leadership, psychotherapy, counseling, parenting, teaching, training, and all other significant relationships are not neutral and may affect people (and performance) "for better or for worse."

The second proposition is, "All effective interpersonal processes share a common core of conditions conducive to facilitative human experiences." Those leaders, managers, counselors, psychotherapists, teachers, parents, trainers, and significant others who are supportive, facilitative, and action motivating will be more effective than those leaders/helpers who are not.

These propositions—and the research on which they were based—roughly cut the edge of a new movement within counseling, one toward the education and training of a wide range of people in the skills that only counselors and therapists previously learned. The new focus on skills training for members external to the "expert" psychologist community marked the beginning of a new awareness of the need for facilitative interpersonal and counseling skills in many fields.

It used to be that managers appreciated the value of communication skills and that "communication" was—and often still is—the buzzword for management training. Now many managers want further training in how to deal with followers' deeper issues and with the problems in their own personal and professional lives. When a rich body of transferable knowledge and skills is available to managers to help them develop personal effectiveness and leadership potency, then why make use of it?

Since the late 1960s, this movement has taken these face-to-face human resource development skills into a wide range of environments, from elementary school classrooms to corporate boardrooms. Most colleges and universities now offer competency-based courses in interpersonal and problem management skills, but these skills-oriented courses are often limited to social work, counseling, corrections, and education departments. In more progressive business, law, and medical schools, systematic competency-based courses have begun to appear during the past ten to fifteen years.

In response to demands from the professional community, Ivey (1987) has developed a well-researched and effective helper training program that has been taken by a wide range of people—from executives, managers, doctors, social workers, nurses, social services workers, and corrections workers to parents and volunteers in community service agencies.

The need for all people to become good people-problem managers is on the increase as problems in our world increase in intensity and frequency. Transformative leaders can pass on some of these important skills to others they help and lead as we move toward the new millennium—perhaps when problem management will likely be most needed.

The Conditions that Facilitate Effective Problem Management

The following "core conditions" are found to be facilitative when present in the behaviors of leaders who are helpful:

1. **Genuineness:** The willingness and ability to be role-free, honest in a kind way, and open about oneself to others makes leaders more free to open up and explore themselves without fear of judgment.
2. **Empathy:** The willingness and ability to perceive others' world views, to see through others' eyes, and to communicate back to them an accurate understanding of their feelings and ideas encourages others to trust you and explore problems more deeply and specifically with you.
3. **Respect:** The willingness and ability to actively show that you highly value the people with whom you work—regardless of their present performance—is an important quality to communicate to others when you need their respect and participation in reaching goals.
4. **Specificity:** The willingness and ability to be highly specific when using language to describe others' views and experiences can help others increase the clarity of their understanding and solve problems more effectively.

Transforming Leadership and Counseling Are Integrally Linked

When leaders learn to apply counseling skills and the problem management process to themselves and in their work with others, they internalize a powerful set of knowledge and skills at a deep and personal level.

Good leaders understand the problem management process both cognitively, when analyzing an organizational problem, and affectively, when understanding the inner workings of self or another person. They understand the stages and steps in the process and are able to deal with their own personal and interpersonal problems. It is important that a leader's personal life be in good shape so that he or she is not distracted by internal unresolved emotional or interpersonal problems at home or at work. Good leaders are personal, interpersonal, and organizational problem solvers and managers, directly in their own lives.

Transforming leaders also help other people solve problems. If an employee facing a personal problem is not seeking outside help for it, which often is the case, a transforming leader is able to respond with genuine caring and effective counseling skills. This leader may be a school principal counseling a student, a teacher or counselor on staff, or a parent. The leader may also be an executive who intimately and quietly assists an executive teammate who is having marriage, family, drug, alcohol, or stress problems—problems typical to some executives.

Counseling skills are an integral part of *Transforming Leadership*'s problem management skill repertoire because some problems are simply inside individuals. Whether a leader is managing a problem within self or others or between self and others, mediating a conflict between others, doing a performance appraisal counseling interview or a career planning interview, or assisting a person or employee to overcome a personal difficulty, basic counseling/problem management skills are invaluable.

Style Shift Counseling: a Developmental Approach

Anderson (1987) has developed a theoretically integrated and developmentally based helper-style assessment and training instrument and leader's manual. While Style Shift Counseling integrates familiar concepts from a number of theoretical approaches, it is novel in its usage of them because assessment and intervention are presented from a developmental perspective. In this chapter, we will briefly discuss the *Developmental Level Assessment Grid*, which integrates developmental theories into a counseling tool for assessment, intervention planning, and tracking progress.

Style Shift Counseling is a systematic counseling plan that organizes psychotherapeutic methods into a working model that provides guidelines for the appropriate use of helping and developmental approaches and interventions. For the purposes of this book, a review of the basic assumptions of the approach is summarized as follows:

1. No one approach works with all people.
2. No one approach always works with the same person.

3. It can be difficult to decide which approach will work best.

4. It is difficult for most helpers to use more than one approach at one time or shift from one approach to another.

5. It can be easy to get discouraged and give up when working with failure-oriented or undeveloped people.

6. A more practical and flexible approach to counseling that would allow for client individuality and facilitate development and performance is needed.

7. A method for assessing a person's developmental readiness to receive help is needed, which would also allow for helper flexibility in shifting to fit people's helping style preferences and ability levels.

8. Helper training often acquaints students with a wide range of counseling theories, but seldom gives them a framework for the appropriate application of those theories and methods in a systematic and integrative manner.

Style Shift Counseling offers such a framework for the effective application of theory. The developmental theories and counseling approaches that form the basis of Style Shift Counseling can be examined in Anderson's (1987) leader's manual.

Understanding Developmental Levels for Situational Effectiveness

The following developmental levels are presented in order for you to gain additional understanding that different levels of functioning exist due to varying levels of development. This is a very important reality to observe in people because it will help you learn to adapt your methods and approach to the level of the person with whom you are dealing.

Level 1—Resistant or Undeveloped Individuals: People who function at level 1 are distinguished by low levels of individual readiness and willingness, which often result in their becoming detractors in the helping and problem-solving process. They are predominantly preoccupied with self, underdeveloped, reactionary, unaware of problems, and/or deny ownership of and responsibility for personal problems. People who function at this level sometimes attempt to escape reality by trying to live in fantasy.

Some examples of level 1 client populations might include preschool children, drug addicts, alcoholics, severely mentally handicapped or mentally ill people, autistic children, "hard-core" juvenile delinquents who are highly resistant, and potentially violent prisoners.

Level 2—Rational Individuals: People functioning at level 2 demonstrate some readiness and willingness to be helped, but usually at a cognitive level only.

They are willing to think and talk about behavior change but need help defining problems in concrete terms and often need follow-up support and reinforcement programs. These people can be good observers who notice many things but seldom take corrective action without support and follow-up from others.

Some examples of level 2 client populations might include underdeveloped teenagers, "soft-core" juvenile delinquents, immature high school and college/university students, underdeveloped adults in general, and mildly mentally handicapped or mentally ill people.

Level 3—Reflective Individuals: People who function at this level tend to seek self-understanding, are willing and able to explore internal personal problems that may interfere with performance, are often more willing to take ownership for personal problems and behaviors, have the ability to learn independently with occasional support, are often concerned about interpersonal development and problem solving, care about others as well as self, and are better able to make lasting commitment to change.

Some examples of level 3 clients might include mature teenagers, responsible adults, some college and university students, and personal development seekers in general. These are the people who make ideal employees and followers because they are ready and willing to learn and take responsibility for their own performance.

Level 4—Resourceful Individuals: People functioning at this level tend to be independent learners, good decision makers, and creative problem solvers. They are often able to teach others, have developed a self-responsible life style, and often are only in need of additional information, resources, additional perspectives. They seek and use expert consultative advice.

Some examples of level 4 clients might include successful professionals, creative homemakers, educators, plumbers, electricians, managers, artists, etc.

The Style Shift Counseling model provides a clear way to assess levels of development and functioning. Each level has corresponding helping styles, behaviors, and interventions that best match levels of readiness, ability, willingness, and preference. A foundational concept of the model is that it is the helper's responsibility to shift his or her counseling style to fit the client's willingness and ability to receive that approach. For a review of the literature that forms the base for this approach, see the leader's manual for *The Therapeutic Style Indicator* (Anderson, 1987).

The Developmental Level Assessment Grid

The assessment grid presented on page 168 can be a useful tool to do a quick assessment of a person's general level of functioning in relation to a specific task he or she is attempting to do or a task you may ask the individual to complete. The developmental level of a person is task specific. It includes the following dimensions: general functioning level, cognitive, affective, interpersonal, ego development, and needs hierarchy level. An example of a person with different levels of functioning in two areas of life is a prisoner doing a life sentence for molesting and murdering children and who is also an accomplished concert pianist. In controlling his abnormal sexual impulses, he is functioning at level 1, but he functions at level 4 on the piano.

The *Developmental Level Assessment Grid* shows that it is possible to estimate what levels of functioning or development a person moves in and out of depending on the situational context. Assessing a person's functioning level will assist you in planning the approach you should generally take in relation to a specific problem that individual is facing.

Four Intervention Styles

Four styles of intervention correspond to the four functioning levels. What we do to help people move ahead in their development must be more appropriate to their readiness and ability levels for our interventions in order to be more catalytic to their development. Four levels with appropriate strategies of intervention are listed in the chart of *Helping Tasks Appropriate to the Four Developmental Levels* on page 169.

These guidelines are meant to be a useful beginning—a starting place for you to learn to use developmental considerations when approaching people facing problems. If you are interested in further information in this area of using developmental considerations to plan your interventions, you can take courses in developmental psychology or counseling theory and practice or read Ivey's book (1986).

Facilitative Leaders Are Not Psychotherapists

The field of psychotherapy—not counseling or helping, as the terms are used in this chapter—includes those therapists who use predominantly one or two orientations of therapy and generally work with emotionally disturbed or mentally ill people over longer periods of time (months or years). Psychotherapists, at least in the beginning, tended to work with institutionalized patients, including both inpatients and outpatients. Helpers are people who have developed counseling skills and who work with members of the general public concerning issues of social adjustment and/or minor emotional and behavioral problem solving. The relationship is usually short term in comparison to psychotherapy and often is educationally related. Leaders can have a transforming impact without pretending to be psychotherapists.

Developmental Level Assessment Grid

Developmental Levels

Assessment Dimensions	Level 1 Resistant/ Undeveloped	Level 2 Reasonable	Level 3 Reflective	Level 4 Resourceful
General capability	Unable, unwilling, and/or insecure	Unable as yet, but willing	Able, but somewhat insecure	A degree of competence with creativity
Cognitive functioning (neo-Piagetian)	"Magical," unrealistic, or illogical thinking	Concrete, rational thinking— linear, simpler	Formal operational, self-reflective thinking— more complex	Dialectic, abstract, creative thinking
Ego/ affective functioning	Lacks inner controls or denies emotions— lacks self-worth and self-confidence	Begins responsible integration and controlled expression of emotion	Integrates own emotion with appropriate control and responds to others' emotions	Has integrated emotion and can understand and care for feelings
Inter-personal functioning	Self-oriented detractor	Self-oriented observer, interacts for self-interest	Minimally capable of intimacy and two-way communication	Seeks to develop relationships and to develop others
Conscious-ness level	Blind belief or imagining	Unvalidated rigid belief based on understanding of a system of belief	Validated belief based on examination of alternatives	Direct sense of "knowing" self and "life"

The differences between counseling and psychotherapy can be summarized in the following statement by Pietrofesa et al. (1984): "Counseling focuses more on developmental–educational–preventative concerns, whereas psychotherapy focuses more on remediative–adjustive–therapeutic concerns." *Transforming Leadership* focuses mainly on the developmental, educational, and preventive concerns.

Helping Tasks Appropriate to the Four Developmental Levels

Structure	Coach	Counsel	Consult
With Resistant People	**With Relational People**	**With Reflective People**	**With Resourceful People**
Design safe environments	Gain credibility	Establish rapport in relationship	Do problem management
Structure therapeutic environments	Clarify problem behavior	Explore problem situation with the person	Consult and give expert info
Control violent people with restraints	Clarify problem behavior	Assist person to take personal responsibility	Provide life-planning consultation
Provide constructive releases	Coach problem thinking	Specify internal problems of person	Personal development (advanced)
Provide positive reinforcement	Plan for improved behavior	Focus on problem which has good potential	Focus on new perspectives
Administer humane discipline	Confront irrational assumptions	Confront person's internal discrepancies	Challenge in a mutual way
Temporary isolation programs	Set action goals and programs	Mutually set action goals and programs	Explore goal options
Evaluate and communicate progress	Mutually evaluate progress	Mutually evaluate progress	Explore possible scenarios

Performance Appraisal and Discipline Interviews Require Facilitative Counseling Skills

The one situation where you do not need "permission" to shift into a counseling mode is when you are doing performance appraisals or reprimand interviews. Then, it is your role and job to assist employees in specifying problems that block performance and even job security. Your position gives you the right to specify problems, goals, and action plans with employees. Under these more difficult circumstances, it is even more important that you be positive, skilled, and wise in your approach.

Conclusion

You may be feeling somewhat intimidated by the complexity and difficulty of these skills, or you may be saying to yourself that you have been doing these things all along but did not have specific names for them. In either case, having gone through this material gives you the advantage of greater intentionality in the use of the skills—a perspective from which to evaluate your own counseling behavior and a model to use in planning your own professional development.

In Chapter 7, we will examine how to build upon the interpersonal, counseling, and problem management skills to intervene in a consultative role in groups or organizations to make a transforming impact. This is the most cognitively complex mode in which to function because you constantly and directly interface with dynamic human systems and organizations. Then in Chapter 8, we will examine the concepts of style, skill, and role shifting for greater appropriateness and effectiveness. That will complete Part II of the book, and we will then move into learning to use the tools of *Transforming Leadership*.

Research has established that basic counseling skills and core facilitative conditions are foundational to most successful relationships. Counseling roles and skills, as part of a leader's transforming tools, are not to be taken lightly. Neither are they to be neglected, avoided, or overused.

References

Anderson, T., *The Therapeutic Style Indicator,* Amherst, MA: Microtraining Associates, 1987.

Berenson, B. and K. Mitchell, *Confrontation for Better or Worse!* Amherst, MA: Human Resource Development Press, 1974.

Bergin, A.E., The evaluating of therapeutic outcomes, in *Handbook of Psychotherapy and Behavior Change,* A.E. Bergin and S.L. Garfield, Eds., New York: Wiley, 1971.

Bergin, A.E., Negative effects revisited: a reply, *Professional Psychology,* 11, 93–100, 1980.

Carkhuff, R., *Helping and Human Relations,* Vol. I and II, New York: Holt, Rinehart, & Winston, 1969.

Carkhuff, R.R. *The Development of Human Resources,* New York: Holt, Rinehart & Winston, 1971.

Carkhuff, R. and B. Berenson, *Beyond Counseling and Therapy,* New York: Holt, Rinehart & Winston, 1967.

Egan, G., *The Skilled Helper,* 4th ed., Monterey, CA: Brooks/Cole, 1990.

Egan, G., *The Skilled Helper,* 5th ed., Monterey, CA: Brooks/Cole, 1994.

Emrick, C.D., A review of psychologically oriented treatment in alcoholism, *Journal of Studies of Alcohol,* 36, 88–108, 1975.

Ivey, A., *Developmental Therapy,* San Francisco: Jossey-Bass, 1986.

Ivey, A., *Intentional Interviewing and Counseling,* 2nd ed., Monterey, CA: Brooks/Cole, 1987.

Ivey, A. and J. Authier, *Microcounseling: Innovations in Interviewing, Counseling, Psychotherapy, and Psychoeducation,* 2nd. ed., Springfield, IL: Charles C Thomas, 1978.

Janis, I., *Short-Term Counseling,* New Haven, CT: Yale, 1983.

Kouzes, J.M. and J. Posner, *The Leadership Challenge,* San Francisco: Jossey-Bass, 1988.

Kravetz, D., *The Human Resources Revolution,* San Francisco: Jossey-Bass, 1988.

Landman, J.T. and R.M. Dawes, Psychotherapy outcome: Smith and Glass' conclusions stand up under scrutiny, *American Psychologist,* 37, 504–516, 1982.

Larson, D., *Teaching Psychological Skills: Models for Giving Psychology Away,* Monterey, CA: Brooks/Cole, 1984.

Levitt, E.E., Psychotherapy with children: a further evaluation, *Behavior Research and Therapy,* 1, 45–51, 1963.

Marx, R., Improving management development through relapse prevention strategies, *Journal of Management Development,* 5(2), 27–40, 1986.

Mays, D.T. and C.M. Franks, Getting worse: psychotherapy or no treatment—the jury should still be out, *Professional Psychology,* 11, 78–92, 1980.

Orwin, R.G. and D.S. Cordray, Smith and Glass's psychotherapy conclusions need further probing: on Landman and Dawes' re-analysis, *American Psychologist,* 39, 71–72, 1984.

Peters, T., *A Passion for Excellence: The Leadership Difference,* New York: Random House, 1985, 367–368.

Pietrofesa, J.J., A. Hoffman, and H.H. Splete, *Counseling, An Introduction,* 2nd ed., Boston: Houghton Mifflin, 1984.

Smith, M.C. and G.V. Glass, Meta-analysis of psychotherapy outcome studies, *American Psychologist,* 32, 752–761, 1977.

Smith, M.C., G.V. Glass, and T.J. Miller, *The Benefits of Psychotherapy,* Baltimore: Johns Hopkins University Press, 1980.

Watson, D. and R. Tharpe, *Self-Directed Behavior,* 3rd. ed., Monterey, CA: Brooks/Cole, 1981.

7

The Skills of Team and Organization Development

There are three types of executives in the world. There are those who can get short-term results and haven't a clue where they're going to take the company in the future. Conversely, there are those who have a great ten-year plan but are going to be out of business in ten months. And then there are those who can get short-term results in conjunction with a vision for the future. These are the good ones. But they are in unbelievably short supply.

—Al Dunlap
Former Chairman of the *Scott Paper Company*

It [leadership] happens in the symphony, in the ballet, in the theater, in sports, and equally in business. It is easy to recognize and impossible to define. It is a mystique. It cannot be achieved without immense effort, training, and cooperation, but effort, training, and cooperation alone rarely create it. Some groups reach it consistently. Few can sustain it.

—Schlesinger, Eccles, and Gabarro (1983)

Introduction

As the police leader peruses the data on a computer screen or responds to an urgent page using a cellular phone, there may well be reflection back to not so many years ago when the police call box was the only form of communication available. As the leader struggles with the latest round of cost-cutting and budget restrictions, there may be reflection on the political "law and order" days of the 1970s when levels of government appeared to have endless reserves to fund policing. As the leader ponders the latest appellate court decisions on individual rights, there may be reflection on the repatriation of the Constitution in Canada and enshrinement of the Charter of Rights and Freedoms—an event that impacted policing more than any other event in recent history. As the leader prepares to attend the endless number of meetings with the local police board, police commission, government council, or community group, there may well be reflection back to the time when policing was shrouded behind the "blue veil" of autonomy. As the leader peruses the latest list of well-educated and culturally diverse police recruits, there may well be reflection to a time when hiring was influenced by nepotistic practices or simple physical stature. The "business" of policing has been swept up in technological and sociological revolutions unlike any other time in history.

Faced with this unprecedented social and political climate of fast, unsettling change, both police organizations and individual leaders tend to react in predictably self-defeating ways. They feel understaffed, underfunded, victimized, under increased public scrutiny, and overwhelmed and work compulsively harder, doing the same things, or try to pretend everything is fine. According to David Noer, author of *Breaking Free: A Prescription for Personal and Organization Change*: "The only response that works is the positive willingness to learn and meet change head-on. Learning to learn is the best tool for growing beyond the victim mentality."

In this chapter, you will be exposed to knowledge and a set of skills that address this need to face change head-on and learn to learn instead of being overwhelmed, entrenched, or retreating into denial. Although these skills are increasingly abstract and more difficult to learn and integrate into your work and life, they are also the most powerful in their potential to get larger scale results. They build on the knowledge and skills presented in previous chapters. By putting all these skills together into one process, you will have the capacity to become a more effective transformational change agent as you lead.

A transformational change agent is another descriptive phrase for a transforming leader: a leader who has developed the awareness, knowledge, skills, and caring to exercise a significant impact on the development of individuals, teams, and organizations to accomplish a premeditated purpose for the community. Leaders who can act as change agents are needed now and will be needed in the years to come. In policing, leaders will compete with other agencies for limited resources. Demands from better educated and more "worldly" employees will require innovative human resource practices. Those to whom police are sworn to serve will accept no less than "great performance," The payoff for all the hard work required to bring a team or organization to the point of high performance is described by Robert Quinn (1988): "The interface of big dreams, hard work, and successful outcomes is potent. The sensation that accompanies the phenomenon is a feeling of exhilaration." It is important, therefore, that leaders light the way toward **strategically managed change** and innovation. When they are acting in the consultative role, they not only ardently practice experimentation and problem solving but also develop the tendency in others to be more explorative and prudently adventuresome. Your organization will not become a learning organization until the leaders in it build a leadership organization of competent leaders who learn to lead change and protect and value people in the process. A police leadership organization can set its own course, based on a thorough assessment of the needs, concerns and problems of its members and community members. In order to take this kind of bold lead, however, it is imperative that leaders be equipped with not only the management skills that are required but the leadership skills as well. This chapter explores the skills of the consultative role and how they can impact positive change in policing organizations and their communities.

The following *Transforming Leadership* skills are discussed in this chapter:

TL Skill #37	Informal Assessment Skills	Page 196
TL Skill #38	Formal Assessment	Page 196
TL Skill #39	Problem Management Facilitation	Page 199
TL Skill #40	Need Clarification	Page 202
TL Skill #41	Readiness Checking	Page 203
TL Skill #42	Values Alignment	Page 205
TL Skill #43	Vision and Purpose Consensus Building	Page 208
TL Skill #44	Strategy Consensus Building	Page 212
TL Skill #45	Inplementation Planning	Page 216
TL Skill #46	Strategic Plan and Team Performance	Page 216
TL Skill #47	TQM Leadership	Page 219
TL Skill #48	Building Accountability	Page 221

This chapter is divided into two sections. In the first section, "An Overview of the Consulting Role," we will look at the nature of the consulting process. You may want to skip this part and go straight to the second, which deals specifically with the skills you feel are your weakest, but be sure to read the first section at some point. The overview and principles described in it are essential in helping you to be most effective in developing and mastering the complex skills in this skill set. In the second section, "Twelve Skills in the Consulting Role," you will explore the various skills appropriate to the consultative role.

In summary, although more difficult and abstract in nature, the knowledge and skills presented and assessed in this chapter are more powerful and far-reaching in their implications. As a communicator (Chapter 5), you saw that you have significant impact on the quality of relationships with others in an organization. In the role of counselor and problem manager (Chapter 6), you recognized that you can have specific preventative and remedial capabilities. In this chapter, by acting in the role of consultant, you will gain awareness and ability as a change agent to increase your impact with individuals, teams, and organizations. Then, in Chapter 8, we will explore application of the various skills to a wide range of settings and review the advantages of learning to shift style, skill, and role to maximize leadership effectiveness. First, however, let's examine the importance of intentionality when effecting the development of teams and organizations.

An Overview of the Consulting Role

Is This Stuff Too Academic?

Some police managers who have taken my courses at the Justice Institute have said at first glance, "This stuff is too academic for me to apply." One even said, "Don't you know that cops don't read!" I challenged them that leadership is complex and requires study, intense practice of skills, the development of competency, and the building of other leaders. I asked if any of them did not want to get on with that agenda. Some said they had not seen how leadership could work in policing—only management. Others said we should cut the B.S. and get on with the training. Still others stated that they were already implementing some of the skills in this chapter. I began talking about the necessity to believe that it is possible to make change happen on the inside as well as on the outside, or we should all just go home because leadership is just a pretentious joke. The first major point to be made in this chapter is that leadership must be intentional and conscious.

Intentionality: A Cornerstone of Transformation

The main difference between a professional and an amateur is that an amateur often uses the trial-and-error method whereas the professional has a backlog of knowledge and experience as an inner guidance system. The professional "knows" what he or she is doing. As an example, consider the brain surgeon who specifically analyzes the exact part of the brain to cut in a keenly refined surgical intervention. He or she does not put a surgical instrument to the patient's brain unless established procedures are being followed. Only a person with a skilled and experienced hand, with the highest level of training, would dare intervene in such an invasive way. Finally, such an operation would occur only in concert with constant monitoring of the patient's physical system during the surgery. In many cases today, the patient remains awake to report to the surgeon. Unfortunately, in policing there is not the same degree of control of the environment as in an operating room. The skills and knowledge required to succeed in leadership are more numerous and complex than those of a brain surgeon, and we shall see why as this chapter develops.

However, intentionality is a notion not foreign to police. One need only consider what happens when a police officer responds to a domestic dispute. There is a required intervention into one of the most private and personal of areas, that of an intimate relationship between two persons. Like the surgery, this is not a time for trial-and-error methods. The police officer is trained not only in the "hard" skills but also in how to interact in this situation with the utmost care, as if a counselor or family mediator. The police officer is trained to consider a unique balance—the objective intervention of law versus a need to intervene in a positive and directive manner that stabilizes rather than destabilizes the incident at hand and the family in the longer term. The intervention skills of the police officer will likely have an effect far beyond that moment in time.

In a like manner, intentionality is a direct factor in the nature of successful intelligence gathering and conducting criminal investigations. At all times, police investigators and project managers must consider not only intended goals of an investigation but also the vulnerabilities, weaknesses, and obstacles that must be managed simultaneously along the way. Without careful balance and consideration of the trappings in their path, the police team can suffer losses in investigative opportunity, breach of intelligence, or physical harm to team members. Furthermore, intervening to produce results in teams and organizations requires even greater care, caution, and planning than most other policing responsibilities. The outcomes of poor or good leadership can affect hundreds and even thousands of lives.

Building the Consultant Inside of the Police Leader

As a police leader becomes increasingly capable of being objective by seeing an overarching view of situations, there is greater opportunity for the strategic kind of intervention seen in the examples of the brain surgeon and the police officer responding to a domestic dispute. The manager becomes a leader with an objective perspective, able to "touch" teams or organizations with more precise effects to achieve agreed-upon and justifiable ends. Oddly enough, like successful brain surgery, good consultative leadership intervention seems very impersonal, removed, objective, or even aloof. Yet, at the same time, it is intimately personal, as it gets at the very nerve roots of teams and organizations and produces healing effects with developmental impact; alternatively, it is possible for a leader to exert a destructive or neutral effect. Certainly, however, every intervention has a consequence for better or for worse; even actions that seem neutral in their impact are rarely without consequence.

The leader in the consultative role can have many functions and "wears many hats"; each of these hats—which can be put on or taken off—has its own requisite set of skills. The consultative role may include such functions as catalyst, developer, researcher, strategizer, trainer, analyst, motivator, group or team facilitator, problem solver, organizational auditor, mentor, and coach. The range of consultative functions leaders can play in organizations is as varied as the organizations in which leader–consultants find themselves. In many instances, several roles are played at the same time. The skills involved in fulfilling these functions are the skills of *Transforming Leadership* outlined in Chapters 4 through 8. These skills are generic in that they are basic to, and flexible enough to fulfill the demands of, the various consultative roles and functions. For a more in-depth analysis of the various roles and skills consultants can use, see Menzel (1975). At this point, you might be saying to yourself, "No wonder so many leaders are inept. If it is this complex, maybe I will never really be very good at it. Maybe I should avoid leadership responsibility and just be a play-it-safe administrator and not try to make that much change happen." If you are saying these kinds of things to yourself, you need not be overly concerned. Many leaders develop into transforming leaders over time. Further examination of the roles and skills of leadership as outlined below will demystify things for you.

The Importance of Consultative Roles and Skills in Transforming Leadership

The following example illustrates the diversity of roles and stages that naturally occur in the course of a consultative intervention. Either a leader from outside an organization or team or someone on the inside can perform the behaviors outlined below. An example from a business I worked with will be used to illustrate this point.

During the initial assessment phase of a consulting contract, a vice-president and general manager of a manufacturing firm confided in me that he had "tried everything" to increase employee productivity (a problem not unknown to police). He had put pressure on managers and supervisors to up the production quotas, threatened to fire people if production did not improve, and tried to "pump" all the managers with "excellence" audio- and videotape programs. He even instituted a "Quality Is Free" program. In my interviews with his managers, supervisors, and frontline workers, however, it became clear that the company was experiencing what I call "excellence burnout." The workers were pushed to the limit of what they believed was reasonable for what they were receiving in return—and they weren't willing to give any more unless they could see where there would be "something in it" for them. As a team, they were, according to industry standards, functioning at only about 60 percent of the real potential of the equipment they had to work with—and the vice-president made sure they heard this on a daily basis. The more he pushed, the more they complained about being overworked and underpaid. As in some union situations, the people who did the work decided how much work was going to get done, and anyone who stepped out of line to perform above this norm would be disciplined by the work group members in very quiet and effective ways. Sound familiar?

Upon further investigation through interviews with frontline staff (the ones who directly control productivity), it became clear they were angry. This anger came across in virtually every interview. I listened carefully for many hours, without allowing the interviews to turn into sessions that could be seen as "encouraging whiners to whine," as the vice-president put it. During my thirty interviews, which included a random cross-section of frontline staff, I made a list of complaints and a list of what the staff appreciated about working for this company. Their complaints, in order of priority of importance, were as follows:

1. Nobody cares about us around here. Why should we put out for them? They won't even fix up the rest rooms, locker rooms, and lunchroom around here. They treat us like migrant workers. (This one complaint about the rest rooms and lunchroom was the most frequently mentioned of all complaints!)

2. They (management) say they care about us "people" and that "people are important to the company" but they really just talk the talk, but don't walk the walk. When Bill was seriously injured on the job, they just called an ambulance. Not one supervisor, manager, or executive in this place even visited him in the hospital for two weeks. That's sick. (The fact was that a manager did make a visit but then they had to go out of town for a week. Not all 197 staff members knew this.)

3. Some low performers connected to the president's family get to stick around and continue to "sluff off" their responsibilities on the job, and we have to pick up the slack. The boss plays favorites, and we aren't his favorites. (From the boss's view, this one person was an old-time friend

of the family, and out of kindness and respect for this person's age, the boss decided not to fire him.)

4. Good performance is not even noticed or rewarded around here. Why should I put out my best when we don't get raises even when production does go up for a whole month? If I put out more on the job, then I get pressure from most other workers to fall back into line so they don't have to work harder.

5. People can be fired at any time around here, and without enough of a chance to better their job performance. They fired three receptionists in the head office without even giving them any training to do the job. Other people have just disappeared around here and no one knows why. You wonder if you are next! (The boss did not fire the receptionists; they could not do the job, so he released them at the end of the probationary period. They could not keep up with a position around which two positions were later built, due to the complexity of that job role.)

6. I've been here for four years and I still don't know if I will ever get a promotion. I don't know if I'm seen as "just another worker" or not. I think I could do a good job as a supervisor, but I have taken the training, and no one will tell me if I should have any hope or not. I'm looking for another place to work where there is more opportunity. (This was remedied by including the issue of career path planning in the performance review process.)

7. Management continues to change its minds about how things should be done, doesn't involve any of us in making changes, and doesn't even ask us how the changes are working! (This problem area was been remedied through more effective team meetings.)

From these complaints, which I collated and summarized into a brief report, the vice-president and I arrived at the following understandings:

1. Managers who are not listened to and shown respect by the vice-president often do not listen to and show basic human decency and respect for their workers.

2. Managers demonstrated role, skill, and style rigidity in the traditional "old-school" fashion.

3. People will not work hard over the long haul for people they do not like.

4. The president of the company had set the "impersonal tone" of the corporate culture by treating previous executive and management staff with a "transistor" approach to management: If it doesn't work, unplug it, throw it away, and put another one in. There had been a 35 percent turnover in managers and supervisors during the past three years, when the company had really gotten off the ground, and a corresponding 40

percent (per year!) turnover in frontline staff. No one calculated the cost of training or hiring people who did not fit their jobs.

5. No one in management acted as an internal consultant to the organization. No one was reading the "nonrational" factors in the workplace to respond to things like fixing up the rest rooms and lunchrooms (at the least)—considered to be the major sign of disrespect by management toward the employees (who were 65 percent women).

During the last few years, I have worked as a consultant with several executive teams of police organizations. The above five conclusions fit all but one of those police organizations. It was clear from this list of complaints that I had discovered, in my role as external consultant, a series of problems that could be remedied if I could get the understanding and cooperation of the vice-president and the president. In a series of meetings and planning sessions, we came to the conclusion that some changes were needed in the way people treated people in this organization. Changes were immediately made to address the specific complaints of the workers. The rest rooms, locker rooms and lunchroom were upgraded. Human resource systems were put in place to find, hire, place, orient, and train the right people to fit the jobs available. Profit-sharing and employee recognition programs were evaluated and installed. The results were that the company increased its productivity significantly. The employees who stayed on accepted Crosby's Quality Is Free program, with the resulting effects of decreased turnover, decreased absenteeism, increased performance, and higher morale.

In police organizations, similar dynamics are at play, with some notable differences. Although police executives, managers, and supervisors have functional roles similar to the corporate example above, the rank and file are police officers with considerable power and responsibilities. They cannot be assigned the task of maintaining public peace as community leaders and role models and then be treated as subservient employees internally in the organization. A high level of cynicism can quickly envelope such an organization. If you ask police board members, community members, and employees, they will probably tell you that a consultative and cooperative leadership style is essential and preferred. Along with the ability to be participative, police leaders also have to make final decisions, call shots, and answer to internal investigative teams when things go wrong.

Leaders are often expected by those under them in the organizational hierarchy to act in a traditionally independent and decisive manner, but as we can see in the above example, in day-to-day affairs, they are more likely to need to use the skills of consulting with others in a collaborative manner. Ideally, all people involved would arrive at decisions for which there is team commitment and consensus. If the vice-president had been the internal consultant, it would have been ideal! "Team leadership," once called participative management, is becoming even more popular in policing because of the results achieved through team efforts in many business environments (Peters and Austin, 1985) and because such a style is appropriate when planning and implementing community policing initiatives.

In another important and innovative work, referred to above, Philip Crosby (1979) has developed a book and training program for managers called Qu*ality Is Free*. This program outlines many of the critical factors that appear to be required for organizational success. Although Crosby places importance on the role of managers as internal quality consultants to the organization (calling them "quality managers"), he does not provide a means for training those managers to become skilled transforming leaders. The success of his program rests on the existing competencies of those who implement it, however undeveloped they may be.

Crosby's focus on developing "management participation and attitude" is a good start, but if we want to go the full distance, we need to provide a means to develop the manager into a skilled and competent internal consultant to the organization. This manager will be a leader who can do more than manage a good system for quality or productivity improvement. It is preferable to develop the capacity within each manager to set up, monitor, and develop people, morale, and unique systems to facilitate an organization's success. But let's not sell Crosby short—he himself is an example of a transforming leader and does provide a tested system for improving quality and productivity. A program such as this is being developed in conjunction with the Royal Canadian Mounted Police, the Federal Law Enforcement Training Center and the International Association of Chiefs of Police: It is called "Every Officer a Leader." (To find out more about this specific program, contact one of the agencies listed above.) The skills in this program have about an 80 percent overlap with the skills in this book.

Interpersonal communication, counseling, problem management, and consultative skills are required to carry out successful team and organizational leadership and community leadership. Even though it is important for those exerting leadership influence to shift at times from a mutually communicative to a helpful counseling role, it is perhaps even more important that they be able to shift from the communicative and counseling roles to the consultative role.

The Nature of the Consultative Role

The consultative manner of dealing with people and problems is an innovative and creative one—a more "global" one. It is characterized by careful assessment and strategically planned action combined with empathy toward others. The consultative role also requires pronounced detachment and objectivity about the team and/or organizational context in which a team's problem is occurring. The skilled leader is capable of transforming people and organizations by moving from a mutual communication role to a counseling and problem management approach, and then shifting to a consultative role when the situation requires this type of "skill and role shifting" (discussed in depth in Chapter 8).

Many police leaders demonstrate role, skill, and style rigidity based on their role perception founded in cultural conditioning. This lack of receptivity and responsiveness to change and to people limits their potential to function effectively. This is attributable, at least in part, to the culture that develops within the organization. Police organizations are usually steeped in tradition and modeled unabashedly on the military. Each rank, each position, each function is carefully delineated and documented for all to see. In *The Leadership Challenge*, Kouzes and Posner describe how standard operating procedures are established and become the "habits" of the organization. These regulations and orders manifest themselves as cultural norms and present "especially potent barriers in times when innovation is required" (p. 65). These regulations and orders may be formalized even more through their inclusion in statutes such as police acts. This inclusion now gives these procedures the "force of law." Developing consultative awareness—objective awareness of the process and the context of people and events—and skills will assist you to be more effective in the consulting process. The multifaceted and flexible leader functions in this "fluid" manner, not closing down options or opportunities. He or she uses both intuition and rational calculation—theorizing, strategizing, and then taking action—only to reevaluate the impact and shift again.

This type of circular modus operandi is similar to what Tom Peters calls MBWA, or management by wandering around. There is a certain informal quality, a genuine and mutual—but expert—quality of leading in this manner. A consultative leader, while having the ultimate authority to make final decisions, can be more of a humble "servant," attempting to discover and meet needs to facilitate the accomplishment of agreed-upon goals while keeping the "big picture" in mind at the same time.

This image of leading while wandering around talking with people for a purpose captures the spirit of the "high-touch" but objective and result-oriented leader who can function in the consultative role and the other two roles—communicating and counseling—alternatively or in a blended fashion.

Difficulties in Developing Consultative Skills

As mentioned above, the consultative role, and the skills that are appropriate to it, are more difficult to develop than the communication and counseling skills, because they are more complex. They require a more comprehensive awareness of self, others, teams, technical know-how, and the organizational and environmental contexts involved in each changing situation.

When functioning in the consultative role, it is as though a part of yourself is reserved and "perched upon the roof," looking down into the context of the team or organizational setting in which events are taking place. When you shift into the consultative role, you practice seeing patterns in the environment, much as the eagle soars above—constantly "casing the territory," looking for movement, irregularities, or patterns below. In working with executive teams, the objective is to get them up on the "roof" of their organizations so that they can begin to work "on" the organization instead of just "in" it.

The consultative skills also require a strong base of communication and problem management skills to be most effective. Many people in positions of authority have few skills that they consciously and deliberately employ. Some people in positions of responsibility over others seem to have one or two sets of skills. Few managers seem to have developed all three sets of skills and integrated them into practice. Until the introduction of objective instruments such as assessment centers in recent years, the promotion systems within policing have tended to promote those seen as "worthy" by their superiors. As noted by Paul Whisenand and Fred Ferguson, "Typically, as small boys imitate their fathers, organizational members with leadership aspirations often strive to be like the leaders they admire." The deficiency of certain skills in police leaders often reflects a lack of skill development programming (which can include education, training, coaching, and longer term mentoring) for supervisors and managers. The practice of using competency-based development and selection models is not yet common but is very important. Therefore, it falls to the leader to take responsibility for recognizing deficiencies and take the appropriate steps in order to develop needed skills.

Even though the consultative level of awareness, and the skills that accompany it, are the most difficult to develop, they are perhaps the most influential. Therefore, they are potentially the most rewarding. The challenge for the transforming leader, functioning in the role of consultant, is to stay open, to deal with complexity, and **to be at least as complex as the complexity of the situation at hand requires**. The capacity to be complex and versatile is vital to both effective processing of information and creativity.

The consultative role includes such roles as listener, interviewer, observer, data collector, reporter, teacher, trainer, coach, educator, sponsor, support giver, advisor, challenger, mediator, mentor, advocate, researcher, problem solver, entrepreneur, and creator. All of these roles capture the complexity of leadership and require all three sets of skills in *Transforming Leadership*. With this complexity in mind, you now have an opportunity to familiarize yourself with the steps in the consulting process.

The Consulting Process

Egan (1988) outlines a practical systems-based model for changing and developing organizations that results in action that leads to valued outcomes:

1. **Current scenario:** Find out what is not going right or what is going wrong in terms of problems, unmet needs, unused resources, unmet challenges, and so forth.
2. **Preferred scenario:** Determine what the organization, organization unit, or project would look like if it were in better shape. A preferred scenario deals with what an organization needs and wants, not with how it is to be achieved.
3. **The plan for getting there:** Develop an action program or strategy for moving the current scenario to the preferred scenario. This stage deals with how results are to be accomplished. It projects action plans that lead to valued outcomes.

In Egan's model above, there is a systematic and objective attempt to gather and interpret relevant information for the purpose of gaining insight about the nature of a need, problem, or overlooked strength. This "diagnosis" provides the consultant with the information needed to design interventions that are more likely to result in improvement of performance, morale, and/or climate of a particular person, team, or organization.

There are many models of strategic planning, implementation, change management, and evaluation that could be referred to here, but I have distilled these into steps that may be appropriate for you to use when you attempt to facilitate positive change in your organization. Outlined on the following page is an amplified summary of the consulting process so that you can gain better perspective on the steps involved.

Step 1: Assessing of Needs, Wants, and Problems

During this first step, some kind of organizational needs assessment or organizational audit can fruitfully be undertaken. This needs, strengths, or problems audit can take the form of administering standardized questionnaires for organizational assessment, conducting interviews with key people in the organization, or a systems effectiveness analysis conducted by an outside specialist (i.e., an accountant, engineer, etc.). Although the identification of problems and unmet needs is essential, it is also critical to pinpoint strengths and unrealized potential and communicate them to all members of the organization. Assessing both the technical and relationship aspects of a problem is equally important.

The leader must ensure that the audit process provides the data relevant to activities that will follow. There may be a tendency to use existing audits such

Steps in the Consulting Process

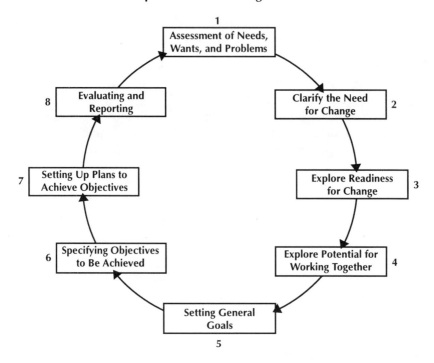

as those used for administrative reasons or legislated audits as required by police acts. The audit must be specifically designed to discover those areas, in terms of both strength and weakness, that will establish the basis for Step 2. An organizational survey called the *Organizational Assessment Review* can be used to do a comprehensive assessment of all areas of the organization. In diverse police organizations, this tool needs to be administered at an organizational level as well as within each activity stream. In policing, the entire audit or review process is under examination globally, with an eye toward making it more useful to policing agencies.

After appropriate assessments are conducted, and the facts are put on the table, it is important to help leaders and those they lead to understand and buy into the need for change.

Step 2: Clarifying the Need for Change in a Language Others Will Understand and Accept

The consulting process is very similar to the problem management process in that problem identification and specification is a most critical phase. The more specific and careful the definition of the problem or need, the greater the likelihood of a successful intervention.

There are both informal and formal ways of defining problems and assessing needs. Some informal ways include small group interviews with representatives from various parts of an organization, small group simulations of problem situations perceived to be occurring frequently in the organization, or anonymous surveys with key work teams, supervisors, and managers. More formal methods of data collection will be specifically explored below. The problem must be communicated to the team in such a way that leaders and members will be able to usefully identify it as a valid problem or need. The following scenario captures the danger of not acknowledging that there is a valid problem. During a review of the administrative procedures of a municipal police organization, a situation that created a service deficiency was discovered. Citizens' calls to the uniformed supervisors' office had apparently been handled poorly. Each area supervisor kept a separate filing (reference) system for his or her service area. If the supervisor for the area being queried was not on duty, the question often went unanswered because the recipient of the call did not know where to find the required information. The solution appeared very simple. To resolve the issue of information retrieval, a generic subject file index system was created so that the on-duty supervisor could access other supervisors' files. However, when presented at the supervisors' meeting, there was almost total rejection of the idea. The supervisors felt that their own administrative systems worked very well for them and saw no reason to change. Someone even went so far as to say, "Nobody has any business in my files," and that sentiment was supported. The issue of quality service outside of the respective areas had not been articulated, and therefore the supervisors' frame of reference for change was specific only to their own areas. In other words, they saw no need for change. A simple solution in another police agency was suggested and implemented. All citizen complaints were input into Maximizer (a client management software program), and all those authorized to examine complaint files received access codes to the networked program. Anyone with authority to access the files could do so immediately. This required some training on the part of a few dinosaur officers, but after they got used to the system, they preferred the instant, constantly updated files.

Even when people understand and accept the need for change, sometimes they are not necessarily ready to participate in making change happen.

Step 3: Exploring Readiness for Change

As each team or organization endeavors to make a positive difference, the change agent and the individuals involved must assess one another's willingness and ability to make the change happen successfully. There are many obstacles to effective change and many forces that can promote change effectively. Personal insecurity, interpersonal or interteam conflict, financial pressures, political forces, and timing can all affect a change attempt adversely. As noted by Scott Cunningham at the 1993 Society of Police Futurists Symposium, "Because of this conservative, status quo nature, law enforcement has evolved into an entity that is slow to change if not outright resistant. It is para-military by historical design, and bureaucratic partially due to its governmental aspects. These two characteristics further reduce the acceptance of innovation and change."

Recently, a police organization was experiencing difficulties with the implementation of its reengineered strategic plan. Members of the management team agreed that the plan was innovative and far superior to the previous one. It had been assumed that it would be embraced by most if not all of the organization. Sessions held by facilitators with members of the organization revealed a pervasive "tired of change" feeling. This feeling was the consequence of years of constant flux within the organization. There were continual staffing changes at the executive level. There were "new policing styles" and "new policing initiatives." The police officers simply wanted for a period of stability, something management apparently had not considered. The police officers expressed their discontent in the only way they thought would be effective—through resistance to the planning initiatives. When intervening in a consultative role, regardless of your role, it is a good idea to do a "force field analysis," identify all the possible blocks, and test to see if there are ways to remove some of the blocks before they hamper the effectiveness of change efforts.

For example, the principal of a large elementary school asked me to assist her in planning professional development activities for her teaching staff. During my mandatory interviews with some of the teachers, a few of them confided in me that nothing would likely be well received because the principal did not consult with the teachers about what they felt was needed in the coming year. She was just planning to mandate some training, the way some training programs are presented to frontline officers whether or not they really need it. The resentment was so strong that I confronted the principal with this perception. We thought through how we could overcome this block, and the principal decided to hold a meeting to specify the teachers' areas of need, using me as a planning facilitator.

The teachers appreciated that the principal had asked an outsider to facilitate staff consensus on training events because her communication and leadership styles were autocratic and authoritarian in nature. The principal did not want to change her management style because she feared losing some of the authority and control she thought she had established. However, because she was participating in the planning process as a mutual leader/member of the team, instead of the "boss," she was also able to get many of the things she wanted into the program.

Because people on her team who perceived themselves as mature or as deserving more respect resented being "bossed around" by her in the past, we had to overcome this block before a positive difference could be made. She had to develop some additional style versatility in dealing with these followers or delegate some leadership to one of them to get the results she wanted. She also had to learn basic interpersonal communication skills because she had never been trained in them. She grew up in a family that had taught her to be the way she was.

The principal subsequently used the same consultative role that she saw me use to solve two other problems that arose in her teaching team—with good results. Her performance was under review that year by her school district's director of instruction, and she was greatly relieved by the increasingly positive evaluations she was receiving from her teachers. Her readiness for change, inspired by her observations of how the consultative process can solve problems without losing authority, increased as time went by. This resulted in the teachers changing their perceptions of and approaches with her, much to the relief of everyone. She made small changes that resulted in big payoffs.

Today, in policing, as in many corporations, the readiness for change within the membership and the stark reality that change is being rapidly instituted because of budget cuts, shortfalls, and restructuring of organizational priorities creates a potentially severe imbalance. It is incumbent on police executives and managers to locate and equip consultative "change agents" within the organization (regardless of rank or position) and employ their positive energies and skills. When these leaders form a leadership team that has as its purpose to initiate planned change, it can be very powerful.

Step 4: Exploring the Potential for Working Together in Concert

A good working relationship is imperative if you are to make the positive difference you would like to make. Establishing bonds of common values, beliefs, or approaches can help in developing trust with those with whom you work. Being open about differences can also be important when it can prevent future gaps in expectations and clashes in values or styles, and that can allow you an opportunity to work through to agreement about how you will deal with problems and resolve the conflicts that will inevitably emerge. The *Values Preference Indicator* and the *Personal Style Indicator* can be used to help team members understand their strengths and accept their differences.

When expectations are not clear, anxiety levels often escalate and arational, even irrational, behavior can result. One of the ways to manage arationality is to be clear about what you will not do and what you can be expected to do. Then see how much support you can get from the people with whom you are working on key issues. Not only can you test to see how much potential compatibility or conflict there is among three or more people, but you can also communicate a certain degree of willingness to respect the values and approaches of others involved in the change effort. Establishing clear and agreed-upon values and procedures in any group can help create compatibility in your work relationships with others.

I was asked to accept an eight-month contract as an organization development consultant with a juvenile correctional facility. Prior to beginning this contract, I became aware that the administrator was perceived by most supervisors and workers as a "spineless jellyfish"; I told this man there was a lot of evidence from initial surveys and interviews that his behavior was being perceived as inconsistent. He was also seen as too easily pressured by various kids or staff to change his mind on key issues. I informed the administrator that this behavior was causing specific problems, including undermining the behavior-modification reward system. There were also morale problems among the staff and kids due to his being seen as "playing favorites"—and financial problems because he had approved spending by one department and left little money in the bank for some of the other programs.

I decided to work on getting a commitment from him that he would meet weekly with members of his senior staff and consult with them about the likely consequences of various actions before he made major decisions that would affect them. Otherwise, I told him, I was doubtful that my presence as a consultant would make a positive difference. He agreed to the consultative sessions, possibly he hated saying no. Actually, he was greatly relieved to get some assistance in making some of the more difficult management decisions. He had never received training in leadership or management, and as a result of our meetings together, he decided to quit his position and become a counselor in an alcohol and drug treatment program. He realized that the administrative role really was not for him. We developed a good working relationship over the eight months of the contract. Without developing these clear working agreements with him and his staff, my efforts to unblock and develop this organization would likely have been entirely foiled.

Step 5: Setting General Goals

A parallel to this step in the counseling role outlined in the previous chapter would be the goal-setting step. In this phase of the process, agreement is reached with others about what achievements or accomplishments are being attempted. These goals need to be stated concretely enough—and usually in writing, as much as most people resist doing so—so that their attainment can actually be observed and measured. General goals are stated as things we hope for: "We want to improve our hiring process," or "We want to use time more wisely in our meetings." It is important to come to consensus about general goals before moving on to seek consensus among members of a work group or team. Otherwise, you may be attempting to set more specific objectives to be achieved when there is no real commitment to do so. These goals can become an important part of a written contract, if this more formal type of agreement is appropriate ("If it isn't written, it doesn't exist").

Exploration by the police leader may reveal that most staff has relegated the concept of goal setting to executive offices and boardrooms. Planning and its associated activities have traditionally been the domain of the "executive row." Police leaders must communicate and promote the concept of conjoined goal-setting activities that lead to ownership and effective implementation. The concept of consensus among members of a work group must be articulated, and real consensus must be reached if optimum performance is to be achieved. You may have to spend time assisting them in establishing an adequate knowledge base in the area of planning so that they fully understand each phase of the process and are prepared to participate in reaching consensus. The police leader must also ensure that they do not succumb to the idea of setting "official" goals to satisfy external influences such as police boards, commissions, or other political interests. These external goals can often be important as well but must be owned by those who will implement them if real progress toward reaching them is to be achieved.

In some police organizations, goal setting and management has recently been delegated to specific unit-manager levels in such areas as finance. An individual manager has the opportunity and responsibility to use financial spread sheets in order to project costs (based on anticipated activities) and then manage the process to stay within the projected financial guidelines. However, it is easy for an organization to reward the poor performer and punish the good manager. A manager who is not good at projecting and implementing his or her own unit resources can find himself or herself in a deficit position before the year's end. A common way of dealing with this in the past was to "borrow" funds from other units and activity areas to compensate, usually from good managers who were meeting or exceeding their targets and goals. Training in goal setting, establishing, and implementing is essential.

Step 6: Specifying Objectives to Be Achieved: A Practical View of a Preferred Future

For most people busy "doing the "job"—whether that job is leadership at home, in a classroom, a school, a hospital ward, a company, the military, or law enforcement, there is some reluctance to take the time to do careful planning. It takes time and stretching one's imagination. It is hard work to be specific with language! It is risky to announce to others that you have a plan, because then you will be asked whether or not your plan worked. Therefore, people often just go along with the status quo; they don't rock the boat or set even slightly risky goals that could later prove to be embarrassing if they are not achieved. Some of the early attempts to set objectives in policing produced inadequate results. Organizations struggled with such concepts as subjective versus objective evaluations. Because police organizations were traditionally judged on a statistical basis, there was a tendency to demand that everything be objectively quantified. By creating this demand, there was a need to create the instruments for gathering the statistical data—a task for which most police organizations were ill prepared. Still other police managers believed that organizational activities were highly influenced by factors outside of police control, such as calls for service. How can the organization plan activities when controlled by external forces? This "reactive mentality" tended to support the status quo. An example from another environment is used here to demonstrate the importance of being specific and concrete in setting objectives and planning action steps.

The director of a large church youth group asked me if I could assist him in developing the team of people involved in working with about 150 youths in the church. The staff consisted of one full-time director, three paid part-timeers, and twenty-five adult volunteers. The youth program had been going along steadily for about seven years with the same director, but no long-range planning or annual goal setting had taken place at the team level. It was "top-down" leadership, where the director, to this point, had taken most of the responsibility for structuring activities and motivating the youths, with other volunteer leaders following along ,whether or not they liked the way things were going. They did not want to confront the leader's authority because they valued showing respect to a leader by not "disagreeing" with him or her. As the church became larger, the need for more staff and more diverse programs became evident.

One primary problem became clear. No one had systematically determined what the needs and wants were from the point of view of the youths, and no one had assessed the needs, skills, and abilities of the staff or twenty-five volunteers. They were hired or accepted as volunteers based on their personal qualities and their willingness to serve. This scenario is typical of most volunteer groups and committees, where one leader takes most of the responsibility and the followers are not specifically qualified for the roles they are assuming. I spent one day with the four leaders and their spouses (they worked together as couples) to decide what they would like to do to strengthen their team effectiveness and the impact of their work with the youths in their church and in their community. With my assistance in wording their objective statements, they wrote out the following:

1. We will conduct an informal needs assessment (personal interviews) of the youth in our church and community and also use a more formal questionnaire approach to see how well the two match.
2. We will create a comprehensive mission, goals, and programs statement based upon the above needs assessment of youth in our church and community.
3. We will write a proposal to the board that will include an outline of our departmental statements and a budget that will outline the financial requirements to achieve our goals; this proposal will be given to the board on May 1 for its consideration.
4. We will involve youth in the decision-making process about programs we are planning for them in the future by getting their ideas and input at planning meetings we schedule each month.
5. We will engage in staff training for ourselves when we determine areas of need and will assess the training needs of our twenty-five volunteers, and provide training for them, and we will begin both training programs in June.
6. We will discover and appreciate one another's strengths and create job descriptions for ourselves that reflect our individual abilities. We will communicate these job descriptions to one another and review their appropriateness every six months.
7. We will bring in people external to our church to assist in meeting needs we don't have the expertise to meet, i.e., career and life planning seminar for senior high and college-age youth, self-esteem seminar for junior and senior high youth, premarital and marriage seminars for those who marry young. We will provide longer term professional counseling for youth who have emotional and family problems.

The group members needed assistance in specifying their objectives because they clearly would not have put them together in this complete and specific way without external assistance. It would have been best, however, if someone within the church organization had consultative knowledge and skills to accomplish this end without external consultation. The board was so impressed with the clarity of this department's plans that it funded all of the proposals without reservation and promoted the youth pastor to assistant pastor. In the past two years, I assisted two police chiefs in implementing a similar process with positive results.

Step 7: Setting Up Plans to Achieve Objectives

Strategic planning is 5 percent of the equation for success, and implementation is the other 95 percent. After objectives have been set with the agreement of those involved, you will be in a much better position to plan and implement the objectives in a step-by-step fashion, with time lines for implementation. You will also be more likely to assign the most appropriate people to do various parts of the task if you have specified exactly what needs to be done. However, history has shown that "appropriate" is a term that is subject to interpretation. To implement the organization's plan, one police agency executive directed section managers to select the "appropriate" person to present the plan and facilitate strategy development. One of the managers, with good intentions, saw this as an opportunity for a subordinate to "be seen" just prior to a promotion opportunity. Of little weight in the choice was the fact that the soon-to-be champion of the plan had virtually no knowledge of the strategic planning process and very little knowledge of the organization's plan. Members of the implementation team have to be ready, willing, and capable! Plan implementation must be stated in terms of action to be taken and accomplishments to be achieved so that the team can achieve its goals and purpose within specified time frames.

The importance of this step cannot be overstated. Many police organizations with well-developed plans have stumbled at this stage. It is estimated that most police departments, if they even have a strategic plan, have less than a 30 percent implementation rate. All too often, strategic plans end up as SPOTS (strategic plan on the top shelves). The cause of this poor performance can be traced to an inordinate commitment of resources in the planning stage at the senior management level. It was assumed that a quality plan would automatically result in quality implementation. This left little in the way of resources to ensure effective plan implementation and often resulted in the "big binder" syndrome—a thick, well-written, academic document that was read by few and implemented by none. Success was seen as the beautifully bound document proudly displayed on bookshelves and tables and presented to anyone who asks, "Do you have a strategic plan?" Care must be taken to select (and/or develop) those people within the organization who possess the skills and competencies necessary to facilitate the implementation process. If required, the organization must be prepared to commit to the development of people so they can provide the support and guidance during the implementation process. Only a plan that shows consistent and regular efforts (at least a monthly review of progress meeting) toward implementation, with deliverables, time lines, responsible people, and evaluation of progress, has a high chance of success.

Step 8: Evaluating and Reporting the Impact of Your Intervention

It is important to assess the impact of your interventions as you intervene at set intervals during a project. Normally, some type of assessment would be done after the first session, another half way through, another two-thirds of the way through, and one at the end. This regular evaluation will assist you in setting a new course, as your planned intervention will need some fine-tuning to hit the mark perfectly .

When you have determined that there is a problem, you will need to communicate that challenge to the group and give members an opportunity to suggest alternative solutions. These suggestions can be integrated into an overall plan for improving their approach or strategies. You will win the respect of group members when you can "head problems off at the pass," rather than ignoring or avoiding them. It is far better to "correct course" than to stick to the plan and run the ship aground.

One example of how this type of evaluation can be effective is to use the same survey both before and after a time of planned change. The *Organizational Assessment Review* can be used to assess the current state of an organization and to measure change after a specified period of time. Also, the strategic planning and implementation document itself can act as a reference point to determine how well the plan has been implemented, because you can determine the extent to which you have achieved what you intended.

Another illustration of this type of evaluation and reporting is in my own practice teaching at the university level. At the beginning of each session, I hand out three-by-five-inch file cards to all the students and ask them to jot down on one side what worked, and on the other side what did not work in the class, with suggestions for improvements. When I read all thirty or forty cards, I know how to better approach the class the next session. I tell the students what I have learned from their feedback and thereby model being open to suggestions and criticisms. By opening up this simple channel of evaluative communication between myself and the students in my classes, I have prevented many problems from developing and have received many exciting ideas from students. My teaching evaluations have improved over the years as a result of this practice, and so has my teaching effectiveness. I suggested to one police chief that he request similar and frequent feedback from members of his management team. He got the feedback—and learned a great deal!

Twelve Skills in the Consulting Role

The skills in this part of the chapter are summarized and explained in concrete terms so that you can gain insight into what is required to perform each one. Reading about these skills often is not enough, however. As with the communication and counseling problem management skills, to develop these skills to their fullest, you will need a coach or a mentor or at least some kind of competency-based training (where you get feedback about how well you are performing a skill) specific to your areas of need.

TL Skill #37. Informal Assessment Skills:
Walking Around Talking with People

This area of skill involves using all the communication skills outlined in Chapter 5. This requires you to informally engage in assessing and reporting needs, wants, fears, problems, opportunities, or threats in several different ways. It can be done in a casual way by walking around talking to people, or it can be done by scheduling one-on-one interviews over coffee with key people, to gain insight into their concerns or to learn their perceptions about issues you have determined are important. Good leaders stay in touch with the people implementing the team's strategies and help those in the trenches, on a daily or weekly basis, to prevent and manage problems. This kind of leadership cannot be done without informal interviewing on an ongoing basis. Some of the very best information I have received has been from this type of "grapevine" communication. After you gather information, you can introduce it in a team or executive leadership meeting for further consideration and discussion.

Consider how often a police executive goes on a ride-along with a patrol officer on the graveyard shift to observe his or her working environment and challenges. On one ride-along, a patrol officer said that he did not go into a certain part of town at night. The reason he gave was a shortage of resources: he would most certainly see criminal activity in that part of town, which would commit his time, thus making him unavailable to respond to calls.

I am reminded of a psychology professor who told me about his experience in trying to research morale issues when he was in the army. His team designed questionnaires, did surveys, collected data, and crunched numbers, yet the team members felt they were not in touch with what was going on with the more than two thousand officers in their charge. Finally, after months of investigation, the four researchers decided to go out and talk with the people face to face. The information they collected made the "data" come alive with meaning. This has also been true in my own experience. It is important to talk with a cross-section of the people who do the work and who have the concerns. This is the *qualitative* aspect of researching needs, concerns, or problems. These individuals can design and implement solutions to many of their own problems, when they come up with the solutions themselves. People implement ideas they help create. This qualitative approach to assessing and pinpointing problems and needs adds depth to otherwise dry but informative quantitative approaches.

TL Skill #38. Formal Assessment:
Research, Interviewing, and Reporting

All too often, police agencies are "surveyed to death" and the results of the surveys are not utilized. University students and professors want to do research in their areas of interest without asking police leaders what information they need to put on the table in order to make more informed decisions. Every policing agency needs to have research on its agenda and needs to have a specific committee to deal with it. Larger police forces have their own research divisions, but smaller departments often have nothing and even keep their own statistics in a haphazard manner due to lack of technology, process, and procedure for gathering data and recording and reporting statistics.

This skill area is critical to the success of the change process, because without careful and accurate assessment of needs, wants, and problems in a team, organization, or community, there can be little or no effective intervention. To make a positive difference, goals must to be accurately and specifically stated and programs implemented so that targeted problems are solved and perceived -needs are met. The following are examples of such information gathering:

1. A leader does a survey of what a work group or team members would most like to do during a given session.
2. A teacher assesses the reading levels of students to plan individually tailored reading programs.
3. A manager or supervisor does a job satisfaction survey each week to determine problem areas and takes appropriate action based on feedback.
4. A salesman reviews monthly data by geographic sales area to better target achievement of next month's sales objectives.
5. A consultant assesses the factors related to absenteeism in a large company in an attempt to alleviate the problem and increase overall productivity.
6. A university president conducts an institutional self-study to determine areas of effectiveness and potential problems or to identify unmet needs.
7. A parent has a family meeting to determine needs, problems, and wants and creates some strategies for meeting them.
8. A consulting accountant provides cash flow or sales projections to plan effectively for future capital expenditures or project sales or for the results needed to achieve a business goal.
9. A police manager accompanies patrol officers on duty to make sure that executive-level decisions take into account those factors that will influence frontline workers.
10. A police agency conducts a crime analysis survey in order to determine the type of resources to allocate to various parts of the city.

The information-gathering and interpreting process follows a number of steps adapted from Kilmer (1978), as outlined below:

1. Clarify the purpose of gathering information so that the information will assist people to make better decisions in specific areas.
2. Formulate expected results so that you can compare the real results with the expected results.
3. Use proper assessment tools, surveys, interviews, questionnaires, or tests so that the information you collect will be focused and useful.
4. Sample all or a representative selection of the members of a team or organization so that you can have confidence that your results reflect the needs or problems of the whole team.
5. Analyze and interpret the information so that the results can be used to make better decisions about solving problems or meeting needs.
6. Summarize and present the results of the information gathering in a way others can understand and use them.
7. Make decisions based on careful assessments instead of "hunches," intuition, "gut feelings," opinions of team members, or "revelations."

The data-gathering process can be assisted by using previously validated instruments or questionnaires appropriate to your environment. However, specific ones that meet your exact needs may not be easy to come by, and you may have to create your own. Often, it is more effective to design the key questions for an interview or a questionnaire because you can then be somewhat more assured that the questions asked are appropriately focused and address real concerns.

A cautionary note is warranted about administering questionnaires or conducting surveys in an organization. Before designing or administering various measures, first discover if the people responding to the questionnaire or survey will perceive it as worthy of their response. Sometimes people are "surveyed out," or they have no confidence that spending their time responding to a survey will result in any change they view as positive.

General Guidelines to Use for Considering the Various Approaches to Gathering Information

Small Groups (four to fifteen): If the members are relatively mature, simply ask them what you want to know, using direct and pointed questions that require a yes or no answer, or ask open-ended questions that can be answered in any way the respondents choose. With a group of shy teenagers or slightly paranoid adults, you might ask them to write down their concerns anonymously and place the notes in a "hat" for later reading and response.

Larger Groups (sixteen to sixty): Use a simple questionnaire that can be developed with the assistance of a few key members in touch with the general concerns of the group. Keep the size of the questionnaire to one or two pages each time you administer it, and make the response time no longer than just a few minutes, to increase the response rate. Ask both closed and open questions, as appropriate. Alternatively, ask each of the key people in the group eato ch approach five members with the same questions. Ask the key people to record the answers and report back to the group leader when the interviews are complete.

Large Groups (sixty to two hundred): Groups of this size can be approached in a similar manner but can often be more effectively assessed by using a more involved and carefully designed questionnaire that, ideally, can be scored by computer. For a group this large, the time involved in collecting the data and collating it into meaningful interpretation can be unruly. It is easier if you have access to a computerized organizational assessment program, such as Campbell's Organizational Survey, or if you know how to use a software program such as Statistical Program for the Social Sciences (SPSS).

Groups Larger than Two Hundred: These groups require high-tech research methods or the time and expense of distribution, collection, collation, interpretation, and presentation of the data becomes unwieldy. As a part of the assessment skill area, in more advanced assessment projects, you may need to develop these research and statistical skills yourself. Questionnaire development and scoring software programs can make many of these more difficult tasks quite "user friendly." A working knowledge of the research process and statistical analysis would be an asset in providing you with a greater sense of confidence that the information you have collected is representative of your total population and not a biased sample. You can take courses in research tests and measurements and in statistics, or you can call on those more experienced in this area if you need assistance in developing these skills. You can also delegate this task to qualified researchers if you are in a position to do so; this can be especially important if the research you are doing requires high levels of confidentiality or impartiality by the investigating parties. In politically sensitive situations, you do not want to be accused of being a biased researcher, data collector, or reporter.

TL Skill #39. Problem Management Facilitation: Leading Teams Through Resistance to Change

This skill of leading people through resistance to change is required to lay the groundwork for change. People do not want to change simply because there is a need for change. People must understand the need for change, the benefits and downsides of change, and what is required of them, and they want to know how their future will look after the change has taken place. Without support, many people become anxious, negative, and unproductive—until they can embrace a clear vision of how change can result in a preferred future. Your job is to use your problem management skills to uncover the "shadow side" of resistance to change, help people understand why changes must be made, get them to see what's in it for them if they help you, and get them to enlist in making necessary change happen. Some theorists call this the "unfreezing" stage of change management, where people get help to become unstuck from old ways of thinking and acting. Most people need help and encouragement to move "out of the box" of what is familiar and step into new territory.

For example, a new police chief was hired in a mid-sized community. He was selected from among many qualified candidates because of his track record of expertise as a leader and a manager. He was a top-flight commander of a large police force and a visionary leader of people. He came to the new police force only to find that most of the members of his management team were not prepared as leaders. They were doing fairly well at managing the status quo but were not innovative leaders or builders of high-impact teams. Their credibility in the ranks ranged from moderate to low. Their motivation levels ranged from medium to low. Several were nearing retirement. After I met with them as a team, the chief confided in me that he could not see a way to build the organization and meet community needs with these team members, yet he felt committed to honor their years of loyal service and contribution to the community. I coached him to be forthright with them by showing them the new job descriptions that he and I had developed for the executive team roles. They could see that they did not have many of the people skills, technical skills, and team skills that would be required to do the new job. They also did not want to take the necessary training to make the transition into the new job roles.

I conducted career and life-planning sessions with the members of the management team. Two of them decided to get additional leadership training and continue on modified management roles, two took early retirement, and one was subsequently fired for harassment of a subordinate officer. We had to prepare these senior officers for change, honor their years of service, and sensitively work through career or retirement solutions that were suitable to each of them. (Compare this humane approach to another police agency where "heads rolled" when the chief "cleaned house.") As a result of these changes, the new chief was able to select and build a competent team with executive members who had high levels of credibility, competency, and motivation. The chief had a responsibility to the community to put a highly competent leadership team in place even though it was a difficult challenge and not an easy transition for anyone. Most chiefs would likely have tolerated the status quo. This chief proved himself to be a transforming leader.

In another example, I worked with a CEO to administer an *Organizational Assessment Review* to evaluate how his $50 million company was doing in twelve areas of performance. I also assessed his own strengths, talents, gifts, personal vision, and life goals in light of what the company needed from a CEO during the current period of rapid growth.

When the CEO looked over the results of the survey, he decided to change his role to that of a more visionary president and to bring in outside professionals to oversee the operations. Previously, his responsibility included overseeing the operational aspects of the company with a team of managers who had come up through the ranks. A few had been with the company for thirty-five years. None of the managers wanted any "new blood" from the outside because each felt deserving of the title of vice-president and all were threatened by the unknown executive vice-president and general manager who could hold them accountable to new standards. To facilitate the organization's leaders through this impasse toward change, I suggested to the president, and he agreed, that I could help him implement the following steps to deal with the resistance to change:

1. Meet with the existing managers to share the results of the *Organizational Assessment Review* (available from Strategia at http:// www.strategia.com or from Consulting Resource Group at http:// www.crgleader.com) and the CEO's newly clarified role and goals.
2. Assess what they feel is needed for the organization to move ahead.
3. Ask them to catalogue their own strengths, talents, and motivations in helping move the organization from an entrepreneurially run company to a professionally run business.
4. Inform them that the decision has been made to hire an experienced and previously successful vice-president of operations. The plan is to advertise and find a person in whom most managers can have confidence and with whom they can work agreeably.
5. Involve them in the final interviews to select the person who will, in a practical sense, become their new day-to-day leader.
6. Allow any of them to apply for the job if they feel their expertise and qualifications surpass those of the final short list of applicants.

After the meeting, the managers agreed on the desirability of at least looking for someone outside the company who might be the best person to lead the organization into its next stage of development. Of course, it was difficult for them to disagree with the CEO, but they all had the opportunity to process how they felt about the proposed change. They were relieved to learn that they would have a say in of selecting the new leader of operations and felt a sense of excitement about the CEO's commitment to learn and move ahead into a preferred future for the organization.

TL Skill #40. Need Clarification:
Clarifying the Need for Change

Before people are really willing to embrace change, they have to be convinced it is truly necessary. None of us wants to change just for the sake of change. It takes work, understanding, patience, and persistence to get key team leaders to the point where their heads and hearts are committed to change. Sometimes people's heads are convinced, but their hearts are reserved or even resistant.

The managers in the example above still did not fully buy into the need for the impending changes in the organization or their job roles. In particular, two of them were very negative and began bad-mouthing the whole venture—blaming me and the CEO for "messing up what has worked for so long." The CEO and I discussed this lack of enlistment to move ahead into a preferred future, as they saw it. The following happened as a result of our discussion:

1. We had another team meeting with the managers.
2. We reviewed the results of the *Organizational Assessment Review*. This helped the managers pinpoint some changes they wanted to improve things from their points of view, and the CEO agreed to help them move ahead with those changes.
3. The managers reported that they liked these new meetings where their concerns and views were heard and where response was immediate with decisions and action.
4. The CEO further explained his own personal need to move out of the role of operational overseer into the role of ambassador for foreign projects, vision-caster, political figurehead in negotiation sessions, etc.
5. He also told the managers he could not make the best use of his time and talents if he continued in his current role. They agreed with him that he was not the best operational manager.
6. I explained the differences between an entrepreneurial-style organization and a professionally run one, and the "lights began to go on" in terms of the benefits of this difference. The managers agreed that they wanted to see the organization move ahead from $50 million to $100 million in the next few years.
7. The managers agreed that they too needed some changes in their roles. They suggested hiring a vice-president of human resources, in addition to the vice-president of operations, so they could get on what they each did best in a less distracted way. They also agreed that the overall profitability of the company would most likely increase (beyond the cost of the salary for the position) as a result of hiring a vice-president with a proven track record.

The managers finally got the message that making planned change happen could benefit them and that they could trust it and the CEO—and even me, an external consultant. They started to "gel" as a team in a new way. But their full enlistment and wholehearted commitment were not yet secured. More is required, as you will see when we explore the next skill in this leadership skill set.

TL Skill #41. Readiness Checking: Overcoming the Real Blocks to Change

Helping people get ready for major change is difficult, complex, and fraught with the unexpected. It is difficult to manage the "shadow side" of the events that inevitably emerge. There are "skeletons in the closet," old resentments among team members that go "way back," and fears about the uncertainty of an ill-defined kaleidoscopic future. Sometimes the real obstacles to change have to be ferreted out and confronted head-on.

The CEO and I met again after the final session with his managers. He was both troubled and encouraged. He was encouraged that we had gotten this far; he had frankly expected far more resistance or even refusal to move ahead from a few of the managers. He was troubled because there was one person on his team whom he could not trust.

He felt that five of the twelve managers were "on board" and ready for the launch of a new and better organization. He also felt empathy for five who were still passively looking on and was stumped by the two who were negative in their attitudes. He was determined to give all seven a reason to either get "on the bus" or not continue to work with the organization.

He did not want more of the poison he had tolerated in the past. He realized that he was no longer willing to tolerate the draining negativity and pessimistic attitude of two of his team leaders in particular. He realized that he wanted to communicate to people in the organization that mediocrity, acceptance of negativity, and minimal performance were no longer acceptable. After a long conversation and some soul searching, he asked me to assist him with the following tasks while I coached him in the further development of his interpersonal, problem management, and consultative skills.

1. We asked all managers to rewrite their job descriptions based on what they *really* did and what they *must* do to make the strategic plan happen. Their current job descriptions were so outdated that many of them started with a clean piece of paper. We asked each to prioritize the tasks on their new job descriptions in order of what they did best and what would best achieve their departmental goals and the organization's strategic plan. The managers went through the same process with the supervisory level

below them, delegating some things to various supervisors who wanted some of the tasks the managers off-loaded.

2. We then met with each manager and revised his or her job description to reflect what we could all see were the best uses of the manager's time and talents. We helped the managers see how they could delegate the rest of the tasks that were distracting them from performing from their strengths. We also reengineered their work roles so that they were relieved of tasks that were not as strategically important to accomplishing what was most critical for their department or the success of the organization.

3. The CEO shared and revised his job description based on feedback from each manager. He off-loaded some of the things that had been "on his plate" for years to the new vice-president of operations or other managers who had the talents to perform the tasks well.

4. From the implementation part of the organization's strategic plan, we added a prioritized list of projects and accountabilities—with time lines for accomplishment—to the last page of the job descriptions, and the CEO and each manager signed off on them. In this way, what they had was an agreement for the work they were committing themselves to do in the coming year.

5. We agreed that this job description document would be open-ended because a new, upcoming strategic review session was planned to further clarify roles and responsibilities for the coming year.

6. We dealt with the most negative person, whom the CEO could not trust because that person had engaged in some manipulative behaviors: lying to protect himself, lording his authority over key supervisors, and refusing to own up to these and other negative behaviors. All the managers felt intimidated by this one fellow because of his history of threats, destructive put-downs, and spreading false rumors that hurt people's reputations. Because the man refused to take ownership of his destructive behaviors, he was given the choice of losing his authority and function as an advisor to another manager or leaving the organization. Interestingly, he chose the former option. Because of a medical problem, he had to reduce his stress level in the few remaining working years before his retirement. He also abandoned most of his negative approaches because he could not make them work without the position power he once wielded.

The result of going through this process was that each of the managers now felt that the major obstacle to team harmony and progress had been removed! The one manager who had been demoralizing the rest of the team had been repositioned and dethroned. The other fellow with a negative attitude turned around because he was no longer in the clutches of the leader who represented the "old-guard" values of the organization.

The values of the organization throughout the decades of its existence had remained predominantly authoritarian and a "good ol' boy" network. In other words, if you got promoted, it was likely because the boss of your division liked you or you were a relative of someone higher up. Many people had received raises based on their connections rather than their performance. This practice is found all too often—masked in sneaky or "quick-and-dirty" personnel selection procedures. Some low performers got raises and their slack performance was tolerated because of whose sons or daughters they were. People of lesser "status" in the kingdom were given the more difficult and stressful jobs. It was just the way things had been done from the beginning. Was this culture difficult to change? Yes! It was similar to some military, police, or correctional cultures in some ways. The need for a new charter, new culture, new values, new vision, and new strategy was at hand.

A police, fire, ambulance, court, or correctional organization may, at first, appear to be so entrenched in bureaucracy and military tradition that this type of restructuring is difficult or impossible. One only has to look at the wholesale changes that are made when faced with severe budget cuts to know that change can be made if the desire is strong enough.

TL Skill #42. Values Alignment

After getting people ready to accept change, the next step is to classify the operating values of the organization. Some consultants would argue that this should be done as the first step. Based on my experience, if we had done that, our major obstacles would not have been removed and the probability of achieving some measure of real consensus around operating values would have been decreased.

Values Must Make a Difference

Many people are sick of the whole values-clarification and consensus-seeking process because they have been through the exercise of specifying organizational and team values before, and it didn't make any significant difference. The values became mouthed, notional values, rather than action-based, guiding values in reality. Once articulated and agreed upon, the values must carry some weight!

For example, Norm Stamper, chief of the Seattle Police Department, made a public statement on local television that if any employee of the police department was guilty of discriminating against anyone because of race, belief, gender, or sexual orientation that person would be dismissed immediately. This put the commitment to values in plain sight for everyone to see. Chief Stamper did this based upon consensus developed about the preferred values of those who worked in the organization. He also made this announcement because he is upholding what he believes to be the worth of all people and the value of the Constitution.

Agreed-upon values must become *operational* values that carry genuine consequences when they are not followed. More importantly, behavior in alignment with the desired values of the organization must be recognized, appreciated, and rewarded or those values will have a tendency to fade.

Bill Bean and Ron Ford have written and produced a workbook entitled *Turbocharging Your Business* (available from Strategia at http://www.strategia.com), which includes a team-based exercise to identify and prioritize organizational values. This technology also provides a fine model and process to accomplish strategic planning and implementation planning that involves key stakeholders. The steps in the model are very similar to the skills outlined in the last part of this chapter.

Clarifying Values at the Organizational and Then Team Levels

Both team and organizational values may need to be specified. Organizational values are more global and are often agreed upon at the executive or management level. Acceptance and adoption of these values are sought by people in all areas of the organization. Once the organizational values are specified, then teams can identify their own team values that are based on the organizational values. Teams must have some cohesion to exist over time. Cohesion is made up of good reasons to get together—to meet one another's needs, to solve problems, and to reach goals.

The failure to clarify and communicate global values may result in a perceived values conflict. While working with the police board of a First Nations police service, the board members expressed to the facilitator concern over the fact that the young police officers were spending an inordinate amount of their time off the Reserve and in the nearby town assisting the local police. A values identification session subsequently conducted identified strong feelings on the part of the board members for the protection and preservation of the cultural values and traditions of the nation. This cultural emphasis was high on their list of values. This was clearly a priority for them and tended to influence their perception of how policing should be delivered to the people of the Bands they represented. Their focus was to blend policing into the cultural environment, and they had concerns that the police officers did not subscribe to similar values.

When a similar session was held with the First Nations police officers, it was found that they too had strong feelings for the cultural values and heritage.

However, the focus of these young officers was to blend the cultural environment into policing. As police officers, their focus and priority were on delivering a policing service while remaining cognizant of the cultural issues. There was simply a lack of understanding between the two groups in terms of how each perceived the process of policing in a culturally sensitive manner. When each was apprised of the other's perceptions, the ability to reach consensus was greatly enhanced. Soon they developed action plans that provided traditional policing activities in a manner that demonstrated a commitment to the cultural issues.

When team members are at odds with one another about how people should be treated, about how rules and regulations should be interpreted or followed, about how to conduct meetings, or about who has leadership and final decision-making authority, then the team will be divided and dysfunctional and may merely exist in mediocrity for years. Therefore, it is of critical importance that the issues of team norms (rules, regulations, manners of treating people, and solving problems), values (priorities, importance), and beliefs (assumptions about what is good, true, worthwhile, etc.) be addressed in the first stage of a team's development.

In the same manner as outlined above for specifying a purpose, a team can be facilitated to seek and arrive at consensus about the issues of norms, values, and beliefs. Where conflict is not resolvable, team members must compromise, follow the authority of a leader given ultimate decision-making authority by the team or a higher authority—or leave the team.

Problems Incurred from a Failure to Secure Values Alignment

When values alignment is not handled in the development of a team or organization, there is bound to be undue and ongoing conflict, strife, and unresolved problems. I am not suggesting that all people should believe the same things and have the same priorities or values, but I am asserting that when people do not agree that it is okay to disagree, there is often an intolerable clash of expectations and hard feelings, coupled with people blaming one another for the demise of the organization or team.

College faculty members had a departmental meeting and sought consensus on, and then agreed upon, their written purpose, goals, norms, values, and beliefs statements. One person only pretended to "buy into" the statements because to resist the team's momentum would have meant she was clearly out of line with the very basic human values prized by all the other team members. She neither wanted to give up her values in favor of the team's nor be openly at odds with the other team members. So she just quietly operated from her own opposing values without the team's immediate knowledge.

Over time, several of the team members began to notice that students were being treated in an arbitrary fashion, without due respect or according to principles that the other members of the department did not value. This kind of internal sabotaging of a team's key values happens in organizations when people who claim they have a certain type of character are hired and then turn out to be the exact opposite. These problems are the more difficult ones to solve. They represent the "shadow side" of the organization and are more difficult to manage.

A police officer who is "assigned" to participate in a special project team but who is not in alignment with the values, objective, and goals of the project has a great capacity to "derail" the whole process internally and in the eyes of his or her peers. Care to ensure "buy-in" is an essential component of a team's success and credibility.

A comprehensive program entitled *TeamLead*, by Everett Robinson, is available from Consulting Resource Group (at http://www.crgleader.com). In this program, a team values assessment and prioritization activity is outlined. More than twenty other assessments and activities designed to build high-performance teams are also available.

TL Skill #43. Vision and Purpose Consensus Building

Many visionaries or strategic planners use an analytic approach to planning that does not unify people into a force for change. This approach has the following characteristics:

1. It begins with an assessment of the current state, issues, and problems.
2. It breaks the issues or problems into their smallest components.
3. It solves each component separately (i.e., maximizes the solution).
4. It has no far-reaching vision or goal—it merely seeks the absence of the problem.

Transforming Leadership takes a systems approach to envisioning and problem solving. The systems approach has the following distinctive characteristics:

1. It begins with a vision of a preferred state of affairs in the future.
2. It articulates ways to know when the preferred state is reached.
3. It assesses the current state of affairs.
4. It then articulates a strategy to get to the preferred state of afairs, to close the gap between the current state and the preferred future state.

The following graphic and description of the systemic approach to strategic planning were developed by Ron Ford of Strategia Resources (www.strategia.com).

**The Elements of Strategic Planning:
A Systems Approach to Envisioning and Problem Solving**

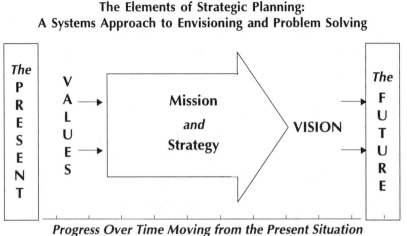

*Progress Over Time Moving from the Present Situation
to the Desired Future*

Description of Key Elements in the Systems Approach

Element 1: Vision. The role of vision is infinitely more powerful than the average leader realizes. Vision pulls us toward the future with an image of what that future could look like. It gives us a compelling reason for the sacrifice and effort needed to accomplish something significant.

Element 2: Values. The values held individually and corporately are primary sources of motivation in the enterprise. Priorities and activities that do not reflect our values are easily procrastinated, compromised, and even abandoned. Values drive us and empower us for accomplishment.

Element 3: The Present. Every determined step toward the future—no matter how bright and promising it appears—must always begin upon the ground of the present. Present realities must be understood and considered as future planning takes shape in your thinking.

Element 4: Mission. The mission of the enterprise is the tactical and operational focus for the company's resources and efforts. While vision concerns what you are ultimately seeking to build in the company, mission is more concerned with the actual business activities in which you will be engaging in the immediate and short-range future.

Element 5: Strategy. With all of the above in view and in proper perspective, a careful, comprehensive plan can be developed. This will consist of priority actions, which will leverage corporate resources and opportunities, and accountable assignments, which will ensure that the plan gets done.

An experienced leader knows that you cannot enlist people in moving toward a preferred future unless they are willing to do so. If people are involved in creating or defining the vision—instead of having one "laid on them from on high"—they are much more likely to accept it and work hard to achieve it. This is one of the most difficult skills for leaders to develop and practice.

Most of the leaders with whom I have worked have had difficulty projecting beyond the next few months in their corporate lives or their personal lives. This is a major challenge, especially for organizations experiencing or desiring rapid growth. Planned change is obviously preferable to spastic change. I often hear, "I can't plan anything because everything is changing so fast, I can't count on things staying the same for very long." Although this is true to an extent, it is still a fact that some people lead market changes and other types of major change. In Switzerland in 1954, Mr. Seiko was laughed at when he proposed a quartz watch at an international watchmakers conference. No one is laughing now.

Bill Bean, in his book *Strategic Planning that Makes Things Happen* (1993), differentiates between vision and mission/purpose. The following clarifications (even formulas) are offered:

1. A vision statement answers the question, "Where are we going?"
   a. What will our primary products or services be in five years?
   b. What will our primary markets be in five years?
   c. Who will our primary customers be in five years?
   d. What will our exclusive differentiating benefit be in five years?
   e. What will the geographic coverage of our enterprise be in five years?
   f. How big will our enterprise be in five years in terms of total sales, total number of employees, locations, types of locations, etc.?
2. A mission/purpose statement answers the question, "Who are we and what do we do?" Look at the examples below for clarification.
   a. XYZ company delivers performance technologies and profitability systems (what we intend to accomplish/provide),
   b. resulting in enhanced performance for our clients and proper returns for our stockholders (results to customer and owners),
   c. based upon a foundation of integrity and respect for the individual (values and beliefs).

Examples of Vision and Mission Statements

The following conceptual statements were developed by Consulting Resource Group to articulate its understanding of its long-range vision and their shorter range mission.

Vision Statement

Consulting Resource Group (CRG) is a global resource that strengthens and develops growth and leadership in individuals, families, and organizations.

Mission Statement

CRG creates, produces, and teaches innovative learning and leadership systems for key leaders around the world, so they can teach these systems to others.

Once there is some reasonable level of consensus regarding the vision and mission/purpose statements, it is then time to move on to developing a strategy that will close the gap between the current state and the future state. Most companies find vision casting and arriving at true consensus to be very difficult. It is, however, the foundation of all else that will occur in the enterprise—and it must be dealt with in a genuine and honest way. Kotter (1996), in his book, *Leading Change*, is emphatic when he states, according to his research at Harvard University, that there are eight major reasons why organizations fail. Several of them relate to the issue of vision:

Error 1	Allowing too much complacency
Error 2	Failing to create a sufficiently powerful guiding coalition
Error 3	Underestimating the power of vision
Error 4	Undercommunicating the power of vision by a power of one hundred
Error 5	Permitting obstacles to block the new vision
Error 6	Failing to create short-term wins
Error 7	Declaring victory too soon
Error 8	Neglecting to anchor changes firmly in the corporate culture

Finally, by way of example, let's return to the company discussed earlier in this chapter. When it came time to articulate the company vision and mission, it was incredibly difficult to do so. No one could seem to articulate how the future might look three to five years down the road. This was a very established, mature organization, accustomed to success (like General Motors and IBM before the competition gained on them).

The company is currently vulnerable because it is building a strategy for the next year, to carry on doing what it now does, but hopefully better. Change seems to be especially difficult for more mature businesses or for government organizations. The future trends that are forming must be discerned and responded to in a proactive way to catch the next "wave" with a creative new "surfboard" that people will want to buy. That is why we turn now to the issue of strategy. Two strategies are needed: one to strengthen and improve current business and one to anticipate and prepare for a preferred future that keeps moving around on us.

TL Skill #44. Strategy Consensus Building

The words *strategy* and *consensus* are combined here because a strategy is not implemented without consensus. Ken Blanchard, in his new book, *Mission Possible*, puts it well when he says, "Getting people to break out of their current world view while continuing to operate within it is difficult even for the best of us. Yet in today's hyper competitive markets, it must be done. We have no choice. We must work on the present and the future at the same time."

The *Strategic Planning Technology* process (available at www.strategia.com) designed by Bill Bean and Ron Ford does exactly this. This process is highly recommend for planning because it is extremely practical, comprehensive, systems based, as simple as possible ("Everything should be done as simply as possible, but not simpler," as Einstein said), and is based on a review and further development of other approaches to strategic planning.

Another comprehensive model and process for strategic change management that is more detailed and has even more supportive materials can be found at the Centre for Strategic Management in San Diego, California (this model is more appropriate for sophisticated audiences). Steve Haines's comprehensive strategic planning workbook, entitled *Reinventing Strategic Planning for the 21st Century: A Systems Solution,* is based on his book *Sustaining High Performance* (1995).

Bill Bean's and Steve Haines' approaches cover many of the skills outlined so far in this chapter and are recommended reading for understanding in greater depth and with more precision what the strategic change and planning process is about. Most people have never seen a strategic planning document with an implementation plan attached to it. It would be very helpful to obtain a copy of one of the above references so that you can learn more about it than space permits here.

Plan a Two- or Three-Day Strategic Planning Retreat

Unless you already know how to carry out strategic planning, find a consultant who has a track record of doing it very well and hire him or her. A good plan and a leadership team that can function with consensus will produce far more benefits than the cost of the consultant. A leadership team, consisting of senior management and representative leaders throughout the organization, must be present for such a planning session. Otherwise, it will be difficult to attain any measure of consensus, acceptance, and enlistment in the plan.

Strategic planning can be done in regularly scheduled meetings, but if you are like most leaders, planning just doesn't get done well unless you can get away for a few days each year for focused reflection and planning. Many leaders do their own review of progress and long-range planning at regularly scheduled times, both corporately and personally. This can become an annual tradition that is both refreshing and challenging.

The description of the skill of strategy consensus building,is as brief as possible here, specifying what a leader must learn in order to have the transforming impact that is sought and expected. This skill involves leading, or having a facilitator or consultant lead, your leadership team through reviewing past performance and setting goals and objectives to close the gap between the present and the preferred future you have articulated. If a facilitator or consultant is brought in from the outside and will not be staying on to help, you or someone in the organization must be prepared and available to lead the implementation process. Failure to give sustained, determined leadership to the implementation process means it will likely falter.

The steps involved in this skill are as follows:

1. **Review all data.** This can be the data you collected when you did the informal and formal assessments using Skills #37 and #38. There needs to be some type of organizational assessment in order to pinpoint successes, failures, strengths, weaknesses, opportunities, and threats.

2. **Conduct an SFSWOT** (an expanded version of what used to be called the SWOT [strengths, weaknesses, opportunities, and threats analysis] SF means success, failures and an external environmental scan. For obvious reasons, it is important to include facing failures and celebrating successes in the assessment formula. This involves an honest appraisal of the organization and using this information to identify and prioritize all of the above issues so that they can be addressed. The *Organizational Assessment Review* or other similar tools can be used. Often, they should be used in conjunction with interviews to gain a better sense of what is currently occurring in the organization and its surrounding environment. This can also be done interactively in a meeting or at a retreat. It is best to have objectively collected data, through questionnaires, and subjective data from face-to-fact interviews. The findings from each source should support the other or you should begin to suspect the validity of one approach or the other. One thing you don't want is information that is false or wrong!

   The *external environmental scan* is also a very important piece of data that can make or break the future success of a justice agency. For example, the funding formula for the New Westminster Police Department was such that, like other police departments, it was given funds to pay a certain number of officers based on the number of people who live in the community at the time. Sometimes, as happened in New Westminster, this funding formula is based on assumptions that do not encompass all of reality. A traffic and crime analysis study revealed that over 300,000 vehicles from out of town moved through the community every day, and that over 70 percent of all crimes committed in the community were committed by people who did not live there! Therefore, if this force continues to work under this kind of understaffed conditions, the result will be both burnout and failure to provide even barely adequate policing services to the community.

3. **Prioritize five to seven major goals that will move everyone toward the vision.** Steve Haines calls these major goals **key success factors** because when accomplished, they will result in successfully realizing at least a part of the preferred future scenario. It is fine to have more than five to seven goals, but most teams find it difficult to focus on five to seven main goals at a time. This is based on the "80/20 rule" which suggests that you want to spend 80 percent of your time doing the 20 percent of the things that will achieve the results you want to achieve. The other goals are important as well, but not nearly as important as the success factors that will transform the organization and its people from where they are now to where they want to be. The goals should be stated in concrete, believable, achievable, and challenging language. The following are examples of clear goals:

XYZ Company Strategic Goals List

Goal #	Goal Description
1	Develop comprehensive, leadership-supported marketing plan.
2	Refocus total quality management plans to align with overall XYZ Company strategic plan.
3	Develop formal cost-control program.
4	Develop comprehensive new-hire recruiting and training plan.
5	Develop continuous workload plan, with backlog and smooth flow.
6	Review health insurance coverage and make recommendations.

Ideally, the following will result if you are skilled enough to facilitate the strategic consensus-building process or smart enough to have an experienced planner do it if you are not ready or are not the right person to do so:

1. You will leave your planning meetings with a living document—a strategic plan that does not become like the familiar SPOTS (strategic plan on the top shelf).

2. You will have a plan on which the attending leaders agree and that they will take back to their teams for review and editing—only to bring it back to the next meeting for additional refinements.

If you ask the people who do the work, they will tell you if they have agreed to "buy into" the plan. And ask them! **If they do not buy into it, the plan will not be implemented very well.** In one government organization, six leaders attended the planning retreat. They then returned to the workplace to meet with twenty-four supervisors to explain the plan and get their input and revisions. The final draft was discussed with each supervisor's work team members—by the supervisors in face-to-face, one-on-one interviews—and further revisions and refinements were made.

Through this process, people found that they could be heard, that there was a pipeline to senior management, and that their comments were taken seriously. No one said he or she was not consulted or heard when an individual made objections or suggestions! Some employees recommended fundamental changes in the workplace and processes that enabled better customer (both internal and external) service, better working conditions, improved communications, lower stress, and higher morale. Frontline workers had a transforming effect on the organization. Union members found themselves more willing to engage in two-way communication and problem-solving sessions with management. They were transformed into team members who felt important and were, in fact, significant to the overall health and performance of the organization. They also implemented about 85 percent of the plan—a good score compared to most teams!

Once the plan has been accepted by a critical mass of people in an organization (at least 60 percent of all staff and 90 percent of all leaders), it has a chance of succeeding. This is especially true if you deal proactively with the negative leaders, who can put a damper on progress in making change. Negative team members can do the same thing but on a smaller scale. Jack Welch dismissed many of the managers when he took over as CEO at General Electric because he was not willing to work with people who either were not high performers or whom he believed would not support his vision. Chief Stamper of the Seattle Police Department challenged every leader in the organization to get on board with the vision, values, and plan—or get off! Most got on board; some got off or were asked to get off. Most people would agree that it is a better place to work now. There are still a few grumblers, as always.

In a small organization, it is possible for the implementation planning to take place in one leadership team and then be delegated to team leaders. In larger organizations, it is likely that each leader will do implementation planning in each department and meet with the senior leadership team to ensure cross-functional team communication and effectiveness. Once goals are set, implementation planning can take place. Let's look at the skill that is involved and the process of planning itself.

TL Skill #45. Implementation Planning: Specifying and Implementing Steps, Dates, and People to Expedite the Achievement of Goals

This skill involves formulating a set of steps that translate the general goals into action-oriented language to make them more achievable and exciting. Being as specific as possible about these steps, time lines, and responsibilities for action can bring team members together and cause a synergistic, energy-releasing effect that gets results.

The increased energy released by careful implementation planning is well worth the trouble and time it takes to formulate such a plan. A thorough plan makes it possible for you to clarify, in the minds of team members, who will do what, why they will do it, and how they will do it. A brainstorming approach is often most effective in stimulating a discussion of a wide range of options for possible implementation.

An example of an effective goals and planning sheet is presented on the next page. This sample of what Bill Bean calls a chronological action plan list is a key step in turning carefully crafted goals into action and results. Without translating goals into clear, time-bounded, person-responsible actions, it is unlikely that disciplined implementation will ever occur. If we carefully plan our interventions, we will create more effective scenarios and implementation will be enhanced. Some planners even use project planning software to track the implementation of the strategic plan.

Once developed, the list of action plans can then be sorted according to due dates. This then becomes a vital tool for use by the leadership of the organization for tracking and managing the ongoing strategic initiatives of the company or group. It provides a simple method to stay focused on a monthly basis in a way that maximizes clarity, specificity, and accountability for action.

TL Skill #46. Strategic Plan and Team Performance

For some reason, the moon shows up every month as some kind of reminder that a cycle has occurred. There are monthly financial statements, invoices, bills, etc. How about a monthly meeting to discuss what we all said we were going to do to move the strategic plan ahead and to review and improve our team performance? Even among committed partners, this is extremely difficult to do. If you discipline yourself to do it, however, you will enjoy the following results:

1. You and other leaders will celebrate together the various accomplishments you have achieved.
2. You will track how realistic your plan is and make course corrections early.

XYZ Company Chronological Action Plan List (Unsorted)

Goal #	Action #	Action Plan	By Whom	By When
1		**Create comprehensive marketing plan**		
	1A	Analyze XYZ product performance and profitablity matrix and develop recommendations	Carl	June
	1B	Develop international strategy with selected joint venture partners and selected country priorities and next actions	Jim	July
	1C	Develop hiring plan and timetable for new marketing director	Mary	July
2		**Refocus total quality management plans**		
	2A	Assess current state of XYZ TQM process with business unit leaders and identify key areas for remedial action	Jack	Sept.
	2B	Make simple company-wide announce-ment of refocused TQM direction	Jack	Oct.
3		**Develop formal cost-control program**		
	3A	Analyze current XYZ budgets and develop recommendations	Helen	May
	3B	Design plan for transforming business units into cost centers	Larry	July
4		**Develop hiring and recruiting plan**		
	4A	Identify new hire volume requirements for next eighteen months	Jane	Feb.
	4B	Design new recruitment and employee-interviewing system	Jane	Mar.

3. You will keep minutes up to date so that all team members have a brief record of plans and results.

4. You and other leaders will report on what you said you would do to hold one another accountable.

5. You will balance the long-term plan with the demands of daily operations.

6. You will keep the "big picture" view of your organization and discuss how to improve current operations and prepare for the shifting future.

The globally competitive marketplace has driven the excellence movement. Now we must do excellent strategic planning and operational implementation of the plan, or, as Tom Peters said, "we may die in the marketplace." I believe that Bill Bean's monthly executive review meeting (Bean, 1993, p. 235) is more important than anything you can do to ensure that implementation is achieved in the most effective way possible. I have had the greatest success in building executive teams in the context of this type of meeting because we develop the team, learn the skills of teaming, and get the job done at the same time. I have seen this in operation with my own clients and a number of Bill's clients.

I have also seen many, if not most, strategic planners and well-meaning, busy executives fail to teach and install a review system that really functions on a monthly basis. This is a matter of critical importance. If you have designed a beautiful and versatile plan but do not implement it, what use is it? The following sample agenda from Bill Bean illustrates how the relationship between planning and implementation can be strengthened to achieve maximum potential.

XYZ Company Monthly Executive Review

Agenda

I. Review of key indicators
   A. Financial indicators
   B. Business indicators
   C. Other indicators
II. "Two-minute" drills
   A. Each person presents key highlights from his/her area
   B. New issues to be addressed in plan (see IV.A)
III. Review of strategic action plans
   A. Past-due (done yet?)
   B. Current (on time?)
   C. Upcoming (on track?)
IV. Address new items/adjust strategic plan
   A. Discuss new items, reach closure
   B. Assign new action plans as needed

Adapted from Bill Bean and Ron Ford, *Turbocharging Your Business,* Cardiff, CA: Strategia, 1996. Used by permission.

To build the monthly executive review into your executive team's agenda, it is necessary to understand the benefits and the process. Outlined below are a list of the benefits:

1. It stimulates getting the job done.
2. It is extremely time efficient—one to two hours per month.
3. It ensures that the strategic plan becomes a living plan, continuously updated with new action plans as necessary.
4. The right people are kept up to date with the right information at the right time, with the right level of executive focus and individual accountability.
5. You have the benefit of a monthly check of the two critical components of performance: monthly operational performance and strategic action plan implementation success. The process involves having those leaders responsible for the implementation of the strategic plan meet together in person or via teleconference or televideo conference to review the agenda items.

TL Skill #47. TQM Leadership: Leading Teams Toward Continuous Learning for Continuous Improvement

As stated in various parts of this book, we must build a leadership organization that can have its act together enough to implement such complex change as total quality management (TQM) to become what Senge has called a learning organization. Senge describes the new leader as a "designer, steward, and teacher responsible for building organizations where people continually expand their capabilities to understand complexity, clarify vision, and improve shared mental models." He says that such leaders are responsible for making sure that learning happens.

Whether or not you choose to implement a full-blown TQM program as recommended by one theorist or another is not as important as whether or not you make the commitment to learning. You need to commit to learning what customers want, what your staff wants, and how you can continuously do better to meet and exceed customers' expectations.

TQM theory states that quality is defined by the customer. TQM is a systems approach to being accountable for checking to make sure we are in communication and are being responsive to both internal and external "customers." We want to create return customers who are "wowed" by the way we treat them. We push the Golden Rule—treat others the way we would like to be treated—to the maximum. TQM is characterized by this customer focus, total organizational involvement, continuous improvement of processes, and fact-based decision making.

The use of the word "customer" in police organizations is a recent phenomenon and not without controversy. A long-standing notion is that the type or quality of service delivered by the police is best determined by the police. This was predicated on the concept that the police "know best" what the customer needs. After all, the police are the experts. Customer "wants" were of little consequence. Perhaps the local community advisory group would provide information that the community concern was traffic related. Once presented to the police, the issue may well have been ignored by police in favor of more "significant policing issues" as determined by the police agency. This paternalistic attitude by some police managers offered substantial resistance to the idea of a customer-generated definition of quality service.

An acknowledgment of the concept of internal customer service was exhibited several years ago in the detective branch of a municipal police department. The organization had established goals and objectives related to community (customer) satisfaction. In an innovative step, the detective unit formulated strategies which acknowledged that the uniform branch of the police service was a customer to which it provided a service. The strategies contained within the strategic action plan recognized that the detective unit had an obligation to provide a quality response to requests for further investigation and file disposition forwarded from the uniform branch. The measurement of success of the strategy was based on the level of "customer satisfaction" as determined by complaints received during scheduled uniform-branch supervisor feedback and on number of file dispositions. The supervisor feedback showed an almost immediate drop in the number of complaints received and the file dispositions increased.

In police organizations that provide services to agencies other than their own, TQM is a more familiar concept. The other agencies or government departments are seen as clients that expect a professional level of service delivery. Checks and balances to ensure service quality are more the norm in these cases. Forensic laboratories are a prime example of this type of police service.

A transforming leader leads a quality movement within his or her own organization—with his or her executive teammates and partners. These people used to be called employees. Space is not available here to go into the detail needed to do justice to an introduction to TQM, but it is important to learn more about it. Consider reading *Juran on Quality by Design* (1992) or the most recent and innovative addition to the literature on TQM leadership by Michael Cowley and Ellen Domb (1997). These resources will give you a more in-depth understanding of the nature and applicability of the quality improvement processes that have revolutionized—not evolutionized—modern business in the past thirty years.

TL Skill #48. Building Accountability

It is possible to install accountability at all levels within the organization so that everyone experiences what I call "no-doubt contracting." This means that all interchanges, both verbal and written, are characterized by agreements between people.

For example, all job descriptions can become working agreements if they are perceived as living documents that describe what we promise to do for one another, what we hope to accomplish, what roles we will play, etc. Having fair, equitable, nondiscriminatory personnel policies is another way to be accountable. It is also possible for all partnership agreements, contracts with clients, and customers, both internal and external, to reflect agreements that took place in conversations characterized by two-way communication and mutual commitment. To be accountable, you can use executive monthly review meetings and initiate TQM initiatives. In other words, no-doubt, no-surprise contracts and commitments can become the dominant way of life in your organization. And everyone wants this.

The International Standards Organization (ISO) wanted accountability and no-doubt contracting among countries when it started the ISO 9000 series in 1945 as a preferred way of doing international business. As a result of this commitment over fifty years ago, you may have to certify and register your company with ISO in the future to engage in certain types of international business because some of your customers will not do business with you unless you are registered.

Accountability Is a Part of Honest Leadership that Leads to Credibility

In *Credibility*, Jim Kouzes and Barry Posner (1993) share strong research evidence that this may be the most important factor in determining success as a leader. They quote a study by the Columbia University Graduate School of Business in which over 1,500 top executives in twenty countries were surveyed. The study reports that "ethics are rated most highly among the personal characteristics needed by the ideal CEO in the year 2000. Respondents expect their CEO to be above reproach." In addition to honesty, being forward-looking, inspiring, and competent were among the top characteristics Kouzes and Posner found to be preferred by those who may be willing to follow someone's lead.

Based on the above, it seems clear that it is best to be seen by team members as honest, caring, competent, inspired, informed, knowledgeable, capable, likable, in a position of authority, and trustworthy—if you are to be given the trust you need to unify and move a team in a particular direction. This can first be accomplished by making sure that you are, in fact, leading a team that you have some real ability and knowledge to lead. Talk about yourself openly, but not boastfully. The team members need to know something about your background and why you deserve to be in this leadership position (e.g., because of your confidence, experience, knowledge, power, etc.).

Kotter (1979) studied many of the ways leaders gain credibility and power in teams and organizations. He illustrates how many of the "success" behaviors of influential leaders can be learned. Your personal credibility will be better established if you can follow Kotter's general guidelines:

1. State your own purpose (based on your own inner clarity) for being in your role as leader. Let team members know you are in harmony with and attempting to achieve your organization's purposes in ways that uphold the organization's values.
2. Communicate and check for the validity of the needs and wants you hope to meet. In this way, you will gain awareness of the degree of real or imagined consensus about these critical issues. This can save you the embarrassment of attempting to meet needs or solve problems only perceived as relevant by a few.
3. Communicate how you intend to work in a respectful and helpful manner. This is critical if you want people to feel comfortable and have a sense of trust in you. If they perceive you as a potential threat or a noncaring person, you will not get their support to accomplish goals.
4. Value the worth and potential contributions of the other members of the team. Look for opportunities where team members can gain various kinds of recognition or rewards for being involved in the work group's endeavors.
5. Model good team-member and leader behaviors, which include all of the communication and problem management skills outlined in the previous two chapters. In this way, you will gain acceptance and trust more readily.

In the next chapter, we will discuss how the knowledge and skills presented in previous chapters can be applied in a creative, flexible, and responsive manner through style, role, and skill shifting. This will assist you in developing the versatility skills so important for *Transforming Leadership* success.

References

Bass, B.M., *Leadership Beyond Performance Expectations,* New York: The Free Press, 1985.

Bean, B. and R. Ford, *Turbocharging Your Business,* Cardiff, CA: Strategia, 1996.

Bean, B., *Strategic Planning that Makes Things Happen*, Amherst: HRD Press, 1993.

Blanchard, Kenneth H., et al., Mission Possible: *Becoming a World-Class Organization While There is Still Time*, New York: McGraw-Hill, 1997.

Burns, J.M., *Leadership*, New York: Harper & Row, 1978.

Cowley, M. and E. Domb, *Beyond Strategic Vision: Effective Corporate Action with Hoshin Planning*, Newton, MA: Butterworth-Heinemann, 1997.

Crosby, P.B., *Quality Is Free: The Art of Making Quality Certain*, New York: McGraw-Hill, 1979.

Cunningham, Scott A., The Empowering Leader: The Key to Managing Organizational Change, presented at the Society of Police Futurists International Symposium, Baltimore, 1993.

Egan, G., *Change Agent Skills (Part B): Managing Innovation & Change*, San Diego: University Associates, 1988.

Haines, Steve, Sustaining High Performance, Boca Raton, FL: CRC Press, 1995.

Juran, J.M., *Juran on Quality by Design*, New York: The Free Press, 1992.

Kilmer, G.R., Consumer survey as needs assessment method: a case study, *Evaluation and Program Planning*, I, 286–292, 1978.

Kotter, J., *Power in Management*, New York: AMACOM, 1979.

Kotter, J., *Leading Change*, New York: AMACOM, 1996.

Kouzes, James, et al., *Credibility: How Leaders Gain and Lose it, Why People Demand it*, San Francisco: Jossey-Bass Publishing, 1995.

Kouzes, James M. and Barry Z. Posner, *The Leadership Challenge: How to get Extraordinary Things Done in Organizations*, San Francisco: Jossey-Bass Publishing 1987.

Menzel, R., A taxonomy of change agent skills, *Journal of European Training*, 4(5), 289–291, 1975.

Morgan, G., *Riding The Waves of Change: Developing Managerial Competencies for a Turbulent World*, San Francisco: Jossey-Bass, 1988.

Noer, David, *Breaking Free: A Prescription for Personal and Organization Change*, San Francisco: Josey-Bass Publishing, 1996.

Peters, T. and N. Austin, *A Passion for Excellence*, New York: Random House, 1985.

Quinn, R., *Beyond Rational Management: Mastering the Paradoxes and Competing Demands of High Performance*, San Francisco: Jossey-Bass, 1988).

Schlesinger, L., R. Eccles, and J. Gabarro, *Managerial Behavior in Organizations: Texts, Cases, and Readings*, New York: McGraw-Hill, 1983, 486.

Senge, Peter M., *The Fifth Discipline: The Art and Practice of the Learning Organization*, New York: Doubleday, 1990.

Whisenand, Paul M. and Fred Ferguson, *The Making of Police Organizations*, 3rd ed., Englewood Cliffs, NJ: Prentice-Hall, 1989.

8

The Skills of Versatility in Style, Skill, and Role

Think about the productivity of employees who bring motivation, imagination, and energy to their work—who have spirit. If you wish all your employees were that way, you know that work spirit is a serious, not soft, subject.

—Sharon L. Connelly

Introduction

It is one thing to compose or begin to play a piece of music; it is quite another to practice and develop one's potential enough to play well. Quality, productivity, motivation, imagination, the willingness to sweat and persist in the face of stress and occasional exhaustion—all these factors, when blended together, can produce unforgettable performance. People who are willing to "go all out" are doing so for good reasons. Someone has mobilized them with clear vision, hopes, ideals, and expectations of rewards and has instilled in them some enthusiasm. Star athletes are an example of those who train until their maximum potential is unleashed.

In a similar way, *Transforming Leadership* has the potential to empower leaders and their teams of leaders to achieve higher levels of impact to motivate and move people to take new action and reach for new levels of achievement and reward. This can simultaneously stimulate the development of all those involved together in the endeavor. To achieve these heights, leaders do not necessarily have to be charismatic. But they do have to be effective in shifting to meet the needs of people and the changing demands of fast-moving surroundings.

The following *Transforming Leadership* skills are discussed in this chapter:

TL Skill #49   Assessment of personal styles   Page 230
TL Skill #50   Style shifting   Page 230
TL Skill #51   Assessment of roles   Page 240
TL Skill #52   Role shifting   Page 240
TL Skill #53   Assessment of skills   Page 249
TL Skill #54   Skill shifting   Page 249
TL Skill #55   Recognition of organizational   Page 250
                      development stages
TL Skill #56   Facilitation of organizational   Page 254
                      development stages

The following specific objective statements summarize what will be accomplished in this chapter:

1. Learn about *Transforming Leadership*'s facilitative, "style, role, and skill shifting" approach, which leaders can use to facilitate individual, group, or organization development
2. Learn about the developmental stages of a group or organization to assess what interventions are appropriate in each stage and thereby intervene more effectively
3. Learn the steps and processes to design and set up a group or organization
4. Explore the future of *Transforming Leadership* as a new practice of designing and managing change

In his fascinating book entitled *Leadership Is an Art*, Max DePree (1989) states:

> ...it is fundamental that leaders endorse a concept of the value of persons. This begins with an understanding of the diversity of people's gifts and talents and skills. Understanding and accepting diversity enables us to see that each of us is needed. It also enables us to begin to think about being abandoned to the strengths of others, of admitting that we cannot know or do everything. The simple act of recognizing diversity in corporate life helps us to connect the great variety of gifts that people bring to the work and service of the organization. Diversity allows each of us to contribute in a special way, to make our special talents a part of the corporate effort.

Essential to the *Transforming Leadership* approach are concepts that relate to the acceptance and integration of diversity in others: the concepts of "style shifting," "role shifting," and "skill shifting." Learning to recognize different personal styles in others' behaviors can lead to more appropriate leadership responses and can bring forth the best in others. Moreover, trying to shift roles appropriately—which also involves shifting sets of skills—to respond accurately to individual differences and preferences can improve communication, problem management, learning, and leadership effectiveness. Thus, style, role, and skill shifting are presented together to provide a more comprehensive and versatile model to subtly capture many of the important aspects of leadership complexity. The model is defined, however, so that it will be practical and applicable in a wide range of settings.

With the new understanding gained in this chapter, you will find yourself responding more flexibly—and therefore more appropriately—to others and to situations. This chapter builds upon the knowledge and skills in previous chapters so you can develop expertise and even finesse in expressing your own individual approach to leadership—especially when your goal is to facilitate team and organization development. The final thrust of this chapter will be to examine how to do more than just develop a team or organization. Some direction on how to transform a well-functioning team or organization into a dynamic one is presented. At this end of this chapter is the case study of how the Royal Canadian Mounted Police have endeavored to achieve this in communicating and arriving at consensus across Canada about the organization's vision, mission, and values.

The Impact of Leadership in Teams and Organizations

Organizations do not have a life of their own separate from the individuals in them. Wittingly or unwittingly, it is the leaders in particular who shape the climate that influences performance and morale. They can and do have a tremendous influence on how people think, feel, and behave. If you look back into the history of your own life in the context of the social systems that have surrounded you, you will become more aware of how many social factors and certain leaders have had profound effects on your own development. When we consider the staggering impact that all social systems—and especially the leaders in these systems—can potentially have on the development or destruction of the morale and fabric of people, the need to develop innovative approaches to design and develop positive organizational spirit becomes evident. As Bass (1985) has concluded from his research, "...transformational leadership will contribute in an incremental way to extra effort, effectiveness, and satisfaction with the leader as well as to appraise subordinate performance beyond expectations..."

Transforming Leadership moves the development of a leader one step further toward effectiveness and competency. It goes beyond communicating the important quality of charisma, the kindness of empathy, the insight of intellectual stimulation, and the benefits of providing rewards. *Transforming Leader-*

ship proposes to develop the core of each leader into a more versatile and creative master of positive change. This leader will then design and manage the quality, health, and performance of an organization or group.

Style, Role, and Skill Shifting: Versatile Wisdom for Inducing Positive Change

It is of prime importance in the development of such mastery, as is suggested above, that leaders develop not only skills but versatility as well. The fluid concept of "shifting" styles, roles, and skills was adopted to capture the essence of the artistry and intelligence-in-action that *Transforming Leadership* asserts is so vital. As we move into examining the complexity of effective leadership, you will learn to see your own behavior more keenly within the context of the overall environment. Further definition of terms for each of the three aspects of style shifting will assist you to understand some of the basic ideas that underlie the notion of "shifting."

Style shifting is the ability to assess the personal style of another person and adjust your responses to better fit what is most effective in achieving your purposes, and to do this genuinely, without manipulation, while meeting the needs of the other person.

Role shifting is the ability to recognize which of three major roles is most appropriate in any given moment to thereby alternate among communication, counseling, and consulting interventions as the situation, team, or person requires.

Skill shifting is the ability to move gracefully between three different sets of skills to accomplish various tasks, depending upon the circumstance or the developmental level of a person, group, or organization. As you skill shift more appropriately, you will subtly increase your effectiveness in each of the three major roles.

It is important to develop the ability to act consciously and intentionally but also to spontaneously "oscillate" among and within each of the three roles and sets of skills. This may seem to make the process of leadership complex and difficult. Of course, it is complex, but the style-shift approach breaks down some of the complex reality of leadership behaviors into small enough "chunks" so each part can be learned before integrating it into a more fluid practice.

Effective leadership requires the ability to deal with complexity, break it into manageable pieces, intervene with a continuous alertness to the impact one is making to correct course, and respond afresh to a changing environment. Continuous vigilance to the impact of your interventions will better enable you to shift styles, roles, or skills again and again as it becomes appropriate to do so.

Transforming Leadership's Style, Role, and Skill Shifting Model

Transforming Leadership is built upon a metamodel for lifelong personal and professional development that consists of several skills training modules, the skills for which were outlined in the previous chapters. A new and practical synthesis of the various areas of skill is what the style-shift model attempts to present.

The remainder of this chapter is divided into four sections:

1. Introduction to personal style theory and its application to *Transforming Leadership* in the form of style shifting
2. Role shifting to increase your effectiveness in recognizing and shifting into appropriate role behaviors
3. Skill shifting to increase your effectiveness by recognizing and shifting into the appropriate skills to be used in different situations
4. Application of these various skills to develop and even transform a group or organization into one that functions and performs more dynamically and successfully

The shifting model, in its most basic form, can be expressed visually in the following way:

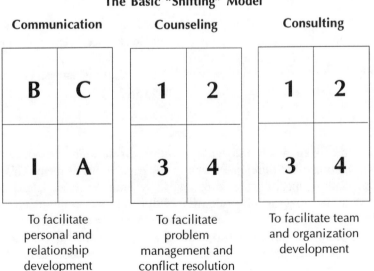

The Basic "Shifting" Model

Communication	**Counseling**	**Consulting**
B **C** **I** **A**	**1** **2** **3** **4**	**1** **2** **3** **4**
To facilitate personal and relationship development	To facilitate problem management and conflict resolution	To facilitate team and organization development

In the **communication** part of the model above, the letters B, C, I, and A represent different quadrants of personal style (to be explained further below). If we are aware of them, they will tend to influence how we approach an individual or even how we approach a group or organization.

In the **counseling** part of the model, the numbers 1, 2, 3, and 4 represent levels of task-specific functioning or development of the individual, which provide indications of how you might best approach that particular person for optimum appropriateness and effectiveness (as indicated in Chapter 6 on counseling skills).

In the **consulting** part of the model, the numbers 1, 2, 3, and 4 represent stages of group or organization development that require different approaches and skills to optimize the results you desire.

Therefore, when utilizing the model above to plan for more effective interventions, we can take into consideration the following.

1. The factor of individual style
2. The appropriate role we should be playing in a particular situation
3. The stage of development and functioning of an individual, group, or organization

Style Shifting for More Effective Leadership Impact

Skills #49 and #50. Assessment of Personal Styles and Style Shifting

Now we examine the issue of personal style assessment and style shifting to various types of behavioral responses to match the needs and preferences of others—which will increase your effectiveness when relating to or solving problems with them. It should be noted that style shifting can also be used with groups and organizations as well as individuals.

What Personal Style Means

People tend to approach and interact with their surroundings (i.e., people, things, situations, and time) based upon their perceptions of them. This part of the personality superstructure is believed, by both Anderson and Robinson (1988 a), to be largely predisposed from birth and further conditioned throughout life and tends to strongly influence individual perception of and response to the environment throughout a person's life. If this kind of natural "filter" through which each individual perceives the environment does exist, then it is important to identify and specify what it is. Personal style theory asserts that such a filter does indeed exist and attempts to provide theoretical constructs that delineate and explain such a phenomenon. Without "pigeonholing" people, the term "personal style" reflects each individual's predisposed and usually preferred way of behaving.

I defined personal style in the above-referenced manual (1988 a) as "a person's habitual way of behaving, or predisposition to act, in everyday situations with most people." Robinson further defined it as "a person's natural predisposition to perceive, approach, and interact with the environment." Thus, personal style includes characteristics of personality and behavior:

1. Preferred manner of accomplishing a task
2. Preferred manner of reacting to individuals
3. Strengths and difficulties characteristic of a person's unique style
4. Natural reaction to stressful events
5. Preferred manner of functioning in a group
6. Propensity to lead or follow
7. Predisposition to be extroverted or introverted
8. Predisposition to be task versus relationship oriented
9. Predisposition to be right or left-brain oriented
10. Predisposition to be verbal or nonverbal

When we can understand others in such a detailed and specific manner, we are in a better position to respond to them in ways that lead them in directions they more naturally go and assign to them tasks at which they are more likely to succeed.

The Process of Style Shifting

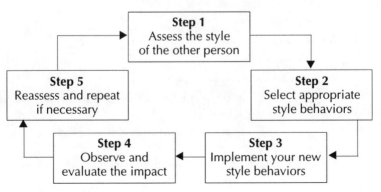

Personal Style Assessment

People who are versatile in their approaches to others will consider the individual style preferences of others and tend therefore to be more versatile and effective than those who do not.

To accurately assess another person's style, you need to be able to observe and predict how a person, or a group, will tend to act. If you have a model for style assessment, you can observe and listen to a person and thereby determine which two or three quadrants of personal style are preferred by that individual.

Because it is a critical factor in the practice of *Transforming Leadership* to appreciate the unique tendencies, needs, and preferences of other people, groups, or organizations, it is important to become more proficient in assessing others' style tendencies so our responses will be much more appropriate and well received.

To gain a general assessment of your own style, read the descriptions of the four general quadrants of personal style (on the following page) extracted from a more extensive instrument that I developed with Everett Robinson (1988 b). After you have read these descriptions of the four style tendencies, you will be able to gain a general picture of your own style tendencies, which have an impact on how you tend to approach others. You can also do a complete *Personal Style Indicator* online interactively at http://www.crgleader.com and get an *In-depth Interpretation* as well. A paper-based learning tool is also available to those who prefer that medium for training groups. Also available for further reading is Robinson's (1997) book on personal style entitled *Why Aren't You More Like Me?*

Now that you have read through the four personal style dimension descriptions, you can do a general assessment of your personal style. After reading the instructions, read through the chart on page 234, "Understanding Your General Style Tendencies." This information will assist you to become more familiar with your own and others' general style tendencies.

Instructions for General Style Assessment

1. Place the number "1" in the quadrant (where you see the word "score") that you believe best describes you.
2. Place the number "2" in the quadrant that describes the style behaviors you would likely shift into next.
3. Place the number "3" in the quadrant that describes behaviors less typical of you.
4. Place the number "4" in the quadrant that least describes how you would act.

Understanding the Four Personal Style Dimensions

Behavioral   ACTION

This style dimension is characterized by a strong tendency toward altering the environment in a way that will achieve well-thought-out goals. Therefore, people who naturally operate mainly from this quadrant of style are likely to seem self-assured and driven, many times oblivious to other people's feelings, and on a track of their own. When their vision is shared by a group, they are often seen as heroes and leaders because they tend to forge ahead to meet challenges with unusual fearlessness. This style position by itself is extroverted and can withstand greater stress. It does not favor artistic, aesthetic, or emotional modes of operating, but prefers a planned method by which previously defined goals and results are achieved. In this style, there is a clear sense of acting upon the environment to achieve these results.

Cognitive   ANALYSIS

This style dimension is characterized by a strong tendency to avoid being influenced negatively by people or environmental influences. This type moves toward goals often perceived as requirements of others in positions of authority. Attention to details and being on the alert for potential dangers or inconsistencies enable people with this style to maintain a better position of security and control. People with this style tend to avoid emotional intensity and unpredictability; they may especially need intimacy because they find that trust in others is not easily attained. This style position by itself is introverted, being more sensitive to stimulation. It does not prefer the sensory, emotional modes of operating, but tends toward logical analysis and correct performance of tasks, with an additional interest in the fine arts.

Affective   EXPRESSION

This style dimension is characterized by a strong tendency to intuitively explore the environment and interact with it to assess the outcome. Spontaneous exploration and expression of ideas and feelings mark the natural tendencies of this style. People with a natural tendency toward this dimension of style are often attempting to influence others through the creative media of speaking, writing, dance, art, or music. They would like to sell others on themselves and ideas or products they believe will be helpful. They will go out of their way to help others, even if it inconveniences them because often they believe in the value of people. By itself, this style is extroverted, not being easily overstimulated by the environment. It does not favor the analytical modes of operating, but is more intuitive and creative in its way of functioning.

Interpersonal   HARMONY

This style dimension is characterized by a strong tendency to adapt to people and surroundings to promote harmony and comfort for self and others. The approach to life and people in a practical, friendly, and naturally warm manner is typical of this style dimension. Adaptation to all other styles is a way of life, providing the desired security and balance needed and preferred by those who score higher in this style dimension. A desire to support others to gain a sense of validation and approval is a natural tendency. This style position by itself is introverted, being more sensitive to stimulation. It favors a practical balance of both the logical and intuitive modes of functioning, thereby avoiding extremes. In this style, there can also be a tendency toward stubbornness, especially if others are being overbearing.

Understanding Your General Style Tendencies

Behavioral—*Action*

Score:

General Orientation:

To tasks:	wants results now
To people:	seeks authority
To problems:	is tactical, strategic
To stress:	doubles efforts
To time:	sees future and present

Typical Strengths:

Acts rapidly to get results
Is inventive and productive
Shows endurance under stress
Is driven to achieve goals
Can take authority boldly

Common Difficulties:

Can be too forceful or impatient
Can often think his or her way is best
Can be insensitive to others
Can be manipulative or coercive
Can be lonely or fatigued

Cognitive—*Analysis*

Score:

General Orientation:

To tasks:	wants quality
To people:	seeks security
To problems:	analyzes data
To stress:	withdraws
To time:	sees past and future

Typical Strengths:

Acts cautiously to avoid errors
Engages in critical analysis
Seeks to create a low-stress climate
Wants to ensure quality control
Can follow directives and standards

Common Difficulties:

Can bog down in details and lose time
Can be too critical or finicky
Can be overly sensitive to feedback
Can seem to be lacking in courage
Can be too self-sufficient, alone

Affective—*Expression*

Score:

General Orientation:

To tasks:	people come first
To people:	seeks to influence
To problems:	intuitive and creative
To stress:	escapes from it
To time:	present and future

Typical Strengths:

Acts creatively on intuition
Is sensitive to others' feelings
Is resilient in times of stress
Develops a network of contacts
Is often willing to help others

Common Difficulties:

Can lose track of time
Can "overburn" and overindulge
Can be too talkative
Can lose objectivity, be emotional
Can be self-orientated, self-assured

Interpersonal—*Harmony*

Score:

General Orientation:

To tasks:	perfoms reliably
To people:	seeks to help others
To problems:	gives practical solutions
To stress:	adjusts to it
To time:	sees present

Typical Strengths:

Promotes harmony and balance
Is reliable and consistent
Tries to adapt to stress
Sees the obvious things others miss
Is often easygoing and warm

Common Difficulties:

Can be too easygoing and accepting
Can allow others to take advantage of
  him or her
Can become bitter if unappreciated
Can be low in self-worth
Can be too dependent on others

Now that you have reviewed your general style tendencies and have become more familiar with the four quadrants of style, you can begin to explore the value of assessing the styles of others and shifting into the various style behaviors they would likely prefer. Keep in mind that you have done only a general estimate of your personal style

Assessing Others' Styles and Style Shifting

According to my field research with Robinson (1988 b) and the experimental investigations of Merrill and Reid (1981), learning to assess the personal styles of others, and to shift into an interpersonal style that best allows others to receive and understand your messages, is an often overlooked and effective skill that can be learned in a relatively short period of time.

To learn some basics of how to assess others' styles and practice this style-shifting skill, see the four-quadrant grid entitled "Style Shifting Guidelines" on the next page. It offers general direction and hints for style shifting effectively with the four style types. Place a person's name (whom you know well) in the quadrant or two near the guidelines that you believe could assist you to approach that person more effectively.

General Style Shifting Considerations

If we examine the various needs and preferences of each style type, we can see why it is so easy to make mistakes out of ignorance with such individual differences among people. Below are some general considerations that can act as guidelines for planning a response to the four types of people.

Behavioral, Action Oriented: If you assess that a person is mainly action oriented in style, then you would give this person "bottom-line" facts in summary fashion and challenging assignments and opportunities. Do not distract the person with too many details or personal issues, get on with the "task" or job at hand, do not challenge him or her personally but provide brief evidence to support your challenge, and respect this person's high need for cooperation from others. These interpersonal behaviors appear especially important to these types of people.

Cognitive, Analytical: If you assess that a person has mainly an analytical, introverted style, then you would provide detailed and comprehensive factual information, give ample time for decision making, announce changes in advance, respect any areas of special competency, and show appreciation for efforts and accomplishments. These things appear to be especially important to people with this style.

Style Shifting Guidelines

Behavioral Styles   *Action*

Wants others to:
Provide summarized facts
Respect his or her judgements
Support him or her to reach goals
Cope with unwanted details
Cooperate with him or her

Gets most upset when others:
Are too slow
Get in his or her way
Talk too much
Try to be in control
Waste time

Responds best to:
Direct, honest confrontations
Logical, rational arguments
Fair, open competition
An impersonal approach
Getting results quickly

Cognitive Styles   *Analysis*

Wants others to:
Give detailed information
Ask for his or her opinions
Not interrupt his or her work
Treat him or her with respect
Do quality work the first time

Gets most upset when others:
Move ahead too quickly
Don't give him or her enough time
Are vague in their communications
Don't appreciate his or her efforts
Are too personal or emotional

Responds best to:
Diplomatic, factual, challenges
Arguments based on known facts
Freedom from competitive strain
Friendliness, not personal contact
Doing tasks well and completely

Affective Styles   *Expression*

Wants others to:
Give him or her opportunity to speak
Admire his or her achievements
Be influenced in some ways
Take care of details
Value his or her opinions

Gets most upset when others:
Are too task orientated
Confine him or her to one place
Are not interested in him or her
Compete for and win attention
Seem judgemental of him or her

Responds best to:
Being challenged in a kind way
An influencing, sales approach
Enjoyable competition
Affection and personal contact
Having a good time

Interpersonal Styles   *Harmony*

Wants others to:
Make him or her feel like he or she belongs
Appreciate him or her for efforts
Be kind, considerate, thoughtful
Trust him or her with important tasks
Value him or her as a person

Gets most upset when others:
Get angry, blow up, or are mean
Demand that he or she be too mobile
Take advantage of his or her goodness
Are manipulative or unfair
Are judgmental of others

Responds best to:
A gradual approach to challenging
A factual, practical approach
Comfortable, friendly times
Respecting his or her boundaries
Conventional, established ways

Interpersonal, Harmonious: If you assess that a person has mainly a need for a harmonious approach to people and the environment, you would shift into providing social behaviors that show recognition and appreciation of services and efforts provided, offer a safe relationship climate relatively free of judgments and high pressures to perform, and provide opportunities for success by service to others instead of achievement of results. People with this style seem to appreciate and respond well to this approach.

Affective, Expressive: If you assess that a person has mainly this type of outgoing style orientation, then you can best relate by giving recognition for achievements and self-presentations (performances, clothes, successes); listen more than you speak; provide opportunity for promotions and for earning money, traveling, and mobility; and do not supervise too closely or you can kill creativity in this type of person.

Developing Style Versatility: A Case Study

The Case of Sandy: General manager for a West Coast paper distribution company that sells and delivers paper to printing companies.

Sandy's Profile: High behavioral (action) and cognitive (analysis). Low interpersonal (harmony) and affective (expressive).

Sandy's Personal Style Graph

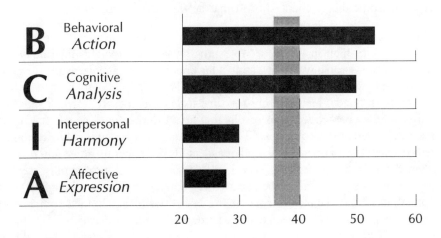

Sandy's Strengths:
1. Often gets quality results the first time
2. Can process large volumes of information

3. Can make objective decisions using a large database of information from many sources
4. Challenges others toward excellence
5. Acts as a model for others
6. Is inventive and original
7. Is careful to avoid pitfalls
8. Provides guidelines others can use
9. Ensures quality control
10. Endures and persists when under stress

Sandy's Difficult Areas:
1. Is impatient with lower performers
2. Can appear smug and as a "know-it-all"
3. Can be insensitive to others' feelings
4. Can be lonely and fatigued
5. Can be too critical
6. Can be "touchy" with critical feedback
7. Can be too self-sufficient
8. Can lack in courage to face emotions
9. Can get lost in details before deciding
10. Can seem to be manipulative or coercive

Upon reading his in-depth interpretation, Sandy laughed. He said that the description of him was better than 90 percent accurate and that he became more aware of some things about himself that he figured were often blind spots.

The Problem: Sandy is in charge of a sales force of nine people who tend to be predominantly high in the affective/expressive and interpersonal/harmony dimensions of style. They resent Sandy's air of superiority and demands for high performance without any promise of rewards. They need recognition and appreciation from Sandy, but he rarely has time to give such "soft" rewards. He has only rewarded people for sales results that affect the bottom line. He has, over the years, demonstrated inflexibility in his approach to others and becomes really irritable with people who do not accept his domineering approach, putting them down in front of others. The increases in company profitability were 3 percent and 5 percent during the past two years, respectively, not enough to keep up with inflation. The turnover rate in the sales division and in the secretary and receptionist positions has been over 34 percent per year, primarily because these employees have had frequent contact with Sandy—and as a result reported that their primary reason for seeking work elsewhere was to avoid working for him. Sandy's wife left him three months ago.

The Intervention: Sandy took a one-day *Personal Style Indicator* workshop and learned that his relationships with the people in his life have been characterized by a rather self-oriented and caustic approach, because he often got short-term results by intimidating people in subtle ways. As a result of the workshop, and the feedback Sandy got from his wife and the other managers just below him, he decided to change the way he treated the high A and I sales and support staff (and his A–I marriage partner); to eliminate "put-down" statements and behaviors from his management style; add more interpersonal behaviors such as expressing appreciation for a job well done, host an awards ceremony every six months for those in the company who achieve agreed-upon reasonable levels of performance; institute an employee-of-the month recognition program for exceptional performance beyond what is expected; and institute interpersonal skills training and team-building sessions for him and his management staff.

The Results: After one year, the turnover rate decreased to 7 percent from the previous 34 percent. Two-way communication improved between Sandy and his employees at all levels. Problems that had previously been "swept under the carpet," because most people avoided Sandy altogether, were solved. Overall profitability of the company increased 14 percent. Sandy's wife decided to try to reestablish their marriage relationship.

This is a dramatic example of how Sandy's developing some interpersonal skills and versatility in his approach to people with styles opposite to his own had a dramatic effect on the performance of his subordinates.

It is important to realize that style shows up in organizational orientations and government leaders' approaches to politics and international relations and that certain style tendencies can pervade whole societies. For example, President Clinton is often perceived as demonstrating an affective/expressive and behavioral/action orientation, acting upon the environment in an assertive and highly verbal manner. The United States and Great Britain, as cultures, are often perceived quite differently from one another. The English, however, have described Americans as appearing to be more "bizarre" (expressive) than they are, and the English are described by Americans as having a tendency toward an analytical approach, being more reserved and "stuffy." The English can be heard to say that Americans are too impulsive and run headlong into situations without thinking through the consequences first.

Of course, England and France have been experiencing "clashes" of style for centuries, in the same way that English-speaking and French-speaking Canada have (although, in general, Canada can be seen, like Switzerland, as having an interpersonal/harmony orientation). The English find the free expressiveness of the French to be overwhelming and even revolting (in the extreme). The stuffiness and formality of the English make the French feel restricted, giving them the impression that the English are "phony." Modern Japan can be seen as having a more complex combination of action, analytical, and interpersonal orientations (with an emphasis on the interpersonal). German culture would likely be seen as action and analysis in its orientation.

Style assessment is complex and difficult, but that style differences can cause difficulties between people cannot be denied. Learning to shift approaches to people can increase our effectiveness with them, reduce conflict, enhance leadership credibility, and facilitate relationship development.

In the next section of this chapter, we will examine the nature of the three major roles—and the tasks appropriate to accomplish in each role the transforming leader fulfills. It is important to keep in mind that a continuing awareness of "style" has a catalytic effect when a person is functioning in all three of the major roles of communicator, counselor, and consultant.

Role Shifting For Greater Effectiveness and Appropriateness

Skills #51 and #52. Assessment of Roles and Role Shifting

Appropriate role shifting makes the leader's responses more effective, and in turn, a follower's response is often more favorable. Proper role shifting as a foundation of appropriateness is needed in order to build the base of influence and trust that leaders need to help develop both people and organizations in a positive manner. It is quite ineffective for a leader to attempt to function in a mutual–communicative or advisory–consultative manner with a resistant employee who clearly needs the problem management approach of the counseling role. It is likewise counterproductive to "counsel" with people who first need to develop a mutual, open-communicative relationship or to see that they can work as effective team members with the leader as consultant and group facilitator.

What Is Role Shifting?

Role shifting is the ability to shift moment to moment among three different sets of skills—depending upon the situations or people encountered. It is important that you become able to shift among these three sets of skills when interacting with colleagues or followers so your interventions will have a greater likelihood of meeting expectations, needs, and preferences. This may seem to make the process of leadership very complex and difficult. It is complex, but a style-shift model breaks down reality into small enough "chunks" that we can learn each part of it before integrating the chunk into a larger picture. Effective leadership requires the ability to deal with complexity, break it into manageable pieces, and intervene with a continuous alertness to the impact we are making.

In keeping with the evidence that effectiveness is related to complexity and versatility of leader behavior, it would assist leaders to be more effective if they could discern which of the three roles is appropriate with each individual, group, or organization in each moment. Further delineation of the three roles involved in role shifting is presented below.

In the Communication Role: Positive interpersonal communication is the appropriate mode in which to be functioning when you want to develop a mutual relationship with a person. It is appropriate with co-workers, family, friends, and even acquaintances on a day-to-day basis. It forms the foundation of all relationships and is usually appropriate at the beginning of a relationship and for maintaining and building relationships. It is the informal "glue" that bonds any relationship, and without it, there can be a kind of robotic formality that can interfere with the fostering of easygoing and effective relating with others.

The police leader finds the building of relationships to be a recurring event that involves both new and experienced police members. For example, a young officer comes into the police culture, where the leader becomes the socialization agent. In this process, the young officer must learn the values and expected behaviors within the culture. There are rituals that must be learned. There is the unique "language" of policing that must be understood. While this regimenting process of organizational socialization occurs, the leader must ensure that channels of communication are not only open but are used by the new hire. This is the time to establish the bond that not only permits but encourages communication in times of question or crisis.

This kind of mentoring relationship is the key channel for the new hire in getting his or her needs met to understand what kind of performance and attitude constitute a job well done. The organization's culture is transmitted in this relationship. Therefore it is imperative that field training officers are carefully selected in order to ensure the transmission of positive cultural values. My recommendation is that, in addition to field training officers for the training of recruits, special "leadership training officers" be selected and trained well so that they learn to mentor new leaders toward competency in leadership.

However, establishing this communication role becomes even more critical and difficult as seniority in the organization and consequently a broader experience base becomes a factor. The socialization process occurs even among the most senior members. Specialized police units are often rife with rituals and ceremonies. The fact of belonging is often displayed by clothing or other visible markings. Experienced police officers will remember the days of the "topcoat and fedora" as the sure indicator that they were in the presence of a detective. These specialized units tend to have a high level of comradeship (some may describe it as elitism) and newcomers often have to "prove themselves" as being worthy of belonging.

The relationship established between the unit leader (either formal or informal) and the new arrival serves a twofold purpose. It provides support to the newcomer and demonstrates to the group that the leader is building a relationship, a sign of acceptance. It also allows the leader to provide direction and, where appropriate, criticism, in a role shift to counseling that assists in both the development and acceptance of the person to the group.

This mode can also include the more difficult aspects of interpersonal communication, such as giving and receiving feedback, assertiveness, and confrontation.

In the Counseling Role: Effective counseling and coaching, which involves personal and interpersonal problem management and personal problem solving, is most appropriate when co-workers, colleagues, or subordinates are having personal difficulties that interfere with their work performance or relationships with others. Your acting as a facilitator of their personal and interpersonal development by assisting them to specify their own problems in relation to a problem situation (and then take effective action) can be a great impetus in keeping people, groups, and organizations "unblocked."

This facilitation may require exposing unpleasant realities to the individual. Such was the case when a senior police investigator sought a transfer to a specialized unit. When the members of the unit heard of the request, they responded almost vehemently to the supervisor. There were significant historical problems with the applicant's relationship with others to the point that he was "a pain" to those within his own unit.

The supervisor had discussions with the applicant over several weeks. As an experienced and self-confident officer, the applicant's attitude was that of a "loner." Over the course of discussions partially based in reflective interviewing techniques, the supervisor was able to raise the applicant's level of understanding of how he was perceived by his existing team. As a result of the supervisor's confrontation, the team's need for harmony became apparent to the applicant.

The supervisor also worked with the team. Team sessions were held in which members had the opportunity to voice their concerns. What became evident was that very few could relate well with the investigator who was seeking the transfer. Their opinions had been formed based on the applicant's "reputation," something that is very common in policing and very often destructive in terms of organizational socialization. Once this "reputation" is locked in, it is difficult to change.

The supervisor was able to bring the team members to the point of acknowledging that their negative predisposition was based on rumor rather than fact. Interpersonal relations were "tainted" even before the applicant had arrived. The supervisor was able to counsel the group into adopting a wait-and-see attitude with the applicant. He had successfully removed the "block" that had been created by the group to acceptance of the applicant as a leader of the team on a trial basis.

When the applicant was transferred to the specialized unit, the supervisor continued in the counseling role. The new member was interviewed regularly and was provided the opportunity to verbalize feelings about what was occurring in the unit. The lack of an adversarial atmosphere in the unit led to positive interactions with the members of the unit. As time passed, the "loner" behavior began to disappear and socialization was clearly evident.

Members were invited to express their observations of the new member to the supervisor. By doing so, each person verbalized the lack of anything that resembled the fears that were articulated only a short time before. Eventually the members began to express their feelings directly to the new member, who responded not defensively but in an understanding manner. He had learned a great deal about group dynamics and member interdependence from the supervisor. The consequence was that it was not long before group members were defending the new member against comments made by those from outside the unit.

This kind of coaching relationship is where the counseling skills in Chapter 6 can be used to guide the development of a subordinate. This occurs by continuous observation and assessment, discussion, guidance, and encouragement so that the subordinate learns directly by practicing new skills, and the manager's own expertise is passed on.

In the Consultative Role: It is appropriate to shift into the consultative mode or role when the person, group, or organization with which you are interacting requires and expects you to do some kind of assessment, intervention, evaluation, and ongoing monitoring. Sometimes you may find yourself under pressure to respond authoritatively or even sternly, perhaps because your position as leader causes others to expect you to be decisive and resolute—especially when time for critical decisions is limited. When you have to make decisions that require an overall awareness of organizational factors of which others may not be aware, then it is especially important to act cautiously and to use this consultative mode. Even if you are not in a leadership position, it can be appropriate at times to act in this role, especially if your action can be seen as effective and appreciated by those in positions "above" and "below" you.

Group identity among police is strong. This is particularly true in the areas that perform specialist functions. If a member of the group is seen as not contributing to the goals of the group, the negative reactions from unit members may range from moderate to extreme. The acts of a single individual may cause the group to become dysfunctional. Because this can be dangerous in critical situations, it is reasonable to expect that members can be upset by even one negative associate.

For example, a senior investigator was transferred to a highly regarded specialized police investigation unit. Although well liked by the group, the person was seen as not contributing to the "professional status" goal of the group. Also, unit members believed that the investigator was not accepting his "fair share" of the work being assigned. In addition, there was an unofficial standard to which all investigators were expected to perform. Subtle peer pressure became more public. Eventually the unit supervisor began to feel pressure from the group members to intercede and resolve the perceived problem.

There had been a history of performance issues for which the senior investigator had received disciplinary counseling on a number of occasions. The unit supervisor tried a mentoring process, but this failed. Clearly, the responsibility of the "leader" at this point was an intervention for the good of the group and, by association, for the overall and long-term good of the individual and the organization.

The interventions began with a performance review interview that included specified and agreed-to performance standards and outcomes. Both the performance level of the investigator and his interactions with the unit members were monitored by the unit supervisor.

The supervisor was, in fact, operating in a consultative role to the individual, the team, and the organization. The investigator required clear and immediate behavior modification to correct the behaviors that the group found unacceptable. Further, these behaviors were also unacceptable to the organization in that they did not meet the level of performance required of a member of the specialized unit, and they were counter to the stated and agreed-to values of the organization. The result of this consultative intervention was that the inadequate performance of the investigator was resolved and this ensured an acceptable level of team performance to the organization's standards.

Blending Roles to Increase Effectiveness

Sometimes situations occur where it is important to accomplish the goals of two or three of these roles. These interchanges are more complex. For example, suppose you have an employee named Manuel who has recently lost his brother in an automobile accident.

In some situations like this, which require greater complexity on your part, you may find it more effective to begin your conversation with role-free communication, with a response such as: "Is it possible you might join us for that round of golf on Saturday that we have been meaning to have?"

Then, as the conversation progresses to more personal material, you can appropriately intervene with a counseling response: "I can understand how you are finding it difficult to get into doing your patrol route this coming week because of the recent loss you have experienced in your family."

Then, intervene with a consultative response as you get into exploring options with Manuel about how to deal with the grief: "I think I can arrange for Bill and Sue to take your route next week if you would like that. The unit members could cover your time off."

Manuel needs time off work to spend with his family, and your caring about his pain by giving him time off will likely be of great value to him. He is an employee who will likely never betray or disappoint you, will likely defend you when others may be unfairly critical, and is likely to find working for you and with you a refreshing change from many other leaders.

The creative combining of the three leadership roles can provide you with greater freedom of choice in how you will respond to another person. By changing roles, role shifting allows you to communicate the value you place on people.

A policing environment offers a very unique challenge for leaders to undertake. In the previous pages, we examined how a new hire in an organization or an applicant for a position in a specialized unit needs to be approached through the three different roles in order to effectively integrate him or her into the police culture and assist the person in functioning effectively among his or her peers. Although the police organization is uniquely different, the primary tasks at hand are fairly consistent with other organizations.

Policing differs significantly, however, in that the new hire, applicant, or seasoned officer must also be able to exercise these same role-shifting skills with the general public. As community leaders, intervening agents, and problem solvers, the police must be able to utilize these skills to deal with the many complex conflicts that the police are daily called upon to mediate. The skill with which the officer is able to recognize the appropriate role to utilize and shift into that role will greatly influence the success of the intervention and proposed resolution. Everyone has heard of the term "rookie syndrome." This often can be attributed to the fact that junior officers' role-shifting skills are not yet exercised and developed. Often, rookies are rigid and lack the ability to skill, style, or role shift. They therefore rely on the hard letter of rules, regulations, and laws to help them make their decisions. This can lead to an inappropriate response in many situations, which can lead to dissatisfaction and complaints on the part of the public or fellow officers.

A unique challenge for the police leader is to assist all officers in the organization to learn role-shifting skills that can be appropriately applied in their day-to-day public interactions. **The better all officers are able to adapt these skills, the fewer public complaints that will be received related to inappropriate officer response to incidents.** This coaching of officers' abilities in various situations must be passed on by their supervisors in the field, which means that these supervisors must themselves possess the knowledge and skills of role shifting.

How Role Shifting Communicates that You Value Others and Builds Positive Culture

The critical difference in *Transforming Leadership* is that it attempts to meet organizational objectives and, at the same time, builds teams and communicates the value of the individuals in each interchange. In fact, one of the organizational objectives in an organization led by a transforming leader is to communicate the value of people to co-workers and followers, and encourage them to understand and communicate that same value to others. In this way, you can better create a value-driven organization that lives and breathes what it believes. This positive culture encourages and nurtures the development of people, which in turn can promote well-being, creativity, and productivity of work groups and organizations.

Compare this vision with that of the rigid, role-bound bureaucratic manager who responds mainly "by the book," who does not "flex" self or procedures for the sake of people. Many police organizations tend to function based on the organization's "book," known as the standing orders, the procedures manual, or the regulations. These "books" attempt to deal with every possible manner of procedural or administrative circumstance that may arise in the course of policing. The bureaucratic manager often uses this type of publication as a "safety net." Decisions are defended on the basis of "it's in the book." Demoralization occurs when people are treated in this depersonalizing manner.

Such was the case when one police supervisor was due for transfer. The supervisor's current assignment was administrative. Aware that a transfer would probably occur shortly, he contacted the department's personnel officer. During the discussions, it was agreed that he should not return to duties as a patrol supervisor, as he had two previous postings in that position. As this was a relatively large police organization, there were many other options available, and he was seeking a new challenge. Shortly after this interview, the supervisor received a phone call from the acting personnel officer, who informed him that he was being transferred to a patrol supervisor position. This was exactly what he did not want. The reason given by the acting personnel director was, "There's a hole out there that needs filling and you're available, so you're going." Obviously, this impersonal approach was not well received and failed to make the highest and best use of the supervisor's motivations. The supervisor was demoralized, demotivated, and felt that in his next assignment he was just going to "do the job—and no more."

By contrast, leading others in the way in which we would like to be led— by considering them and even asking them how we can respond to meet their needs—is leading by the Golden Rule. Using the communication role to make friends and develop relationships; the counseling role to resolve personal, interpersonal, and performance/morale problems; and the consultative role to implement team or organizational interventions will increase the complexity and therefore the effectiveness of your responses.

The Importance of Being Genuine and Respectful When Acting in Various Roles

Most people prefer a leader who is a genuine person at all times and who treats them as individuals. Sincerity and respect are key qualities to communicate in all three roles. If you are genuine and respectful when you attempt to communicate, counsel, or consult with someone, your credibility will increase almost automatically. Making statements that clearly identify your personal opinions and feelings can encourage others to see that you are not "role bound," that you are approachable, and that you, too, are a person who can make mistakes, learn, and develop.

This genuine and respectful attitude and approach communicates the qualities of honesty and humility. Even when you have to exercise difficult leadership authority in stressful situations, you can still communicate this kind of humility, a willingness to serve, and a willingness to be wrong. By communicating these qualities in your language, your tone of voice, and your actions, others will feel more respected and will have a greater sense of trust in, and respect for, you.

Specific tasks are appropriate in each role. These tasks are typical of the kinds of things that you would normally discover need to be handled in each role. Achievement of these three sets of tasks requires the three sets of skills for their accomplishment. These tasks are summarized in the next section to further elucidate the complexity and potential in style, role, and skill shifting.

Role Shifting: The Tasks Inherent in the Three Roles

The relationship among the three roles (or modes of functioning) and the tasks in each of the three roles is illustrated in the chart on the next page. The tasks outlined in the chart are typical of each role. Achievement of each requires practicing the set of skills appropriate to that role. Understanding that these tasks are often necessary to facilitate development of people and organizations is another step toward exerting a transforming effect wherever you go.

Role Rigidity Obstructs Leadership Effectiveness

A parent who cannot become a friend to his or her child is an all too common situation. An overly friendly boss can lose credibility and clout when it comes time for confrontation. Trying to act in the consultative role when others are not asking for it or expecting it can cause others to see you as overly officious or "high-minded." With practice, however, your increased ability to shift roles

Appropriate Shifting of Roles and Typical Tasks

Communication

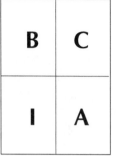

To facilitate
personal and
relationship
development

- Developing trust
- Sharing fun times
- Relaxing together
- Appreciating and attending
- Facilitating two-way, mutual listening
- Showing interest and understanding
- Getting agreement about how to communicate better
- Being assertive and respectful at the same time
- Encouraging, validating, and rewarding others
- Making the work more meaningful and less lonely
- Understanding personal styles of others
- Shifting your style to develop versatility
- Solving simple, external problems
- Challenging others to develop

Counseling

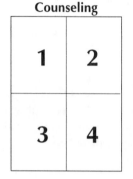

To facilitate
problem
management and
conflict resolution

- Problem management and solving
- Specifying internal problems
- Developing deeper trust
- Specifying personal problems of followers
- Setting goals
- Exploring alternate strategies
- Action planning for problem management
- Confronting low performance
- Giving direction when appropriate
- Mediating inter-personal disputes
- Negotiating inter-personal contracts
- Understanding the developmental levels of others
- Adjusting helping approach based on these levels

Consulting

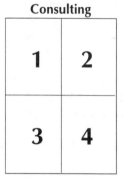

To facilitate group
and organization
development

- Developing more credibility and organization-wide trust
- Specifying internal problems of the organization
- Specifying the vision and purpose
- Communicating organizational goals, values, and norms
- Building organizational culture
- Selecting and training appropriate people
- Building effective work teams
- Evaluating and researching
- Forecasting changes required for success
- Adjusting course based on these forecasts
- Being open to innovations and opportunities
- Understanding the stage of the group/organization
- Adjusting approach based on stage of development

gracefully and appropriately will assist you in meeting the challenge of constant change and complexity in your organization, with groups, and with individuals—at work or at home.

In addition, more appropriate interventions with individuals, groups, and organizations can be better understood by using personal style theory. Once you internalize a clear understanding of the theory, you can learn to better "read" the style tendencies of groups and organizations.

Skill Shifting for Greater Versatility in Leadership Roles

Skills #53 and #54. Intentionally Assessing and Shifting Skills

Assessing the skills appropriate to a particular situation is relatively easy if you know what role is appropriate in the given situation or with a particular person or group. The following examples will help clarify how this skill-shifting approach works.

Shifting into the Communication Role: A few months ago, I was coaching the CEO of a business to build his executive team. He rarely played the consultative role because he did not have the skills to do so. That was not his fault. His MBA had taught him analytical skills he could apply to managing his company well, but he was not taught the skills he needed to build a team, to work on designing and developing a better organization, and to do strategic planning and implementation.

As I coached him, I modeled all three sets of skills. Over lunch, we discussed, in a very mutual way, how difficult it was for me to develop the skills and apply them consistently in my own life and business. I shared with him some ways in which I failed to use what I know. He was relieved and saw me as being more humble and approachable and less the "expert" he had imagined me to be. I intentionally shared my mistakes and shortcomings with him to move our relationship into greater intimacy and mutuality. We were in the very mutual communication role together over lunch, and I became more "real" to him. This was appropriate and a natural development of the personal side of our relationship.

Shifting into the Counseling Role: Then, in the afternoon session with the CEO and his senior vice-president who was not functioning up to the CEO's standards, I had to shift into the counseling role. I asked both parties for their permission to act as the problem manager/mediator in their scheduled conflict resolution encounter with one another. As each voiced his disappointments and concerns with one another, I acted as a mediator to ensure that two-way communication occurred. I also functioned in the closely related counselor role to ensure that each party understood and took ownership of some behaviors in which each engaged that were not effective. We resolved some unresolved issues that had been troubling their work and personal relationship for years. After about an hour, when we finished talking, they both said something very strange. They confessed that they had never really talked with each other before! This is all too typical of many business and marriage relationships. People just don not have the skills to make it work and don not always apply the skills even when they do have them!

Shifting into the Consulting Role: In the late afternoon session, we spent two hours with the executive team in order to conduct the monthly executive review. The CEO chaired the meeting, and I was there to coach his group leadership and meeting facilitation skills. Before the meeting started, I enlisted agreement that I would function, for the most part, in the consultative mode for this afternoon meeting. Everyone wanted to learn these skills because they all had to go back to their functional teams and lead their own meetings. We therefore worked with three agendas all at once: (1) we had a meeting, (2) we had a training session on how to run better meetings and lead better, and (3) we wanted to get real work done. Training, learning, and getting the job done needed to occur simultaneously.

Notice in the preceding chart that the tasks under each of the three roles require the use of the skills in order to do the tasks well. These tasks are the work of *Transforming Leadership*. The skills required to perform these tasks are the three sets of skills that were the focus of the previous three chapters. All the skills build upon one another, sometimes overlap, and at other times are used separately, intentionally.

Recognizing and Facilitating
the Stages of Organization Development

TL Skill #55. Recognition of
Organization Developmental Stages

In this section, the developmental stages of a group or organization and the skills appropriate to each stage are examined.

Stages of Development in a Group or Organization

Understanding stages of development is beneficial to a leader because it enables him or her to accurately assess the stage at which a group or organization is currently functioning. It also facilitates clear planning for the next steps of development that need attention. Without the ability to assess stages of development, the following often-made mistakes may be committed:

1. Trying to build teams before goals are clarified
2. Setting goals and attempting strategic planning before there is a clear purpose in the minds of the people involved
3. Specifying programs to achieve results before identifying specific goals to be accomplished

To be a leader who can demonstrate versatility, it is useful to use some kind of model to understand the development of groups and organizations. There are various models for assessing the levels of development of a group or organization; some are complex and others are relatively simple. Of course, in reality, events overlap in each stage but the details of the five-stage model presented below will help map the territory of group and organization development and thereby respond more effectively as a leader.

Introduction to the Five Stages of Group and Organization Development

Stage 1. Design, Orientation, and Commitment: This stage complements what Adizes (1988) describes as the "courtship stage" in his book *Corporate Life Cycles.* Orienting people to the entrepreneurial, inspiring, or ennobling vision, values, and goals of the organization inspires them to commit themselves to the task of achieving the vision, all critical factors in *Transforming Leadership.*

Informal introduction and orientation processes are appropriate at this stage. These can involve retreats or the "whisper- in-the-ear" approach, where successful group members act as ongoing mentors in the orientation, coaching, or training processes. People usually want to know how they can succeed in the organization or group when they first enter it. Those who meet this prime need are likely to be heard most thoroughly. Often, some kind of emotional experience needs to occur for an orientation "courtship" to be effective. Some companies have effectively created their corporate cultures with their executives at retreats in remote places where the company's norms, values, beliefs, and philosophy were introduced in both a formal and informal fashion.

Commitment by a member to a group or organization is achieved to the extent to which the neophyte "buys into" the stated purpose, philosophy, and goals of the organization in a genuine way. The closer the new member's position is to the group's values and beliefs prior to joining, the more likely there will be a "locking in" or bonding effect. Just prior to commitment, a new member often experiences a sense of "I feel like I belong here." This sense of belonging would appear to be a critical factor in attaining the level of commit-ment required for the achievement of a highly developed corporate culture that leads to exceptional achievements.

Stage 2. Making the Transition—Overcoming Resistance and Obstacles: This stage is similar to what Adizes calls the "infancy stage." Even though a person has psychologically "bought into" the group or organization at the end of Stage 1, there has not yet been a real investment of self, time, energy, planning, envisioning of achievements, and sweat to match dreams. In making the transition to full involvement, group members need to be personally in-volved in formulating some of the general goals and action plans that will later result in programs that will be implemented and evaluated. People need to be recognized and rewarded in ways that are personally meaningful.

It is during this transition stage—where general goal setting and specific objectives are committed to by each member—that resistance and obstacles often rear their heads. Many people will commit themselves to lofty goals and agree to achieve objectives, but when they show up at the next meeting, often they have not achieved what they intended. The way people are handled by leaders during this critical stage can set the tone for the failure or success of a group.

It is also at this stage that the distracting or withdrawn group or team member will often surface. This is the time when some of the individuals who said they "bought in" to the purpose and philosophy of the group or organization often unwittingly reveal feathers of a different color. Conflict ensues, feet drag, and some members just can't seem to "get with it." Resentment can develop on the part of the group members who are "with it." If the leader does not facilitate the group or organization through this stage, it likely will never move on to accom-plishments that fulfill the vision thought to be shared, but may limp along acceptably, minimally, for a time.

At this stage—when goals are set and objectives cast as commitments—leaders who facilitate further development will take actions such as confronting and coaching (or dismissing) poor performers, resolving group-member conflict, working through intergroup clash or confusion, and refusing to tolerate opposi-tion to or undermining of valued corporate culture. If the leader allows conflict and tension to continue to the point of undermining the potential effectiveness of the group or organization, then he or she is either knowingly or unwittingly participating in its demise. If leaders intervene swiftly and effectively at this time, however, great potential lies ahead in the working stage of the group.

Stage 3. Doing the Work of the Group: Adizes calls this stage the "go–go" stage. When individual resistance, group-member conflict, and intergroup clashes are for the most part handled, then the group members can get on with achieving the vision with a simultaneous sense of relief and enthusiasm. When this stage begins, people often sense it! It is a pleasure to work at a place—with a group—in an organization where "unfinished business" does not pile up under the carpet. Leaders are respected when things can move to this working stage; when energy is released, learning and creativity are unleashed. When problems are encountered at this stage, the group or organization has already developed systems and approaches to deal with many of them effectively. New products are launched, new systems are put into place, and there is a fresh sense of being part of a "going concern."

In addition, several other important things occur during this stage. Members have become acquainted with one another; they are more familiar with one another's personal and work styles, strengths, difficult areas, reactions to stress and pressure, and tendencies to lead or follow. This familiarity can breed performance and fine-tuning of the team's efforts. Job descriptions can also be renegotiated and rewritten into working agreements—based on expressed needs for change or newly recognized talents of group members in areas of specialty previously unknown in Stage 2.

Stage 4. Making the Transition from an Entrepreneurially Run Firm to a Professionally Run Firm: This stage is similar to what Adizes calls the "adolescent stage." Typically, this is the most difficult transition to make because the senior leader or owner has to make great changes to establish financial, information, marketing, sales, and quality improvement systems that tax his or her current knowledge and skills limits. This is where the senior leader must learn to work more on the organization and not so much in it. Teams are developed and learn to function well, cross-functionally. They also learn to communicate with customers so that they can answer concerns well enough to demonstrate that they care and will deliver what the customer wants, fast. Many companies fail at this stage because of what Adizes calls the "founder trap"—where the owner cannot delegate or accept input from others and is often unwilling to do the proper planning and implementation that must pave the way to larger scale success. Where the leader does make it through this stage, the organization becomes a leadership organization.

Stage 5. The Mature, Flourishing Organization. Adizes calls this stage the "prime stage." There is a balance among innovation, planning, operational implementation, and integration of systems. The ability to learn quickly from mistakes and to correct course based on facts is greatly enhanced. A key feature of the mature company is that it is wise, anticipates and tests the accuracy of predictions regarding future trends, and is on the cutting edge of creating and responding to new markets and providing new services. This stage represents a fully functioning learning organization.

In today's police organizations, a relatively new phenomenon is becoming a part of every community's policing efforts: the trend toward greater public accountability, interaction, and participation in police efforts. There is widespread implementation of police–community liaison organizations in which the police and the citizens form an organization of sorts to examine, address, and plan police response to community issues.

This new partnering relationship between the community and the police is challenging the abilities of the police leaders in nurturing this new "organization" through the above stages of a developing organization. Many organizations are in Stage 1 (design, orientation, and commitment). Both the police and the community are exploring how they can work together to develop a cohesive and productive working group. Some of these organizations have progressed to Stage 2 (making the transition—overcoming resistance and obstacles). This is where the community liaison group has its greatest challenges. There can be great reluctance on the part of many officers to embrace an organization where the general public has a more significant role in shaping the objectives and goals of the police. There can often be a lack of trust or passive resistance to the successful implementation of this organizational structure and its goals. Perhaps one of the greatest challenges for police leaders in their communities is assisting there officers in becoming functioning, participating, and contributing members of this new organization.

Learning from feedback (both positive and negative), celebrating success, and planning for new levels of achievement can all have a powerful impact on how people experience their membership in organizations and groups. Because developing a leadership organization is such an important part of the preparation for building a learning organization, let's look at the ten steps involved in developing teams and organizations.

TL Skill #55. Facilitation of the Organization Development Stages

Ten Steps in the Process of Developing a Team or Organization

The ten steps in developing a team or organization are examined in detail so that you can gain further insight into the nature of the way groups and organizations develop and how you can act as a catalytic agent to make this development occur.

Step 1. Solidifying and Communicating the Mandate: This step of team or organization development requires that the leader have a mandate or some authority to proceed with a position of power to decide, power to move in certain directions, or a vision or mission that has the sanction of an official body. For example, only when a college president has a mandate from the board or other governing agency to provide a certain level of quality and scope of instruction may he or she proceed with clarity and authority. Furthermore, if an entrepreneur were to start his or her own company, then the government of most free-world states would give that person the right to exercise a self-decreed mandate: to make money by engaging in free enterprise.

It is often necessary and many times desirable that there be a clear mandate (from "on high," as it were) to proceed without coming into conflict with the purpose of the organization or authorities in charge of its overall direction or operation. Volunteer organizations are famous for "splintering" when a "leader" decides he or she needs to achieve a personal purpose not in harmony with the larger (officially) "mandated" vision of the organization according to its constitution. It is desirable to prevent this splintering effect whenever possible by making the mandate clear in the minds of everyone in the group or organization.

Clarity is made possible by publishing the mandate in writing and by initiating an orientation process whereby people understand that going against the mandate will result in their losing membership in the group or organization. One delivery company has issued a mandate of safety at all levels of the organization. Irresponsibility toward the safety of anyone is not tolerated. If, for example, an employee of the company is caught speeding while driving a company delivery vehicle on the freeway, the result is known in advance to be immediate dismissal.

In summary, then, the mandate makes explicit what the purpose of an organization or group can and cannot be. It specifies what is acceptable and what is not. It spells out in no uncertain terms how things will be and often remains quite stable and inflexible throughout the life of the organization, as in the constitutions of various government bodies. The mandate comprises the assumptions, fundamental definitions, and rules that everyone is required to know and follow when dealing with one another and with the organization. Some organizations or groups call the mandate their "terms of reference."

Many individuals resist creating, publishing, communicating, or standing up for a mandate because it can seem to some people to be "authoritarian" or rigid. It does not have to be however, as in the case of a constitution founded upon the democratic principles of freedom of speech, freedom of worship, freedom from discrimination, etc. A humane mandate—built upon the assumption that people are valuable—will be a solid foundation on which to build a group or organization.

Consider the following sample mandate statement of A to Z Community Services Agency:

> Our mandate is to provide support and develop community-based social services mostly to needy members of the community. We cannot

compete with existing government or private agencies, but will supplement their services to fulfill unmet needs where such government services fall short due to funding, staff shortages, or people's inability to pay for such services.

If you can help a group or organization to clarify and communicate its mandate effectively to its members, you will likely prevent all sorts of misunderstandings, misdirection, and conflict from emerging and destroying the integrity and cohesion needed for further development. After achieving this first step, the next one is assisting in the clarification of the organization's purpose, vision, or mission.

Step 2. Clarifying Purpose, Mission, or Vision: As a next step in this first stage, a purpose statement is a further specification and extension of the mandate statement. The terms purpose, mission, and vision are used synonymously to refer to a group or organization's reason for being. Some leaders, such as Dr. Martin Luther King, have a "dream" (in his case, it was an inner vision driven by passion and commitment) that they communicate to their group members. Others have a purpose statement that is perhaps less fiery but nevertheless provides overall direction and reason for being to the members of a group or organization.

Assisting group members to achieve understanding of and consensus around a purpose statement, and what the statement means, is a critical prerequisite to "gelling" the group into one functional entity. If you can get people to "buy in" to the organization's reason for existence as a part of their own reason for being, then you have instant commitment! For example, it wasn't hard for Douglas Aircraft plant workers to arrive at work group consensus about what their purpose was at the beginning of World War II. The employees realized they were an absolutely necessary part of a war machine that, if they built it fast and well, had the potential to save their own lives and the lives of their children.

However, the "buy in" as to the purpose of policing today is not nearly as clear as the reason for Douglas Aircraft's existence during World War II. Policing is in a state of massive flux. The very purpose of policing is being questioned over and over. From the *Vigils* of the first century B.C. in Rome through the *parish constables* of fourteenth century England to the *Bobbies* of Sir Robert Peel, the role of the police in society has constantly changed. What is the purpose of the police organization? The challenge facing the police leader is that there are as many different opinions within the organization as outside it. Many police organizations have seen their efforts to achieve a purpose of collaborative policing with their communities resisted strongly from within. The perception of those within is that the purpose of the organization is to provide services as a separate and distinct entity, not joined in a collaborative effort. One large police organization's executive spent considerable time, effort, and funding to develop what was considered to be a mission statement that could and would be embraced by the community and the members of the department. Instead, the mission statement became the brunt of jokes by the police officers. They resisted it so strongly that eventually the mission statement was scrapped and a new one developed.

The concept of visioning or developing purpose statements can be utilized at each level of the police organization. Recently, the human resources unit of a large police organization entered into this process. This organization, like many others, was struggling to define the role of a human resources unit. The complexities of human resource functions, such as hiring, training, entitlements, performance management ,and labor relations, had left many unclear as to their role. Also, a major restructuring initiative within the department had resulted in significant downsizing. There were significant personnel changes as the team-building process began.

To assist in building this new team, an off-site session was held to establish, within the group, their beliefs in relation to their role in the organization. The session was held at the behest of the group members as they sought clarity, not in the "nuts and bolts" of day-to-day operation but in the global vision of the organization and the unit leader. This group was comprised of senior supervisors who were chosen for human resources because of their experience, skills, ethics, and demonstrated ability to "get the job done." They needed consensus surrounding the purpose for which they worked each day.

By the end of the session, the group had developed a vision statement that the members unhesitatingly rallied behind. Consensus was achieved and the vision statement was adopted as describing how they wanted the organization and the world to see the new human resources unit. They expressed feelings of satisfaction in that they now had "direction" to which they could focus their energy.

Vision Statement of the Human Resources Unit

We are a values-based service provider, widely recognized as a leader in the management of human resources, in support of a progressive, effective police service.

Purpose Statement of A to Z Community Services Agency

Our purpose is to enrich the lives of community members—especially the poor, provide for their basic material needs, offer them personal development opportunities they otherwise would not receive, and provide training and avenues for the expression of volunteer services and financial contributions.

Step 3. Specifying and Gaining Consensus about Philosophy, Values, Beliefs, and Norms: This next step in the first stage of developing a group or organization is also very important. Without a similar philosophical orientation, there really cannot be a cohesive group or organization. A group's philosophy is comprised of values (priorities and importance) and beliefs (assumptions about what is true, good, false, bad, etc.). In addition, without agreed-upon norms (extension of values and beliefs—agreement about ways of treating people and solving problems), people may find they have frequent clashes with one another, and the group or organization will likely either live in disharmony and lose productive energies or may fall apart.

In one organization where I acted as an external consultant, staff members were working with a base of conflicting values, beliefs, and assumptions. They certainly were at odds with one another—with resultant harm to young people in the organization where a mandate was in place to rehabilitate them. In this example, about half of the correctional officers in the juvenile correctional facility honestly believed their purpose was to attempt to facilitate the development of juveniles, with the eventual hope of rehabilitating them as self-respecting citizens of the community. The other half of the staff referred to the residents as "slugs who'll never amount to anything" and treated them with strong disrespect. Staff members fought bitterly with one another and were in conflict daily about this issue of the worth of the offenders in custody. Staff turnover was high as management was blamed by both sides(!) for "hiring a bunch of idiots."

The leaders of the juvenile facility did not attend to this issue of specifying and communicating purpose when they hired the correctional officers. They didn't even ask them or their previous employers their purpose for working with juveniles! The juveniles received these two conflicting messages on a daily basis. As a result, program efforts were undermined and discipline procedures were implemented with entirely opposite spirits—one with a spirit of discipline and the other with a spirit of punishment. The end results were disastrously in favor of the punishing officers' predictions.

At a point of crisis—after a riot during which the youths damaged the facilities extensively—management asked me to facilitate a team development process with the management group first and then with the whole staff. We started with an examination of the mandate that was in the contract the agency had signed with the government funding body. Then we moved on to creating purpose statements on flip charts on the walls until we had as much consensus as possible among the group of twenty-eight staff. It became clear it was going to be difficult to move ahead with the next step of specifying philosophy because the conflict in the air was so thick that it turned everyone to ice.

When we moved into clarifying the organization's philosophy about how to treat kids and staff, the worth of kids, the approach to discipline and control, etc., the frustration was so great among those with a punitive attitude that eight of the "old-school, old-guard" staff quit within days. New staff were soon hired—individuals who "bought in" to the juvenile center's philosophy—and stress and conflict levels decreased immediately. The organization began to "gel" into a cohesive group of people "of the same mind." Within a few weeks, consistent evidence of positive impact on the juveniles was observed. The organization was then in a position to reevaluate its general goals.

The police/community organization faces its greatest challenges in this step. Examining philosophy, values, beliefs, and norms of the police officers versus private citizens can, on the surface, create great levels of anxiety. We have all seen the jaded views of some officers toward private citizens. Some officers have been "street-hardened" through the years. There is often an "us and them" attitude. Likewise, many citizens have a jaded view of "the cops" and what the police are like. Reality often lies somewhere in the middle. Police beliefs about the public have become altered through time and experience. Likewise, public attitudes about police have developed through experience, rumor, media attention, or fear. Breaking down these barriers and developing mutual understanding of philosophy, values, beliefs, and norms is a primary need and challenge in the success of these joint police/community organizations.

Step 4. Formulating General Goals that Meet Needs or Solve Problems: Motivating goals can be effectively formulated only upon a foundation of clear and agreed-upon mandate, purpose, and philosophy statements that are real to those in a group or organization. Perhaps it is true that a band is no better than its worst player—that a band with a drummer who plays to a different beat should suggest the drummer go play jazz fusion somewhere else (unless the band's purpose is to play jazz fusion). If there is no agreement on the general direction and hoped-for accomplishments of a group, then it will not achieve much of what it intends to achieve. If there is agreement on general goals, it will be possible to achieve higher levels of success. The transforming leader's job is to assist—in the consulting mode—in articulating and translating the aspirations of group members or the needs of a group whom they serve (or sell) into goal statements that are motivating, realistic, achievable, worthwhile, and adequate to solve problems or meet needs.

In the case of the juvenile correctional facility, a subsequent consulting intervention resulted in writing down and implementing the following goal and objectives statements:

> **Goal #1.** We will provide a clean, colorful, and socially supportive environment that will encourage the development of residents at the spiritual, intellectual, physical, social, emotional, and creative arts levels.

Objective A: Staff Team E (educators) will implement the Skills for Living Program for life-skills development from January through April of this year.

Objective B: Staff Team P (physical plant maintenance staff) will paint this ugly place during the next month in colors that the kids have a say in choosing.

It is clear from the above results that from the general goal flow specific objectives. Clear general goal statements are the soil from which grow specific implementation plans and commitments.

Step 5. Specifying Objectives: Objectives are statements of commitment with a name and a date attached. They are highly specific in terms of defining what will be accomplished by a certain date. They are based on general goals that reflect known and perceived needs or problems.

To facilitate the achievement of objectives specified, each objective can be recorded on a simple sheet during staff or planning meetings. These sheets can become the "minutes" for any meeting, and they can, in turn, be reviewed and evaluated at the next scheduled meeting. Each team member with an objective to achieve can set up a program of steps to achieve it and can get ideas from team members for the effective implementation of the program plan. In this way, a specific team member has taken responsibility for the objective, but have solicited and received input from the team to share overall ownership.

The format of the overly simplified version of the staff-meeting minutes show that each person at the meeting eventually committed himself or herself to accomplishing a specific objective by a specific date and agreed to give a report on that date about the results of his or her effort. This kind of specific planning and recording by each member of a group or organization has the effect of enlivening meetings, setting up achievable targets, and meeting the needs of staff members to be recognized for their accomplishments. It also allows them to gain assistance and support when their efforts fail.

Step 6. Planning Action Steps: Programs are objectives translated into the smaller, logical, more realistic steps required to achieve the desired objectives within certain time frames. Planning requires experience in the area of expertise being exercised. This is true because if the steps are too large to be achieved, people will become discouraged by failure. If the steps are too small, they will become bored or fatigued with meaningless repetition. Steps in programs need to be large enough to be challenging but small enough to be realistically achieved. Failing to plan realistic but challenging steps is the main reason many objectives fail to materialize into action. Unless this step is accomplished thoroughly and carefully, individual or group objectives may never be translated into achievements.

Step 7. Implementing Plans: Effective program implementation by a group or organization requires follow-through on the leader's part to monitor, recognize achievement, encourage commitment, and reward performance in both formal and informal ways. The consistently successful implementation of a diverse community outreach recruiting program, for example, could likely depend upon the long-term follow-through of a good police manager who realizes that the power of his recruiting force resides within the skills, attitudes, and motivations of the people who recruit for the organization. The police manager will plan regular and meaningful feedback, training, motivational incentives, and various types of ongoing recognition. It may well be that the organization does not possess a formal recognition system for these activities. In this case, the police manager must create informal but valued recognition systems.

This step is likely the most common stage of failure in developing a team focus or direction in a police organization. Often, great effort, with commensurate funds, is devoted to the planning or formulation stage. Forgotten is the importance of facilitating the objectives to an action state where the accomplishment of specified tasks leads to the realization of the organizational goals. This failure to recognize the implementation step early in the planning stages was acknowledged by Mintzberg (1994) when he wrote, "...Every failure of implementation is, by definition, also a failure of formulation" (p. 285).

Step 8. Learning from the Past—Evaluation: Honest and valid feedback to members of a group or organization can either be extremely valuable or destructive. Regular performance reviews can be conducted by leaders who actually observe the performance of a subordinate. Obtaining agreement in advance for such an assessment, so that it will occur on a regular, formal basis as well as on an ongoing informal basis, can alleviate much of the anxiety often associated with such evaluations. One method of beginning the performance review process is to ask group members to critique the performance of their own work team during team development or planning sessions. People in leadership positions can also give and receive feedback about positive and negative impacts that occurred as a result of their actions or practices. One company gave weekly feedback to assembly-line employees about how their performance compared with that of the competition. The employees were embarrassed to the point that they increased their productivity more than 15 percent in the following weeks, 6 percent on average over the competition.

Planning for improved future performance is another event that can occur on a regular basis as a part of Step 8. This step often has to be leader induced because work teams may be resistant to improving their performance when it means they have to work harder. If planning for improved performance will result, however, in an increase in meaningful rewards and recognition, greater enthusiasm for such activities can be expected.

Step 9. Celebrating and Enjoying the Rewards: If genuine celebration can be fostered and allowed to occur, it can seal a group together for long periods of time. Genuine celebration can occur, however, only when there has been some kind of dramatic and hoped-for achievement beyond the commonplace. If leaders can challenge exceptional performance in only one area and provide opportunity for valued recognition and rewards to be earned by group members, there will likely be further commitment to the achievement of other challenging objectives. Rewarding innovation and creativity is another way to promote celebration and recurring high performance.

Step 10. Recycling the Ten Steps: It is important to recycle group or organization members through any or all the steps in the process of developing a group or organization, as often as is needed. Sometimes it is critical to reexamine the mandate. It may need to be adjusted to respond to changing areas of police concern, changing needs of people being served, changing priorities, or the shifting values of those in positions to set the course or fate of an organization. Mandates, however, are perhaps the most stable of all the steps in the process. Unexpected change was required in a police agency that, after much research, published its organizational values. The intent was that all values would be accepted as stated. However, the organization's members quickly observed that of the values given, the one dealing with "people" was listed last. The interpretation of many was that this meant that people were the *least important* of the values listed. Clearly, this was not what was intended. The organization had to withdraw the published values statement and republish the values with the "people" values statement placed first. I have found it most useful to ensure that the value of the vision is renewed in the minds of group and organization members regularly. I have also found it especially helpful to reassess needs and problems to ensure that goals are in line with what is truly important. When failure occurs, it is especially important to examine the appropriateness and workability of objectives and programs.

"Well Functioning" Is Not Enough: Pressing Toward Transformation

Ackerman (1986) describes the essence of what she calls "flow state leadership in action"—a nontraditional view of organizations as bundles of energy-in-motion:

> To increase performance, leaders must be able to release energy that is blocked, to free untapped potential, and to organize in ways that facilitate rather than impede energy flow (p. 245).

The basics of flow state leadership are in sync with *Transforming Leadership*. Removing blocks, creating and communicated a vision, empowering and enlisting people, and enhancing performance factors must be enhanced are key to *Transforming Leadership*.

Groups, companies, or organizations that merely run smoothly often fail to grow and creatively adapt to changing demands and opportunities. They often become boring and generally lack an innovative spirit which, if its potential were released, could generate enthusiasm and energy capable of propelling even higher, more interesting, and more rewarding achievements. Therefore, we will conclude this section with an examination of the nature of the transforming process and begin to explore this relatively new field of how we can transform organizations or groups into dynamic high performers (such as Federal Express, People Express, and Microsoft).

After you have practiced the skills and awareness you have assessed in this book as needing further development, you will have an opportunity to creatively apply the *Transforming Leadership* approaches in your own groups or organizations.

The development and transformation of a group or organization into a dynamic and high-performance entity is an inspiring phenomenon to observe and be actively involved in.

An Illustration of Organization Development and Transformation

As example from my personal life, five of us were at Manuel's place in Southern California on a hot July 1961 practicing rock-and-roll numbers for a dance scheduled the following Saturday night. We had only been playing together for about two years, but were good enough that we enjoyed playing about twenty-five different numbers. Our "organization" had developed to the point that we were a solid group of musicians who had developed enough talent to contract to play-for-pay at some local dances, schools, and fairs. Together, we had agreed on a vision of becoming the best band in Southern California—and winning the upcoming "battle of the bands" at the San Bernardino County Fair (our competition, little did we know, would be the Beach Boys).

That evening, after about two hours of practice, something new happened that began the process of transforming our group into an exciting and dynamic performing group. We were so competent at playing a particular song that we simultaneously forgot to "try"—a feeling of effortless "flowed," a sense of "having it made." Mutual glances and grins spread from member to member, as a fine, clean sound emerged. Most other sixteen-year-old band members would have been "green with envy" to have achieved this kind of "groovy" sound.

In jazz slang, we had finally started to "cook." Prior to that, all we had been doing was cutting the tomatoes and the celery on the cutting board. It wasn't a bad salad, but it became boring after a while. But when our performance "heated up" to the point of excellence, more than twenty of the neighborhood kids (eighteen of them were girls!) often dropped in to listen to us practice. Then we knew we had transcended the "beginner" phase. Our band (organization) had become transformed to a new level of creativity and expression of "spirit"—a spirit of success and freedom that went beyond the commonplace novice performances of our past.

As a result of this new "flowing" sound, an unexpected mystique developed around our band; we were among the first to achieve enough recognition to have "groupies" follow us around to our dances (groups of girls who admired and wanted to date us). We used our profits to buy the best Fender guitars, Showman amplifiers, French Selmer saxophones, a '55 Chevy, a T-Bird, a street rod, a '57 Chevy, and a VW van. A "cool" young culture of dancers and other young musicians developed around our band, and these people regularly attended the dances where we played.

As our excitement and confidence continued to build, we learned to trust that we could practice nearly any song and "glide" (or transcend) into that same clean, crisp, competent sound that moved people to dance and even return to our next performance. As a result, bigger dance promoters began to book us for dances where more than a thousand kids—and on several occasions even over two thousand kids—would turn up. We added some rather simple choreography to our stage presentations (rare in 1963) and became one of Southern California's five most popular bands (known as Manuel and The Renegades).

As a result of all these factors, we earned exciting new jobs at the Cinnamon Cinder Teen Nightclub. We came in second in the "battle of the bands" at the San Bernardino County Fair (yes, the Beach Boys won!) and cut several "surfing"-style records that unfortunately only sold well in Chicago.

Those of us who were The Renegades went through the design, development, and transformation stages of a team without any awareness of what was happening to us. Our experience was so rich and powerful that nearly all of the groups and organizations we have encountered since those days have been pale (and some have been grim) in comparison. For years after we disbanded, we felt a sense of disillusionment with the other groups and organizations to which we belonged. This included some band members' marriages and certain colleges and universities they attended because none of them ever "transcended" the ordinary, "heated up," or creatively "cooked" to the same extent The Renegades had. To my great relief, I finally found another "hot" band with which to play music (The Reactions) during my college years, and to this day, I still find myself playing the audiotape recordings we made at the dances at Running Springs Lodge near Big Bear Lake, California.

The significant thing about this story is that when I first realized that the same type of experiences and performance that flow from being "on a roll," "really high," "on," or "in the groove" can be achieved inside of myself first and then to an increasing extent in family, group, and other organizational settings.

Perhaps the "trick" of releasing the transforming "spirit" in other settings is to learn to transfer the same principles and practices learned in the "hotter" settings to the more mundane ones.

1. Set up the group or organization properly at its inception—with enthusiasm about a clear vision, a worthy purpose, adequate goals, and shared beliefs, values, and norms.
2. Select competent members who genuinely share and "buy in" to the foregoing vision.
3. Gain a refined consensus and commitment among the members about the specific purpose, goals, values, and norms of the group, company, or organization.
4. Learn to play a series of "numbers" well together.
5. Practice until you begin to "cook" with spontaneous creativity.
6. Apply that creative style-shifting power and "flow" you have developed to any number of other emerging situations or problems.
7. Stay open to the potential of positive change and a diversity of approaches that demonstrate themselves as appropriately viable—as long as they are consistent with number 1, above.
8. Play "numbers" or create products or services that meet the emerging needs or challenges of the times.
9. Stay alert to changes in the environment that require a response so that adjustments and developments can be made in a timely fashion.
10. Celebrate the achievement of goals, recognize the unique contributions of each member, share in the "take" so that each member receives a portion of the profits from the endeavor, and look to the future for new opportunities.

The following example from a policing environment illustrates the same kind of synergy. It was much more difficult to achieve the "flow" of The Renegades because of the size of a national policing organization. However, the achievement of consensus around vision, values, and goals is truly significant.

Change in Government:
A Case Study of the Royal Canadian Mounted Police*

Background

As Canada's national police service, the Royal Canadian Mounted Police (RCMP) enforces federal laws across the nation, acts as the provincial police force in all provinces except Ontario and Quebec, is the territorial police in the Yukon and Northwest Territories, and serves as the local police force for more than two hundred municipalities.

The RCMP is part of Canada's federal government and so faces the same challenges that other government departments do. Taxpayers are demanding better, cheaper, and more efficient government. Education and increased sophistication have meant that citizens are demanding more accountability of their governments. These changing demands are having serious repercussions.

According to David Zussman, executive director of the Public Management Research Centre, there is now a clear delineation between policy development as a government function and service delivery. Many services once provided by government are now delivered outside of government, through partnerships between government departments or between the public and private sectors. The final result being that government departments will be constantly challenged over the next five to ten years on *what* they are doing and *why* they are doing it. This scrutiny means that accountability and meaningful performance measurement will take on new importance (Zussman, 1997a).

Studies, such as that done by Ekos Research Associates and Environics Research Group, have shown that public trust in government is low (Zussman, 1997b). This is not unique to Canada, but is certainly evident there. Because of this public environment, Canadians are demanding more say in the workings of government and are more vocal about questioning the decisions made by government. It may explain, at least in part, why there is a trend toward smaller government and fewer resources; big government smacks of waste and inefficiency.

But what of the internal government climate? How is the public service adapting to these changing demands?

While change was the rallying cry of CEOs and politicians alike in the early 1990s, the promise of a new future now fails to motivate a change-weary

---

* Colleen Gareau, Officer in charge, Communication Services Branch, provides communication advice and services to the Office of the Ethics Advisor of the Royal Canadian Mounted Police. For more information on the RCMP or to obtain a copy of the mission, vision, and values statements and values discussion papers, see the RCMP Web site at www.rcmp-grc.gc.ca.

audience. This lack of employee engagement poses a major challenge for organizations that must transform their businesses in order to stay relevant to society's changing needs and to do so during times of fiscal restraint.

Nowhere is this dilemma more evident than in Canada's federal public service, which has been beleaguered with ongoing change for some years with only the promise of more on the horizon.

Job cuts, loss of job security, and increased duties have created a cynical work force. Yet the changes to be made must be carried out by these same disgruntled workers.

The RCMP is a good example of a federal government agency that is facing all of these challenges. What makes it different is the way in which the RCMP has chosen to address them.

The force, like all federal departments, had undergone Program Review I and II. Canada was facing crippling debt, and the reviews were to help the government determine which services it should continue to provide. They examined the business lines of all departments and posed six fundamental questions about the services provided. Paraphrased, the questions were

1. Is the activity in the public interest?
2. Should the activity be carried out by government?
3. Should the federal government carry out the activity?
4. Could the activity be carried out by anyone other than the federal government?
5. Is the activity being carried out as efficiently as possibly?
6. Is the activity affordable?

The bottom line was the bottom line. Based on the results of applying the six test questions, departments had to cut budgets and faced unprecedented downsizing. Industry Canada was cut by about 48 percent over two years and Transport Canada witnessed the results of 30 to 40 percent reductions. The RCMP also faced cuts which saw the end of the RCMP Musical Band and changes in many of its other services.

In late 1995, the RCMP had established an independent body to look at pay and benefit issues for the force. Part of the research process was a series of interviews with managers. During these interviews, the researcher became aware that there was no consensus or sense of urgency among managers as to what needed to be changed within the RCMP.

The Shared Leadership Process

At a regularly scheduled conference in November of that year, Commissioner Philip Murray challenged his senior managers to take charge of the force's destiny. He spoke to them about the importance of their leadership and of fueling a "fire in their bellies." It was time for the force to look beyond its command-and-control hierarchy to develop a shared vision of its future.

Following the conference, the decision was made to proceed with the shared leadership process. The objective of this process was to review corporate values and develop contemporary mission, vision, and values statements for the RCMP which would be used as the basis for cultural change. This was to be a grass-roots initiative with a final submission presented to senior management in June 1996.

The SLV process began with training of RCMP employees as facilitators who represented a cross-section of the force from across Canada. In total, 160 employees were trained and then tasked with facilitating shared leadership sessions. They were charged with reporting back to senior management at the June conference.

Facilitators were excited about the process. S/Sgt. Randy Parks of Newfoundland echoed the feelings of many of the facilitators by saying that he felt hopeful about the process. It provided a unique opportunity for employees to steer the RCMP into the next decade. "This signals a shift in management style from the top-down culture we've become accustomed to, to a bottom-up approach in which we've been empowered to make a difference," observed Cpl. Mike Murphy from Prince Edward Island in *Pony Express,* the RCMP's internal news magazine (Chew, 1996).

Another facilitator, Cst. Mike Frizzell of British Columbia, told *Pony Express*: "If we are to remain the police service of choice in our jurisdictions, we must embrace these ideals and develop a true community-based policing philosophy and vision. We have to make sure we are treating our employees well and upholding these ideals within the organization as well as without. A happy employee will do a better job, and will relate to the community better" (Chew, 1996).

Focus groups were held across the force and approximately 4,000 of the RCMP's 20,000 employees participated. At the beginning of each focus group session, a period for venting was planned to allow employees to get past their grievances and get to the creative stage. Issues raised were consigned to the *parking lot*—a list which would be addressed at a later date by appropriate policy centers.

Each focus group developed mission, vision, and values (MVV) statements which were used to develop divisional (provincial) statements. The divisional statements were then brought to Charlottetown, Prince Edward Island, and for five days prior to the June 1996 conference, forty representatives selected from among the facilitators developed national MVV statements. The parking lot issues were handled separately and had been categorized according to which policy center was responsible for responding to which issue.

The final MVV statements along with commitments to communities and employees were crafted and presented to senior management at the conference, along with the parking lot issues.

According to the August 1996 issue of *Pony Express*, the commissioner identified two main themes which emerged from the shared leadership vision process: service to clients and service to all employees.

"We have got to get beyond the point where we are serving ourselves, and ask how we can help others," Murray stated. "The emphasis must be on service and commitment. We must all approach our day-to-day decisions with a service-oriented focus, no matter what our position or function may be within the organization" (Rauch, 1996).

One of the participants in the MVV process was Supt. Vern Baugh of Saskatchewan. "It is not only necessary to have shared leadership in the 90s, it [was] absolutely inevitable," he said in the *Pony Express* article. "There is a lot of talent out there amongst our employees, and as managers we have got to go directly to the people to find out how we can help them do their jobs better" (Rauch, 1996).

Regionalization

In the meantime, the senior executive committee (SEC) of the force had done more than give its verbal support to the SLV process. In March 1996, a conference was held, this time in Aylmer, Quebec. Over the course of three days, participants (directors, commanding officers, senior officers, and more than seventy other employees) grappled with the dilemma of how to make the RCMP the best it could possibly be for its employees and communities. The result was the *Aylmer Declaration,* which changed the organizational structure of the RCMP to better support a shared leadership style of management. Deputy commissioners would no longer be located at national headquarters. Instead, divisions (provinces) would be grouped into five regions and deputy commissioners would be posted to each region.

Since deputies are part of the SEC, this new structure would better facilitate the flow of information to and from different areas of the country. The deputies would be closer to the front line and, therefore, be able to bring the concerns of their divisions directly to SEC meetings as well as ensure the corporate message was consistent across the country.

In addition, changes in the noncommissioned officer promotion system, a new classification system, and the establishment of a pay council to look at pay and benefit issues, employee recognition, and appraisal systems were accelerated to keep pace with changes in the management structure as well as to ensure congruency with the newly created mission, vision, and values statements.

Sgt. Ken Green, NCO in charge of Rose Valley, Saskatchewan, stated in *Pony Express*: "It will be a real turning point in the history of the Force. The promotion system and employee recognition are the things that will make the difference and have people believing that things are going to change. Telling people 'This will change' and 'That will change' just isn't going to cut the mustard today. It just has to be done" (Johnson and Serry, 1996).

The way that these decisions were made is indicative of the new way of doing business in the RCMP. According to Commissioner Murray, "Getting everyone involved in the process makes for a much better decision because before people leave the room you have everybody on side. To just dictate the decision was our historic way of doing things, but I think we all realize that is no longer the effective way to play" (Johnson and Serry, 1996).

The Parking Lot

The SLV process did not end in Charlottetown, however. After the June conference, the parking lot issues where sent to the appropriate policy centers and two question-and-answer documents were developed. One was on human resource concerns, and the other covered all other issues.

Project Renewal, the group responsible for overseeing the SLV process, developed an action plan to ensure that the divisions carried on with next steps. Video conferences were held with divisions to share information about what was happening to keep the initiative alive. The final MVV statements were produced as posters, and each employee received a pamphlet containing these statements in his or her paycheck.

But Project Renewal would not be around forever. It had originally been established to deal with Program Review, and its mandate ended in May 1997.

Ensuring a Viable MVV

To continue to champion SLV, an ethics advisor had been appointed by the commissioner in October 1996 with a mandate to champion the MVV. Assistant Commissioner Patrick Cummins became the person responsible for this task. He has stated that: "...the ethics advisor's role would be to ensure that the core values identified by the membership at large take on a living meaning in the day-to-day operations of every employee in the RCMP. Be it regular members, public service employees, civilian members or temporary civilian employees—it doesn't matter. That's the objective, and the ethics advisor would be the person who would be available to assist in ensuring that the core values become more than just a plaque on the wall that's there but no one pays any attention to it" (Richardson, 1997).

In previous decades ethics, in police organizations meant adherence to codes of conduct; it was a perspective based on command-and-control hierarchies. Ethics belonged to academia, and its impact on our daily lives was not widely understood. Today, industry, government, and nonprofit organizations recognize that ethics is an integral part of doing business. If the RCMP is to continue to advance its delivery of quality policing services through the application of modern management principles, it must consider ethics as one of these principles.

"The RCMP is no longer a command control organization," the commissioner stated in *Pony Express*. "The fundamental reason for the initiation of the shared leadership vision process was to get input from every level within the organization—and we have done just that."

To begin his task of making the RCMP's mission, vision, and values an integral part of operations, Assistant Commissioner Cummins oversaw the development of definitions for the RCMP's core values to ensure that the values were clearly understood and that they would be relevant to the force. The definitions were developed using the consultative process and validated using a process similar to the MVV focus group sessions. "What we're attempting to do in operationalizing the core values is capture the concepts and the ideas that were discussed by hundreds of people across the country during the visioning sessions..." he said in the January 1997 issue of *Pony Express*. "It's essential to accurately capture what the membership meant by each value; accountability, integrity, honesty, professionalism, compassion and respect... If we don't accurately reflect employees' understanding, then we run the very significant risk of the document just being posted on the wall and not becoming a living part of everyone's daily activities."

Accountability was viewed by employees as the most important value, and certainly this has already had an impact within the force as well as served to stimulate discussion.

One employee in Protective Operations in Ottawa responded to a *Pony Express* article defining the force's values with this: "I enjoyed your article in the *Pony Express* offering brief definitions of each of the core values. While these 'words' are being quoted ad-nauseam by many members they really haven't taken the time to fully consider what they mean. Your article serves to define what they should mean to members. Your article comes at a most appropriate time as PMPDB [protective operations] is in the process of restructuring to place more responsibility at the lower levels and I intend to use your article as a topic of discussion. You have made my job easier."

The impact has also been felt among managers within the force. Until recently, senior managers were given mandate letters from the commissioner. These letters outlined what was expected of the commanding officers and directors. While these letters were to be directly linked to annual performance, they were not terribly effective due to a lack of performance indicators or measurement.

These letters were discarded in favor of performance agreements between the manager and the commissioner. These agreements—new in 1998—are based on mutual expectations and commitments and will, in the coming few years, be developed between all managers and employees. They herald the beginning of new accountability relationships indicative of a new culture and new style of management within the RCMP. It will be very interesting to track the impact of these agreements over time.

The ethics advisor also developed an action plan with input from the divisions to respond to the question: What are you doing to further cultural change within the RCMP? The action plan was presented to the SEC in March 1998.

Certainly great progress has been made to bring the RCMP from a command-and-control type of organization to one of shared leadership. But there is still some way to go on this journey of change. Talk about cultural change including accountability and employee empowerment is welcome, but real buy-in and support of change must be shown by management first before many employees are willing to embark on a new way of doing business.

The Alignment Initiative

And so the *Alignment Initiative* was born. Led by a task force and championed by the commissioner and senior management including the ethics advisor, the initiative will synthesize the force's policies and practices with its mission, vision, and values and with federal government priorities.

Every year, the commissioner prepares a directional statement which provides the foundation for divisional and policy center business plans for the year. The directional statement for 1998 focused on three priorities: alignment, cultural change, and communication. It states: "In this fiscal environment, being all things to all people is not a recipe for success. This approach erodes quality and puts unrealistic stress on employees. We must focus on what we do best, has high impact and high value within the context of client needs…We must realign our resources to support our priorities, to enhance quality and to maximize support to the front line."

The 1998 directional statement outlines the alignment priorities. The Force must:

- Align priorities with those of government
- Align resources and priorities
- Align organizational structure with service delivery objectives

- Align technology strategies with priorities
- Align human resource systems with the mission, vision, and values statements
- Align individual performance/accountability with corporate goals.

The directional statement also details the must-do's for cultural change, including:

- The need for ongoing learning and adapting to the diverse and changing needs of our society
- Valuing our people
- Choosing and managing partnerships strategically based on long-term organizational and individual career objectives
- Developing leaders throughout the organization
- Developing a climate of trust
- Sharing best practices (Murray, 1998)

These issues must be included in all force business plans to ensure that the RCMP is working in sync from coast to coast.

Lessons Learned to Date

As with every undertaking, there is room for improvement. The ethics advisor has identified a number of areas in the shared leadership vision process which could have been improved.

Participaction: In a four month period, just less than 20 percent of employees of the RCMP participated in the initial SLV process. Although this was a significant effort and every employee was encouraged to contribute to the activity, many did not, and this has raised some criticism internally that the results of the process are not representative of the force.

Geography: The RCMP provides service across Canada, which includes some very remote areas. Communication over these vast distances becomes a formidable challenge when trying to solicit participation and increase understanding of a new initiative across the miles. Timeliness is certainly affected, and face-to-face communication is often impossible.

Leadership: It was noted that wherever the SLV coordinators were able to motivate employees and management, participation was greater. This was even true in areas that are traditionally very cynical. Selection of coordinators was obviously very important.

Management: While most senior management articulated strong support for the SLV process, their actions did not always model their words. Some middle managers did not support the SLV process either. This could be attributed to a lack of communication with and understanding by managers of what their new role would be in an organization that embraces accountability and employee empowerment. It is difficult to support something that is perceived as taking away your prestige or position without knowing what will replace it. However, some middle managers made a conscious decision not to participate in shared leadership sessions that their presence would not impede discussion. Unfortunately, employees perceived these managers as not supporting the process, and for this they were criticized. All of these issues had a direct impact on the participation and buy-in of others.

Details, Details: Employees were surprised by the number of issues placed in the parking lot. One of the problems this attention to detail created was an overwhelming amount of minutiae. Not all issues could be easily or quickly addressed. In retrospect, perhaps the top three issues for each policy center could have been chosen, which might have had more impact than reams of detail.

Next Steps

The alignment initiative has formed eight steering committees to deal with the enormous task of aligning processes and practices with the mission, vision, and values statements and with the priorities of government. Working groups have been formed for each steering committee.

The time frame for this initiative is short; the work must be completed by December 1999. A communication strategy has already been developed and an orientation session was held in August 1998.

A best-practices repository is being established, and employees across the force are encouraged to submit examples of what they consider to be best practices to share with other employees. These best practices will be tied to awards and recognition within the RCMP.

At the time of writing, the success or failure of the RCMP in modernizing its management style is unknown. However, in the words of the commissioner, "As a member of the Force, I am proud of our reputation around the world as a police organization built on integrity, professionalism and principle. I am committed to this process. Indeed, I am determined that the RCMP be at the forefront of change and best practices, while providing excellence in service to the Canadian public. Excellence is not achieved through moderation and caution, but through active participation in the building of a strong future for the RCMP" (Chew, 1996).

Appendix I
RCMP Mission, Vision, and Values Statements and Commitments to Employees and Communities

The RCMP Shared Leadership process involved the participation of over four thousand employees over a five-month period. It culminated in a seven-day workshop in Charlottetown, Prince Edward Island, in June 1996 which produced the following national mission, vision, and values statements presented to the commissioner and the senior executive.

Mission

The Royal Canadian Mounted Police is Canada's national police service. Proud of our traditions and confident in meeting future challenges, we commit to preserve the peace, uphold the law and provide quality service in partnership with our communities.

Vision

We will:

- Be a progressive, proactive and innovative organization
- Provide the highest quality service through dynamic leadership, education and technology in partnership with the diverse communities we serve
- Be accountable and efficient through shared decision-making
- Ensure a healthy work environment that encourages team building, open communication and mutual respect
- Promote safe communities
- Demonstrate leadership in the pursuit of excellence

Core Values of the Royal Canadian Mounted Police

Recognizing the dedication of all employees, we will create and maintain an environment of individual safety, well-being and development. We are guided by:

- Integrity
- Honesty
- Professionalism
- Compassion
- Respect
- Accountability

Commitment to Our Communities

The employees of the Royal Canadian Mounted police are committed to our communities through:

- Unbiased and respectful treatment of all people
- Accountability
- Mutual problem solving
- Cultural sensitivity
- Enhancement of public safety
- Partnerships and consultation
- Open and honest communication
- Effective and efficient use of resources
- Quality and timely service

Commitment to the Employees of the Royal Canadian Mounted Police

In the spirit of shared leadership and recognizing all employees as our greatest asset, we commit to:

- Open, honest and bi-lateral communication
- Demonstrating leadership through accountability and responsibility at all levels
- Treating all employees with equal respect and consideration
- Ensuring the safety of our employees by developing and enforcing minimum resourcing standards
- Training that is timely, specific to the needs and relevant to job requirements
- Effective and efficient management of human resources through consultation, teamwork and empowerment at all levels
- Ensuring a safe and harassment-free work environment
- Encouraging and recognizing innovation and creativity
- Fair and equitable systems to deal with
  - * Recognition for good performers
  - * Compensation and entitlements
  - * Financial hardship caused by employees' worksite
  - * Consistently poor performers
  - * Discipline and discharge
- Promoting health, safety and well-being
- Ensuring adequate human, financial and material resources
- Enhancing job security through aggressive marketing of our services

Definitions of Core Values

Integrity is an outward expression of our actions and beliefs, consistent with our other core values, that instills trust.

Honesty is being fair, just and truthful in character and behaviour.

Professionalism is a conscientious awareness of our role, image, skill and knowledge in our commitment to quality, client-oriented service.

Compassion is being sensitive, caring and considerate.

Respect is the objective, unbiased consideration and acknowledgment of the rights, values, beliefs and property of all people and communities.

Regional Definitions

Integrity

Integrity	is acting in accordance with the Mission, Vision, Core Values and Commitments of our organization. (Pacific)
Integrity	is the inner voice, the source of self control, and the basis for the trust that is necessary in one's role; it is an outward expression consistent with all our beliefs and actions. (Atlantic)
Integrity	is consistently doing what is right in the implementation of our actions through guidance of the core values: accountability, compassion, respect, professionalism and honesty. (North West)

Integrity—an outward expression of our actions and beliefs, consistent with our other core values, that instills trust.

Honesty

Honesty	is being truthful in word and action. (Pacific)
Honesty	fair and just in character and behaviour (not cheating or stealing); free of deceit; truthful; sincere; and genuine. (Atlantic)
Honesty	fair and just in character and behaviour, being truthful, sincere and genuine. (North West)

Honesty—being fair, just and truthful in character and behaviour.

Professionalism

Professionalism	is conduct which demonstrates our dedication to delivering the highest quality service which is skillful, reliable and competent. (Pacific)
Professionalism	is outstanding conduct and action that is consistent with excellent service. (Pacific)
Professionalism	is conduct which demonstrates our commitment to an exemplary, skilled, and courteous service. (Pacific)

Professionalism   is the attitude and abilities displayed in dealing with employees/clients and communities, mindful of dress and deportment, and in concert with the Mission, Vision, Values and Commitments of the organization. (Atlantic)

Professionalism   is providing quality, client-oriented service with a conscientious awareness of one's role, image and knowledge mindful of the Mission, Vision and Core Values. (North West)

Professionalism is a conscientious awareness of our role, image, skill and knowledge in our commitment to quality, client-oriented service.

Compassion

Compassion   is demonstrating care in word and action. (Pacific)

Compassion   is caring in word and action. (Pacific)

Compassion   is the treatment of everyone with sensitivity, respect and consideration. (Pacific)

Compassion   is being a supportive listener, offering a reassuring presence, sensitive to the concerns and needs of each individual, and taking appropriate action. (Atlantic)

Compassion   is demonstrating care in what we say and do. (North West)

Compassion is being sensitive, caring and considerate.

Respect

Respect   is the objective and unbiased consideration for all people, their values, beliefs, rights and communities. (Pacific)

Respect   is the regard we display, in an objective and unbiased manner, when acknowledging the rights, values and beliefs of people and properties. (Atlantic)

Respect   is unbiased and equitable treatment of all people, property and values. (North West)

Respect is the objective, unbiased consideration and acknowledgment of the rights, values, beliefs and property of all people and communities.

In Conclusion

The endeavor of creating and managing positive change is really just emerging as a science and an art. This book is a starting place from which to collect what in the past might be effectively transported into what I believe in the future will become a new kind of practice of leadership—a constantly adaptive and evolving leadership.

Police organizations have unique challenges. Therefore, they must effectively implement skills internally, then in community policing organizations, and finally extend these skills into the policing of the community through the membership at large. These are challenges that require new focus in teaching within the police organization to foster these skills in all police officers and nurture their development for the good of the organization and the good of the community.

Many books describe transformation in organizations and illustrate how excellence has been achieved. They do not, however, offer a comprehensive, integrated, competency-based working model that reveals and develops within you the knowledge, skills, and tools for transforming yourself and your organization into a more powerful one—one that can produce both business and human development results simultaneously. There is a wealth of additional ideas regarding the nature of the transformation process and how leadership can have a positive impact (see Albrecht, 1987; Bass, 1985; Bennis, 1966; Beckhard and Harris, 1987; Brandt, 1986; Kirkpatrick, 1984; LeBoeuf, 1980; Martel, 1986; Tichy, 1983; Tichy and Devanna, 1986). I also especially recommend *Strategic Planning for Police*, edited by Dan Ogle (a publication of the Canadian Police College, Ottawa, Canada), and *Police for the Future* by David Bayley (1994). Those serious about reviewing some of the critical works that have come before this, can review any one or all of these books.

To conclude this section, we turn to the words of John Kotter (1990), professor of organizational behavior at the Harvard Business School. He writes:

> Some people have the capacity to become excellent managers but not very strong leaders. Others have great leadership potential but, for a variety of reasons, have great difficulty becoming strong managers. Smart companies value both kinds of individuals and work hard to make them a part of the overall team. But when it comes to grooming people for executive jobs, such firms ignore the recent literature that says people cannot manage and lead, and focus their efforts on individuals that seem to have the potential to do both. That is, they try to develop more leader–managers than managers and leaders, and for one very important reason.

Leadership and management are sufficiently different that they can easily conflict. A firm made up mostly of leaders and managers often polarizes into two warring camps—eventually resulting in one side winning (usually the managerial camp because it is bigger) and then in the purging of the other side. In firms with a large contingent of leader–managers, this rarely happens.

Developing enough leader–managers to help run the huge number of complex organizations that dominate our society today is a great challenge. But it is a challenge we must accept. The more pessimistic individuals among us think this is hopeless. Some people argue there is no such thing as a leader–manager. They are clearly wrong; most of the individuals discussed in this book both lead and manage. At this point, it is simply not clear how many more of these people would emerge if circumstances were right. The only way to find out is to try.

The *Transforming Leadership* approach asserts confidently that any manager who wants to become a better leader can learn to do so! *Transforming Leadership* is an attempt to provide these "right circumstances" Kotter suggests. This book, combined with a program of formalized mentoring or coaching, can be the next step for many who would stretch themselves from the limitations of management into the exciting challenges of leadership. This new development and growth can have positive impact at every level of society: at home, at work, and in our other systems.

To formulate your own *Personal Leadership Development Plan*, turn to Chapter 9, or if you want to do a free online *Executive Coaching Needs Assessment*, you can do so at http://www.consultingcoach.com.

References

Ackerman, L., in *Transforming Leadership: From Vision to Results,* John D. Adams, Ed., Alexandria, VA: Miles River Press, 1986.

Adizes, I., *Corporate Life Cycles,* Englewood Cliffs, NJ: Prentice-Hall, 1988.

Albrecht, K., *The Creative Corporation,* Homewood, IL: Dow Jones–Irwin, 1987.

Anderson, T. and E.T. Robinson, *The Leader's Manual for the Personal Style Indicator and Job Style Indicator: A Guide to Their Significance, Development, Administration, and Practical Applications,* Abbotsford, B.C., Canada: Consulting Resource Group, 1988a.

Anderson, T.D. and E.T. Robinson, *The Personal Style Indicator,* 3rd ed., Abbotsford, B.C., Canada: Consulting Resource Group, 1988b, 4, 6, 14–15.

Bass, B., *Leadership and Performance Beyond Expectations,* New York: The Free Press, 1985, 201.

Beckhard, R. and R.T. Harris, *Organizational Transitions,* 2nd ed., Reading, MA: Addison-Wesley, 1987.

Bennis, W.G., *Changing Organizations,* New York: McGraw-Hill, 1966.

Brandt, S.C., *Entrepreneuring in Established Companies. Managing Toward the Year 2000,* New York: Mentor, 1986.

Chew, Heather, Designing tomorrow today, *Pony Express,* p. 12, February 1996.

DePree, Max, *Leadership Is An Art,* New York: Dell, 1989.

Johnson, Rebecca and Keith Serry, Inside the Aylmer Declaration, *Pony Express,* p. 12, April 1996.

Kirkpatrick, K.L., *How to Manage Change Effectively: Approaches, Methods, and Case Examples,* San Francisco: Jossey-Bass, 1984.

Kotter, J.A., *Force for Change: How Leadership Differs from Management,* New York: The Free Press, 1990, 125–126.

LeBoeuf, M., *Imagineering: How to Profit from Your Creative Powers,* New York: Berkeley Books, 1980.

Lombardo, M., Looking at Leadership: Some Neglected Issues, Center for Creative Leadership, Technical Report Number 6, January, 1978, research sponsored by Organizational Effectiveness Research Program, Office of Naval Research (Code 452), under Contract No. N00014-76-C-0870;NR 170-825.

Martel, L., *Mastering Change: The Key to Business Success,* New York: Simon & Schuster, 1986.

Merrill, D. and R. Reid, *Personal Styles and Effective Performance,* Radnor, PA: Chilton, 1981.

Mintzberg, Henry, *The Rise and Fall of Strategic Planning,* New York: The Free Press, 1994.

Murray, Philip Commr., The 1998 Commissioner's Directional Statement, RCMP, Ottawa.

Quinn, R.E., *Beyond Rational Management: Mastering the Paradoxes and Competing Demands of High Performance,* San Francisco: Jossey-Bass, 1988, 51.

Rauch, Kerry, Focus on shared leadership vision: what's next? *Pony Express,* p. 17, August 1996.

Richardson, Stephanie, Meeting ethics head on, *Pony Express,* p. 16, January 1997.

Robinson, E.T., *Why Aren't You More Like Me?* Boca Raton, FL: St. Lucie Press, 1997.

Tichy, N.M., *Managing Strategic Change: Organization Development Redefined,* New York: Wiley, 1983.

Tichy, N.M. and M.A. Devanna, *The Transformational Leader,* New York: Wiley, 1986.

Zussman, David, Declining trust in government: a global phenomenon, *Insights,* 2(2), 1, 1997a.

Zussman, David, Canadian perspectives on trust, *Insights,* 2(2), 3, 1997b.

Part III

Building Your Personal Leadership Development Plan

In Chapter 2, you completed a personal assessment and developed a profile of your relative strengths and weaknesses in the five *Transforming Leadership* skill sets.

The following diagram was introduced in Chapter 2. It illustrates the dynamic relationship between the leadership skills measured in the *Leadership Skills*

Inventory (*LSI*) and the job of translating your vision, insight, or strategy as a leader into the influence. It is a leader's influence that moves and leads individuals, groups, and organizations. The real potential for change and growth through using the *LSI* is realized only when you take action based upon what you have learned.

Using the Results of This Assessment

The insights you gain from completing this *LSI* assessment can be used to develop a plan for your growth and development as a leader. There are different ways to benefit from the results of the *LSI*:

1. Based upon what you have learned, you can begin to target resources, training events, or classes that would help you to increase your understanding and practice in these various skill areas. You will benefit from paying attention to skills where you already have a degree of strength so you can enhance your leadership influence and effectiveness. You will also benefit from working on skills that are weak. You begin to capture lost opportunities and potential.

2. Share the results of this *LSI* assessment with someone you consider a coach or mentor in leadership, someone more experienced and effective as a leader than you are. This individual can use these insights as a basis for giving you input, direction, and coaching in key skill areas where he or she can help you.

3. Begin to take note of leaders around you in your environment and observe their practice of these various skills in their leadership roles. While this is a common way in which we learn to do what we do anyway, you will be amazed at how much more you will see and benefit with this set of skill categories in mind.

Fewer than one in ten professionals have been observed, in videotaped assessment sessions, to use the whole range of skills (to at least level 4 competency) outlined in this *LSI* assessment. Yet, these skills are critical for success and effectiveness.

Fortunately, effective leadership behaviors can be observed, learned, and transferred to others. These behaviors can be broken down into microskills and can be demonstrated, practiced, and refined, and competency can be developed. But microskills are not wisdom. How you go about integrating the various skills into your personal leadership style is a matter of your individual creativity and requires much intentional practice and development.

Realistic Expectations:
How Quickly Can You Develop Your Leadership Skills?

Most people who aspire to be effective in leadership, and who realize the complexity of the task (and the preparation needed), understand that development does not come primarily because of a course or a book. People usually have to go through the following levels in developing competency and the advanced ability to "pass the torch" along to others:

1. Knowledge about concepts and skills takes a few hours to a few weeks to internalize.
2. Gaining understanding and working knowledge (the ability to try a skill on one's own without supervision) can take up to a month or two.
3. Competency (the ability to perform reliably well) is learned through mentoring, training, coaching, and through making unpleasant mistakes as well as having successes. This stage may take from six months to two years for some of the more complex skills.
4. Dynamic creativity in the application of skills comes after many years of practice and experience.
5. The ability to mentor and train others comes easier when your own skill sets are well established and you are able to be unconsciously competent in a wide range of skills.

Skills Development Plan Worksheet:
Personal Mastery Skills

Review the results of the *LSI* assessment for this skill set in Chapter 2 and fill out the following worksheet. In this way, you will develop an overview of the key skills in this skill set that would benefit from additional focus.

What are your three strongest skills in this skill set?

#	Skill Name
☐	_____
☐	_____
☐	_____

Why are these the strongest? _____

_____

_____

What are your three weakest skills in this skill set?

#	Skill Name
☐	_____
☐	_____
☐	_____

Why are these the strongest? _____

_____

_____

Can you identify any next steps that can be taken to maximize these skills of personal mastery in your leadership role?

Skill #	Action Step #	Action Item	Coach/Mentor/ Target Date
☐	1.	_____	_____ ___/___/___
☐	2.	_____	_____ ___/___/___
☐	3.	_____	_____ ___/___/___
☐	4.	_____	_____ ___/___/___
☐	5.	_____	_____ ___/___/___
☐	6.	_____	_____ ___/___/___
☐	7.	_____	_____ ___/___/___
☐	8.	_____	_____ ___/___/___
☐	9.	_____	_____ ___/___/___
☐	10.	_____	_____ ___/___/___

Skills Development Plan Worksheet:
Interpersonal Communication Skills

Review the results of the *LSI* assessment for this skill set in Chapter 2 and fill out the following worksheet. In this way, you will develop an overview of the key skills in this skill set that would benefit from additional focus.

What are your three strongest skills in this skill set?

\#   Skill Name

☐ _____

☐ _____

☐ _____

Why are these the strongest? _____

_____

_____

What are your three weakest skills in this skill set?

\#   Skill Name

☐ _____

☐ _____

☐ _____

Why are these the strongest? _____

_____

_____

Can you identify any next steps that can be taken to maximize these skills of interpersonal communication in your leadership role?

Skill #	Action Step #	Action Item	Coach/Mentor/ Target Date
☐	1.	_____	_____ ___/___/___
☐	2.	_____	_____ ___/___/___
☐	3.	_____	_____ ___/___/___
☐	4.	_____	_____ ___/___/___
☐	5.	_____	_____ ___/___/___
☐	6.	_____	_____ ___/___/___
☐	7.	_____	_____ ___/___/___
☐	8.	_____	_____ ___/___/___
☐	9.	_____	_____ ___/___/___
☐	10.	_____	_____ ___/___/___

Skills Development Plan Worksheet: Counseling and Problem Management Skills

Review the results of the *LSI* assessment for this skill in Chapter 2 and fill out the following worksheet. In this way, you will develop an overview of the key skills in this skill set that would benefit from additional focus.

What are your three strongest skills in this skill set?

\#   Skill Name

☐ _____

☐ _____

☐ _____

Why are these the strongest? _____

_____

_____

What are your three weakest skills in this skill set?

\#   Skill Name

☐ _____

☐ _____

☐ _____

Why are these the strongest? _____

_____

_____

Can you identify any next steps that can be taken to maximize these skills of counseling and problem management in your leadership role?

Skill #	Action Step #	Action Item	Coach/Mentor/ Target Date
☐	1.	_____	_____ ___/___/___
☐	2.	_____	_____ ___/___/___
☐	3.	_____	_____ ___/___/___
☐	4.	_____	_____ ___/___/___
☐	5.	_____	_____ ___/___/___
☐	6.	_____	_____ ___/___/___
☐	7.	_____	_____ ___/___/___
☐	8.	_____	_____ ___/___/___
☐	9.	_____	_____ ___/___/___
☐	10.	_____	_____ ___/___/___

Skills Development Plan Worksheet: Consulting Skills

Review the results of the *LSI* assessment for this skill set in Chapter 2 and fill out the following worksheet. In this way, you will develop an overview of the key skills in this skill set that would benefit from additional focus.

What are your three strongest skills in this skill set?

\#   Skill Name

☐ _____

☐ _____

☐ _____

Why are these the strongest? _____

_____

_____

What are your three weakest skills in this skill set?

\#   Skill Name

☐ _____

☐ _____

☐ _____

Why are these the strongest? _____

_____

_____

Can you identify any next steps that can be taken to maximize these skills of consulting in your leadership role?

Skill #	Action Step #	Action Item	Coach/Mentor/ Target Date
☐	1.	_____	_____ ___/___/___
☐	2.	_____	_____ ___/___/___
☐	3.	_____	_____ ___/___/___
☐	4.	_____	_____ ___/___/___
☐	5.	_____	_____ ___/___/___
☐	6.	_____	_____ ___/___/___
☐	7.	_____	_____ ___/___/___
☐	8.	_____	_____ ___/___/___
☐	9.	_____	_____ ___/___/___
☐	10.	_____	_____ ___/___/___

Skills Development Plan Worksheet:
Versatility Skills

Review the results of the *LSI* assessment for this skill set in Chapter 2 and fill out the following worksheet. In this way, you will develop an overview of the key skills in this skill set that would benefit from additional focus.

What are your three strongest skills in this skill set?

\#   Skill Name

☐ _____

☐ _____

☐ _____

Why are these the strongest? _____

_____

_____

What are your three weakest skills in this skill set?

\#   Skill Name

☐ _____

☐ _____

☐ _____

Why are these the strongest? _____

_____

_____

Can you identify any next steps that can be taken to maximize these skills of versatility in your leadership role?

Skill #	Action Step #	Action Item	Coach/Mentor/ Target Date
☐	1.	_____	_____ ___/___/___
☐	2.	_____	_____ ___/___/___
☐	3.	_____	_____ ___/___/___
☐	4.	_____	_____ ___/___/___
☐	5.	_____	_____ ___/___/___
☐	6.	_____	_____ ___/___/___
☐	7.	_____	_____ ___/___/___
☐	8.	_____	_____ ___/___/___
☐	9.	_____	_____ ___/___/___
☐	10.	_____	_____ ___/___/___

Leadership Theories Overview

During the 1980s, people and organizations pursued "excellence" with great vigor and determination. And, while creating excellence will probably continue as a mainstay during the 1990s, a new quest has clearly emerged: the pursuit of integration and balance. Individuals, families, organizations, and society in general increasingly see the need for greater harmony among professional career and personal relationships, worldly success and spiritual fulfillment, economic prosperity and environmental protection, accomplishment and peace of mind, tough-mindedness and gentleness, immediate gratification and enduring joy, this generation and future generations.

—Craig Hickman

Goals of This Chapter

The goals of this chapter involve your gaining perspective on the nature of leadership, comparing traditional versus transformational views on leadership, and understanding how these views are related to the *Transforming Leadership* model. This chapter elucidates three important aspects of leadership development history:

1. Philosophies of leadership
2. Definitions of leadership
3. Theories of leadership

Introduction

The police, justice, and public safety sectors have not, so far as can be found in the literature, developed any unique theories of leadership. Most, if not all, leadership theories have emerged from the business and education sectors. However, it is obvious, when one studies these theories, that they are applicable across disciplines and across fields of work. Therefore, in this chapter, leadership theory development is reviewed from a historical perspective so that you can gain familiarity with the various assumptions behind each theory and so that you can see how each theory led to the construction of the next one. This has over time resulted in an increasing complexity and comprehensiveness of theoretical orientations, resulting in the more modern and versatile transformational theories of leadership. *Transforming Leadership* is, I believe, the most recent, integrative, and comprehensive of leadership development models in that multitheoretical perspectives have been synergistically fused together to form a seamless approach to personal, team, organization, and community development.

Comparing Traditional and Modern Philosophies of Leadership

As a first step toward understanding various perspectives on leadership, it is important to grasp the underlying assumptions that have guided various leaders in the past and to consciously formulate more encompassing assumptions to guide you as a leader into the future. This first step in achieving a more balanced understanding can be approached by looking at some definitions.

Webster's New World Dictionary (1984) defines philosophy as "a study of the principles underlying conduct and thought." It is valuable to compare the traditional with the more modern assumptions (principles) because we can then better see the value of both. Gaining a basic understanding of leadership philosophies will assist you in formulating your own integrated philosophy of leadership.

The Operating Assumptions Behind Theories X, Y, Z, and R

The first philosophy of leadership we will look into is outlined in Douglas McGregor's work (McGregor, 1960). After studying a number of organizations and the operating assumptions of those with decision-making authority, he identified a set of beliefs that summarize this early view. He called this first view Theory X. Here it is called a philosophy, not a theory, because it is really a set of beliefs about the nature of work and the nature of workers. McGregor based his work on the work of Maslow. Like Maslow, he was interested in what motivated people toward greater personal development and improved performance. McGregor argued that traditional leader behavior was inappropriate because it was based on questionable assumptions about employees. These assumptions are outlined below.

Theory X Assumptions

1. Employees are inherently lazy and will avoid work unless forced to do it.
2. Employees have no ambition or desire for responsibility; instead, they prefer to be directed and controlled.
3. Employees have no motivation to achieve organizational objectives.
4. Employees are motivated only by physiological and safety needs.

These assumptions form the basis of a philosophy that can be very dehumanizing to others and even to self as a leader. McGregor believed that Theory X assumptions were outdated and that employees would perform better if treated with a very different set of assumptions he called Theory Y. This is the second philosophy, or set of operating assumptions, we will examine.

Theory Y Assumptions

1. Employees find work as natural as play if organizational conditions are appropriate. People appear adverse to work only because their past work experiences have been unsatisfactory.
2. Employees can be motivated by higher order needs such as ego, autonomy, and self-actualization.
3. Employees seek responsibility because it allows them to satisfy higher order needs.

Autocratic philosophy is at the root of Theory X, with the leader initiating all the structure and where the central focus is on production, not people. In Theory Y, there is a more democratic philosophy where leaders "believe the best" about employees and treat them more as "people who work" rather than as "workers who also happen to be people."

Even today, McGregor's work stands as a breakthrough in identifying basic operating assumptions of leaders and the impact those assumptions can have on morale and organizational effectiveness. Much development has taken place, however, since McGregor's findings regarding basic assumptions or philosophies about leadership.

Theory Z Assumptions

In 1981, Ouchi presented a clear set of operating assumptions that have impacted the functioning of a number of companies of the Fortune 500, ILK:

1. Offer people long-term employment, a positive "family" of co-workers and leaders, and clear objectives and they will stick around, do a good job, and have a sense of pride in the work done.
2. Offer people a piece of the pie when it comes to making decisions that will affect their work and they will understand and support the decisions more often and more wholeheartedly.
3. Expect people to take individual responsibility for their own performances as an important part of a bigger "team" and they will fulfill that expectation.
4. Evaluate people over the long-term rather than frequently because this gives them opportunity to develop, based upon their inner sense of integrity, rather than outward pressure.
5. Build trust and integrity into all interactions between managerial and nonmanagerial personnel to develop a sense of the importance of individual contributions to the group effort.
6. Maintain few levels of authority in the organization and emphasize work groups to get jobs done because this maximizes an individual's sense of belonging to his or her group and to the organization as a whole. It also increases individual and group accountability and performance.
7. Use informal rules and regulations, with formalized measures of performance to further encourage individual workers to internalize personal responsibility for achieving group and organizational objectives.

Theory Z takes the spotlight off the individual and puts each person in the context of the group, the organization, and the culture in which he or she is living. This gives the individual a sense of value and importance based upon the accomplishments of the overall organization and takes some of the heavy pressure off each individual in each moment to perform all-out. In Japan, this has created personal and corporate determination to succeed at functioning in groups to reach departmental, organizational, and even national cultural goals.

Critics of the Theory Z philosophy claim that it will not really work in North America because of cultural differences with Japan * (Biggs, 1982). Some of the assumptions have, however, been successfully implemented, especially in some small family businesses, and in larger corporate structures like IBM, Hewlett-Packard, General Motors, and others (see Ouchi, 1981).

It is ironic to consider that North America, previously driven by predominantly Judeo-Christian historical and cultural roots, has found or would find the values of cooperation, support, loyalty, family closeness, intimacy, and caring so foreign to its way of leading businesses and organizations. Individual accomplishment, competition with others, confrontation between labor and management, and an emphasis on self in general have come to the forefront of the value structure of many people since the 1950s. One important reason may be that the reward system of a company is usually skewed to individual performance and is not connected to group achievement.

The Assumptions of Theory R: A Relational Approach

Alderson (1985) introduced a unique set of assumptions into the arena of leadership philosophies. Given the name Theory R, the guiding assumptions underlying this philosophy are as follows:

1. All people need love (affirmation), a sense of dignity (appreciation), and need to be treated with respect (recognition that they are of intrinsic value and that their work is a valued contribution) in the workplace—not just at home or in other environments.
2. Building a person's sense of self-esteem through meeting the foregoing three key needs will have a positive impact on worker morale, quality of work, and productivity.
3. Reconciliation, not confrontation, in leader–follower relations will help to create the needed sense of mutual respect, dignity, and unconditional concern for one another as human beings.
4. Relationships between leaders and followers are the key to productivity, morale, and quality concerns.
5. People have the desire to work hard and take pride in what they accomplish.
6. When people are placed in an environment sensitive to the "value of the person," they will be cooperative, creative, and productive.
7. Treating people "right" is the right thing to do, and that is reason enough to actively value people.

At first glance, these ideas seem too simplistic to have much credence in the "real," complex world. Yet, at least in the hands of Alderson, they worked stunningly well at the Pittron steel foundry in Pennsylvania. Alderson found something upon which both labor and management could agree. Every man and woman in the entire operation had something in common: each wanted to be valued.

Two years after the "value of the person" approach was implemented, the plant went from a $6 million loss to a $6 million profit, from 300 to 1,100 employees, from 600 grievances per year to 1 grievance per year, from 20 percent absenteeism to 1 percent, from poor-quality production to high-quality production, and productivity was up 64 percent! Such dramatic changes warrant our attention. (To read the published story, which outlines the whole case study of Pittron's turnaround, see Sproul [1980].)

Thus, we see a dramatic shift in the evolution of the guiding assumptions of leadership theories, from the autocratic swea shops of Theory X to the humanistic Theory , to the group emphasis of Theory Z—to the value of people of Theory R. But there are more questions we must ask. In the next section, we will compare these more traditional definitions of leadership with new insights into the nature of transformational leadership.

Comparing Traditional and Transformational Definitions of Leadership

Traditional Definitions

Leadership has been defined in many ways by people of varying perspectives over the years. Indeed, there are so many definitions that vagueness and confusion seem to prevail about the whole issue in many minds. It is not surprising, then, that many leaders question their roles, their effectiveness, even their importance, and are questioned by those around them. Presented below is a brief summary of many definitions of leadership, most of which are traditional in nature; some, however, lead toward the more transformative (adapted from Stogdill [1974]) and then give a specific definition of *Transforming Leadership*.

1. Definitions and aspects of leadership: a potpourri
2. Determining group structure, ideology, and activities
3. Coupling leader behavior with the meeting of group needs
4. Keeping one step ahead of the group
5. Innovation in accomplishment of tasks
6. Achieving the most with the least friction
7. Inducing compliance, respect, and cooperation
8. Goal-directed communication that gets positive results
9. Serving others and meeting their needs
10. Persuading others to accept a particular view or strategy
11. Exercising positive power to get desired results

12. Making the most of individual differences to reach goals
13. Being perceived as legitimate, expert, and trustworthy

The range of definitions reveals the considerable differences among these various views of leadership. Few individuals bother to search the literature to discover alternative views. This lack of a working definition of leadership can be a problem for someone who wants to develop leadership potential and become more effective and successful in achieving goals.

In contrast, the next section presents a focused definition of leadership that can assist you in developing a more integrated and applicable understanding of leadership and its more transformative nature.

Transforming Leadership: A Definition

> *Transforming Leadership* is vision, planning, communication, and creative action that have a positive unifying effect on a group of people around a set of clear values and beliefs, to accomplish a clear set of measurable goals. This transforming approach simultaneously impacts the personal development and corporate productivity of all involved.

The transforming leader also transforms self and the nature of leadership itself in a continuing process of learning to lead better. Therefore, everything is affected by a transforming, developing leader who is, by definition, an active agent of positive change. The environment is affected, organizations are affected, groups are affected, interpersonal interchanges are affected, the character of leadership becomes more mature throughout the organization, others are developed, and the leader's understanding is developed in the process. The transforming leader is no "superperson" but rather the subtle, ripple effect of positive leadership can affect all parts of an organization and all the people in it. As a "spin-off," their families at home can be positively affected, and this can even impact the tone of the communities in which people live.

Transforming leaders can be people who are administrators, managers, supervisors, educators, health and medical professionals, counselors, clergy, criminal justice workers, parents, and others who might have the knowledge, skills, tools, and abilities to impact and develop both an organization and the people in it at the same time. Such is the case when the father and mother (the transforming leaders) in a family (the organization) facilitate themselves and their children to grow by combining structuring and nurturing behaviors. It is also the case when an executive structures an organization through long-range planning and policy development and develops teams of people who grow toward increased morale and productivity. How many organizations do strategic planning to increase productivity? Quite a number. How many of those organizations also do strategic planning and budgeting to increase the quality of the work and interpersonal lives for the people who produce that hoped-for productivity? Not nearly as many. Therefore, you can see the potential importance of defining leadership in terms of people who are the producers—rather than producers who also happen to be people instead of robots.

Traditional Theories of Leadership: An Overview

Now that we have reviewed some general definitions of leadership and compared them to the working definition of *Transforming Leadership,* it is useful to review some general theories of leadership and compare them with *Transforming Leadership* theory. A theory is defined in *Webster's* as "a formulation of underlying principles of certain observed phenomena which have been verified to some degree." Important aspects of leadership are contained in many of the traditional views of leadership, and some important lessons can be learned by identifying some of their limitations.

Biological Personality Theories

The Great Man Theory: In 1960, Jennings presented a comprehensive survey and analysis of the "great man" theory of leadership. In summary, this earlier theory advances the idea that certain people are born stronger, more intelligent, more able to lead. Heroes, royalty, and the more successful people in general were thought to have inborn talent and ability that enabled them to stand out from among the masses and achieve unusual successes. This idea that born leaders had certain characteristics gave rise to the related trait theory of leadership, studied and popularized in the 1920s and 1930s by Bernard (1926), Bingham (1927), Tead (1929), and Kilbourne (1935).

Trait Theories: These theories were sometimes intermixed with racial, sexual, and class discrimination to promote supremacy of one race over another, one sex over another, or one social or economic class over another. A king's brother or son (or at least a daughter) would succeed him to the throne because of the "good stock" inherent in the blood. Though it is possible that some strengths are hereditary (as revealed in medical research), it is clear that there are too many surprising exceptions to this theory for us to give it significant credence.

Environmental Theories

Leader-Behavior Theory: This position suggests that circumstances themselves cause a great leader to rise to the occasion. Under the "right" conditions, a leader will emerge as if by nature's necessity or invention. Bogardus (1918) suggested that the type of leadership a group will develop or accept will be determined by the nature of the group and the problems it must solve. Victor Frankl, in his book *Man's Search for Meaning,* cites examples of leadership emerging from the most frail of beings in the terrible conditions of a concentration camp. There have, however, been many crises that have not produced a person equal to the occasion. Therefore, we cannot necessarily give great credence to this theory of leadership either.

Personal-Situational Theory: This theory is the first to propose a complex set of factors involved in the shaping and development of leadership and is the first to be scrutinized by serious research efforts. Westburg (1931) proposed that the critical factors involved in leadership were a combination of the "affective, intellectual, and action traits of the individual as well as the specific conditions under which the individual operates." The idea here is that success in leadership is dependent upon a leader's ability to understand the followers and the surrounding environment and then react appropriately to those people and situations as they change.

Bennis (1961) recommended that theory on leadership should consider the measurement of rationality, the impact of informal organization and interpersonal relations, the positive influence of a benevolent autocracy because it structures relationships between superiors and subordinates, job enlargement and employee-centered supervision that permit individual self-development, and participative management and joint consultation that allow the integration of individual and organizational goals. Bennis emphasized the importance of interpersonal dimension in determining the quality of work life in an organization. He also emphasized the value of the person in relation to productivity.

Interaction-Expectation Theory: In this theoretical orientation, leadership is the act of initiating structure supported by group members because such structure solves mutual problems, conforms or positively transforms group norms, and causes members to expect that success will come from following a leader of such initiative. Leadership, according to this theory, involves both initiating and fulfilling the expectations of followers. Leader credibility is based upon the ability to fulfill expectations generated by the leader (Homans, 1950; Stogdill, 1959).

Humanistic Theories of Leadership

The theories of Argyris (1964), Blake and Mouton (1964), Likert (1967), and McGregor (1960, 1966) are focused on the development of effective organizations through a "humanizing" process of structuring the work or living environment so that individuals can meet personal needs and organizational objectives at the same time. This theory attempts to balance the needs of the individual with the goals of the organization, but has been accused at times of sacrificing organizational "bottom-line" results for the sake of realizing human values such as employee morale, worth of the individual, quality of work life, meaning and purpose in work, mutual trust, and productivity based upon the internal motivation of workers.

This approach can contribute much to our understanding of human needs in the workplace and can cause us to be more cognizant of the "people" side of enterprise, the importance and dignity of human life, and the importance of personal meaning and purpose in work. It has also revolutionized thinking about productivity and performance; basically, it has clarified that people who like what they do, feel respected and valued, and are involved will perform better. Some major contributions from the these authors are summarized next

Argyris pointed out the inevitable conflict between the individual and the organization. He claimed that organizations are most effective when leaders provide avenues for workers to make valuable contributions and be recognized for their efforts in reaching organizational objectives. He also explained how most organizations overplay the rational and underemphasize the emotional—especially the negative emotions (Argyris, 1982). In his opinion, the best organizations recognize and process negative emotions until resolution or at least compromise is achieved.

Blake and Mouton presented a grid to illustrate the relationship between concern for people and concern for production. They created one of the first leadership-style assessment instruments and formulated a theory that suggested that a leader who scored high on both people and production concerns was most effective.

Likert suggested that leaders need to seriously consider the values, expectations, and interpersonal skill competencies of others with whom they work. The positive leader, as defined by Likert, is one who appreciates an employee's efforts and builds self-esteem in others. Task and relationship factors are both important and interrelated.

McGregor is included in this section because some of his assumptions have been verified through observation and research over the years. He developed a theory of understanding leadership behavior along a continuum from "Theory X" to "Theory Y." The leader with a Theory X orientation is thought to be "old school," believing that followers are self-oriented and uncaring about the needs of the organization, and so attempts are made to directly influence and motivate them in the direction of accomplishing organizational goals—without much regard for their own feelings or motives. A leader with a Theory Y orientation is thought to be "new school," believing people are self-motivated and self-actualizing by nature and that leaders should arrange the organizational environment to capitalize on those internal motivations to help employees reach organizational goals.

All of these humanistic theories suggest a single path for leader behavior and are considered today to be somewhat narrow. It has become increasingly clear that no one theory or approach really works best. Depending upon a host of variables, a wide range of interventions may work. This is not to say there are not some key principles that can be applied throughout the leadership process, but for now we will examine the more situational approaches.

Situational or "Contingency" Approaches to Leadership

These approaches reflect important advances over the more simplistic "one-best-way" leadership models. Contingency models suggest more complex diagnosis of the situation at hand and more complex leadership interventions. Situational or contingency approaches reflect the belief that there is a relationship between employees' satisfaction and performance and their environment. The basic premise of these approaches is that if we understand the factors that impact employee morale and performance, and apply that understanding successfully, we can have more direct influence and control over morale and, as many believe, productivity.

Fiedler (1967) advanced a theory called the Leadership Contingency Model, which serves at least three main purposes. First, it supports the idea that effective leadership is situational in nature, that a leader has to attend to a wide range of situational variables to make a wise choice of leader behavior. Second, Fiedler found that more directive leaders were effective in certain situations, and this finding was contrary to the philosophies of the 1950s and 1960s, dominated by human relations theories. Fiedler also opened up the issue of leader versatility and the placement of a leader in a situation where he or she can capitalize on his or her strengths (i.e., "engineer the environment to fit the manager").

A second theory that suggests leader behaviors can influence worker performance and satisfaction is the Path-Goal Model formulated by House (1971). This approach suggests that the leader's job is to increase the payoffs to workers for achieving work goals. The leader does this by clarifying the path to these goals, by reducing blockages that prevent workers from reaching the goals, and by behaving in a way that will increase worker satisfaction while workers are achieving those goals. If workers feel they are capable of doing a good job without direction from the boss, they will be dissatisfied with—and even re-sent—directive leadership behavior. House's model is important because it gives us insight into some ways leaders can increase employee satisfaction.

A third type of situational or contingency theory of leadership is contained in Vroom and Yetton's (1973) Decision-Making Model. According to this theory, it is critical for the leader to decide how much participation subordinates should have when making decisions. They provide guidelines for leaders to decide how much participation is appropriate in each situation. They stress the importance of decisions and information availability and show that acceptance of decisions by subordinates is an important issue in regard to their productivity.

Finally, Situational Leadership was developed and popularized more recently by Blanchard and Hersey (1977, 1982). Even though the roots of this approach go back to Westburg (in Stogdill, 1974), it is fair to mention the impact and importance of this work as a major voice in communicating to many leaders (and trainers/educators of leaders) the value of carefully considering the developmental level of a follower or group of followers and matching the leadership style to the ability of the follower to perform a particular task.

A concern for follower development is clearly voiced, and this approach continues to be influential in shaping thinking and training in leadership flexibility for greater appropriateness and therefore greater effectiveness in face-to-face leadership situations.

Summary

As the foregoing discussion reveals, leadership theory has become more and more complex as time has moved on. The simple authority relationship of boss/employee has shifted greatly toward a realization of the importance of the people factors—factors in each situation that affect overall outcomes—and people and situational factors that interact to affect one another.

Only a few people in a situation rise to the top for a number of complex reasons, and only a few succeed or fail for a number of complex reasons. Each of the theories of leadership is each limited, none is metatheoretical (integrating and including many useful theories into one), and they are all based upon interesting academic or valuable research trends and the philosophical beliefs of a particular decade or era.

For a more complete account of the development of leadership theory, see Stogdill (1974). It is useful to see the historical development of leadership to note the direction in which it has moved in past years and to thereby gain a sense of where it is likely to move in the next decade. Leadership, at all levels, from family to government, will have great impact on how we move into the next century.

A Price to Pay for Complexity

Theories of leadership move from simple to the more complex as we move through time. There comes a time, however, when the richness can become clutter—a time when the complexity goes beyond what is applicable by the average leader. This is the price we pay for more complex theories. They are more difficult to learn, more complicated in their applications, and require more sophisticated training methods. More intricate research methodologies are needed to study their effectiveness.

A Payoff for Integrating the Logically Useful Parts of Various Theories

As we develop more intricate but integrated models of leadership, there is a greater likelihood these models will represent guidelines that can work in the real world. The challenge is to state them clearly enough so they become tools that can be tested and used. Research on leadership effectiveness reveals that, at this point, we are still groping for the "magic formula," that there is some conflicting evidence about the effectiveness of leadership training (Fiedler, 1972), and that each leader is still basically out there on her or his own trying to make a positive difference using the talents, knowledge, and skills he or she has.

Hickman (1990) does an excellent job of contrasting, comparing, and integrating traditional and transformational definitions, roles, and functions of management and leadership. In the preface of his new book, he states:

> In organizations, this gravitation toward balance has encouraged business people to begin integrating incremental strategies with innovative breakthroughs; cultural values with corporate policies; stability and security with change and opportunity; flexible processes with structured systems; and short-term gains with long-term progress. The complex global business environment of the 1990s demands that we go much further in this direction. Given the growing pressures, complexity, change, and competition facing business organizations today, most executives find themselves confronted with an escalating conflict and schism between the managerial and leadership requirements of organizations. An "either-or" mentality dominates at a time when organizations most desperately need the best of both.

Transforming Leadership is an emerging assessment and training model with promise for providing a clearer vision of how powerful and enlivening leadership can be integrated with the wisdom of traditional management, and offers concrete ways we can grow into becoming better "leading managers" through expanding awareness and receiving training in deficit areas.

The second edition of *Transforming Leadership* is currently being used at the Justice Institute of British Columbia, the Criminology and Criminal Justice Program at the University College of the Fraser Valley, and the Abbotsford and

New Westminster police departments in British Columbia. It is being used for leadership development, education, and training at the frontline, supervisory, and management levels.

Internet Resources

General Administration of Justice Gateways

A gateway site is one that contains more subject-specific sites, usually with links to them.

- **Criminal Justice Links:** Provides links to many law enforcement sites and agencies.
- **Links to Criminal Justice Related Sites:** Provides links to federal agencies and offices, state governments, judicial agencies, organizations, etc.
- **National Criminal Justice Reference Service's Justice Information Center:** An extensive source of information on criminal and juvenile justice.
- **Tenny's Law Enforcement Links:** Provides links to periodicals, agencies, and other law enforcement sites.

Law Enforcement

Many law enforcement agencies in the United States and some in foreign countries now have Web sites. They usually contain useful information related to agency functions.

- **Bureau of Justice Statistics (BJS):** This is a primary source for criminal justice statistics. BJS collects, analyzes, publishes, and disseminates information on crime, criminal offenders, victims of crime, and the operation of justice systems at all levels of government.
- **United States Department of Justice:** As the largest law firm in the nation, the Department of Justice serves as counsel for its citizens. It represents them in enforcing the law in the public interest.
- **Justice Technology Information Network:** This network is a service of the National Law Enforcement and Technology Center. It serves as an information gateway for law enforcement, corrections, and criminal justice technology information.
- **Saint Mary's University's Criminal Justice Homepage:** This is one of the more extensive sites on the Web related to administration of justice and is a good example of resources listed by a university department.

Prisons and Corrections

Web sites dealing with prison or corrections agencies or issues provide a variety of information useful to practitioners in the field.

- **Prison Related Resources:** Covers news items, general information, and articles on related issues such as the death penalty.
- **Prison Information and Resources:** Gives information on law and prisoners, Control Unit Prisons, and the like.

Local Law Enforcement Agencies

The following Web sites cover state, county, and municipal law enforcement agencies in California:

- **Santa Clara County Sheriff's Office:** Outlines the functions of the office with information categories, enforcement operations, education programs, and a county-wide radio frequency list.
- **San Jose City Police Department:** States purpose and describes administrative and investigative services.

References

Alderson, W., *Value of the Person: Theory R Concept,* Pittsburgh: Value of the Person, 1985.

Argyris, C., *Integrating the Individual and the Organization,* New York: Wiley, 1964.

Argyris, C., *Reasoning, Learning and Action: Individual and Organizational,* San Francisco: Jossey-Bass, 1982.

Bennis, W.G., Revisionist theory of leadership, *Harvard Business Review,* 39(1), 26–36, 146–150, 1961.

Bernard, L.L., *An Introduction to Social Psychology,* New York: Holt, 1926.

Biggs, B., The dangerous folly called Theory Z, *Fortune,* pp. 48–53, May 17, 1982.

Bingham, W.V., Leadership, in H.C. Metcalf's *The Psychological Foundations of Management,* New York: Shaw, 1927.

Blake, R.R. and Jane S. Mouton, *The Managerial Grid,* Houston: Gulf, 1964.

Blanchard, K. and P. Hersey, *Management of Organizational Behavior: Utilizing Human Resources,* Englewood Cliffs, NJ: Prentice-Hall, 1982.

Bogardus, E.S., *Essentials of Social Psychology,* Los Angeles: University of Southern California Press, 1918.

Fiedler, F.E., *A Theory of Leadership Effectiveness,* New York: McGraw-Hill, 1967.

Fiedler, F., How do you make leaders more effective: new answers to an old puzzle, *Organizational Dynamics,* Autumn, 3–18, 1972.

Hickman, Craig R., *Mind of a Manager, Soul of a Leader,* New York: John Wiley and Sons, 1990.

Homans, G.C., *The Human Group,* New York: Harcourt, Brace, 1950.

House, R., A path-goal model of leader effectiveness, *Administrative Science Quarterly,* pp. 312–338, September 16, 1971.

Jennings, E.E., *An Anatomy of Leadership: Princes, Heroes, and Supermen,* New York: Harper, 1960.

Kilbourne, C.E., The elements of leadership, *Journal of Applied Psychology,* 43, 209–211, 1959.

Likert, R., *The Human Organization,* New York: McGraw-Hill, 1967.

McGregor, D., *The Human Side of Enterprise,* New York: McGraw-Hill, 1960.

McGregor, D., *Leadership and Motivation,* Cambridge, MA: MIT Press, 1966.

Ouchi, W., *Theory Z: How American Business Can Meet the Japanese Challenge,* Reading, MA: Addison-Wesley, 1981.

Sproul, R., *Stronger Than Steel,* New York: Harper and Row, 1980.

Stogdill, R.M., *Individual Behavior and Group Achievement,* New York: Oxford University Press, 1959.

Stogdill, Ralph M., *Handbook of Leadership,* New York: The Free Press, 1974.

Tead, O., The technique of leadership, in *Human Nature and Management,* New York: McGraw-Hill, 1929.

Westburg, E.M., A point of view: studies in leadership, *Journal of Abnormal Soc. Psychology,* 25, 418–423, 1931.

Vroom, V. and P. Yetton, *Leadership and Decision Making,* Pittsburgh: University of Pittsburgh Press, 1973.

Webster's New World Dictionary of the American Language, D. Guralnik, Ed., New York: Warner, 1984.

11

How Building a Leadership Organization Prepares the Way for Learning

Now that we have reviewed previous theories of leadership, we will examine how *Transforming Leadership* can prepare you to build a leadership organization—one ready to become a learning organization. You will see where the skills become so very important in the development of an organization and its people and how the skills also enrich relationships with the customers who drive a business.

What Is a Leadership Organization?

A leadership organization creates and sustains a leadership-centered culture where leaders develop leaders from the top down and the inside out.

Organizations not led by transforming leaders look a lot like a cart with square wheels. The leader is out front alone, head down, pulling and straining to move the organization forward. Meanwhile, the other members of the organization who may well be at the back of the cart pushing (or sometimes pulling in the opposite direction of the leader), exert a tremendous effort—without even seeing the destination, let alone the view ahead. The people at the back of the cart have little to no communication with the leader.

© Performance Management Company, 1993 800-659-1466

In organizations without transforming leaders, the square wheels on the cart too often represent ineffective operations, inappropriate methods, resistance to change, no flexibility, lack of innovation, lack of creativity, dead weight, unwillingness, and a lack of readiness for change.

An organization that looks and functions like a cart with square wheels needs to replace its square wheels with round ones. Otherwise, this organization cannot create an environment where it is natural, normal, and easy for leaders to create and sustain a leadership-centered culture.

There is an answer for organizations with this dilemma. Most probably it is contained in the very cart the leaders are lugging behind them. If they only looked inside the cart, they would probably find more than enough round wheels to put on the axles to create a leadership organization. These round wheels are not only new ideas, other options, and unused assets—they are also the potential capability for every person in the organization to become a transforming leader.

What Would a Leadership Organization Look Like?

For starters, it would maximize the potential of both people and technical systems by developing them in a balanced way. Instead of just concentrating on placing round wheels (technical systems) on the organizational cart, key leaders would develop a team of people with leadership skills who could work together. It would require that leaders provide inspiration, plan strategic direction, make effective operational decisions, work as a team to implement strategies, evaluate accomplishments, and enjoy (and celebrate) the process and results of working together.

It would not only optimize the current operations but would prepare for a preferred future, based on vigilantly crafted forecasts of current trends that develop into the waves of change. Doing the same old thing, selling the same old product, treating customers the same old way just won't work any more. The luxury of staying the same for most services and products is over.

A leadership organization views people as a vital—and at least equal—part of the system, along with its technical strengths. For organizations with a high technical component, this is often a challenge. The consultants at Consulting Resource Group have worked with manufacturers, hospitals, construction firms, security advisors, computer hardware suppliers, chemical testing laboratories, agricultural associations, engineering groups, and resource management firms where the traditional concentration on technical solutions makes it very difficult for these organizations to redefine themselves with an equal emphasis on *Transforming Leadership* skills. In the past, these organizations were often at the forefront of their sectors because of technical excellence. With the rapid spread and assimilation of technical competencies, however, the only way for these organizations to differentiate themselves is to develop the people side of their systems.

Leadership organizations equip and develop leaders, not just to optimize their technical capacities but to optimize individual, team, and organizational performance while they develop other leaders. Leadership organizations recognize that they create a synergy by connecting the development of individuals, teams, and organizations. This synergy has a permanent, long-term multiplier effect on satisfaction and performance at every level.

Without this approach, organizations develop in a lopsided way. They reengineer, restructure, implement total quality management, obtain ISO 9000 accreditation, or simply upgrade technology. They obtain early returns from these sound and practical new systems. But unless these organizations invest the resources to develop leadership skills—or carefully select new and skilled leaders from the outside, the demands of these new structures and methodologies will likely break down. They often fail because of lack of communication, lack of commitment to accountability, and lack of skills to implement the underlying assumption of most of these revised work practices—namely, that everyone is someone else's customer.

A leadership organization with a people-development culture at all levels can avoid the problems of such costly mistakes. From a technical point of view, these mistakes are little more than the equivalent of harnessing the cart with square wheels to a bulldozer or replacing an intelligent living system (people) with brute force (such as a horse). Neither solution maximizes the potential of the whole organization. Moreover, both approaches discourage, anger, demoralize, and disrespect potential leaders.

Why Is Leadership Development So Important?

The amount and pace of change we have experienced in our lifetime is only the beginning of an exponential change growth curve. For organizations to survive in these circumstances, such change must be anticipated and led. Recently, two women explained to me exactly how this truth was affecting their lives.

One, a Canadian travel agent, had known for months that the airlines were going to "cap" their commission structures (i.e., limit how much they paid per ticket). This change was going to seriously affect the revenue structure of every travel agent. She had seen it coming (it had been implemented in the United States the year before), and so she had been restructuring her business, retraining her staff and reeducating her customers in anticipation of this change. Instead of cutting back services, she added new ones and discovered that customers were willing to pay for them. Her first efforts were rewarded with significant revenues, happier team members, and new customers—from other travel agents who had no plan to face these changes in the supplier environment.

The other woman, Margaret Wheatley, author of *Leadership and the New Science* and co-author of *The Simpler Way,* admits that everything she ever learned about managing and leading organizations must now be reevaluated, relearned, and reframed in the light of new scientific discoveries. Concepts from quantum physics, mathematics, biology, and meteorology have changed her perceptions of how people relate with one another and to their organizations.

Change of the magnitude we witness around us every day is stressful. Stress is at an all-time high. Without *Transforming Leadership* skills, organizations suffer the deficiencies that stress can cause. People become unavailable because of physical, psychological, emotional, and spiritual suffering. When people are absent in body and/or mind, it creates more stress on the people who are present. Many of the downsizing efforts have backfired because the people who remained to do the work burned out from overload as they were now doing the tasks two people used to do.

In many workplaces, people are expected to work in teams without a traditional leader (so-called self-directed teams). Flattened organizations and self-directed work teams require more leadership skills in all team members so that they can perform effectively. When everyone has leadership skills, all can assume leadership roles as and when required. This kind of just-in-time availability of leadership skills makes individuals, teams, and organizations more flexible. It also prepares them to respond to global quality standards and is the key to balancing people with technical issues.

If the Value of *Transforming Leadership* Skills Is So High, What Is Blocking Leaders from Developing Them?

The answer must be examined in the light of the readiness and willingness of leaders to develop themselves and create a leadership-development culture. The concept of readiness and willingness has been discussed previously. Transforming leaders develop when individuals have level 3 and 4 readiness and willingness levels. So the question then becomes: Why are many leaders at level 1 or 2 resistant or only thinking about change?

Leaders are often justifiably proud of their accomplishments, position, and recognition. They fear being exposed as inadequate. Many leaders have struggled throughout their careers to work their way up the technical and administrative ladder. It is often a shock for them to learn that they need to learn additional skills—some of which may take years to develop—at a point in their careers when they thought they had completed their learning. An interesting example of this is evident in the health care system. Many women physicians are the most resistant to change in hospitals that want to restructure around program management and patient-focused care. At first blush, this seems difficult to explain until we learn that their success in the "traditional health care system" has been obtained by overcoming many odds along the career path—from simply getting into medical school to attaining departmental leadership status. When these women are asked to give up power and status to share it with others, in newly reengineered organizations, they are often quite unwilling.

Many leaders also fear they do not or will not have credibility when they develop and practice new leadership skills. They have depended for their recognition and credibility on their technical competence in the past. If *Transforming Leadership* skills are new to them, at first they do not feel on certain ground. They fear they will lose credibility in the eyes of others (peers, subordinates, outsiders, colleagues, spouses, children). Adults do not like to be made to feel uncertain or incompetent.

Many of these feelings result from simply a lack of preparation, training, and coaching for new learners. Lifelong learning is still a new paradigm for many people. Most baby boomers still live with the image that their career education was completed before they turned thirty. Few of us have had the benefits of coaching or mentoring relationships or programs to assist us to learn and to develop our *Transforming Leadership* skills on a regular basis. Many men who have chosen technical careers have shared with me that they never expected to need these skills and so they never learned them—or valued them. A new consultant recently shared with me that her clients who work in the resource-based industries still do not understand how these skills would relate in any way to the work they do.

Traditional organizations and traditional managers often have a false trust in the old ways of management. I have been told more than once in my career, "If it ain't broke, don't fix it." Managing without leadership skills can be a dangerous job these days. It opens managers to being blindsided by the behaviors of valuable employees (which may have expensive legal implications), the actions of competition on the other side of the world, or the reactions of community activists.

The other side of this "trust" coin is management's failure to trust people's potential. One retail owner has told me more than once, "It is easier to do it myself than to train someone else to do it. They never do it the 'right' way, anyway." This attitude is self-defeating for the organization as well as the leader. The complexity of our world today means that leaders with this expectation will shoulder an ever-increasing load and innovation will be stymied in the organization. Recent scientific discoveries teach us that diversity and innovation are the keys to transformation. They confirm an old saying: "If we always do what we've always done, we'll always get what we've always got."

Finally, a major block to learning *Transforming Leadership* skills arises because of personal difficulties and/or internal emotional problems. Stress can originate at home and be imported into the workplace and vice versa. If this happens and is not addressed, it can become a self-perpetuating cycle. Leaders need *Transforming Leadership* skills so that they know how to manage this kind of stress for themselves, recognize and assist others who are suffering from it, and keep the round wheels on the organizational cart. Organizations cannot create a leadership-centered culture that promotes learning unless addressing the causes of stress is supported and accepted.

Leadership Organizations Benefit from Transforming Leaders

Transforming leaders prevent and solve people and organizational problems. They develop the perspective of not just working *in* the organization but working *on* the organization. They see the organization as a whole, not just an assembly of parts. They are caring and committed to individuals, teams, and the organization as an integral system. They demonstrate a wide range of competencies, including both technical and people skills. They are forward-looking visionaries who anticipate possibilities for the organization.

"Make no small plans, for they do not have the power to move men's souls." A successful entrepreneur coached a class of developing business owners with that challenge. It speaks loudly to developing a vision for a positive future and linking it with the ability to communicate and energize this vision to others. A leadership organization does not have just one person who can "move souls" but rather a group of people who have the skills and willingness to energize each other on a continuous basis. They have found ways to capture hearts that are tied to a common vision. This moves the exercise of strategic planning onto a completely different plane. It creates an expectation that individuals and teams will act and that success is inevitable.

In fact, "the moving of souls" can produce long-term practical benefits that go far beyond simply celebrating targeted successes. One of the best examples of how practical this can be is told by Bill Gibson. Bill tells the story of Dunsmuir Shell, a gas station in Victoria, British Columbis, owned by Bob Dunsmuir. In the 1970s and 1980s, Bob looked for ways to differentiate his gas station from others, many of which became self-serve operations. He focused on providing not simply personal service but exceptional service.

As a transforming leader, he engaged his young staff in deciding how to demonstrate exceptional service to their customers. They invented many ways that have since been adopted by others, such as running to the pumps, giving flowers away, and vacuuming cars while the owner is waiting. These services won the operation a large and loyal following, and impressed the staff with the impact of their decisions.

Bob knew that was important because gas jockeys are typically young people, often struggling students, or even school dropouts. Bob wanted to keep his staff highly motivated and involved, so he took the unusual step of teaching them how to read Dunsmuir's financial statements, and he shared the results with them on a regular basis. He also set up profit-sharing opportunities for them.

Bob continued to look for ways to create a leadership organization and even taught his staff to consider the next customer as potentially their next boss, as he encouraged his staff to move on to better opportunities. With a highly dependable crew in place, it was not difficult for Bob to take a vacation and know operations would run smoothly. At one point, he found out exactly how fine a job he had done. Bob decided to take a holiday on his motorbike in the southern United States. Unfortunately, he ended up in an accident that put him in the hospital with amnesia—he couldn't remember who he was or where he came from. After some months, Bob recovered his health and memory, but he had been away a long time without any contact with the business. Because of the leadership organization culture he had created, Bob returned home to find the whole operation running as smoothly as and even more profitably than when he had left it.

The Dunsmuir Shell story is a classic example of the mutual benefits that exist for transforming leaders in leadership organizations. It demonstrates that management and leadership are both necessary. They both help to manage change. They are both needed to balance technical and people issues, the present operational and future change issues. If Bob had not developed leadership skills in his management staff, he would have found a floundering operation on his return; if he had not developed management skills along with leadership skills, he would have found an injured or dead business. Leadership organizations need more managers like Bob who do not overmanage and underlead.

Benefits of Transforming Leadership Skills
to Individuals and Organizations

TL Skill Set	Benefits to Individual	Benefits to Organization
Self-management skills	Has control over his or her life Competent in basics Reduces stress Has personal "act" together	Can inspire others Positive model to others More effective Better use of resources
Interpersonal skills	Can communicate with others Can express needs Credibility Values self and others Can listen and hear	Communicates others' needs Can influence others Two-way communication Able to work with others
Counseling and problem management skills	Can manage work/life Manages others Evaluates options Self/other understanding Effective with staff and family Trusts others	Can coach others Can help others Can solve problems Can develop ideas Works with people and technical issue
Consulting skills	Can plan forward Feels in control Evaluates options Has insight, honesty, truth, confidence	Can give direction Can lead Proactive Confident Develops teamwork Serves others
Versatility skills	Can assess styles, skills, roles Can understand others Credibility Open to change Effective Tolerant, patient Empathic Can assess, suspend, shift Versatile, flexible	Manages change Works with teams Organizational development Future oriented Able to change fast Effective

Leadership organizations need transforming leaders who can even go beyond management and leadership. Leadership organizations really need leaders who can focus on development and not just the status quo. Development of people is the secret to transforming the culture of an organization. It has been my experience with all the leaders with whom I have worked that when they develop, the organization develops—and as the organization develops, leaders develop. Development is a bridge that opens new possibilities for everyone.

Leadership organizations are concerned even with the opportunity to transform people along with the organization. Transformation happens when the whole system—person, team, or organization—develops to a new level of performance. A transforming leader demonstrates a wholeness of mind, body, emotions, spirit, and interpersonal relationships that becomes the foundation for organizational transformation. Such leaders not only know they cannot lead everyone directly—they know they need help to lead an organization. They are the leaders who create and develop teams of leaders able to move mountains.

Summary

The greatest satisfaction for transforming leaders is to ask the protégés they are coaching to describe the benefits—to themselves and the organization—of their new *Transforming Leadership* skills. On the opposite page is a collection of comments others have shared when asked to identify the benefits of learning *Transforming Leadership* skills.

In the next chapter, we will examine the components of the Comprehensive Personnel System and how it works to accelerate an organization's performance. Part of what transforming leaders do is transform the whole human resource area of their organization so it has a systems approach to finding, selecting, placing, orienting, coaching, and reviewing the performance of people and teams.

12

Transformation Through Personnel Systems

*If organizations wish to be successful in managing the turbu-
lence of the modern world...they will view their people as a key
resource and value knowledge, information, creativity, interpersonal skills, and entrepreneurship as much as land, labor, and
capital have been valued in the past.*

—Gareth Morgan

Introduction

One of the most important aspects of leadership where a transformative effect
can be realized is in the careful assessment, selection, and development of
people. Finding and retaining high-quality, committed employees or followers
is absolutely critical to the success of any leader and any organization. Why are
these tasks so critical to success? It is not unusual for a large police or other
justice or public safety organization to spend 80 to 90 percent of its budget on
its "human resources" in areas such as salaries and benefits. Although the
percentage will change depending on the size of the organization, there remains
little doubt that the human resource is the most expensive of an organization's
resources. Whether an organization reaches its goals will depend to a great
extent on how these resources are recruited, selected, trained and evaluated.
These activities are commonly referred to as personnel or human resource
management.

This book has to this point introduced you to knowledge and skills that can assist you in improving your effectiveness as a leader. It is critically important to understand that it is the people who affect everything that occurs in an organization on an ongoing basis and that you, as a transforming leader, can have a positive impact on your organization through the effective and efficient use of personnel systems. In this way, you, as a transforming leader, can become a "systems manager."

To illustrate the need for enhanced personnel systems, pause for a moment and reflect on your own organization. When you walk into your human resources or personnel office, do you see row upon row of five-level filing cabinets, each bursting with dog-eared and yellowed papers of dubious usefulness? Are your requests for information met with looks of "I hope you don't mean anytime soon"? When you are reviewing candidates for a transfer, are you able to obtain records on training, experience, and education? To what source do you refer when someone asks, "Exactly what is it that I'm responsible for?" Does your organization have an effective performance management system? What has your organization done to help you plan *your* career? What does your recruiting section do to ensure that the organization is hiring not only the best recruits but also those who possess the qualities to become the best future supervisors and managers? You probably have many effective field training officers, but you likely have no leadership training officers. Where are all those who prepare leaders to assume the actual responsibilities of the positions into which they are promoted? Who has been *professionally and competently trained* in your organization to manage and lead the human resource management function? People who are promoted into human resource manager positions often are "rotating" in from some other section of the department without any previous training in human resource management!

Let's begin with a brief introduction to the concept of a "system." There are four basic parts to any system: input, process, output, and feedback. Although it is somewhat of an oversimplification, we can view **input** in policing as the "humans" who will become police officers. The **processes** in a personnel system are separately identifiable but interdependent. A process can be the selection and training of a new recruit or the development of police officers to become supervisors and managers. The **output** is the product in terms of quality. Do we have quality police officers, quality supervisors, quality technicians, and quality leaders? To add complexity to these systems, we include subordinate activities as subsystems. Your role as a transforming leader is to introduce, change, facilitate, or manage the system and subsystem processes that will maximize the "human resource" contribution to the organization. Lastly, you use **feedback** to evaluate the effectiveness of your systems and the people in them.

It is important before proceeding further to acknowledge the way in which information technology and information systems have changed the way we do business, particularly in the human resource field. All industries and occupations, private and public, are directing organizational resources to personnel functions. To better comprehend the degree to which industry is committed, all one need do is log on to the Internet and "surf" for human resource pages. Using only "human resources" as the search parameter, one search engine provided over 488,000 hits. When the search parameters were restricted to "human resources software," the search produced 118,000 hits. These large numbers demonstrate the importance of human resource issues in the workplace today.

The Internet can also provide us with some useful information in terms of the type of activities and human resource tools that should be found in a modern organization. This can be done through the review of specific sites, particularly those that offer a service in the human resource area. For example, one such site listed support in applicant tracking, employee testing, training administration, performance management, career development, human resource planning, Human resource information systems, computer-based training, and many other areas. Consider which of these areas are relevant to your organization.

If it has not already occurred to you, one purpose of this chapter is to assist you to continue to make a "paradigm shift." Hammer and Champy (1993) write of the need for managers and executives to stop thinking *deductively* and start thinking *inductively*. Inductive thinking is recognizing the solution followed by identification of the problems that the solution will resolve. The solution for the human resource management problem is the technology of personnel systems management and human resource information systems.

The questions asked of any organization vis-à-vis personnel issues, are virtually without limit. The purpose of this lengthy introduction is to demonstrate the complexities of the human resource function within an organization and the need for leadership in human resource management. When complexity arises, the transforming leader is responsible for seeking and implementing the strategies that will optimize the efforts of the human resources staffing the organization. Now it is time to identify those areas where problems will have a significant negative impact on an organization's ability to reach its goals. You already have the solutions as an *inductive* thinker.

As you are by now probably even more painfully aware, the issues surrounding human resources in your organization are many and complex. So that this chapter does not become a book unto itself, it is necessary to focus on specific identified problems. To do that, we will draw upon information obtained through the use of a paper-based human resource instrument known as the *Comprehensive Personnel System* (CPS) (Anderson and Zeiner, 1989). More information about the CPS can be found at http://www.crgleader.com. The CPS was originally designed in 1986 as a paper-based introductory seminar program entitled "Selecting and Developing Exceptional Employees." It was field tested between 1987 and 1991 with over four hundred small to medium-sized companies. The program was evaluated very positively, and many of the companies have implemented parts or all of the CPS in their day-to-day operations. Most of the company owners and personnel managers who attended the one- or two-day sessions either had not taken a course in personnel management or had not implemented the principles to which they were introduced in such courses. Therefore, to their satisfaction, many of the staff problems they encountered on a day-to-day basis were addressed in the seminar.

As a group, they reported that the following fifteen of their most frequently encountered problems were causing them moderate to serious concern, from time to time. The information that grew out of the CPS seminars will be used as a starting point in our examination of personnel issues. Since the original seminars, and subsequent consulting interventions in the police, corrections, customs, immigration, and private security fields, we have discovered that there is a commonality of personnel issues regardless of whether an organization is in the corporate, justice, health, or public service sector.

The fifteen most common problems identified were

1. Not hiring the right person for a job
2. Failing to communicate clear performance expectations
3. Fear of telling employees the truth about their performance
4. Forgetting to reward or recognize positive performance
5. Losing track of personnel information
6. Failing to collect personnel information
7. Seeing employees make the same mistakes repeatedly without coaching them
8. Fearing legal repercussions when firing low performers
9. Misplacing files or information in files
10. Employees not motivated to perform well
11. Employees not doing what you want them to
12. Failing to capitalize on strengths and talents
13. Absenteeism rates that are too high
14. Believing employees can't problem-solve on their own
15. Believing that training takes too much time, is not cost effective, or is almost always ineffective

Take a moment to reflect on this list. Are these comments that you would have made? Does your organization misplace files? Does your organization fail to capitalize on strengths and talents? Does your organization fail to communicate clear performance expectations? Is yours a "sick" organization with inordinately high absences? If you are answering yes, then this chapter deserves your special attention. Because we cannot deal with all of the issues presented in the CPS seminars, the focus here will be on the first few critical issues: ensuring you select the "right people for the right job" and continuing the development and performance management of your human resources.

Selecting and Developing Exceptional Employees

Often, we are "caught" without a key person in a given position. This may be due to a poor "front-end" selection process that ignored future needs, failure to identify performance-specific needs in the position, a lack of succession planning, or simply a failure to properly identify organizational needs. Usually it is not one activity (or lack of it) that results in this "weak link" in the organization. It is most often a number of interrelated events or activities. Sometimes these events are synergistic and can cause significant problems within the organization. And these problems increase significantly where no coordinated human resource management activities occur. To reduce this circumstance, it is your responsibility as a leader to pursue those activities that will help your organization select and develop the human resources that will support your organizational mission. As you will see in the nine-step process presented later in this chapter, every person in the organization can contribute to the betterment of the human resource processes.

There are twelve key things you can do to select and develop the people critical to the performance and productivity of your organization:

1. Screen applicants more thoroughly, accurately, and efficiently
2. Build a database of applicant and employee information
3. Create relevant, behaviorally based interview questions and use them
4. Assess work behavioral style of the applicant or employee
5. Assess work behavioral style of each job
6. Assess past work-performance history and references
7. Match knowledge and skills of employees with jobs
8. Contract for employee performance enhancement
9. Conduct and record performance reviews without being officious
10. Develop employee career plans and career path plans as an annual and ongoing process
11. Reward and recognize employee performance and loyalty
12. Communicate on a regular basis, using a shared language

Now pause for a moment and reflect on each of the twelve activities listed above. Reflect in terms of how your organization deals with each issue. Does your organization have a database of applicant and employee information (human resource information system)? How does your organization assess work behavior in terms of both behavior required and behavior demonstrated by applicants? Do you conduct and record performance reviews? If you do, how effective is the instrument and process (performance appraisal) that you use? How do you reward and recognize employee performance? The level at which you conduct these activities and the quality of instruments used will determine the "output" in terms of quality human resources as described in the chapter introduction.

Results You Can Expect When Using Personnel Management Systems and Human Resource Information Systems

To this point, we have looked at the importance of an effective human resource/personnel management system. Problems have been identified, and you have had an opportunity to reflect upon the competency level of your own organization. A list of the most commonly identified problems based on the CPS was provided. This was followed by a list of the twelve key things you can do to select and develop your human resources. We now acknowledge that appropriately designed and used management and information systems and subsystems with related tools and instruments add productivity and efficiency to your organization or company by assisting you to more carefully manage all aspects of the human resource function. The four key components of an effective system are

1. How you select, orient, place, train, and evaluate people
2. How you organize things and people in the work environment in order to make the best use of people's talents
3. How you record and track all personnel data
4. How you use ideas to improve performance and morale on the job

The primary aim of personnel systems and their related human resource tools and instruments such as the CPS is to provide you with the knowledge and tools needed to lead others effectively toward increased productivity, effectiveness, and efficiency. Because employees differ in regard to motivation, age, maturity, experience, competency, and style of approaching people and tasks, it is important to understand each employee or applicant on an individual basis. These types of instruments (when combined with other data within an organization's human resource information system) will assist those in your organization who are responsible for developing human resources to get to know each applicant or employee more quickly and carefully. It will also enable you to have a record of this information that can be accessed instantly. Thus, you will be able to make more effective personnel and leadership decisions.

Nine Steps in the Personnel Assessment and Development Process

To further focus our studies in the area of personnel systems and human resource management activities, the following nine-step process is presented. The topics are again derived from the CPS. These steps will help you to assess the areas you think need attention in your organization. Reflect on each area in terms of your own organization. Where you feel your organization is lacking, you may have identified a problem for your organization and you as a leader. Remember the concept of *inductive thinking*.

1. Specify Knowledge and Skills Required in a Position

Both skills and knowledge areas need to be delineated for each position in your organization. Relationship, task, and leadership factors also need to be specified. Job analysis is the first step any organization should take after identifying a position as an organizational need. A variety of methods are available. Internally, you can use questionnaires and interviews of incumbents and specialists, or you can use specifically designed, commercially available instruments to provide insight into the specific knowledge and skills required. These are used to specify all of the skill areas required by an employee so that he or she will be most effective in a given job. It is important to remember that the more carefully the job analysis is done, the more accurately the requirements for that job will be understood and communicated to those doing the interviewing to select new personnel.

One of the more comprehensive methods to date for determining the knowledge and skills required for a position is the assessment center. This approach, which originated in the mid-1950s, uses a series of exercises under the watchful eye of trained assessors. The assessors evaluate against a predetermined set of "dimensions" or qualities that are indicators of future performance. This method will be addressed in Step 5. Suffice it to say at this point that the research methods used by the center to determine the appropriate dimensions involve job studies, questionnaires, and similar tools. The center data can provide significant information on the relevant knowledge and skills required in the performance of a specific job function.

The Comprehensive Personnel System

Job Analysis—Job Specification—Screening

1. Job Analysis	2. Job Description	3. Screening Process
Identify Required:	*Specify in Writing:*	*Rate Applicant's:*
• Results	• Results expected	• Skills
• Job tasks	• Job tasks	• Knowledge
• Job skills	• Job roles	• Work history
• Social skills	• Extent of authority	• Extent of training
• Behavioral styles	• Job-style pattern	• Extent of education
• Difficulty level	• Performance criteria	• Application form
• Training requirements	• Progress evaluation date	• Decide on short list

Selection—Placement—Orientation

4. Application Review	5. Applicant—Job Fit	6. Orientation Process
Assess Applicant's:	*Rate Applicant's:*	*Contract for or Inform re:*
• Skills	• Skills	• Work tasks
• Knowledge	• Knowledge	• Expected results
• Work style (i.e., *PSI*)	• Training required	• Work behavioral style
• Perception of job (i.e., *JSI*)	• Work/job style fit (*PSI/JSI*)	• Appraisal criteria
• Past work experience	• Interview performance	• Appraisal dates
• Interview impressions	• Past work performance	• Work team placement
• Testing results	• General suitability	• Length of probation

Performance Appraisal—Career Path Planning—Research

7. Performance Review	8. Develop Plans	9. Career Path Plan
Give Feedback about:	*Facilitate Agreement re:*	*Specify Agreements re:*
• Results achieved	• Present strengths	• Future job potential
• Problem areas	• Past successes	• Plans for development
• Performance of tasks	• Areas to develop	• Completion dates
• Relationship factors	• Plans to develop	• Lateral transfer options
• Work style/job fit	• Plans for training	• Research to validate selection criteria
• Performance goals	• On-the-job coaching	
• Probationary status	• Date of next review	

These dimensions were developed in a process of cooperation between the Police Academy at the Justice Institute of B.C., Canada and active police officers. Numerous questionnaires were completed, interviews held, and statistical data examined and analyzed. If the information gathered was correct, then the center should be able to validate in terms of the actual performance of former center candidates. This has been done at the Justice Institute of British Columbia in a longitudinal study by Darryl Plecas (1998).

2. Specify Appropriate Work Style Behaviors in Each Job

The job analysis for any position requires the inclusion of work style behaviors. These "dimensions," as they are referred to in the Assessment Center, are those behaviors that are deemed acceptable for the position sought and are included in the job description. For example, a position can require the demonstration of sensitivity when dealing with issues. Such positions could include the coordinator of an employee assistance program or an investigator in the unit responsible for sexual offense investigations.

One of the instruments available to determine the appropriate range of work style behaviors is the Job Style Indicator (JSI). The JSI is a pencil-and-paper job-style analysis tool that is used to specify a work style behavioral profile so that it can be compared to an applicant's work behavioral style profile. By seeking agreement on a range of scores on each style dimension of the JSI, managers and supervisors can agree upon an appropriate work style for each position in the organization. Asking employees who do a particular job to complete the JSI is also useful in arriving at their understanding of the job they do. More information regarding the JSI is available at http://www.crgleader.com.

This style (or range of acceptable behaviors) can be included as a part of each job description if you want to print or view the JSI scores for a job role. This agreement can be achieved by using the JSI to define the appropriate work style for each position in the organization, as above. Those employees assessed as being very successful in a position should have input into describing the requirements of that position so that managers who have never done that job can appreciate and consider their successful workers' points of view.

Doing a good job analysis requires a careful assessment of all of the dimensions of a job. An annual (or even more frequent) review of job requirements often reveals that jobs change over time.

3. Specify a Job Description

Through an effective job analysis and the use of instruments such as the *Job Knowledge and Skills Inventory*, the organization prepares a job description for every position. A job description must provide a clear explanation of the duties to be performed and the conditions under which they will be performed. It contains the job specification, which outlines the required skills and knowledge (Step 1) and abilities and characteristics (Step 2) necessary for the satisfactory performance of the job. This description will include the core competencies of the organization. These are the basic but essential qualities required for the position and relate to what the organization does or would like to do well. For example, the ability of a new police officer to mediate a domestic issue is not only a skill possessed by the officer but also a "service" that the organization wishes to deliver well. It is critical that each position has a clear job description that attaches all of the information obtained in Steps 1 and 2 and also the following:

1. Any objectives and time line performance requirements
   - If evaluation is results based, specific performance objectives must be provided
2. A clarification description of roles in relation to other positions
   - How this job fits in with other jobs, including any functional relationships
3. A clarification of the extent and limits of authority in the position
   - Defining responsibilities and accountability, particularly important for functional (staff) positions
4. A clear line of authority (who is above and below)
   - Defining reporting responsibilities, particularly relevant in this era of flattened organizations and work teams
5. Information on how problems can best be solved
   - What is the performance expectation in problem solving? What problems is the employee responsible for solving?
6. Progress evaluation criteria (how the employee will be evaluated)
   - How is success in the position measured?
7. Incentives or rewards that will be given if goals and performance criteria are reached
   - Necessary in a system of incremental promotions
8. Performance evaluation dates and who is to conduct them
   - For new hires on incremental system and a standard evaluation cycle for others
9. Terms of probationary appointment
   - As a new hire or for a position that carries a probationary period (e.g., promotion, specialist unit)
10. Conditions of termination or transfer (behaviors that will definitely cause an employee to be fired for cause or lose the position)

Again it is time to stop and reflect. The critical question you need ask is whether your organization has up-to-date job descriptions for all positions. If not, why not? Many traditional police (and other rank-based organizations) have emphasized rank rather than function. In a recent review of job descriptions in a relatively large police organization, job descriptions were found that had not been revised for twenty years. Consider how much policing has changed in twenty years and how relevant those job descriptions must now be. Some managers prefer generic job descriptions because they proffer the "flexible" management style.

This lack of clarity can cause significant problems for you as the leader. For example, at one large police organization, it was decided that the operational and administrative roles at the middle management level within an operational unit would be separated and staffed by two employees rather than the previous one. A section of the organization was restructured to show the two separate positions, one operational and one administrative. The two positions reported to a single senior manager. A problem was created in that up to ten operational supervisors, in effect, would now report to both positions.

This organization did not see the need to make one of the positions a "staff" position and remove it from the operational chain, providing functional rather than operational authority. Because policing positions are often based on rank deemed appropriate to fill the position rather than function, the ten supervisors saw only the two equal ranks above them without clear direction in terms of to whom they had accountability. The result was a gross violation of the standard principle known as "unity of command." The operational advice received depended on which of the middle managers was present during the supervisor's shift. Soon the supervisors began "cherry picking." If they knew they wouldn't get the answer they wanted from one of the middle managers, they simply went to the other. Accountability and reporting must generally be to only one person. Even when functional authority becomes an issue, areas of authority and lines of accountability must be very clearly specified.

Now that we have spent considerable time extolling the virtues of very detailed job descriptions, a significant *caveat* must be raised. Recall the story earlier in this book of the personnel officer who called the supervisor and said, "There's a hole out there and you're available." There is a tendency in organizations to look for "perfect fits." That is, staffing personnel look only for those skill sets that are outlined in the job description. The mind-set is to the present need. There is also a tendency to train only to those skill sets. The result is often the loss of beneficial skills and qualities that a person possesses outwardly or innately. Growth in the person is not encouraged. It is requested and sometimes demanded that the person do only those tasks specified within the job description, and behavior outside those parameters is seen as inappropriate.

When preparing job descriptions, do not build "boxes" from which there is no escape, no chance for freedom, no chance to grow and contribute in new ways to the position and to the organization. Every position should be seen as simply a stepping-stone, whether vertical or lateral, to other areas in the organization.

In a recent consulting contract with a policing agency, I coached the chief of police to not stop at developing comprehensive and accurate job descriptions, but suggested that these job descriptions become the criteria on which all performance reviews are based and be elevated to the status of **working agreements**. This meant that the chief and a new hire would both sign the document to indicate that there was an agreement between the parties that the job description had been read, understood, and agreed upon. This seals the document as a **working document** that gets reviewed while a new employee or a newly promoted employee is being coached on the job and when it comes time for a scheduled performance review.

4. Screen Applicants on "Paper" Qualifications First

Paper screening is relevant at all levels of the organization. Selection processes (such as assessment centers) are very costly and not welcomed in this time of budgetary restraints, unless they can be shown to be cost effective and efficient. Every effort should be made to ensure that the "right" people move into appropriate job roles. It is at this point that the need for an effective human resource information system becomes especially evident. All information pertaining to an applicant must be centralized in a database. For a new hire, the information is generally limited to a resume, background check, educational transcripts, references, employment records, questionnaires, employment application, medical information, and hiring pretests. A note of caution is required here. Ensure that your hiring pretests and hiring processes comply with the provisions of the appropriate labor legislation in your jurisdiction. If screening an applicant for promotion or placement, the database becomes considerably larger. It includes service records, training records, awards, disciplinary actions, and posthiring education that must be compared to the job description/specification.

Instructors in the use of computers often use the expression "garbage in–garbage out." Your ability to make reliable decisions at this stage depends almost entirely on the reliability and validity of the accumulated information. This information may be in the form of human resource instruments such as **applicant tracking and employee testing** or references, applications, education transcripts, pretesting, and investigations. These documents provide the opportunity to evaluate the extent of each applicant's training and experience.

This will also provide you the opportunity to arrive at a short list based on close examination of paper applications, letters of reference, and resumes. Given the significant costs associated with the selection process, early screening is essential (but premature screening should be avoided). If the job specification within a job description requires a specific level of training or education, the selection and placement of a person into the position without the required level is counterproductive.

Having said that, it is important to reflect on the above comments. You must examine the paper qualifications in terms of ability to do the (entry-level) job *now*, the apparent ability to learn the job during the training provided, and the apparent abilities that will provide the organization with individuals capable of moving well beyond entry-level positions. Do not just look for good police officers; look for future supervisors and managers. Some recruiters disagree with this approach because they believe in be hiring people who are good frontline officers who do not seek promotions. The authors disagree because they would rather hire the greatest potential possible.

5. Assess Information and Prepare for the Interview

By this stage in the process, you have clearly defined the skills, knowledge, and behavioral qualities required to fill the position. How well you have constructed the human resource information system database on the applicant will profoundly affect the value of the interview process. As limited time is available, the primary purpose of the interview will be to focus on the critical factors in job performance. The employment record may reveal a pattern of frequent job changes. This needs to be explored. If it is due to the applicant's inability to socially adapt within the workplace, it should "raise a flag" in relation to the policing culture. Is there anything in the database that suggests an integrity issue? Do some areas appear unusually vague? Did you provide a realistic job preview, such as time in a reserve police program or victim services unit? What was the evaluation of the applicant? Does pretesting show anything contrary to information provided by the applicant? Assess the relevance of each piece of information. Does it apply to job performance?

While assessing this information, it is important that the appropriate weighting be placed on areas relevant to the job function. If there is an identified weakness in an easily corrected skill area, should this be given as much weight as an attitudinal area that may be difficult to correct? Numerous evaluation instruments are available for assessing an applicant's suitability for employment. However, whatever is used must comply with the labor legislation in effect for your area. If you are not familiar with the labor laws that effect your hiring processes, you should familiarize yourself with them as soon as possible.

A very significant source of information is the assessment center mentioned in Step 1. Each level of the center is designed with specific dimensions for the level in the organization to which an individual aspires. This may be entry level (recruit), supervisor, manager, or executive. Although, as mentioned in Step 1, the assessment center process has been validated, it is not without controversy. Take the case of the manager assessment center where the exercise was interviewing a troubled employee. The information provided indicated the likelihood of an alcohol abuse problem. The candidate had just completed the Senior Police Administration Course at the Canadian Police College, Ottawa. The candidate scored well in the interview portion of the course in Ottawa. However, at the assessment center, he was given a failing score. A review of the assessor's notes revealed comments such as, "Obviously unsure of himself. Kept answering questions with questions." Clearly, the assessor was unfamiliar with the reflective interviewing technique that the candidate was using. This technique is generally accepted in situations that deal with troubled employees where an effort is made to have the employee accept responsibility for his or her problem. As a consequence of the assessor's lack of knowledge, the candidate received a low score, which resulted in his elimination from the promotional competition. Despite this "anomaly," an assessment center provides valuable insight into candidates.

Although the assessment center method can be costly and time consuming, it demonstrates validity in matching people to jobs. To do this, it is critical that the skills and knowledge required to perform a job satisfactorily be determined and documented.

6. Interview Short-Listed Applicants

The purpose of the interview is twofold: Does the applicant have the knowledge and skills to do the job (after training, if relevant)? Where does the applicant rate in relation to other applicants?

Superior interviewing skills are critical at this stage. The interviewer must maximize the interview time. Given that a structured format (use of standard questions prepared in advance, often to comply with labor issues) guides most interviews, the interviewer must have the ability to present problem-solving questions and ethical scenarios to further test the applicant's skills, knowledge, and character. Also, the use of open-ended questions provides a skilled interviewer the opportunity to lead and focus on areas of concern where more information is desired. Behavioral interviewing is another useful approach that is often used to elicit greater specificity of information from applicants. This involves probing into when, where, with whom, and how an applicant has demonstrated specific skills.

There is a propensity in policing to attribute the ability to perform selection interviews to individuals based on other factors. Consider the skilled investigator who must possess the skills to perform the investigative function. Certainly some of the basic interviewing skills are similar. However, an interviewer must have intimate knowledge of the selection process, the job requirements of the position being applied for, the relevant labor laws, and how to probe for those important hidden qualities that have the potential to affect the organization in a positive or negative way.

Also, it is a fact that no one is endowed with skill by virtue of rank. It is an unfortunate reality that police organizations (and other paramilitary organizations) promote people into positions where the skills required to perform the job are automatically attributed to them by rank. Not all detectives/investigators make good selection interviewers. Not all officers make good personnel/staffing officers.

7. Hire, Orient, and Train New Employees

As soon as the applicant is hired, the socialization process must begin. This is socialization not only with peers, trainers, and supervisors but with the organization itself.

There are two performance expectations for a new hire. First, there is a learning expectation in the form of achieving training standards that are clearly articulated. Although this training usually occurs somewhat in isolation by a training section, unit, or off-site facility, the recruit must understand the organizational consequences of not meeting the training standard. The extreme is that failure to meet a training standard may result in termination of employment. Also, organizational expectations regarding standards of behavior must be outlined. This is particularly true if the training facility is off-site and operated by either the organization's training staff or a nonorganizational training facility. Even if the training is conducted outside your organization, never let the recruit feel abandoned. Take steps to ensure he or she always feels "connected" to the organization.

The real orientation to the organization occurs when people receive the informal "whisper-in-the-ear" approach. Positive or negative role models let new employees know what is "really" expected of them in terms of acceptable performance. Some very positive values or some very negative values are transmitted at this time!

During the orientation process, you should provide your new employees with the following information if you want to get maximum performance with a minimum of confusion:

1. The vision, mission, purpose, philosophy, and goals of your organization. If you have a displayed vision or mission statement, provide a copy. (You obviously want your new employees to "buy in" to how and why you want them to accomplish things.)
2. The policies, practices, and procedures the new employees will need to know to be most effective and least confused. (Ideally, you would already have prepared a staff manual with all this information in it. If you do not provide a manual, make sure a copy of the policies is easily accessible to them.)
3. The job descriptions and working agreements for their new positions, which will include everything (mentioned above) that is needed for employees to understand what is required of them.
4. A formal letter describing the terms of their appointments, including length of probationary periods and vacations, amount of pay, etc.
5. How the performance review and promotion system works in your organization, and when the first performance review will occur. If the training facility is off-site, ensure they understand that it is a collaborative evaluation process.

8. Conduct Performance Reviews

No other segment of personnel systems seems to have caused as much controversy and discord in policing and other justice and public safety sectors as performance reviews. How do you evaluate employee job performance, whether a new recruit on probation or a veteran officer seeking promotion? This topic could be and has been the topic of many books. The purpose here is not to define the instruments and techniques but to generalize the "when and why and how."

There are numerous occasions when an performance appraisal is required. These may be administrative in nature, such as an incremental pay raise, or in response to an employee who asks, "How am I doing?" New hires are subject to a high level of evaluation during their training. This is usually followed by an on-the-job evaluation. The results for most are an incremental promotion from the probationary stage. Performance appraisals are required as part of a complete performance management program. It is essential that both the employee and the employer have a clear picture of the employee's level of performance. Promotion, assignment, or even continued employment may hinge on a series of appraisals.

There are a number of issues with which you must be concerned. The performance of the individual must be compared only with established standards of performance or performance objectives. Setting standards of performance is a task that requires specific skills. When some parts of the job are quantifiable, such as the number of traffic violation notices for traffic officers, setting standards is relatively easy (provided, of course, that the person writing the standard remains realistic). However, when a part of the job is not quantitative but qualitative, such as relationship with peers, the task becomes very difficult. Failure to establish the standards results in performance reviews that contain comments such as, "Looks good in uniform" "and Gets along with peers." Of what value are these comments? Nil!

Your organization must seek out the various types of performance appraisal instruments available today. What type of rating scale should be used? Graphic? Behaviorally anchored? What type of training will supervisors and managers require to use the instrument? How much will it cost? How does the organization change unsatisfactory behavior? What behavior is considered unsatisfactory? What will be done with the appraisal? The answer to this last questions is not as obvious as it appears. One organization forwarded its appraisals to the staffing department, where the front scoring page was removed. The balance of the document, which contained all the dimensions and observed data, was "thrown" into a box in a corner, where it was left for a year and then shredded. When this information became known, you can well imagine how much effort went into doing a meaningful appraisal.

What you do with the appraisal is important. When you conduct an appraisal interview, you must keep in mind the purpose of the interview. Are you interviewing an "up-and-comer" with outstanding performance and no deficiencies noted or a young police officer who, if behaviors do not change, will be at risk for termination of employment? Although the interview style will be different, the outcome should be the same. Both are apprised of observed behavior that relates to the performance of their current jobs or is relevant to a future position (e.g., leadership). Both should be asked for commitments to future behavior. One is continued growth and the other is a commitment to change.

The appraisal interview of an employee whose performance does not meet the standard presents unique issues. It is especially important with these employees to highlight the positive things they have done and to identify, write down, and commit to agreements for specific changes. Supervisors also need to commit to giving the necessary coaching and support to get the desired results. Then, later, if the employee meets the specified requirements, he or she will have hope of being taken off probation.

To develop morale and encourage minimal performers, you have to communicate to them that you believe their developing into good employees is a real possibility; otherwise, their next three to six months will be too stressful (or boring) and will add to their anxiety—or to their low performance, while they find another job at your expense. Give them support and feedback every week or two for a while, until progress is sure.

Because termination of employment is a potential consequence, the employee's commitment should be in writing. You are unlikely to see grievances from legal or union sources when you have fairly told the employee ahead of time that certain tasks had to be performed to specific standards in order for him or her to remain in the position and if there is documentation on paper that he or she, in fact, did not do so. Most employees will not argue with facts stated in terms of behaviors that they agree they have done or failed to do adequately. When in doubt, however, you should always refer to legal counsel and to the labor laws in your jurisdiction. Commitment cannot be open-ended. If a change in behavior is required, time lines must be set. This is similar to individual goal setting, where the change must be specific, measurable (observable), and time constrained.

9. Career Path Planning

For those employees who demonstrate leadership or managerial potential or some other needed expertise in the workplace, a career path can be identified and discussed with them in advance of an opportunity or job opening. With the trend toward flatter organizations, "vertical climb" and career path are no longer synonymous. Lateral movement within the organization is a modern-day reality. Few promotional opportunities exist, and providing a meaningful career path horizontally is a major human resources task.

Career path planning is a collaborative activity between the employee and the employer. However, the ultimate responsibility lies with the employee. Only the employee can agree to and follow up on the steps deemed necessary to achieve his or her chosen career path. Nor is up to you to decide what success is. Think of success as a state of mind. For example, the police officer who becomes a member of a forensic identification unit begins a carefully scripted path of education and experience to become the best forensic identification officer he or she can be. There is a very real possibility that others, who have been socialized in the traditional hierarchy where success is traveled vertically, will refer to the individual as "dead-ended" in the job. They do not see the growth that is occurring in the individual and how this person's perception of success is to be the very best at what he or she does..

Career path planning requires honesty on the part of the organization and the leaders who represent it. During a promotion competition in one police organization, a section manager approved and forwarded a request by one of his staff to enter the competition. The process guidelines were such that by forwarding the request, the manager was acknowledging the member's readiness to compete. Within a few days after the request was received, the staffing unit received correspondence from the same section manager now requesting the member's transfer due to his inability to meet even minimal performance standards.

Instruments such as the *Job Style Indicator* and *Personal Style Indicator* can help an employee understand the style behaviors appropriate for current and future positions. This can help the employee formulate a motivating internal career plan and a personal development plan, feel more challenged by the work, and assume more responsibility. This combination of factors will likely even more strongly motivate him or her to seek specific positions.

People Information Is Performance Information!

By using personnel systems, you will come to know those who work for you better. You will find that if you know them well enough, you come to understand what challenges them as individuals. If you can come to know what areas of responsibility they want to assume, then you have incredibly motivating information! People information is leadership information!

Frederick Herzberg (1989) asserts that we cannot motivate people by improving work conditions, raising salaries, or shuffling tasks. He asserts:

> KITA—the externally imposed attempt by management to "install generators" in employees—has been demonstrated to be a total failure. The absence of such "hygiene" factors as good supervisor–employee relations and liberal fringe benefits can make workers unhappy, but the presence of these factors will not make employees want to work harder. Essentially meaningless changes in the tasks that workers are assigned to do have not accomplished the desired objective either. **The only way to motivate employees is to give them challenging work for which they can assume responsibility.**

In order that we might challenge people, we need to select, hire, and train the "right people for the right jobs." We need to provide challenging work with rewards that are meaningful. We need information systems that will allow us to do all of these things in the most efficient and effective way. We need well-designed personnel systems such as performance management, career development, and computer-based training. All of these things have a significant cost, but the cost pales in terms of the cost of not having a well-motivated, committed, and ever-developing work force in our organizations. People are the most expensive resource your organization will have. Treat this resource well and you will see a monumental "return on investment."

If we can communicate with followers clearly enough to understand and appreciate the desires of their hearts—and provide opportunities for them to find the realization of these desires to some extent, we will likely find increased performance, loyalty, and longevity as a result. In achieving this result, we will have been transforming leaders.

References

Anderson, T. and B. Zeiner, *Comprehensive Personnel System (CPS)*, Abbotsford, B.C.: Consulting Resource Group International, 1989.

Herzberg, Frederick, *The Motivation to Work*, New Brunswick, N.J.: Transaction Publishers, 1993.

Hammer, Michael and James Champy, *Reengineering the Corporation,* New York: HarperCollins, 1993, 84.

Plecas, Darryl and Paul Tinsley, *Validity of the Police Academy Assessment Centre,* British Columbia: Justice Institute Library, 1998.

13

Security in the Policing Environment

Introduction

In my service in the Royal Canadian Mounted Police (RCMP), I spent a significant number of years in ensuring the security of police facilities, including a standard detachment (precinct), headquarters facilities, forensic laboratories, and other special-purpose police buildings. In each of these facilities, there are common elements of security which have proven to have a dynamic impact on the overall operational security of each type of building.

Outside the RCMP environment, I provided security consulting services to other federal government departments in addressing their security issues through audits and ongoing security consultation advice on new building construction. Since my retirement from the RCMP, I have been providing similar services through my private consulting corporation (SRG Security Resource Group) to clients throughout North America. These clients have been from government at municipal and provincial (state) levels, institutions (universities and hospitals), industry (warehousing, transportation, shipyards, manufacturing, national newspapers), transit (commuter and light rail systems), corporations (national chains, high-tech, office services, national standards testing facilities, art galleries, theaters, hotels, sports complexes, and banks), and policing organizations of various types.

In each of these consultations, there has always been a common thread of threat and risks, specific vulnerabilities, and appropriate solutions to problems that are often unrelated to what the client thought was needed as a solution. This is because, in my approach, I try to determine the cause of the problem and then apply solutions to that cause. This often provides opportunities to solve problems at much lower costs.

Getting Beyond the Symptoms

My consultations are effectively completed when the client is provided with the most cost-effective solution presented in a clear implementation path for correcting the various security problems. This is often a combination of policy and procedure changes, security education, and other administrative and operational security issues.

Beyond this, there are many organizational security issues that need to be addressed to effectively create a security program that is comprehensive, yet in many respects transparent.

Physical security measures such as landscaping, lighting, structural security, and doors and hardware are evaluated in conjunction with the above subject area to ensure that the facility passively provides for the appropriate level of security to meet the identified risks. Where this is not possible, electronic security measures are considered to meet those deficiencies.

Finally, security personnel requirements are analyzed. The ongoing operational expenditure of a guard force usually ends up being one of the most expensive security measures in the long run. For this reason, the use of this resource is carefully analyzed to ensure that it is recommended only when internal policies and procedures, structural change, or electronic security systems will not meet the client's needs.

SRG Security Optimizer™ Model

The development of the model of getting beyond the symptoms of the problem to the actual cause has led me to the development of a model for the consistent delivery of consulting services to my clients. This is included on the following page so that discussions in the remainder of this chapter can be read with an understanding of my overall approach to security consulting.

Model Overview

Step 1   The organization identifies that it has security problems. The problems could be increases in theft, employees feeling unsafe, or any number of issues or deficiencies.

Step 2   The leaders in the organization make a decision to act appropriately, utilizing security consultants to correctly identify and correct the problems with the most appropriate solutions.

Step 3   A current-state assessment is completed. SRG security professionals come in and analyze the current and historical internal and external influences on the organization's security. SRG professionals look at all aspects of the organization, its structure, traffic flow, and so on.

Step 4   SRG professionals undertake a four-step threat and risk assessment. This includes asset identification, vulnerability assessment, impact analysis, and a review of existing security measures.

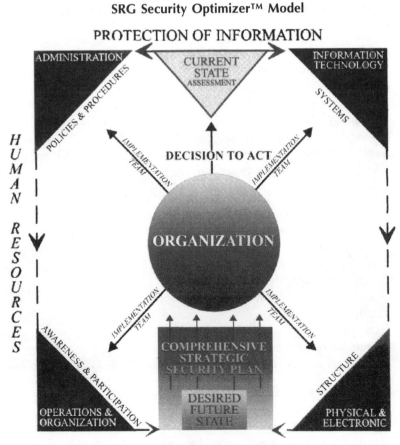

SRG Security Optimizer™ Model

Step 5   SRG defines the desired future state, with the organization's input.

Step 6   SRG puts together a comprehensive strategic security plan. This is a document that clearly articulates the solutions that will address the identified problems in the most cost-effective and efficient manner, addressing priorities.

Step 7   The implementation process is a team action, where the agreed-upon recommendations are implemented in order of priority in conjunction with budgetary limitations.

Service Breakdown

The above model displays the four corners of the overall security audit process. The specific areas that are addressed in each of these cornerstone groups are as follows:

Administrative security
- Policies and procedures
- Employee selection
- Contingency planning
- Emergency planning
- Business resumption planning
- Security orientation and training
- Workplace violence issues

Operational security
- Threat and risk assessments
- Identification issues
- Security department and management
- Janitorial service examination
- Facilities management examination
- Smoking in the workplace (security issues)
- Personnel security
- Executive protection
- Counterterrorism issues
- Security issues relevant to organizational units within client environment

Information technology security
- Information access controls
- Confidential waste security
- Confidential record handling and storage
- Physical, environmental, and organizational security for information handling

- Hardware/software
- Communications (data and voice)
- Internet security
- Encryption issues
- Data recovery
- Discrete computer crime investigations
- Intellectual property issues
- Industrial espionage issues

Physical and electronic security
- Environmental design and crime review
- Landscaping
- Parking areas
- Fencing
- Lighting
- Security markings and signage
- Electrical and auxiliary power
- Natural gas supply and gas storage
- Perimeter security
- Structural security
- Glazing (windows and mirrors)
- Elevator security
- Doors and hardware
- Master key and key control systems
- Display security
- Access control systems
- Intrusion alarm systems
- Closed-circuit television systems
- Integrated electronic security systems
- Specialty security systems

Police Building Security Audit

Effective leadership in police, justice, and public safety organizations requires that leaders give more credence to issues of security. We live in a time when the security of buildings, vehicles, people, and information has become increasingly vulnerable. It seems that many leaders are not inclined to face these facts until there is a crisis. Or, it could be that leaders are so busy with day-to-day operations that the need for stringent preventive security measures just does not come into focus until something significant occurs.

This chapter explores the issues surrounding security and a policing organization. This is not a discussion of internal investigation issues. Instead, it is a discussion about how the security audit methods discussed in the introduction of this chapter reveal vulnerabilities that are common to police facilities as well as buildings in other environments. Additionally, security issues unique to the policing environment are examined.

I will to take you through a security audit of a police facility, discuss some of the findings that are common, and review the assumptions or attitudes that occur in police facilities and the resultant vulnerabilities that are created.

Many departments effectively look after certain areas of security, but few have an overall comprehensive program. Some readers may think that a police facility would provide the ultimate in security because of the nature of the work. But just remember the plumber's leaky faucet or the carpenter's broken stairs. Often, the expertise and energies of individuals are directed outward toward the clients of the service. They quickly go from their own base to the client without focusing on their own environment in enough detail.

This is not to suggest that police buildings are not protected against outside attack of many types. It does suggest, however, that there are security issues that may not be readily recognized for what they are—a weak link in the security chain.

The Attitude

One of the interesting things that is found in conducting a security audit of a police building, especially as a private consultant, is the preconceived attitude among the police personnel that they are experts on security and that their facilities are sound. Additionally, personnel feel that a private consultants cannot understand the types of issues or resulting security concerns that police personnel and organizations face. In these assumptions and attitudes lie the opportunities for policing personnel to miss security vulnerabilities within their facilities.

In conducting security assessments in dozens of police facilities, the following findings are typical:

1. Security policies and procedures require updating to reflect current operational needs and regulatory requirements of a department.
2. Information access protocols often provide too much information about secure operational environments within a policing organization.
3. Smoking policies within the building that houses a police facility contribute in a significant way to the security of the personnel, the building, and the information assets of the police organization.

4. Vehicle movements in out of a police facility can often create vulnerabilities for secure police operations because of countersurveillance activities.
5. A secure facility is often visually compromised due to inappropriate or unusual activities in the neighborhood where the facility is located.
6. The main entrance to a police facility often creates security vulnerabilities for the civilian or police officer staffing the desk.
7. Control measures for master key systems, key control records, and access card records are often insufficient and outdated, yet assumed to be effective.

Administrative Security

Policies and Procedures

One very common thing that is found in the corporate, institutional, and governmental environments is that the policies and procedures that provide directives and guidelines to the personnel on security issues are often not up to date, relevant to today's vulnerabilities, or in existence at all. In a police environment, there is once again an assumption that the police building is relatively secure. On examination of policies and procedures in many different client environments, we have found consistency in this issue.

In a police environment, some of the policies and procedures that should be in place are as follows:

1. Building security
2. Escort of all visitors
3. Guard tour patrols
4. Building maintenance (not security related)
5. Cleaning staff escort's and security clearance requirements
6. Access control cards (normally, only authorized persons are entitled to receive cards, but there is often no list of the authorized persons)
7. Press releases
8. General information release requirements
9. Access to central records
10. Security of police radios

Another issue affecting policies and procedures is the use of updating bulletins. As situations change, these changes are often reflected in bulletins. The bulletins are added in as supplements to policy and procedure manuals. As time goes on, unless there is administrative review and updating, the bulletins begin to overpower the manual and the policies and procedures are lost. Ongoing bulletins that are put into a manual in chronological order, without being integrated into the manual itself, makes the organization of the manual chaotic. This provides ample opportunity for personnel to not be informed of relevant security information.

Security Orientation and Training

In any policing organization, there is a formal training program for new skill sets that are to be learned by officers and civilian support staff alike. However, when it comes to learning about security vulnerabilities and mitigating actions that can be taken to reduce these vulnerabilities in the policing environment, training is often ignored. There should be a formal security orientation manual for new employees and a training program for the security administrator and the security guard force (or front-desk) personnel. Consistency in the application of security depends on personnel working from similar guidelines. These guidelines are usually contained in a security policy and procedure manual and/or orientation material.

Identification Issues

One of the extremely interesting habits of policing organizations is a reluctance to adopt photo identification systems within policing buildings. It is assumed by the membership that everyone who works within the building knows each and every person in that environment. This is consistent in smaller police buildings as well as large. This behavior often occurs in corporate environments as well and is not unique to policing environments.

The common habit adopted is for the membership not to wear identification and for visitors to be required to wear some sort of identification. This often takes the form of a card that reads "visitor—escort required." If the visitor is another police officer or other trusted visitor, the card often reads "visitor—no escort." The problem with both of these methods lies in the fact that staff members do not wear cards. A visitor only needs to remove his or her card to appear to be a staff member.

Photo identification cards should be created in such a way that the background of the cards is unique to the particular environment. Cards that are very plain in nature are relatively easy to duplicate; a unique background makes this much more difficult. It should be understood that there are people and organizations that have something to gain by accessing police buildings and information. Policing organizations cannot assume that they are not subject to surveillance or infiltration from the outside.

Operational and Organizational Security

Threat and Risk Assessment

Visibility: Most people would agree that police buildings are generally highly visible, unless the police building is secretive in nature. Even under such circumstances, neighborhood residents and businesses frequently know there is an unusual tenant in a particular building. Therefore, one must always assume that the general public has knowledge of the location of the police building.

Overt Security Equipment: Even when the location of the police building is guarded, or the building itself is kept nondescript, the security equipment installed on the building will often give away significant clues about the tenant. Equipment such as closed-circuit television cameras, special door hardware, coated windows, or other measures make identification relatively easy.

Security Incidents: If one examines the number of times police buildings have come under some form of attack by persons who have been the subject of targeted investigation, prosecution, or some coordinated intelligence probe, it is justified to be concerned about this type of vulnerability. When examining your police department, ask yourself how many individuals would like to get at your police information or personnel. Then ask yourself what the relative skill level of these individuals is.

Vehicle Traffic: Think about how often police personnel are involved in surveillance of suspect criminals. If you consider all the methods that are used to observe, follow, listen to, photograph, or otherwise surveil suspected criminals, you will get a firm understanding of the different ways that the criminal element can gain information about police personnel, vehicles, activities, and buildings. Vehicles coming to and from a police building not only establish activity patterns but provide the opportunity to determine such things as the number and identity of persons on a shift and the types of vehicles used. The complete identification, including license numbers, of the vehicles is easy to obtain by basic surveillance techniques. It is very easy to find an observation site when looking at various vantage points offered by neighboring buildings. How often do you look at your building from the point of view of a person trying to observe your actions? Do you know the identity and background of all the neighbors surrounding your building? Do you make inquiries on a regular basis to determine changes in the dynamics of your neighborhood? Do you know if any individuals living in proximity to your building are subject to police investigation?

You need only use your imagination to determine what information could be gained by knowing what vehicles the police drive, where these vehicles go, whose is visited at the destinations, and other relevant information. Think about all of the information you try to gain on criminal activities through surveillance. Countersurveillance of police activities can reveal information just as valuable to criminals. To believe that the criminal element is not capable of the same surveillance techniques is potentially dangerous.

Smoking and Security

In today's health-conscious environment, smoking has become a less frequently tolerated habit in the workplace. It has become extremely common for employees who smoke to be told that they must smoke outside the building. Often, smoking rooms are not provided.

If you want to determine easily where the smoking staff go for their coffee or meal breaks, you need only look around the parameter of the building. Wherever you find a doorway that is protected from the elements (wind and rain), you will find evidence of smoking. If you look at the security arrangements at those locations, you can find where vulnerabilities are being created in your operational environment. How often have you seen a rock used as a wedge to hold a perimiter door open while staff go outside?

Think about the way security should be layered within your environment,and then look at how it is breached by creating a nonsmoking environment without consideration of the smokers. It will make you question the way in which the issue of smoking is addressed.

Insecure Work Activities

One of the other issues that is common to both corporate and policing environments is that working files are often left insecure on desks during coffee and meal breaks. If you think about the investigative files that are left on desks or in review baskets, you will start to see some of the vulnerabilities to which this information is exposed. People who do not have security clearance or access to these files are brought into the police environment for statements and other investigative purposes and are left unattended. When this happens, they could access the information without being detected. Additionally, witnesses and suspects are frequently taken to areas within a police facility that are clearly restricted security zones because of the operational layout of the building.

Locating interview rooms near the main entry enables effective interrogations and interviews without disturbing the operational activities or providing a tour through the police facility.

Insecure Personnel

Generally, there is an acknowledgment that personnel within a police facility must be afforded some protection beyond that of a normal office environment. Even when there are weaknesses in the overall security, this acknowledgment is still in place. It appears in measures such as tinted windows, protective door entry systems, security surveillance systems, and ballistic walls and windows. Personnel within the building are generally afforded reasonable security. The operational policies of the department must also be considered.

Issues such as the smoking policy, addressed earlier in this chapter, create a working environment where some staff are segregated out of the building to promote a clean-air work environment. This is not an unreasonable approach when viewed by itself. However, when you acknowledge the extra construction precautions taken to protect personnel against increased threats and risk and then place some personnel outside this protective barrier because they smoke, smoking really can be hazardous to one's health—in more ways that one!

Workplace Violence Issues

In the United States, OSHA regulations guide how employers must protect staff from workplace violence. Canada has equivalent regulation at the provincial level through Workers Compensation Boards. In both cases, where there is an environment in which violence can reasonably be expected, the employer must take reasonable steps to ensure against physical harm of the personnel. This is especially true for those staff in a police environment without police officer powers, self-defense training, or weapons.

Security Personnel

In most large police buildings, dedicated security staff control access to and from the building and monitor the security system. By providing up-to-date security policies and procedures, these personnel are effectively equipped with tools that enable them to do their job in a professional manner. Policing personnel, by nature, are often prone to try to bypass the security that is there to protect them. How many times have you seen police personnel walk right by the front desk, trying not to sign in on entry logs or show their identification to the security staff?

Janitorial Services Security

The personnel that provide cleaning services within a building are often contracted from an outside source. These contracts are often awarded on the basis of the lowest bid. In these competitive situations, contractors provide services with personnel at the lowest rates possible. This often creates an environment where the janitorial staff works for very low if not minimum wages. These personnel complete their cleaning activities from an hourly wage, not a career, point of view. Often, a person who cannot come to work calls in at the last moment and a replacement is required. The replacement may not be familiar with the site and may not have security clearance if that was not a specific contractual requirement. Additionally, cleaning services personnel are generally not focused on the security of the building, as it is not part of their job function.

When you look at the above examination of the type of services that are provided and then consider at what time of day these services are required, you see another vulnerability. Nighttime janitorial services provide the least disruption of administrative activities in a building, but create the greatest security risk. This is not to imply dishonesty on the part of the cleaning staff. It only suggests that their duties are generally focused only on cleaning. If you want to ensure that the security of the building is maintained, you need to consider daytime janitorial services or make special arrangements to cover security needs at night.

Physical and Electronic Security

There are numerous things within the physical environment itself that should be considered in order to ensure effective security within a police facility. Just as a police investigator looks for ways to penetrate the criminal environment in order to find evidence against criminals, the police environment can be penetrated to access investigative information. Additionally, the threat of an attack on a facility in order to free a prisoner, access police exhibits, or further a terrorist cause poses a real danger that needs to be addressed. Remote facilities such as vehicle garages need to be afforded protection similar to the main facility.

Environmental Design

Layered Security

Security within any facility should be layered to ensure that the most vulnerable or valuable assets are within several security barriers. The building should be generally divided into public and restricted access zones. The public access zone provides uncontrolled areas that can be freely accessed by the public during open hours. The reception zone is an area that functions as a physical entry point where there is initial contact between the public and police personnel, where services are provided, information is exchanged, and access to restricted zones is controlled. Persons accessing the building should not have immediate uncontrolled access to the building interior on arrival at the main entry. This reception zone should be physically separated from the operations zone by physical barriers that are suitable to meet the specific threats and risk. This can include such items as a ballistic barrier between the inquiry counter and the public vestibule, with effective speech ports and a document or parcel pass-through in this counter.

The restricted access zone includes an operations zone where access is limited to persons who work there and to escorted visitors. This is usually the standard working area and offices for police and civilian staff. Security zones are strictly controlled areas where access is limited to authorized persons and properly escorted visitors. Additional safeguards are required in these areas (exhibit rooms, investigation project rooms, computer server rooms, telephone rooms, prisoner cell areas, or other areas requiring special security measures). Each of these special rooms requires security measures consistent with the function therein.

In any of the zones, approved security containers can create additional levels of security when required.

Security Lighting

Lighting surrounding a police facility should provide adequate illumination for several functional reasons:

1. To provide effective illumination for closed-circuit video system monitoring
2. To remove visual shadows so that persons close to the building can be easily seen
3. To provide adequate lighting for police activities such as moving prisoners from police vehicles into the building

Lighting is consistently one of the security elements that provides effective increase of prospect at night, in addition to deterring activities that may otherwise go undetected.

Underground Parkades

Effective security in underground parkades is a mixture of good functional control over entry into the building, effective lighting, and good control of access to interior elevator vestibules. Additional issues such as closed-circuit video system monitoring and security alarm requirements need to be looked at on an as-required basis.

The sequencing of the vehicle entry doors and the duration for which they are kept open create one of the largest areas of vulnerability. The other main problem area in the garage is the security of the fire egress doors.

There may be a need to control vehicles entering or leaving the garage beyond the normal access control requirements. The use of the garage by vehicles that are not authorized to enter the facility or other operational issues may require the use of more strict control over access to or egress from the garage. If this is a requirement, proximity tags can be added to authorized vehicles to enable the overhead doors to maintain audit control over which vehicles enter or leave the garage.

Security Vestibules

The need for physical barriers was discussed earlier in this chapter. In addition, consideration can be given to creating a "mantrap" configuration on the doors that provide access to security vestibules. Basically, this means that if a perimeter door is opened, then no doors that provide access to restricted access zones from that vestibule can be opened at the same time. This helps to prevent a situation where someone can charge through the outside door and access the interior door.

Exhibit Storage

Access to the exhibit room is an area that often causes great problems and concern for police. The continuity of exhibits for court purposes can become the sole issue in the success or failure of a criminal prosecution. It is paramount that this area receive one of the highest levels of security within a police building. This includes consideration of card access control and/or security alarm zone controls that enable positive identification and create an   audit trail of any persons entering this area. Failure to have electronic audit controls in place may mean that all persons accessing a particular area must attend court to establish that they *did not* have any involvement or contact with an exhibit.

Utilities Security

The security of building utilities is one area that is not usually adequately addressed. Rooms such as telephone, electrical, fire safety system, and emergency generator rooms should be effectively controlled by key system restrictions and security alarm protection. Additionally, the room in which security equipment is located (often the telephone room) should be protected by the security alarm system.

After reading this statement, you would probably acknowledge that the telephone room (housing security system interface and computer system data mux equipment) is usually left unprotected. Additionally, it is often a dual purpose room where the janitorial staff stores mops, buckets, and brooms. There should be no unauthorized unrestricted access to this area.

Structural Security

The perimeter walls to a building are, in most cases, relatively well looked after. Inside the building, however, there is often a tendency to utilize demountable partitions for individual room walls. These partitions extend from the structural floor to the suspended ceiling very often used in modern construction. This type of wall construction provides opportunity for persons to climb over the partition wall into security rooms. This can create continuity breaks in control of the security of the special-purpose rooms. Walls in these areas should extend from structural floor to structural ceiling. In cases where there is a need to accommodate ventilation and electrical equipment, expanded metal mesh needs to be secured from the structural ceiling to the demountable wall.

Doors and Hardware

There have been many instances in the opening of a new police building when I have noticed how poorly the doors and hardware have been detailed in the construction process. This is a critical issue in ensuring the overall physical security of a facility. Yet it is often left to the contractor's discretion to determine which lock functions and levels of door security should be given to a police building. In numerous cases, hardware has been incorrectly installed on the doors, creating not only a breach in the level of security but actually a guide for unauthorized entry. This becomes a critical issue when the police personnel feel that they have a new facility with appropriate levels of security through the new construction process. Very often, that is not the case.

Master Key and Key Control Systems

Once the doors and hardware are installed, control of the keys to a building needs to be established effectively and early. If the keys are not controlled from the date the system is installed, then there is potential compromise and loss of the control to critical access areas through unmonitored key access. Imagine the potential damage that could occur if unauthorized persons can enter a police building at will.

Storage

Once information has become inactive, it is usually stored for a given retention period in case it is required for review, renewed investigation, or audit purposes. The length of time information is stored depends on the type of information and the protocols or requirements of the department. In any case, the volume of material can become quite significant, necessitating storage in basement or off-site areas. These storage areas are often only visited when additional storage material is being added or the retention period for items has been reached. There are significant periods of time when individual records and/or files are not viewed or scrutinized. This creates an overall vulnerability as someone could remove records and it would go unnoticed for periods up to years. This can also be true for some types of exhibits.

The security measures afforded archived record storage areas should generally be consistent with measures for active areas such as central records storage, or other areas that contain vital, protected, or other investigative information. Controlling access to all information assets is a fundamental component of effective security.

Confidential Waste

Once documents are no longer useful, it is critical that they are disposed of properly. With an effective classification system for documents in place, controls implemented on the different classification levels, and overall awareness of those controls, then disposal of documents is easily achieved.

It is important to ensure that the systems established to dispose of all paper waste do not create vulnerabilities of their own. Recycled and classified waste receptacles should not be adjacent to each other, so that confusion over how to dispose of particular documents does not occur. Additionally, highly sensitive document waste should be shredded immediately by the owner of the document.

If a shredding service is used, effective control over the contract with the service provider should include knowledge of how documentation is bundled, transported, stored, destroyed, and recycled. Very often, shredding companies that do not shred on-site compact documents into bales that are transported to their storage facilities, stored in dry but insecure areas, and then transported to pulp and paper mills for recycling when stored volumes are sufficient. In this type of operation, there is ample opportunity to access documents from the bales.

Access Control

Modern construction often includes electronic access control to provide convenience for personnel, discrimination control over access to particular areas, and audit trails of access activity. This type of access strategy requires as stringent a system and information control mechanism as a master key system.

Security Alarm System

Generally, there is a need for some level of security alarm system(s) within a police facility. Some of the areas typically covered include:

- Perimeter doors
- Security zones
- Special-purpose zones
- Duress alarm at the public reception counter

In all cases, systems of control must be in place that are consistent with access control, master key system control, or other systems such as computer system password controls. On several occasions, I have found the alarm code written on the inside cover of a keypad because some of the staff have difficulty remembering the code. This is almost as common as finding computer passwords attached to monitors with self-adhesive notes. Both of these examples sound absurd, but they are true.

Closed-Circuit Video System

Closed-circuit television (CCTV) monitoring of a police building should be considered wherever there is an opportunity to include live monitoring or a particular problem area needs to be recorded for potential investigative purposes. Generally, when these very basic guidelines are followed, the use of CCTV is restricted to incidents and locations where it can contribute to effective control measures. Widespread use of CCTV is often seen where there is no provision for live monitoring and very little chance of investigative requirement. Security equipment dollars can very often be spent much more effectively. There is some deterrent effect in just the visual presence of cameras, but this is a very dangerous premise on which to base your security.

Another very common useful implementation of CCTV is for the continuous monitoring of prisoner activities by the custodial guard staff. This way, the staff can visually observe behavior in between physical inspection tours of the cells.

Integrated Security Systems

New electronic security systems, to the extent possible, are integrated in their control measures. This is most often accomplished by ensuring that equipment is ergonomically positioned to work from a single station. Alarm and access control systems are often integrated into a common software interface at the security desk. Asset management systems can also be added to interface with the access control/security alarm system. Open architecture of software enables many systems to tie into current access control/alarm systems, when appropriate.

Conclusion

I have worked in a detachment where one of my colleagues working the front desk was shot (not fatally) by a man who had a negative attitude toward police. I have investigated a cell block security incident where a prisoner had escaped through a locked door and seriously injured the custodial guard. I have seen exhibit rooms and other critical areas left totally vulnerable because door hardware components such as astrigals were incorrectly installed. I have also repeatedly seen unauthorized persons walk right into police buildings because they had the appearance or attitude of a police officer.

Police executives and managers have a responsibility to understand the vulnerabilities and corrective security measures appropriate to their type of work environment. Most of the time, very simple and inexpensive measures can mitigate the majority of these issues. Even in cases where a capital expenditure is required and must be budgeted for, security can be increased if there is understanding and acknowledgment of the vulnerability. This enables corrective actions to be put in place until physical changes can be made.

This chapter does not present an entire security consultation process. It is intended to shed some light on particular security issues relating to police facilities and some of the corrective measure that can be taken to mitigate vulnerability. In order to understand more fully the issue of security in your facility, several publications are available through organizations such as the American Society for Industrial Security. Additionally, further information and assistance can be obtained from this writer at http://www.securityresourcegroup.com.

A Futures Perspective on Leadership Development

As a social scientist, my first inclination was to provide a review of *future* trends in leadership, with special attention to trends in police leadership, followed by analyses and conclusions from the data. But as a *futurist*, I realized that this approach would not only be inadequate but would deprive the reader of the perspective gained by adding futures research to the equation—from societal trend monitoring to technological scanning to bellwether, Delphi, brainstorming, scenario development, and numerous other methods—and providing a *vision* of the future that synthesizes data from a plethora of sources. Certainly the review of relevant futures leadership literature was involved in the synthesis, but this chapter focuses on the role of futures research in leadership and the character-istics—starting with *vision*—needed by future police leaders. This approach is predicated on a belief that early twenty-first century policing will seek to *bring peace to neighborhoods* rather than fight endless, costly, and fruitless wars on crime.

Vision is the number one prerequisite of leadership. Without *vision*, where does the leader lead?

Vision can be as simple as understanding, adopting, and pursuing a depart-mental mission or goals statement or as complicated as unilaterally seeing the gold-paved path to success in the future and communicating it successfully to others, much as a "cult" visionary (e.g., Christ, Muhammad, Buddha).

In other words, the leader's vision can be his or her own creative development or can simply be adopted or adapted from the vision of others—from lawmakers who established the mission statement to local political officeholders who have articulated their goals for the larger community, police administrators in other locations who are much admired, citizens whose expressed needs and desires are being served, a synthesis of futures research and its indications about the future world, or, at best, a combination of all of these. However acquired, *vision* and the ability to interpret it, communicate it, sell it, and challenge others to join in its pursuit is critical to leadership.

What makes this particularly important in evolving police culture is the trend toward *all* police having to be leaders—from the traditional director/commissioner/chief down through supervisory levels to the street officer. In community-oriented policing, the commanding officer must have the broad vision for the total department/community, while supervisors must adopt/adapt that vision and communicate it to field officers, who in turn must interact within the framework of the vision with citizens in their neighborhoods as well as with their "partners" in the community and in government and private service agencies. Feedback from the street level, indeed, will be critical in maintaining, revitalizing, reformulating, and—sometimes—rethinking the vision altogether.

Whereas this is certainly a new role for many police at all levels, one can look at evolving culture and clearly see it is an idea whose time has come. Contrary to popular myth, the generation joining police agencies as we enter the twenty-first century is vision driven. Members of the so-called Generation X and beyond have been found to not only desire but indeed require vision in order to maintain interest and be productive in their work lives.

In *Naked Management,* psychologist Marc Muchnik (1996) declared that given clear, consistent communication of vision, positive recognition, considerable autonomy and trust, and a collegial atmosphere, Generation Xers often become the type of creative, dedicated colleagues we all desire. "Bean counters: No! Better bean creators: Yes!"

This is the generation moving through the ranks in police departments today, and if anything, the generations to follow will require and demand still more respect, autonomy, and direct communication, along with "meaningful work." The day of the standard operating procedures automaton is over. The day of the dedicated, vision-seeking, problem-solving, better-world-creating "partner" is dawning (Muchnik, 1996; Tulgan, 1996).

In other words, this independent-thinking worker—who does not blindly follow orders but who genuinely wants to make a difference—is exactly what is needed as a variety of community-oriented, problem-solving approaches move toward becoming the *norm* in police departments everywhere.

In many ways, the convergence of new mission and new employee type is a product of another idea whose time has arrived. It is in harmony with the structure and needs of the emerging society—in which the mechanistic, assembly-line thinking of the *industrial age* (with its militaristic, law-enforcement-oriented policing) is rapidly being replaced by the rapid-and-constant changing, creative-thinking-demanding *information age* world. Quick adaptation, flexibility, and networking (e.g., partnerships) are the keys to individual and agency survival in this new environment.

A leader applying futures study techniques moves from being a strategic planner who relies on primarily data on the past with a few trend predictions to a confident visionary armed with significant *data on the future*. This leader can finally *plan for the future world*.

Futures research provides many tools for this twenty-first century leader: *trend analysis* and *forecasting* to help him or her keep ahead of the curve, *"future facts"* to provide a preview of soon-to-be-available technology as well as direction of social change, *bellwether* to allow adaptation of cutting-edge experimental programs, *Delphi* studies to get expert opinion on the future, and *scenario* development to put alternative futures in perspective. Each of these is reviewed briefly below before turning to a discussion of the roles and characteristics needed in future police leaders.

Trend analysis is based on collecting and evaluating data on the past and present and forecasting it into the future. For example, if there were 100 burglaries five years ago, 110 four years ago, 120 three years ago, 130 two years ago, and 140 last year, what would you forecast for this year? Next year? The year after that? Since the number of burglaries rose consistently by 10 per year over a five-year period, the obvious forecast would be to add 10 more each year for the foreseeable future—to 150 this year, 160 the next, and 170 the year after that. If the past five years were 100, 90, 95, 85, 90, the logical forecast would be 80, 85, 75, 80, 70—ten down, five up, ten down, five up, ten down—for the next five years.

Consider that the U.S. Bureau of Census (annual) forecasts that the "graying of America" will be an ongoing process for the foreseeable future. The percentage of the U.S. population 65 or older, which was 8.1 percent in 1950 and 12.7 percent in 1998, will reach 16.5 percent in 2020 and 20.4 percent by the middle of the next century. The same trend is forecast for other industrial countries (e.g., Canada, 12.5 percent in 1998 to 18.2 percent in 2020; Germany, 15.9 percent to 23.2 percent; Japan, 16.0 percent to 26.3 percent).

For police, this raises serious issues to be considered in planning for the future. For example, how do we cope with the possibility of increased crime by and against the elderly, and how will we head off intergenerational warfare between the politically potent elderly and frustrated adolescents? To assist in this process, we might collect further data, such as economic predictions for the elderly. For example, increased poverty among those over sixty-five likely would equal more crime by them, and more multigenerational households—as the elderly became wards of their children and grandchildren—could bring additional conflict in homes and communities.

At the other end of the spectrum, U.S. Bureau of Census (annual) data indicate that a baby boomlet in recent years will result in a 30 percent increase in the crime-prone fifteen- to -seventeen-year-old population in 2010 compared to 1995. This projection led Northeastern University criminologist James A. Fox to predict a crime wave among juveniles in the first decade of the twenty-first century (Fox, 1996).

One warning here, however. Whereas trend analysis and forecasting are helpful—even necessary, they should not be used in isolation in identifying issues and planning for the future. First, trends do not reflect changes in technology; second, they do not accommodate social change; and third, they do not reflect major events. For example, the computer and decoding of DNA have changed crime and investigative techniques considerably, as have changes in the economy and events such as schoolyard shootings by preteen youths. Beyond this, in the preceding example, the violence rate among juveniles actually declined in the late 1990s, leading to significant revaluation of twenty-first century forecasts. Thus, methods beyond trend analysis must be employed and included in the synthesis of data needed for good visioning by police leaders.

One excellent tool is **scanning for future facts**—ideas, products, services, processes that are a year or more away from marketing and use but are likely to result in significant change in society (or at least procedures) once they appear. Future facts can be found in reports of laboratory research, think tanks, academic/scientific journals, special-interest and technical magazines, and even popular media including newspapers and television reports.

For example, television was unveiled at a 1930s world fair but did not come into widespread use until the 1950s. This *incubation* period between discovery and development to deployment in society gives futures thinkers time to consider impact and develop contingency plans, as well as include the "future fact" in the vision process.

Some currently developing future facts include a sober-up pill that will block the impact of alcohol and other drugs on the brain, a universal low-cost translating device that will accommodate immediate translation from any language, a hand-held scanner that will allow remote body-cavity searches, listening devices and cameras that hear and see through walls, and bionic ears and eyes that can utilize new listening and watching devices (think "In Plain View Doctrine").

In the biotech area, soon there will be nanosized computer chips that can be placed in neural networks (such as the human brain) to give the recipient access to billions of gigabytes of instantly accessible data (such as criminal records of suspects or modus operandi files). Knowledge of future facts, then, can play an important role in visioning.

Bellwether is another useful tool. Most seemingly new phenomena that police face—from a new crime (identity theft) to a new criminal technique (housenapping)—have also occurred in other locations as well, possibly earlier. Thus, scouring the nation (or now the world) via the Internet or other modern low-cost communication systems might result in finding someone coping, possibly even successfully, with the phenomenon. If the approach can be adapted to deal with the dilemma in your jurisdiction, you save time and money and still solve (or at least alleviate) the problem. For example, years ago when Charleston (South Carolina) Police Chief Reuben Greenberg found that ATM machines were attracting nighttime muggers, he scanned the country in search of solutions and found that placing the machines in commercial establishments open twenty-four hours a day seemed to work best. At that time, there were few such businesses in Charleston, so Greenberg convinced banks to put their ATMs in the twenty-four-hour-a-day police precincts around the city. Thus bellwether involves cutting-edge, trend-setting ideas/programs/approaches that can be emulated or adapted for use.

Similar to bellwether is the **Delphi method**, where experts are sought out and consulted in a search for answers to an emerging situation. For example, if computer fraud has begun to affect families as well as businesses in your community, you might identify and query a group of computer security experts. You could have worldwide access to their input via the Internet. In 1984, then FBI Special Agent William Tafoya decided to use the Delphi method in his Ph.D. dissertation research at the University of Maryland on "The Future of Policing." After identifying a panel of a score of cutting-edge police administrators, scholars, and legal experts, now Dr. Tafoya asked them to provide a series of forecasts about the future of policing. After compiling their ideas and eliminating duplication, he then asked them to take the total list and put a date beside each item or write "never" by the ones they did not believe would happen. Finally, Dr. Tafoya (1986) compiled a consensus chronology of policing from the data. For example, Delphi indicated that crimes using high technology would become so complex by the year 2000 that police would be unable to do more than take initial reports. In response to this and other Delphi forecasts, Dr. Tafoya, who taught a course in police futures at the FBI Academy, founded an organization of Police Futurists International, which is at the forefront of "spreading the word" on the needs of police to be effective in the twenty-first century.

Two other futures research techniques that are helpful are **opinion polls** and **brainstorming**. For example, in the South Carolina Fear of Crime Poll (College of Criminal Justice, University of South Carolina) conducted by this author, it was found that by the mid-1990s drug abuse in the community was a concern of more than 95 percent of respondents, and 75 percent said they would be willing to pay higher taxes to alleviate the problem. When asked whether they thought law enforcement or prevention/education was the more effective approach, two-thirds chose education/prevention. Armed with these data, a police leader could go to the city council/county commission or elsewhere and seek additional funding for Drug Abuse Resistance Education (DARE) and other education/prevention programs while possibly shifting some existing funds toward these approaches and away from dependence on undercover operations and arrest efforts.

Brainstorming is a way of taking data obtained from futures research and developing ideas for their use through creative interaction. For example, after collecting data for more than a decade on the youth-at-risk problem and possible solutions, including future facts (such as computerized crying dolls for teenage parenting classes, which are now available), this author began fifteen years ago holding brainstorming sessions with students, academics, and practitioners to develop plans for coping with this continuing problem. The results, which include recommendations for comprehensive community partnerships to provide everything from nonviolent conflict resolution programs to mentoring to community service opportunities, have been published in *The Futurist* and distributed by the National Consortium on Alternatives for Youth at Risk to its membership of juvenile and family court judges and social workers, among others.

Finally, the **scenario** is an excellent tool for synthesizing findings from all the methods discussed above into a story set in the future. Scenarios provide an opportunity to creatively think about what all these trends, forecasts, and future facts could mean on the job and in everyday life in years to come. Every word or phrase in a scenario should have a specific purpose, to illustrate how an *expected* future technology or social or demographic trend, for example, might be manifested. Consider, for example, the following line in a scenario about police patrol in the early twenty-first century: Wang Hernandez lazily hovered above the city, soothed by the subliminal implant that kept him calm, cool, and collected as he patrolled. Here, the name Wang Hernandez indicates the multiculturalism that will escalate in society, while "lazily" indicates crime is not perceived to be out of control, and "hovered" we learn later means he is using a jet pack for transportation. The "subliminal implant" means social control technology has been applied. Later in the scenario, we learn that a burglar was overcome by nerve gas when he illegally entered a computer-controlled "smart" house. Officer Hernandez quickly "hypodermically administered an antidote, took a blood sample, and checked the DNA bar code obtained with the criminal files database built into his unit."

This research technique becomes even more useful when **alternative scenarios** are developed. For example, a *standard* or *surprise-free* scenario can be developed from trend forecasting, while a *pessimistic* scenario can indicate what could go wrong in the future, and an *optimistic* scenario can show how new technology could be melded with expected social and demographic changes via enlightened policy-making, training, and application to create a desirable future. For example, in another version of the scenario discussed above, no break-in takes place thanks to a policy of "providing tax credits so citizens can afford low-cost, computer-controlled Smart Houses."

In 1990 in San Antonio, some three hundred judges, court administrators, lawyers, law professors, and law reformers gathered to consider the future of the courts with the help of Dr. James A. Dator (1994), director of the Hawaii Research Center for Futures Study. The method used was to envision alternative scenarios for the twenty-first century court system. Seven scenarios were developed, each focusing on a different direction the courts could take—from a *judicial leadership* model in which judges played a greater role in controlling the agenda to a *multidoor courthouse* approach in which neighborhood justice centers offered a range of culturally appropriate dispute-resolution techniques to a *global high-tech* system in which appearance in the courtroom was unnecessary and artificial intelligence was used to decide cases.

All of the techniques above provide tools for the future leader—a way to develop vision with more *data on the future* and more *thinking about the future*. The task of the leader is to use them not only in developing vision but also in *managing change creatively*. Clearly, the twenty-first century begins as a period of increasingly rapid change, with little likelihood of a slowdown in pace in the near future. Such an environment requires a different approach to leadership. James Ogilvy (1995), of the Global Business Network, succinctly captured the new direction in the following summary: "As more jobs succumb to automation, the work that remains demands higher levels of mindful creativity. There are fewer rewards for following standard procedures, fewer opportunities for human automata. A capacity for innovation is as important in an information economy as the need for standardization was important to the industrial economy."

Thus, future (and the future is *now*) police leaders will face coping creatively with constant change. But creativity has always been a major part of the police role, as the officer learns bits and pieces of a situation—from a bank robbery to a domestic crisis to a neighborhood disturbance—and must put the puzzle together—fill in the gaps and create a whole picture. Already, there are numerous examples of creative police leadership, such as the police officer who dressed as a clown and went trick-or-treating on Halloween. His "trick" was serving subpoenas on some hard-to-catch defendants. Many "sting" operations have been used, such as invitations to a party or the promise of a generous price for stolen goods, to attract wanted felons. Working with communities, police have sued criminal gang leaders for damages to the neighborhood and created citizen patrols armed with cellular phones to serve as the eyes and ears of the community. In Charleston, Chief Greenberg holds periodic "Police Tactics That Really Work" conferences to exchange creative ideas with other agencies, such as providing cameras to all officers with instructions to take flash pictures of all suspected drug dealings because, Greenberg says, "Our goal is to destroy the business of crime." Another good source for exchanging creative policing ideas is the Community Policing Exchange of the Community Policing Consortium in Washington, D.C.

Other excellent networks for futures-oriented police leadership assistance include the California Commission on Peace Officers Standards and Training, in Sacramento, which administers the California Command College and other leadership programs; the Canadian Police College in Ottawa, which houses the Police Leadership Forum; and the Florida Criminal Justice Executive Institute headquartered at the Florida Department of Law Enforcement in Tallahassee; as well as Police Futurists International (http://www.policefuturists.org/).

Over the years, much has been written about *principles* of leadership. This entire volume, for the most part, has served to illuminate such principles. Like others, this author has thought long and hard about this subject and, thus, in closing, presents here his "seven principles of effective community-oriented policing (COP) leadership":

The COP Leader

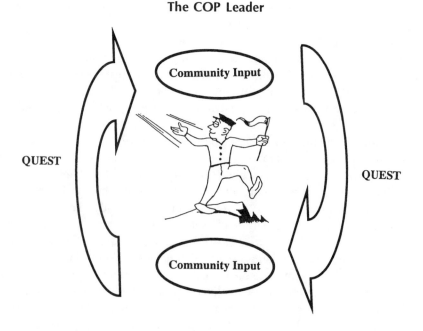

QUEST

Community Input

Community Input

QUEST

1. **Bottom-up leadership**. The good COP. leader, whether at the chief, supervisor, or street-officer level, is listening to the constituency—the citizens of the community and, in the case of the chief and supervisors, the employees closest to the people, the street officers. Thus a flattened pyramid is necessary for success, as a collegial atmosphere is required not only to get top performance from Generation Xers and beyond but to accomplish the task of identifying and solving crime-breeding situations and the mission of keeping "peace in the neighborhood."

2. **Leader as visionary**. With bottom-up leadership come "listening" and "researching," which in turn allow the leader to synthesize input into vision. Each level listens and scans in order to develop and operationalize the vision necessary to accomplish the goals of the agency.

3. **Leader as interpreter**. The leader, at whatever level, must put events (e.g., a senseless murder, a neighborhood disturbance) into perspective in order to avoid activities or redirection away from mission and vision accomplishment. Of course, if events, especially a series of occurrences, indicate a serious flaw in the vision, reconsideration may be necessary. Once redirected, however, the leader needs to keep the path to mission accomplishment open and clearly articulated.

4. **Leader as clarifier**. Vision and mission must be in congruence, and it is the leader's role to translate the vision into a clear mission statement and clearly delineate the path of the vision quest. Again, Generation Xers are vision driven for the most part, but must have a clear understanding if coordinated effort is expected.

5. **Leader as facilitator**. Twenty-first century leaders will spend much time clearing the path, acquiring the tools, creating the partnerships, and, in general, seeing that needs are met for those on the vision quest. Again, this ranges from community officers facilitating community programs to supervisors facilitating street officers and administrators facilitating at all levels. Among the facilitating tasks is taking the lead in establishing community when none can be discerned. After all, how can a community be assisted if there is no community? Identifying needed partners and developing trust-based relationships are also the facilitator's role, as are carefully listening to needs at the street level and acquiring the resources to meet them.

6. **Leader as mediator/arbitrator**. In any quest, there will be disagreements—differences in vision and/or how to achieve it. The leader, again at all levels, must negotiate conflicts by seeking to gain consensus agreement (mediation) or by developing, articulating, and implementing an equitable decision in the case of impasse (arbitration).

7. **Leader as #1 cheerleader**. Everyone needs encouragement and appreciation. The leader must maintain an optimistic environment for the quest and utilize positive reinforcement in a variety of ways and often along the way. As chief morale officer, the leader enthusiastically guides partners toward the quest, even as the vision itself is often reevaluated and sometimes modified.

Finally and above all, the twenty-first century police leader must have *courage*—the fortitude to try new ideas even when there is a chance or even the likelihood of failure. No leader who accomplishes a great vision will be able to navigate the new milieu of the next few years without making mistakes. Trial and error will be required; recklessness, of course, is not acceptable, but creative approaches based on solid futures research will be needed in a rapidly changing environment. As leadership/management expert Tom Peters (1992a, 1992b) said, "If you're not taking risks, you probably lose automatically. If you try and fail, you always learn something from it" (1992b, p. 4B).

Thus, police leaders must make it clear to their colleagues, their constituents, and their partners that they will be as diligent as possible in the vision quest, but mistakes will be made and rectified as the mission and even the vision are constantly reevaluated and redirected in a rapidly and ever-changing society.

Acknowledgment

Special thanks go to Dave Hall, Bureau Chief of the California Commission on Peace Officers Standards and Training and a chief architect of the futures leadership focus of the California Command College. It was Dave Hall who recommended this chapter be included here and provided valued counsel concerning the content.

References

College of Criminal Justice, University of South Carolina, *South Carolina Fear of Crime Poll.* Columbia, SC: College of Criminal Justice, University of South Carolina (annual).

Dator, J.A., Inventing the future of the courts and the courts of the future, in *Judicial Foresight in the Hawaii Judiciary,* S. Inayatullah, Ed., Honolulu: Judiciary, State of Hawaii, 1994.

Fox, J.A., Trends in Juvenile Violence: A Report to the United States Attorney General on Current and Future Rates of Juvenile Offending, Washington, D.C.: Bureau of Justice Statistics, U.S. Department of Justice, 1996.

Muchnik, M., *Naked Management: Bare Essentials for Motivating the X-Generation at Work,* Boca Raton, FL: St. Lucie Press, 1996

Ogilvy, J., *Living without a Goal,* New York: Doubleday, 1995.

Peters, T., *Liberation Management: Necessary Disorganization for the Nanosecond Nineties,* New York: Knopf, 1992a.

Peters, T., Gales of creative destruction blowing, *USA Today,* p. 4B, December 8, 1992b.

Tafoya, W., A Delphi Forecast of the Future of Law Enforcement, Ph.D. dissertation, University of Maryland, 1986.

Tulgan, B., *Managing Generation X: How to Bring Out the Best in Young Talent,* Oxford, UK: Capstone, 1996..

U.S. Bureau of Census, Current Population Survey, Washington, D.C.: U.S. Bureau of Census (annual).

Supplemental Reading

Didsbury, H.F., Jr., Ed., *Future Vision: Ideas, Insights, and Strategies,* Bethesda, MD: World Future Society, 1996.

Stephens, G., Challenges of 21st century policing, in *Strategic Planning for Police,* D. Ogle, Ed., Ottawa: Research and Program Development Board, Canadian Police College, 1991, 127–163.

Stephens, G., Crime and the biotech revolution, *The Futurist,* pp. 38–42, November–December 1992.

Stephens, G., The global crime wave and what we can do about it, *The Futurist,* pp. 22–28, July–August 1994.

Stephens, G., Crime in cyberspace, *The Futurist,* pp. 24–28, September–October 1995.

Stephens, G., The future of policing: from a war model to a peace model, in *The Past, Present, and Future of American Criminal Justice,* B. Maguire and P.F. Radosh, Eds., Dix Hills, NY: General Hall, 1996, 77–102.

Stephens, G., Humanizing 21st century justice: balancing "freedom to" and "freedom from," in *International Rights and Responsibilities for the Future,* K.W. Hunter and T.C. Mack, Eds., Westport, CT: Praeger, 1996, 91–102.

Stephens, G., Youth at risk: saving the world's most precious resource, *The Futurist,* Special Section, pp. 1–7, April 1997.

Stephens, G., Saving the world's most precious resource: our children, *USA Today Magazine,* pp. 54–57, May 1998.

Stephens, G., Thinking globally, acting locally: bringing peace to everyone's 'hood, *Crime & Justice International,* 14(18 and 19), 9–10, 32–33, 1998.

Appendices

APPENDIX

Appendix A: Stages in the Development of a Personal Faith Position

Cornerstone Principles

There are cornerstone principles that can make an important difference in our lives. Before looking at the stages of faith development in greater depth, these principles are presented, discussed, and explored. If these cornerstones are not used to build teams, organizations, families, and individual clarity, then the consequences can be serious. Briefly, these cornerstone principles are

1. Individual clarity precedes commitment.
2. Individual commitment precedes motivation.
3. Motivation precedes individual high performance.
4. Individual performance precedes team performance.
5. Team values alignment precedes high performance.
6. Goal clarity precedes team high performance.
7. Higher performance is important in a competitive world.

An Example from Sweden

A year after publication of the first edition of *Transforming Leadership*, I went to Stockholm to conduct a seminar for Swedish executives. Many of them had recently read the Swedish translation of my book *Transforming Leadership: New Skills for an Extraordinary Future*.

For the past few decades, the Swedes have been ahead of much of the rest of the world in their innovative approach to team management. Even so, they were interested in hearing more about how the principles and practices of *Transforming Leadership* could help them strengthen team leaders to build world-class teams that could better compete within the pressures of globalization we all face.

They also sought answers to some other problems they saw as unique to their culture, such as individual identity and motivation in a previously affluent society and a commitment to a vision of the common good through individual effort. These problems are similar in nature, but perhaps more intense and obvious than those of the seventeen-to-thirty age group in North America (called "baby busters" by sociologists and marketing specialists).

I trust they gained some useful ideas from my seminar, but I was the one who left Sweden with some useful insights about how incredibly important managing the future with clarity and meaning is. If you are like me, you will be able to immediately apply these insights in creating and managing your own future by considering the Swedish experience.

Learning about Clarity from Sweden's Unique Experience

Sweden has produced an economy and form of government that are socialistic in the extreme.

1. If you want to go to a college or university, it is government funded, for as long as you want to go.
2. If you are unemployed (by choice or not), you are likely to earn as much as if you were employed.
3. If you have a medical problem, your medical fees are paid by the socialized medical plan.
4. If you are absent from work, you are paid anyway.

As a consequence of these and other forces, a number of companies, like Volvo, have to hire 30 percent more employees than they need to get the work done. On the average day, 30 percent of the employees are absent! In some ways, this can seem like a kind of utopia from the employees' perspective. I overheard one of them say, "I owe it to myself to take one or two days off per week; I'm paying for it in my taxes—and if I didn't take the time off, my fellow workers would hassle me!" When you listen to executives talk about the negative consequences of these conditions, you don't get the impression of utopia at all.

Please, Come to Work!

What some of these executives told me is that they have a hard time finding employees who want to work hard when they are at work and an even more difficult time finding employees who will come to work at all on a regular basis. This disruption of the work environment due to absence and low motivation has eroded team synergy, quality, performance, and morale in many companies. Many people, both young and old, have lost their inner desire to work. Why is this?

At first, I thought this was the same problem many companies in North America face, especially among younger generation employees who seem to lack commitment to the work ethic and who have lower motivation and morale—unless they get to do what they want to do. Then, as I listened more carefully, I heard things that revealed deeper causes.

1. "Our people have become used to being taken care of, from the 1970s until recently, having all the opportunities laid out for them, and now that things have changed and they have to take initiative on their own, they just don't feel like it—they don't believe they have to."
2. "They have lost a sense of reliance upon themselves and have become dependent upon 'government' to get their basic needs met. As a result, their souls have gone dry."
3. "We have lost our spiritual roots. We have become 'secularized' to the point that individuals have no life stance, and as a people we have no common world view—this has weakened our ability to act as a nation. For example, even though 95 percent of us claim to be Lutheran, less than 10 percent really believe in Christ and practice the Christian life-style."
4. "Some cling to the cultural and social history of our royalty but no longer acknowledge or seek to understand the deeper mysteries of life. We don't like anything that smells of religiosity (which we have experienced in the past as social control)—so we avoid spirituality altogether. This is a form of throwing the baby, as it were, out with the bathwater. But we haven't found anything to replace what we have rejected. Perhaps some of us have even forgotten that we need to have deeper meaning in our lives in order to be inwardly motivated."
5. "I find that we no longer have beliefs in ultimate things. In fact, I suspect that we are even curiously lacking in a definition of what the word 'belief' means—there is no directly translated word for it in Swedish. I have heard a number of executives saying that this is the single most interesting aspect of your book and your seminar presentation. We want to know what you mean by the word 'belief.'"

As I reflected on these comments, I found them to be not very different from those of our colleagues in North America. The problem is perhaps more intense, and possibly more clearly articulated by our Swedish friends: People without a vision, without foundational assumptions, are vulnerable to a whole host of difficulties and experience an inner emptiness. Lack of clarity breeds lower motivation; lower motivation results in lower performance and morale. Less optimism and hope are the end result—a downward spiraling of individual lives, corporate life, and family life.

Personal and Corporate Issues of Spirit

Many key leaders are keenly interested in looking into deeper personal and corporate issues of spirit—spirit in self and spirit in the workplace. Spirit is that innermost part of us that, while remaining somewhat of a mystery over our lifetimes, can be fathomed more and more as we grow.

It is that part of us that wants to know answers to ultimate questions, that wants to find some kind of relatedness to the ultimate, to grasp what we cannot see. It is that quiet center that can experience peace, joy, clear vision, and assurance of truth. It has been called "the still, small voice within." It is the part beyond the psychological—the mysterious consciousness part that cannot be explained by psychology. It is in the spirit of a person that clarity can come. I offer the following insights that have, in part, emerged from extended conversations with my Swedish friends.

Clarity of Beliefs, Identity, and Purpose
Is the Foundation of All Commitment and Action

Beliefs, identity, and purpose are intertwined, but beliefs are the foundation of the three. To become a motivated person who loves your work, I suggest that, if you have not done so, you seriously consider embarking on an exciting lifelong journey to seek clarity about why you really want to do anything.

This journey involves an exciting venture to seek greater truth about what life means, who you are, and what your purpose is. Vision, values, and goals are surely important but have much more power when they are based on inspiring and motivating beliefs, identity, and purpose.

In more detail, actions you can take to delve into these three parts further, are as follows:

1. Clarify options for your belief stance and choose one to test the reality of it—this involves studying the belief options and acting from a clear foundation of belief.
2. Clarify who and what you are as a person—with an inner life that gives you guidance and direction for personal and career life. This involves being authentic with others about who you are (your beliefs, strengths, preferences, purpose, values, goals, etc.) in ways that respect them rather than preach at or judge them.
3. Clarify a primary purpose for your life by writing it, speaking it, and living it—this involves pinpointing what sets you on fire, what could be a lifelong mission that you can feel wholehearted about, and getting into action to realize it.

If you are already well along on this "road less traveled," I encourage you to continue traveling it to gain more depth. If you are just beginning your conscious journey toward clarity, I encourage you to move ahead boldly for very good reasons.

These three primary issues—clarity about beliefs, identity, and purpose—are at the heart of what motivates individuals, allows groups to commit to common goals, and results in increased organizational performance. If neither the leaders nor their constituents have clarity about these critical issues, they cannot reasonably be expected to be motivated about getting everyday work done. Moreover, if they have conflicting beliefs, identities, and purposes, they will work in a house divided against itself, and this house will likely fall or falter. Clarity and consensus are critical if people are to feel they belong and want to perform well.

Therefore, to become more clear about what you believe, who you are, what you want, and why is to become free of vagueness, confusion, and lack of direction. The added clarity will give you a laser-like focus that will fuel your motivational system.

The more clear your self is, and the more sure you are, the more you will commit to bring results into reality. Going through this clarification process consciously, rather than unconsciously, is what gets people moving forward to realize their visions and dreams—because they have them clearly in mind.

If some things do not become clear to you at first, that is to be expected. Clarity comes as time goes by, as you study and meditatively focus, as you talk with others, and as you continue to seek it. As your beliefs, identity, and purpose become more clear, your vision of an ennobling future, values, and priorities will also become more focused. Then goals and plans more easily crystallize as well.

Clarity as a Foundation for Leadership

In a complex and fast-paced world, we cannot afford to be without clarity in the center of the storm. We can choose to be clear. From this base of clarity, we can more consciously choose those with whom we wish to work, marry, partner, team, and live. Watch for the next article entitled "Clarifying the Muddy Waters to Build Strong People, Groups, and Organizations." That article will expand on the main points here and provide operating definitions of the key terms outlined in this article.

Like our Swedish friends, perhaps all of us, no matter how much we think we know now, can take a positive step forward toward greater clarity, commitment, and fulfillment of our mission in life. I invite you to begin or continue your journey of intentional living now. Those you love and serve will be the direct benefactors.

To develop this clarity, let us first examine a summary of the developmental stages of belief delineated by Fowler (1981).

Clarification: A Developmental Process

Fowler describes the clarification and development of clear beliefs from a developmental perspective by outlining what he calls "stages of faith."

Stage 0: This is a prestage called **undifferentiated** faith. The seeds of trust, courage, hope, and love are sown here during infancy and correspond somewhat to Erikson's psychosocial stage of trust versus mistrust. When thought and language begin to converge, then the child moves through the transition to Stage 1.

Stage 1: This first stage is called the **intuitive–projective** faith stage. Between ages three to seven, fantasy and imitation powerfully and possibly permanently form some basics of a belief system. Fluid thinking, the beginnings of self-awareness, and the verbalization of learned doctrines and concepts (mixed with imagination) are expressed, and the child begins to become more concrete in thought, separating fantasy from "doctrine," and gets ready to move into Stage 2.

Stage 2: **Mythical–literal** faith is characterized by the emergence of concrete, causal thinking, which is able to separate fantasy from the stories, doctrines, beliefs, and observances that have been taught in order to belong to the family or surrounding community. Symbols are taken literally, as are moral rules and attitudes. This is the faith stage of the school child (age seven to twelve), although this stage is found in many adolescents and adults.

People at this stage are able to be deeply affected by stories and dramatic presentations (and are therefore highly vulnerable to influence) but are not able yet to consciously reflect on the meaning or possible errancy of such presentations (television included). Because of a lack of reflective or relative thinking capacity, they may seem to be "legalistic," black-and-white thinkers.

The transition to Stage 3 is marked by a breakdown of literalism. Contradictions in stories or reflective logic can cause disillusionment with previous teachers or teachings (including parental influences and early religious training). Formal operational thought makes such reflection possible and necessary.

Stage 3: This stage is called **synthetic–conventional** faith. It emerges most often in adolescence, but for many adults becomes a place of nonresponsible comfort, fun, or avoidance of further development. This is a "conformist" stage because a person's security and identity are defined and dependent upon others. A person in this stage does not have enough inner—and autonomous—judgment or solid faith to build and maintain an inner resolution about beliefs. The Stage 3 person believes, but often not in a wholehearted, well-examined manner, and constantly scans the environment (especially the social environment) to see if what is believed is popular and accepted.

The adolescent is using the beliefs and assumptions acquired in childhood in a sense to "get by" during the turbulent and insecure teenage years, until full formal operational thinking capacity develops; then, a full and thorough examination regarding the source, validity, and utility of a belief system (and therefore an inner identity) can be independently begun. Quite often, crises occur (such as a failed a love relationship or parents' marriage or leaving home), which precipitate the breakdown of Stage 3 and the need to move into the "crisis of the deeper life," which can prove to be the most critical, but also most rewarding, transition.

Stage 4: Stage 4 is called **individuative–reflective** faith. At this time, a person realizes how alone he or she really is in deciding everything, even if there has been relegation of that responsibility to others. A person's self-awareness causes a painful realization that "my decisions are in my own hands." Many adults do not reach this stage, perhaps because they are, for a number of reasons, unable. Many who do turn away from the burden of responsibility for their own consciously chosen life and turn to the age-old philosophy of Numbism, supported in full force by the increasingly available forms of "soma" (alcohol, drugs, eating, television, and other "give up" paraphernalia described by Glasser [1998]).

This level is extremely difficult to face, especially alone. There are fewer and fewer people more developed than you to give you help as you move up the stages of development! If the call to higher belief definition is heeded, the reward is a sense of being beyond the definitions others offer and beyond the roles one happens to be in at the time. For many people in this stage, a certain sense of the reality of a "higher being" has been reported to be especially strong and clear in a personal way.

At this level, the ability to critically reflect on one's own self-identity and upon various outlooks or ideologies is greatly enhanced. The ability to be increasingly objective is a danger, however, in that there can come a kind of cognitive self-assurance that closes off a continuing deeper search and trades it in for "settling for security." For many people, however, a certain restlessness, sense of flatness, or sterility to life creeps in that prompts or even urges a higher search for greater meaning and intimacy with what ultimately is to be discovered. This stage has been called by many the "mid-life crisis" and seems to often occur in the early to mid forties.

Stage 5: Stage 5 is called **conjunctive** faith. Often, the potential power in symbolic meanings comes alive for people in this stage. This can be called a kind of second naivete, where the emotional and/or spiritual impact of one's beliefs becomes quickened or alive in each moment—"becoming as a little child," if you will. A reworking of the fabric of one's past into the garment of the future must be attended to. In mid-life, when this stage usually occurs, there is a seriousness that emerges, and a person knows the realities of defeat, the irrevocability of certain commitments and acts, and is in full appreciation that life is more than half over (at best).

This is the sobering, deepening time when the search for inner resolve and resolution is contrasted with a curious openness to new depths of spirituality and the possibility of personal revelations. A sense of the ironic—the paradoxes of life, the unsolvable mysteries—makes life both more magical and the individual more able to be in a state of wonder and awe. On the other hand, some people become bitter or reach a state of complacency or cynical withdrawal if the power of faith is not sufficient to withstand a more full awareness of the inescapable presence of death and the unknown.

While many people in this stage report deep peace, inner resolution, and interrelatedness to their supreme being and loved ones, others report a sense of hopelessness and futility and excruciating hollowness when they arrive near the top of this developmental climb. In only a few cases, people who arrive at this stage are moved or committed to move on to the stage of radical actualization called *universalizing faith* (Stage 6).

Stage 6: Universalizing faith is characterized by a person's radical commitment to the sanctity of all being, all life, justice, love, and selfless passion for a transformed world. People in this stage are not pushing what they personally wish to see happen (as Hitler or the Reverend Jim Jones), but are committed to a transcendent vision, as were Gandhi, Martin Luther King, Jr., Mother Theresa, and many others who had "no greater love than this, than to lay down their lives for their friends" (Jesus, approximately 33 A.D.). They seem to have a "subversive" character that challenges the status quo, governments, and/or individuals to reach past their own usual patterns of self-orientation to the higher path of love for others.

Fowler says of these Stage 6 people:

> It is my conviction that persons who come to embody Universalizing faith are drawn into those patterns of commitment and leadership by the providence of God and the exigencies of history, heated in the fires of turmoil and trouble, and then hammered into usable shape on the hard anvil of conflict and struggle (p. 202).

These people in Stage 6 have a clear vision of what life is "meant to be," are able to feel the injustice and suffering imposed on others, are nearly always heralded for their uncommon courage and faith, and are willing to die for the cause of justice and the liberation of any and all people. Not many of us are able or perhaps willing to take the full leap into universalizing faith.

Admittedly, the six steps outlined above are "Western" in their orientation, much as are the developmental stages of Piaget. These stage-specific theories do not seem true to some people in other cultures. Fowler, however, has at least given us a starting place in understanding the development of what many people would call the spiritual part of people.

Steps in the Process of Clarification of Your Belief Stance

The process of clarifying your beliefs involves several steps. By following these steps, your own belief stance will become clearer as time passes. The steps for clarifying beliefs can be done by yourself, or you can help an individual or group of people to gain resolution by coaching them through the following steps.

1. As best you can, specify in writing your present answers to life's major questions as outlined in Chapter 4 (or attempt to answer your own problem questions).
2. Search out the sources of your beliefs and write down these sources for later comparison.
3. Examine your criteria for accepting these beliefs as true, and write down the various validations for the beliefs that you accept.
4. Write a clear and concise position paper about your stance on life's major questions and issues.

5. Read this paper over once a week while you consistently attempt to take on this position in a real way, living it out on a daily basis as congruently as you are able.

6. Review your position statement every three to six months and examine how your position helps you to deal with problems or better appreciate the joys of life.

7. Note any "holes" or inconsistencies in your belief positions that you think may be invalid, incomplete, or problematic.

8. Examine other differing belief positions (ones you think are incomplete or false, if any) that validate for you how true your position is, or note how parts of other positions seem to have truth in them on the premise that "truth is truth wherever it is found." To assist you in getting started with this step, I suggest that you read Chapter 9 in *Megatrends 2000,* by Naisbitt and Aburdene. This will give you a factual overview of what is occurring in the world of beliefs. Using this chapter as an introduction, you can move ahead with a more thorough study of each of the various philosophical or religious belief positions.

Students who have generally followed this series of steps in my courses on self-awareness and interpersonal communication have reported in course evaluations that this exercise was the most challenging and meaningful of the semester. Some even reported that it was the most important step in their lives.

The Downside of Failing to Clarify a Life Stance

People who avoid the whole issue of belief clarification—or give up on its resolution—perhaps are less deeply "rooted" in a life position. They may be more easily influenced to move in a number of directions, depending upon which way a personal, social, political, or economic "wind" is blowing at the time; they often claim that "flexible" tendency to be a strength—that they are "open-minded" or willing to "change with the times." They also often say that they have little inner peace, that decision making is difficult without a clear reference point, and that their relationships suffer because they often clash with people who have clear beliefs.

I believe those who have a metaphysical understanding of and orientation to life (answers to the "why" questions) have a distinct advantage—even if their orientation may ultimately be incorrect. I believe they are more solid, act more consistently, can get feedback from the environment as to the validity and workability of their actions (because they have a position as a reference point), and many times are better able to understand others' positions, an important "tolerance" skill when leading people.

Beliefs form the solid foundation of a clear purpose in life; clear values are structures upon which to build goals, strategies, and actions. With only values to live by, the "why" of life is not addressed, explored, or resolved in the least. Beliefs address the "why" and "what" questions of life directly.

When people can share some basic beliefs, they are more likely to join together to create something productive. This is true in a marriage or in any other of endeavor in business, education, community development, or human services—where team effort is required.

Furthermore, if you understand others' beliefs, you are more likely to comprehend why they have given their "hearts" to their beliefs, why they feel they need them, and why they need to keep them, and you can become even more tolerant.

If you want to move ahead toward greater clarity, turn to Appendix B and complete the process called *Deep Structure Strategic Planning.*

References

Erickson, Erik, *The Life Cycle Completed: A Review*, New York: Norton, 1982.

Glasser, William, *Choice Theory: A New Psychology of Personal Freedom*, New York: HarperCollins, 1998.

Gruber, Howard and J. Jacques Voneche, Eds., *The Essential Piaget*, New York: Basic Books, 1977.

Naisbitt, John, et al, *Megatrends 2000*, New York: William Morrow, 1990.

Appendix B:
Deep Structure Strategic Planning: A Process to Optimize Personal, Team, and Organizational Clarity and Performance

"Sharpening the Inner Edge" for Morale and Performance Improvement

A great many strategic planning programs deal with strengths, weaknesses, opportunities, threats, vision, and goals. These aspects of planning are inadequate by themselves. There are important, deeper issues that need to be included in personal and organizational strategic planning if extraordinary and lasting results are to be achieved.

First, we need to clarify the murky waters of the many critical concepts in strategic planning to identify the important differences among them. The critical concepts are **beliefs, identity, vision, mission, purpose, values, ethics, and goals**. Most individuals do not have clear definitions or descriptions of these separate and important parts of their inner lives. Neither do most organizations. This vagueness is demoralizing and undermines meaning, strong motivation, and performance.

For example, leaders often express their values as though they were their beliefs. They state their missions as though they were their visions or values. This murky, but likely unintentional, practice prevents visions from solidifying, blocks consensus for team development, and thereby undermines performance improvement. In an attempt to dispel this confusion, I will provide, in the paragraphs that follow, with the most discrete operating definitions of these transforming concepts I have seen anywhere.

Once you understand the differences among these concepts—and see that you can use each concept to gain important life-changing insights, you will want to go through a process of becoming clear at each level. We should have had the opportunity to do this on an ongoing basis since our school years, but who had the know-how to assist us?

First, let's get a visual picture of the components that form a strong inner architecture. As illustrated below, each component forms a solid foundation for the next.

The Hierarchy of Key Success Factors

| Focused Results |
| Action Plans and Steps |
| Goals Specification |
| Ethics Clarification |
| Values Identification and Prioritization |
| Vision Clarification |
| Purpose Specification |
| Identity Clarification |
| Beliefs Clarification |

Developing Inner Clarity to Achieve External Results

The process of inner development and formation of internal "architecture" is not entirely linear (as illustrated above). It seems to develop rather organically—sometimes with unexpected bursts of clarity at various levels. It does make sense, however, to pay attention to the more foundational matters, like beliefs, identity, purpose, or vision, before attempting to formulate our goals or plans. Most people, without realizing it, start with goals and omit clarifying the motivating reasons of beliefs, purpose, vision, or mission that could jump-start and sustain their performance.

It also helpful to understand there is a process for building strength and clarity inside individuals, within groups, and in organizations. This process can be step by step, as indicated above in the preceding hierarchy of key success factors. It is even more helpful to put this process into action by focusing separately to gain clarity at each level. This process is what I call Deep Structure Strategic Planning. This kind of deeper structure strategic planning involves considering the nearest and dearest motivations of each individual and blending them into a team and corporate culture that results in exceptional morale and performance. The literature on high-performance teams and companies attests to the fact that clarity and consensus get results.

It is most difficult but most fruitful to begin at the foundation with beliefs and purpose. People often fail to adequately attend to "why" issues (beliefs and purpose) because they are more difficult to articulate and express. Most people have general goals but do not know *why* they might want to be a police officer, business manager, teacher, nurse, or technician and do not consider what *consequences* might follow (personally, for their family, or financially) or what deeper or higher purpose a particular personal vocation or corporate strategic plan might fulfill.

If you leave out or skip over one of the building blocks, your "building" will not have the strength it needs to withstand the storms of change or the power it needs to push ahead with vision toward an ennobling future. Investing the time to make each block strong, clear, and solid builds confidence, and this confidence increases your morale and performance. Outlined below are the main building blocks, with some suggestions about how you can gain clarity to strengthen them. Consider this outline an introduction to the concepts that would be covered in depth should you participate in a *Deep Structure Strategic Planning* workshop/seminar or individual coaching session.

Beliefs Are Your Assumptions About:

1. What is going on here in this universe?
2. What is true, real, false, unreal, good, and bad?
3. How can I validate what is true? What criteria are reliable?
4. What is the origin, source, and purpose of life?
5. What is at the foundation of life?
6. Why does life exist? My life?
7. How should I conduct my life and how should I love?
8. Should I even concern myself with these types of questions?
9. How do I know my life has meaning?

These are, of course, tough questions. Your beliefs are the foundational cornerstones of *everything* you think, judge, plan, hope for, and seek to achieve. They form the basis for all moral and ethical decisions. They are the screen through which you filter and interpret your world. Your beliefs also determine your mental attitude to some extent, in terms of being basically hopeful, neutral, or pessimistic about life.

Some people have very clearly defined assumptions about what they believe, but most people are just not clear. Others dismiss the issue as "philosophic fuzziness" that they don't want to deal with right now. The caution is, **be careful how you assume things to be, because for you, that's how they are right now!**

I should say here that I believe that some beliefs are in error. For example, I cannot subscribe to fascism or any type of authoritarian rule that overrides individual free will because I believe that free will is integral to commitment, motivation, morale, and performance. You can continue to clarify your beliefs over time, and as you do so, you will discover greater depth of meaning in life and work.

In the Space Below, Write a Point-Form Summary of Your Key Beliefs

-
-
-
-
-
-
-
-
-
-
-
-
-
-
-
-
-
-

Your Identity Is Based on:

1. *Who* and *what* you believe you are
2. Experiences with family
3. Experiences with social groups and school
4. Successes, failurees, and traumatic experiences
5. A vision of what could be possible for you
6. An internal image of how you think others see you

Your identity is shaped and limited by the boundaries of your beliefs. You can only think of yourself in ways you assume are true about the nature of people and the nature of life itself. For example, if you assume, as the existential philosophers do, that life is absurd and has no meaning, then you will consider yourself to be nothing but a speck of sand on the shore of a drifting, chaotic universe that may be washed away at any moment. The consequences of such a belief system are that people often adopt a philosophy of *carpe diem* (seize life!) or, translated into "baby-busters'" language (age seventeen to thirty): "Party on, dude, for tomorrow we may die!"

If, on the other hand, you assume you are a spirit created by an intentional Being who knows and cares for you and all people, then your view of your identity will be that you and all people are extremely precious—the most valuable of all life-forms and more valuable than the most expensive crown jewel. Would you trade someone you love for such a gemstone? This is just an example of how our beliefs shape what we can conceive ourselves and others to be. This conception, therefore, shapes our beliefs about our own and others' worth.

If you want to gain clarity about how you see yourself now, you can list words or phrases that describe *who* and *what* you believe you are (such as "visionary leader," "protector of the people," "cool dude," "great musician," "serious scholar," "child of God," etc.). These phrases can help you to remain conscious of how you see yourself. How you see yourself limits or expands what you will do with your life in a serious way.

In the Space Below, Write a Point-Form Summary to Describe Your Identity: What Is Important and Exciting to You?

List the ten most important events in your life.

-
-
-
-
-
-
-
-
-
-

List the ten most exciting events of your life.

-
-
-
-
-
-
-
-
-

Complete the sentence, "I am a person who…" _____

_____

_____

Now look over your list and identify what it was about these events that made them important or exciting. This will assist you in painting your future vision. You do not need to know why they are important, only that they are. For example:

Exciting event: Presentation to five thousand people

Excitement was: Speaking to a large group of people, preparing the presentation, telling people about the event

This process will assist you in gaining greater clarity about the kind of person you are—in terms of your interests, abilities, and the significant life experiences that have shaped your current understanding of your identity to this point in your life.

Vision Is a Mental Picture of What
You Believe to Be Possible for Your Preferred Future:

1. For a preferred future
2. To inspire and motivate self and others
3. Regarding dreams that could come true

We can only envision what we can conceive to be possible because of our beliefs and our identity. If I believe I am "stupid" because of previous negative experiences at school, I will not envision myself receiving a Ph.D. years down the road. If I do envision myself as having a Ph.D. years hence, it is possible that this could occur! If I do not, it surely will not. So, vision is at the beginning of most things we end up doing, *whether we are conscious of our vision or not.*

Consciously held visions often take on power and energy and come into being, but if visions are not consciously in focus, they tend to lie somewhat dormant. If you want to get a start on clarifying your vision, write a brief statement that outlines what your life will be like, what you will be doing, where you will be living, and with whom you will be living and working in five years and in ten years. Revise your vision as time goes by and as your understanding increases. This is a powerful exercise that gets results!

In the Space Below, Write a Point-Form Vision of Your Future

In five years

-
-
-
-

In ten years

-
-
-
-

Purpose Is a Public Statement:

1. Of *why* you intend to move ahead toward your vision
2. Of what you intend to accomplish
3. That sets you on fire
4. That could be lifelong, but is updated often
5. Of purpose that emerges from a deep and clear sense of vision

Purpose cuts to the chase, goes to the jugular vein of our lives, and helps us to get in touch with what truly moves us in our hearts and guts. Having a clear sense of purpose is to understand the reason that underlies what you want to do with your life—and with your career.

So many people do not search for and find a sense of clear purpose. They do not find it because they do not search. As a result, their lives are hollow and they feel they are stuck on treadmills over which they have no control. Over 80 percent of workers in one survey reported not finding satisfaction in their work. More than 80 percent expressed confusion about where they would go and what they would do if their present careers were to come to an end.

Life does not have to be that way. It is possible to gain a clearer sense of purpose by *continuing to consciously seek greater clarity,* the same way as outlined in the preceding sections on beliefs and vision.

Sometimes it is difficult to get in touch with this issue of purpose within oneself. It is very important to do so, however, because it can build your motivation level.

1. The greater the clarity of purpose, the more intense the laser-like motivation.
2. The greater the motivation, the easier it is to concentrate.
3. The easier it is to concentrate, the greater the success.

As an example of a purpose statement, one person who wants to become a leader wrote:

> It is my purpose to lead people toward realizing their talents, interests, identities, and sense of purpose. My leadership of their personal development will positively influence their loyalty to my company, will enhance their performance, and we will all move ahead toward success together.

If you want to attempt to move toward additional clarity of purpose, write a first draft of your own purpose statement and continue to revise it as time goes by. Post it in a place where you can review it each morning and evening. It will become emblazoned in the forefront of your mind and will drive your motivation and accomplishments.

In the Space Below, Write a First-Draft Summary of Your Purpose Statement

Values Are Personal Priorities about
What Is Important to You:

1. They determine *how* you go about getting things done.
2. They determine how you treat people.
3. They determine your real priorities.
4. How you spend your *time* is a true measure of values.

Once we have a clearer sense of beliefs, vision, and purpose, it is easier to sort through all the possible values priorities we could embrace in life, and begin to limit ourselves to a focus on the ones that are *most important* to us. This process of narrowing down our options, called **values clarification or specification,** is difficult but rewarding to do.

Most people do not really think seriously about this issue. As a result, they set goals, get jobs, and five years later wonder why they are trapped in a job that does not fit their interests, abilities, and purpose. Now they have kids, a mortgage, a car payment, and credit-card bills and find it difficult to find time to seriously search—let alone go back to school or start a new business.

This pattern is scary and far too common. The values priorities they unconsciously held when they laid the foundations of their adult lives were fun, money, relationships, etc. But because many people do not do these kinds of things for a higher purpose, they lose a sense of deeper meaning in their work. or they base their lives on their career goals rather than base their career goals on their plan for living a purposeful, value-ordered life. The unexamined life can feel like it may not be worth living, if it goes to the extreme.

In the Space Below, Write a Point-Form Summary of Your Operating Values

- *Example*: Honesty and integrity

-

-

-

-

-

-

-

-

-

-

-

-

-

-

-

-

Ethics Are Formal Codes of Conduct that Are:

1. Based on values
2. Agreed upon between parties
3. Shared by an association of people
4. Breakable, and penalties are often imposed for ethical breaches (Dishonesty and manipulative gain are two examples.)

Ethics are ways of acting that conform to the agreements between people who belong to certain groups or associations. For example, psychologists, doctors, lawyers, and accountants all have professional codes of ethical conduct (confidentiality, for example) that they must follow if they want to continue to practice. If they breach their ethical oaths, they can be prevented from working for a period of time, and for serious enough offenses and breaches of ethics, they can lose their licenses to practice.

In the Space Below, Write a Point-Form Summary of Your Ethics

•

•

•

•

•

•

•

•

•

•

Goals that Lead to Success Are:

1. Set after beliefs, vision, purpose, and values are specified
2. Well-defined targets for accomplishment
3. Concrete and specific
4. Bound by time lines
5. Worthwhile achieving
6. Realistic and achievable
7. Committed to wholeheartedly

Goals help bring substance to your vision of your future. If you write down a goal statement, you are far more likely to accomplish it than if you just think about it. If you post your goals in a place where you will see them regularly, check your progress, and reward yourself for achievement, your list of accomplishments will increase. A written goal becomes a commitment to get results by a specific date. The more specific and well defined your goals are, the better your chances of reaching them will be. Goals, once they are translated into accomplishment statements, become achievable as part of a step-by-step plan. These goals can be personal growth goals, educational goals, career goals, spiritual goals, and/or physical goals.

In the Space Below, Write a Point-Form Summary of Your Personal Goals

-
-
-
-
-
-
-
-

Action Plans and Strategic Steps Are:

1. Agreed upon by individuals
2. Supported by team consensus
3. Challenging enough to stretch performance
4. Realistic enough to be achievable
5. Defined in concrete, actionable terms
6. Accountable on a schedule for review
7. On someone's job descriptions
8. In your or someone's time schedules

This step is critical to the implementation of your plan. This is really the most important step of all because it is the one that will result in achievement of your goals. It is on this page that you want to summarize action steps for the achievement of each of your goals. These action steps are translated to your schedule or to another team member's schedule for implementation. You will meet with yourself or others to review and celebrate accomplishments, analyze failures, and plan for further success.

In the Space Below, Write a Point-Form Summary of Action Steps and Strategies for the Achievement of Your Goals

Action Steps	Completion Target Dates
•	___/___/___
•	___/___/___
•	___/___/___
•	___/___/___
•	___/___/___
•	___/___/___
•	___/___/___
•	___/___/___
•	___/___/___

Appendix C: Competence in Using Skills

The following is a summary of the results of two studies conducted by Anderson and King (1996a,b). The first two tables summarize police supervisory skills competencies as perceived by self and as other supervisors. It should be noted that all the skills on each of the lists were evaluated by all supervisors and managers in the police and public safety sectors in British Columbia as necessary and relevant in the proper performance of their daily duties as police, justice, and public safety leaders.

Competence of Self in Using Skills:
Police Supervisory Skills (Median Results[a])

	Competence				
	Extremely	Very	Somewhat	Slightly	Not at all
Resolving interpersonal conflict		☑			
Written communication skills		☑			
Designing and making effective presentations		☑			
Interpersonal communication skills		☑			
Evaluating employee performance		☑			
Recognizing training needs		☑			
Problem solving and decision making		☑			
Time management and organization skills		☑			
Understanding and applying ethical standards		☑			
Supervising a new recruit		☑			
Supervising a veteran employee		☑			
Mentoring and coaching skills		☑			
Supporting a positive learning environment		☑			
Addressing harassment in the workplace			☑		
Dealing with an underperformer			☑		
Dealing with a stressed employee		☑			
Enhancing work area morale/motivation		☑			
Working with the union contract			☑		
Working with the Police Act			☑		
Recognizing/rewarding performance		☑			
Dealing with the public		☑			
Multiculturalism and diversity issues			☑		
Team development and performance		☑			
Goal setting in your work area			☑		
Budgeting			☑		
Personnel deployment and shifting		☑			
Strategic planning			☑		
Using new computer technology			☑		
Research skills			☑		
Dealing with violence against women			☑		
Future trends in policing			☑		
Planning and implementing community-based policing initiatives			☑		

☑ = frontline.

[a] The median represents the point where at least 50 percent of the respondents fall.

Competence of Peers in Using Skills
(Median Results[a])

	Competence				
	Extremely	Very	Somewhat	Slightly	Not at all
Resolving interpersonal conflict				☑	
Written communication skills			☑		
Designing and making effective presentations			☑		
Interpersonal communication skills				☑	
Evaluating employee performance			☑		
Recognizing training needs			☑		
Problem solving and decision making			☑		
Time management and organization skills				☑	
Understanding and applying ethical standards			☑		
Supervising a new recruit			☑		
Supervising a veteran employee			☑		
Mentoring and coaching skills				☑	
Supporting a positive learning environment			☑		
Addressing harassment in the workplace			☑		
Dealing with an underperformer				☑	
Dealing with a stressed employee			☑		
Enhancing work area morale/motivation			☑		
Working with the union contract			☑		
Working with the Police Act			☑		
Recognizing/rewarding performance			☑		
Dealing with the public		☑			
Multiculturalism and diversity issues			☑		
Team development and performance			☑		
Goal setting in your work area			☑		
Budgeting			☑		
Personnel deployment and shifting			☑		
Strategic planning			☑		
Using new computer technology			☑		
Research skills			☑		
Dealing with violence againstwomen			☑		
Future trends in policing			☑		
Planning and implementing ommunity-cbased policing initiatives			☑		

☑ = frontline.

[a] The median represents the point where at least 50 percent of the respondents fall.

Training Priority for Police Supervisory Leadership Skills

The last table in this series reflects respondents' opinions regarding the priority that should be placed on individual skills during training. Municipal frontline supervisors identified more "highest priority" skills (4) than the other constituent groups. The "highest priority" skills identified by the municipal frontline supervisors were

- Interpersonal communication skills
- Problem solving and decision making
- Dealing with a stressed employee
- Team development and performance

Results of Manager Survey in the Justice and Public Safety Sectors

Part 3.2: Skills Competency—Self

Please take a few moments and indicate **how competent you personally feel** using these skills in your current job. Circle the most appropriate response.

	Competence				
	Extremely	Very	Somewhat	Slightly	Not at all
Communicating interpersonally with others		☑			
Understanding own ethics/values and those of others		☑			
Understanding and applying ethical standards		☑			
Encouraging a willingness to work on difficult problems		☑			
Ensuring that mentoring and coaching occur			☑		
Appropriately and effectively delegating responsibilities		☑			
Establishing corporate vision and enlisting others			☑		
Reinforcing a positive working environment		☑			
Ensuring a fair and objective disciplinary process			☑		
Working with independent advisory groups			☑		
Responding to change in a planned and deliberate way			☑		
Ensuring a meaningful performance evaluation process		☑			

	Competence				
	Extremely	**Very**	**Somewhat**	**Slightly**	**Not at all**
Moving the corporate vision toward results		☑			
Resolving problems using consultation and consensus	☑				
Anticipating and resolving problems using creativity			☑		
Establishing relationships of trust		☑			
Speaking and making presentations before groups			☑		
Building consensus around corporate vision			☑		
Actively seeking feedback on own performance			☑		
Lobbying for legislative change			☑		
Establishing measures of organizational effectiveness		☑			
Evaluating organizational effectiveness	☑				
Addressing sources, not just symptoms, of problems		☑			
Building/changing corporate culture			☑		
Communicating so others understand and cooperate	☑				
Ensuring a fair and objective promotional process		☑			
Ensuring a quality training/ employee development system		☑			
Managing financial resources efficiently	☑				
Managing human resources efficiently	☑				
Fostering organizational change to meet future challenges			☑		
Making difficult decisions in a timely fashion		☑			
Establishing positive linkages with other agencies			☑		
Enhancing morale and motivation		☑			
Planning and implementing community-based initiatives			☑		
Addressing and preventing harassment in the workplace			☑		
Conducting, implementing, and evaluating a strategic planning process			☑		

☑ = represents the median where at least 50 percent of the respondents fall.

Skills Competency—My Perception of Other Leaders

Please take a few moments and indicate **how competent other leaders in your field** are in using these skills. Circle the most appropriate response.

	Competence				
	Extremely	**Very**	**Somewhat**	**Slightly**	**Not at all**
Communicating interpersonally with others			☑		
Understanding own ethics/values and those of others			☑		
Understanding and applying ethical standards			☑		
Encouraging a willingness to work on difficult problems		☑			
Ensuring that mentoring and coaching occur		☑			
Appropriately and effectively delegating responsibilities		☑			
Establishing corporate vision and enlisting others			☑		
Reinforcing a positive working environment			☑		
Ensuring a fair and objective disciplinary process			☑		
Working with independent advisory groups				☑	
Responding to change in a planned and deliberate way			☑		
Ensuring a meaningful performance evaluation process			☑		
Moving the corporate vision toward results			☑		
Resolving problems using consultation and consensus			☑		
Anticipating and resolving problems using creativity				☑	
Establishing relationships of trust			☑		
Speaking and making presentations before groups			☑		

	Competence				
	Extremely	**Very**	**Somewhat**	**Slightly**	**Not at all**
Building consensus around corporate vision			☑		
Actively seeking feedback on own performance				☑	
Lobbying for legislative change				☑	
Establishing measures of organizational effectiveness			☑		
Evaluating organizational effectiveness	☑				
Addressing sources, not just symptoms, of problems			☑		
Building/changing corporate culture				☑	
Communicating so others understand and cooperate			☑		
Ensuring a fair and objective promotional process			☑		
Ensuring a quality training/ employee development system			☑		
Managing financial resources efficiently		☑			
Managing human resources efficiently		☑			
Fostering organizational change to meet future challenges				☑	
Making difficult decisions in a timely fashion		☑			
Establishing positive linkages with other agencies				☑	
Enhancing morale and motivation			☑		
Planning and implementing community-based initiatives				☑	
Addressing and preventing harassment in the workplace			☑		
Conducting, implementing, and evaluating a strategic planning process		☑			

☑ = represents the median where at least 50 percent of the respondents fall.

The Meaning of the Discrepancy in Self versus Other Scores

The self and other perceptions in the supervisory study above reveal a discrepancy, as does the managerial study. This discrepancy between self-perception and the evaluations of others is not rare in such surveys, but highlights the tendency for others often to see us in a more critical light than we see ourselves. Perhaps reality lies somewhere between the two ratings. In any case, there was agreement on the part of most of the officers that they needed further training in many of the skills that they agreed were important in their jobs.

References

Anderson, T. and D. King, Managerial Leadership Training Needs Assessment in Justice and Public Safety, Justice Institute of British Columbia, New Westminster, B.C. Canada, 1996a.

Anderson, T. and D. King, Police Supervisory Leadership Training Needs Assessment, Justice Institute of British Columbia, New Westminster, B.C. Canada, 1996b.

Appendix D: RCMP/FLETC Competencies

The Royal Canadian Mounted Police (RCMP) has further delineated its competencies list to include a plan to deliver various skills at different levels in the organization. This competency list is also similar to the "Every Officer a Leader" program that was developed by the Federal Law Enforcement Training Center (FLETC) and the RCMP. Permission has been granted to publish these competencies in their current form with the understanding that this is not the final version of the skills list for either the RCMP or FLETC.

Assumptions

- All employees are leaders. They may lead themselves, their peers, their subordinates, their supervisors, their managers, their executive and/or their organization. Core Values underpin Core Competencies.
- Core competencies:
  - Are clusters of behaviours of all employees;
  - Are observable/measurable;
  - Are continuously improved upon;
  - Identify successful performance;
  - Are essentially the same across all levels, however varied in complexity with the responsibilities of each level; and
  - Translate the mission, vision and values of the organization into the actions all employees must display for the organization to be successful.

Core Values

- Integrity
  - firm adherence to a code of values
  - consistency of actions over time cornerstone of all other values
  - uphold the law
  - support the administration of justice
- Honesty
  - straightforwardness of conduct
  - trustworthiness
  - dependability
- Professionalism
  - high standards maintained in all actions
  - all treated with respect
- Compassion
  - sympathy for one another
  - desire to alleviate others' distress
- Respect, consider worthy
  - conduct is courteous
- Accountability
  - held responsible for one's actions
  - answerable
- Fairness
  - freedom from self-interest, prejudice and favouritism
  - impartial and just treatment
- Courage
  - control under adversity
  - act under conditions of difficulty, fear or danger

Core Competencies

Change Management

- Learns continuously
  - Improves self and engages in ongoing development for self and environment by:
    - Continuously seeking new ideas and concepts and keeping abreast of research by reading; using multi-media; seeking appropriate experiences; communicating with peers, supervisors, etc.; training; community involvement; and/or any other formal or informal means
    - Seeking knowledge, skills and experience for developmental reasons (i.e., future goals and career aspirations)

- Develops self-awareness and self-discipline
  - ◆ Recognizes one's personal belief system (i.e., rational/irrational thinking and/or behaviour)
    - – Recognizes one's preferred style of interacting
  - ◆ Engages in self-assessment/reflection
  - ◆ Seeks and accepts feedback openly
    - – Discards ineffective and inappropriate behaviours and replaces them with new/more effective behaviours
    - – Handles failure/criticism in a constructive manner
  - ◆ Is self-directed and self-motivated
- Balances personal/professional competing interests
  - ◆ Maintains a well-rounded perspective on competing interests of self, family, social and professional demands
  - ◆ Establishes a course of action including mission and personal goals
  - ◆ Does first things first
- Practices stress management
  - ◆ Maintains personal energy through attention to physical and emotional health requirements
  - ◆ Manages demands on time
    - – Does first things first
  - ◆ Recognizes the impact of stress on others
  - ◆ Tolerates ambiguity
  - ◆ Recognizes stressors and warning signs
  - ◆ Seeks assistance from appropriate sources at appropriate time
- Recognizes and promotes the concept of the learning organization
  - ◆ Improves the organization by:
    - – Learning on an ongoing basis how to develop the organization
    - – Continuously seeking opportunities to improve upon organizational initiatives, efficiency and service delivery
    - – Challenging rules and regulations when they prove to be barriers to align systems to the goals of the organization
    - – Using relevant current knowledge to initiate action in a positive manner
  - ◆ Pioneers and integrates technology
  - ◆ Creates a culture where all employees are leaders
- Develops and enunciates vision
  - ◆ Identifies local and global trends
  - ◆ Aligns the organization to the future
  - ◆ Promotes corporate mission, vision and values
  - ◆ Articulates and directs intent clearly
  - ◆ Gains and sustains the interest and support of others for a shared vision

- Invites, accepts and promotes change
    - Manages change
    - Encourages constructive questioning of policies and practices
    - Tolerates ambiguity
    - Predicts, assesses and takes action to maximize the human dynamics of the organization during the change process
    - Adapts approach and style to different leadership demands of downsizing, turnarounds and re-structuring
- Promotes organizational and community harmony and awareness
    - Builds and maintains cooperative relationships

Communication

- Listens/reads attentively to understand the message
    - Consults appropriately to ensure others' views are reflected in communications
    - Listens actively and empathically
    - Pays attention to non-verbal clues
- Communicates ideas clearly
    - Asks appropriate questions (5Ws and H)
    - Chooses appropriate medium and time (i.e., timing)
    - Uses appropriate non-verbal communication
- Connects at the appropriate level
    - Aligns the format, vocabulary and official language to the audience
    - Captures interest and gains support
    - Conveys the organization's messages and information accurately and appropriately

Relationship Building

- Interacts sensitively and respectfully
    - Validates
        - Affirms their worth as unique individuals
    - Accepts
        - Accepts others for who they are and not what they do
    - Listens
        - Listens to people since they are worthy of attention
    - Understands
        - Seeks first to understand, then to be understood
    - Empowers
        - Strives to provide and maintain a positive and safe environment for

interpersonal growth
- Creates and enhances relationships
  - Establishes open communications
  - Builds trust, commitment, loyalty and respect
  - Appreciates the contribution of others
    - Listens to and understands other perspectives
    - Modifies approaches to better communicate or achieve results
  - Challenges rules and regulations when they prove barriers to sensitive or quality interactions
- Practices the art of carefronting
  - Challenges others' behaviours using tact to maintain relationships
  - Empathetically establishes open communications with others in high-stress situations
- Builds on diversity
  - Conveys the organization's messages and information accurately and appropriately to diverse groups
  - Interacts sensitively and respectfully with diverse individuals and groups to advance the work of the organization
  - Ensures diverse human resources are searched out, utilized and applied to maximum benefit
- Acknowledges conflict as positive by focussing on the solution .
  - Cooperatively identifies and solves problems through consultation, negotiation and consensus building

Service Orientation

- Is client-centred
  - Recognizes and evaluates opportunities for partnering to ensure quality service to clients
  - Measures current business systems, client needs and market opportunities for continuous improvement
  - Is sensitive to client need
    - Demonstrates an understanding of who the clients are, their needs and expectations, the service standards and the importance of meeting the standards
  - Balances the competing interests of clients and stakeholders
  - Evaluates organizational performance by seeking client feedback
    - Uses formal and informal mechanisms to stay in-tune with clients/ partners
- Creates and enhances partnerships
  - Collaborates with partners in meeting project objectives

- – Ensures comprehensive understanding, buy-in and commitment by the partners through open communication
  - – Promotes and maintains a "win–win" situation
  - – Ensures cooperative approaches to service delivery
  - – Contributes to consensual solutions for better quality outputs
  - ◆ Balances the competing interests of partners
- Delivers what is promised
  - ◆ Responds to client/partner needs effectively, competently and thoroughly consistent with the organizations' mission, vision, values and service standards
  - ◆ Accepts responsibility for quality products
  - ◆ Reliably delivers on promises and honours commitments

Critical Thinking

- Challenges assumptions and analyses present paradigm
  - ◆ Critically evaluates, questions, challenges status quo to stimulate creativity and continuous improvement
- Evaluates risk and potential outcomes of action
  - ◆ Takes ownership and responsibility for decisions even with a risk of failure
  - ◆ Handles failure/criticism in a constructive manner
  - ◆ Evaluates choices and opportunities
    - – Explores options before deciding
  - ◆ Deals with complexity
  - ◆ Foresees barriers/obstacles and determines possible solutions
- Makes decisions objectively and through the lens of mission, vision and values
  - ◆ Bases decisions on relevance/priorities
  - ◆ Does right things in the right way at the right time for the right reasons
  - ◆ Bases decisions on whether they are Moral, Ethical, Efficient, Effective, Affordable and Legal (MEEEAL)
  - ◆ Focuses on client/partner interests, needs and expectations
  - ◆ Evaluates patterns, trends and/or causes and their effects
  - ◆ Translates analyses of problems/issues into sound recommendations
  - ◆ Establishes a course of action
  - ◆ Balances competing interests
  - ◆ Evaluates patterns in multi-dependency systems, showing understanding and balanced decision-making

Action Management

- Plans
  - ◆ Develops a mission
  - ◆ Assesses internal and external environment (strengths & weaknesses)
  - ◆ Identifies feasible strategic options
  - ◆ Evaluates alternatives
  - ◆ Selects a strategy
  - ◆ Sets goals and objectives
- Organizes and implements
  - ◆ Sets course of action to meet goals and objectives
  - ◆ Works within the accountability framework
  - ◆ Clarifies roles and responsibilities
  - ◆ Identifies the scope of work
  - ◆ Identifies, allocates and manages required human, financial, and material resources
  - ◆ Contributes to and/or manages teams
  - ◆ Allocates and manages time
    - – Does first things first
  - ◆ Deals with problems/crises simultaneously
  - ◆ Takes calculated risks
  - ◆ Monitors performance
  - ◆ Evaluates results

Sharing Power and Creating Opportunity

- Enables the development of others
  - ◆ Counsels, mentors and/or coaches others towards performance improvement
  - ◆ Develops others' skills and abilities
- Entrusts responsibilities to others
  - ◆ Collaborates with others in meeting project objectives
  - ◆ Empowers others to accomplish goals and objectives
- Creates the environment for empowerment
  - ◆ Removes obstacles and barriers
  - ◆ Creates freedom to learn from mistakes
  - ◆ Stimulates and supports creativity and innovation in others

Inspiration and Motivation

- Influences others in attitude and demeanour
  - ◆ Elicits improved performance

- Motivates others to work towards a shared purpose in the best interest of the organization, the employees and the clients/stakeholders/partners
  - Inspires risk taking by setting challenging and achievable goals
  - Recognizes contribution and celebrates success
  - Plans small wins
  - Leads by doing
  - Inspires others to perform to the highest standards
- Builds trust through consistency
  - Demonstrates consistency by upholding the ethical and social values of the organization in both word and action
- S-T-R-E-T-C-H-E-S followers
  - Encourages others to think outside the box

Index